Northwestern University Publications
in Analytical Philosophy

THE

Concept

OF

Knowledge

Panayot Butchvarov

Northwestern University Press

EVANSTON · 1970

*Panayot Butchvarov is Professor of Philosophy
at the University of Iowa*

TO
Sue

Contents

PART ONE   *Primary Knowledge*

1. Introduction   3
2. The Senses of Know   13
3. Knowledge as True Belief Based on Sufficient Evidence   25
4. The Degree of Evidence Sufficient for Knowledge   39
5. The Usage of Know   54
6. The Nature of Self-Evidence   61
7. The Principle of Unthinkability   76
8. Knowing That One Knows   88
9. A Priori and A Posteriori Knowledge   93

PART TWO   *The Objects of A Priori Knowledge*

1. The A Priori and the Necessary   99
2. The Standard Logico-Linguistic Theories of Necessary Truth   105
3. The Appeal to Rules of Language   124

Contents

4. The Synthetic A Priori   140
5. The Concept of Necessary Truth and Ordinary Thought   142
6. The Subject Matter of Necessary Propositions   152
7. Necessary Truth and the Problem of Universals   167
8. Intuition   178

PART THREE   *Primary Perceptual Knowledge*

1. The Argument from Illusion   185
2. Bodies and Perception   197
3. The Publicity and Mind-Independence of Bodies   205
4. Three-Dimensionality and Solidity   214
5. The Nature of Perception   221
6. Pure Perceptual Statements   239
7. Pure Perceptual Objects   249
8. Incorrigibility   262

PART FOUR   *Derivative Knowledge*

1. Knowledge and Rational Belief   267
2. The Concept of Defining Criterion   274
3. The Concept of Nondefining Criterion   278
4. Nonequivocating Multiple Criteria of Evidence   287
5. Nondefining Criteria in Specific Fields   292
6. Are Epistemic Terms Evaluative?   299
7. Nondemonstrative Criteria of Knowledge   302
8. Induction   307
9. Skepticism   312

The Concept of
Knowledge

PART ONE

Primary Knowledge

1. Introduction

THIS BOOK HAS as its subject matter the conceptual foundations of epistemology. Its central task is the account of the concept of knowledge, but in the course of the inquiry detailed accounts are also offered of the concepts of necessary truth and sense perception. And much of the discussion is concerned with the notions of evidence, rational belief, and criterion.

Answers to questions such as whether all knowledge is founded in and derived from experience, or whether we can know what things are in themselves and not only what they appear to be, are likely to be inadequate if they are not based, in part, on an adequate answer to the question, What is knowledge? But it is equally true that an account of the nature of knowledge cannot be satisfactory unless it is tied to, and throws light upon, more specific issues such as why, if at all, there are both a priori and a posteriori knowledge, how one can know something without relying on one's knowledge of something else, and why perception plays a crucial role in the acquisition of knowledge. For example, if a general theory of knowledge claims that it is essential to knowledge that it be based on experience, then the theory must include a thorough, detailed account of the nature of the truths usually supposed to be necessary and a priori. It must demonstrate either that they are really a posteriori or that they are not truths at all and thus not objects of knowledge. An adequate account of the concept of knowledge must avoid empty formality as well as blind detail.

Part One of this book attempts an account of the general concept of knowledge, especially as it is employed in what I shall call *primary epistemic judgments,* that is, judgments of the form *"A* knows that *p"* which would not typically be in need of justification by appeal to other epistemic judgments. (Epistemic judgments that are in need of such justification I shall call *derivative,* and I shall make a corresponding distinction between primary and derivative knowledge.) We shall find that this account leads to, indeed demands and at the same time illuminates, the division of all knowledge into a priori and a posteriori. But unless then a detailed elucidation of this division is provided, the general account of the concept of knowledge would remain skeletal. There are two questions in particular that such an elucidation must answer. First, what are the objects of a priori knowledge? Second, what is the nature of primary a posteriori knowledge? Our account of the concept of knowledge, like most such accounts, requires that the object of knowledge be a certain truth or fact. But what, if anything, could be an a priori (or necessary) truth or fact? Our account, again in common with most, requires the distinction between primary and derivative knowledge. But can this distinction be made good with respect to our sense-perceptual knowledge of the "external" world of bodies, which is the paradigm and most extensive segment of a posteriori knowledge? That the answers to these questions are not at all settled should be obvious. Yet, unless it includes such answers, an account of the general concept of knowledge cannot be accepted as satisfactory. Part Two of this book will attempt to provide an answer to the first question, and Part Three an answer to the second.

The consideration of a posteriori knowledge in Part Three raises with particular urgency the question of the possibility and nature of derivative knowledge. This is not surprising. That question concerns chiefly derivative a posteriori knowledge, the nature of derivative a priori knowledge being largely the concern of formal logic and its possibility generally unquestioned. The crucial issue regarding derivative a posteriori knowledge is the legitimacy of nondemonstrative inference. In Part Four we return to our inquiry into the general concept of knowledge, but this time with special attention to the issue of nondemonstrative inference and to the nature of derivative knowledge in general, and provide further reasons in support of the chief thesis of Part One.

I shall not, however, discuss the usual philosophical problems about the validity of certain particular kinds of derivative knowledge (e.g., of the future, of bodies, of other minds). Each of these requires careful, detailed treatment in its own right; nothing is gained by sweeping proclamations or refutations of skepticism. And since these problems constitute the familiar subject matter of the theory of knowledge, I offer here only an introduction to that branch of philosophy and not a theory of knowledge as such. Indeed, as is well known, the sort of theory of knowledge one proposes, and most of its tenets, are largely determined by the account one offers of the fundamental epistemic concepts. It is important, however, that such an account be given first and that it be uninfluenced by one's epistemological convictions. For, true or false, these convictions have philosophical value only insofar as they are justified, and their justification cannot be attempted without an account of the key concepts involved. Thus the reader may come to think that our inquiry leads to skepticism. In this, as I shall explain, he would be mistaken. But even if he were not, I would regard such a consequence as acceptable, as long as the rejection of skepticism is not itself grounded in investigations such as ours. Our respect for common sense must not be confused with the possession of a philosophical answer to skepticism. In philosophy, as in any other purely theoretical discipline, it is better to be wrong as the result of inquiry and argument than to be right as the result of mere conviction. The layman who takes the existence of an external world for granted may be right, and the philosophical skeptic whose inquiries lead him to deny the existence of an external world may be wrong. But the skeptic is the philosopher, and the layman is not.

A word may be needed here about what I mean by an account of a concept, although I would prefer to rely on the example of the accounts offered in this book rather than on abstract explanation. It is often supposed that to offer an account of a concept is to analyze it, that to analyze a concept is to describe its content as it is actually found in thought and language, and that to describe this content of a concept is to describe the meaning of a certain word. But, I suggest, a philosopher

5

should be concerned with a concept mainly, if not solely, as a way of achieving a clearer, deeper, and more adequate understanding of the world around him and of himself. If such concepts are already available in the common store of the human race and if they can be discovered in the linguistic practices of men, well and good. If not, then surely the philosopher's task is the delineation of such concepts. Indeed, it is unlikely that he should engage in actual *conceptual synthesis,* as traditional philosophers have sometimes supposed. The concepts that he needs are likely to be already present in our ordinary conceptual framework or at least to be modifications of such concepts. But the philosopher would be better able to discern the conceptual treasures we already possess if he were committed to an account of the concepts we ought to have rather than to an account of the concepts that we in fact do have. He should be engaged, therefore, in what may be called *conceptual criticism* rather than in *conceptual analysis.* And this book is an essay in conceptual criticism, not in conceptual analysis.

What I have said about the sense in which I shall speak of an account of a concept suggests the sense in which I shall employ the word *concept* itself. I shall employ it in the fundamental sense of a way of holding together before the mind, a manner of classifying, a means of thinking about, a place in thought for things or characteristics in the world. A concept thus has an intimate relation to the meaning of a descriptive word. For to apply a descriptive word to an entity is, at least implicitly, to classify it, and to know the meaning of a word is, at least in part, to have a way of classifying certain things or characteristics in the world, that is, to have a way of grouping, a way of viewing them together. But there is no reason for supposing that one cannot have a way of classifying without knowing an appropriate word or that one cannot revise the meaning of a word or even introduce a new word in order to express a novel, and perhaps more appropriate, way of viewing certain things in the world. Therefore, it would be a mistake to confuse a concept with the meaning of a word.

What is involved in the classification of things? Surely, primarily it is the recognition of the similarities and differences among things, our rendering them intelligible to ourselves, the understanding, the grasping, of what they are. To develop a classificatory system is to develop a conceptual framework. And to aim at developing a satisfactory conceptual framework is to aim at reflecting adequately the similarities and differences among the things constituting the subject matter of the framework, the various degrees of these similarities and differences, their hierarchy. (According to the traditional philosopher, the aim of knowledge is the discovery of the essences of things; the essence of a thing is what is stated in its definition; and what is stated in the definition of a thing is the genus under which it is to be classified and the differentia that distinguishes it from other species in the same genus.)

Thus an inquiry into those concepts that would be vehicles of a clearer and deeper understanding of a certain subject matter is in fact an inquiry into the most general and essential features of that subject matter itself. In the case of philosophy, such an inquiry, that is, conceptual criticism, would in fact be metaphysics. Our preference for saying that we are concerned with concepts rather than with the nature of things is due mainly to our awareness of the difference between a philosophical and a scientific description of the nature of a thing. The features of the world that constitute the subject matter of philosophy are on the highest possible level of generality, and thus their description consists, in effect, in the illumination, revision, and perhaps construction of a whole conceptual framework; scientific description, on the other hand, is usually a contingent application of such a conceptual framework to special subject matters. This difference is the reason for the nonexperimental, but hardly for that reason nonfactual, character of philosophical inquiry: a thing's most general classification cannot be determined by experiment, for it is presupposed by the very character of any experiment to which the thing may be subjected. The currently fashionable supposition that the world can be described only by science is due either to a pedestrian conception of what it is to describe or to a romantic view of the powers of science. But the philosophical preference for the terminology of concepts is also, and more obviously, due to the fact that the most general features of the world, or at least those that cause philosophical wonder, are conceptually recalcitrant: they do not fit easily into the ordinary conceptual framework, they seem to have no real home in our thought, and they bear no definitive likenesses to other, more easily accommodated, features. With regard to such features, the question of their natures seems misplaced. We must locate them before we describe them.

Conceptual analysis is of course also metaphysical in motive and in goal. (One cannot forsake metaphysics in philosophy, though one may be under the illusion of doing so.) At its best it is an inquiry into the conceptual framework we in fact have. And this is an inquiry of philosophical importance, even though it is in constant danger of degenerating in one age into psychology, in another into philology. But the conceptual framework we in fact have, doubtless to some degree expressive of the most general features of the world, is not likely to be so expressive to the highest degree. It is, quite properly, subject to philosophical appraisal and criticism.

It may seem, whatever the merits of a metaphysical description of the world, that knowledge itself cannot be one of its objects, for knowledge is *of* the world, not *in* the world, or at least not only in the world. But there is nothing that is not in the world. The supposition that there is, in this case, is largely due to a picturesque conception of the Self and a related conception of Knowledge which have dominated most of continental philosophy at least since Fichte, although Hume warned against them in 1739. They may be roughly described as the conception of an Ego facing the World (somewhat like an astronaut in orbit facing a planet!) and of knowledge either as the Ego's stare at ("consciousness" of) the World or, worse, as the Ego's fall into the World or the World's fall into the Ego. But such conceptions, I suggest, are only pictures, whose long hold on the philosophical imagination can hardly be excused. I will return to this topic in section 2 of this Part.

It may also seem that I am assuming that *know* is a descriptive word. Indeed, I am, but this is not a mere assumption. This book may be regarded as a defense of this assumption, indeed as the only sort of defense that would be appropriate. For one can prove that a word is descriptive only by describing what it describes. We would be impatient, for example, with a man who tries to prove that *good* is a descriptive word by abstract argument; such a method may be appropriate to a proof that a word is *not* descriptive, but surely not to a proof that it is. Tell us, we should ask instead, what is that which *good* describes? If his reply fits what we mean by *good,* we would agree with him. If it does not, we might still have had our attention drawn to an important feature of the world, even though one not captured in ordinary talk.

Philosophers sometimes scornfully reject what I have called conceptual criticism as being committed to the view that there is a true classification of things, whether writ in heaven or in nature, which may be known and consulted and which our linguistic conventions may more or less approximate. Their scorn is due mainly to the proper but irrelevant conviction that things never *force* us to classify them in a certain way. Yet this conviction does not entail that some classifications are not more appropriate, more illuminating, more adequate to the world than others. We do not have to classify lions as cats or whales as non-fish. Such a classification does violence at least to a child's conceptual framework. But part of what is meant by knowledge and understanding of lions and whales is the knowledge that lions are more like house cats than like bears and that whales are more like dogs than like salmon. A man who sees a way of dividing the country which is different from the one used on the ordinary map need not be advocating an eccentric new notation or proposing an exercise in gerrymandering. He could be offering us a map in which facts of geography would be reflected in a way that the old map ignores (the United States, for example, may be divided into economic regions rather than into states).

A second reason for philosophers' scorn of the idea of a true classification is the belief that since all resemblance is in respect to something, therefore all resemblance is, at least in part, determined by our language and our subjective interests. But the premise is false, and the conclusion does not follow.[1] That the color blue is more like the color green than it is like the color yellow is intelligible without specification of a respect of the resemblance. (Imagine saying that colors resemble each other in respect to color!) And even when a resemblance must have a specifiable respect, it still is an objective fact independent of our language or our interests. An American mailbox is more like the sea than it is like an English mailbox, although only in respect to color. We might not have noticed the resemblance had we no word such as *blue* or a certain interest in colors. But that the color of the first is more like the color of the second than it is like the color of the third is an objective fact that has nothing to do with human purposes, interests, or ways of speaking. The resemblance is there, whether we notice it or not and whether our language is capable of reflecting it or not. When made explicit, rather than obscurely hinted at, linguistic transcendental idealism is no more persuasive than psychological transcendental idealism. In fact it is less so.

A third reason for rejecting a philosophical attempt at an adequate classification and description of the most general features of the world is the belief that the classification and description embodied in our actual

1. I have argued against this belief in detail in *Resemblance and Identity: An Examination of the Problem of Universals* (Bloomington & London: Indiana University Press, 1966).

language is superior to any classification or description a philosopher may achieve by modifying ordinary language. But I am unaware of a demonstration of this belief. The classification of animals embodied in ordinary language is presumably not superior to that offered by the natural historian. And while the natural historian would be acquainted with the former, he need hardly regard a detailed study of it as even preparatory for his own work. Are the natures of mind and matter, knowledge and truth, perception and thought more likely to be adequately reflected in ordinary language than are the natures of cat and lion, whale and fish? In any case, such a belief can hardly be accepted a priori. If true, its truth can only be shown as the result of specific conceptual inquiries such as ours. It must not be allowed to precede and thus stifle these inquiries.

A fourth reason for scorning the idea of a true classification is the quasi-psychological view, usually assumed rather than argued, that one cannot think about and know the world except through the use (whether overt or internal) of one's language and thus that one cannot judge the adequacy of one's language to the nature of the world. Thinking, we are told, is essentially the activity of operating with signs, and to distinguish between the world as known and thought about and one's language is to treat one's language as if it were a foreign tongue. But, surely, this view is at best an exaggeration. The fact is that to much of our thought language is only peripheral. The cook's recognition, comparison, and thought of the finer shades of taste; the patient's knowledge of the special characteristics of his pains; the man of the world's extraordinary knowledge of facial expressions and manners of speech, and of their likely significance; the sailor's thought about sea conditions and weather signs—none of these is likely to have language as its vehicle, and their overt or internal linguistic expression is likely to be grossly inadequate, not because they are mysteriously ineffable but because of the difficulty of having language match the subtlety of thought. Indeed, even in the case of far more ordinary kinds of thought and knowledge, the full specificity and richness of their content is likely to remain unreflected in their linguistic expression. I can see, think, and know that the chair before me has a certain specific color, and *say* that it is yellow, but I do not *see, think,* and *know* just that it is yellow but that it is *that* specific shade of yellow, which I can recognize and compare with others but probably cannot name or adequately describe.

But even if the above quasi-psychological view were true, it would be irrelevant to the question of the possibility and desirability of what I have called conceptual criticism. Let us suppose that thought about the world and our knowledge of the similarities and differences in the world are incapable of life outside language. It would not follow at all that such similarities and differences are in any sense *determined* by language or that language determines the results of our thinking about the world, any more than it would follow, from the fact that we cannot know colors unless we can see, that the colors objects have are determined by our sense of vision. And thus it would not follow that our thought and knowledge of the world cannot change and grow by adjusting more closely to the similarities and differences in the world, even if such change and growth would also be a change and growth of our language.

But after all this has been said, we must remind ourselves of the lesson that Wittgenstein has taught us: the philosophical account of a concept cannot be performed in a conceptual vacuum, and filled conceptual space is to be found only in natural, ordinary thought and language. The failure to recognize this has been the cause of much of the obscurity, even unintelligibility, of parts of traditional philosophy. And, what is even more important, it has been the cause of the irrelevance of many conceptual accounts to the issues that occasioned them. This is true both of parts of traditional metaphysics and of contemporary constructional philosophies such as Carnap's and Goodman's. It is not the establishment of technical notions in philosophy or the drastic revision of natural notions that is objectionable; the worst consequence of these would be puzzlement. What is really objectionable is the illusion of answering the original philosophical questions that aroused our interest in the concepts involved by substituting for these concepts something so different as to drastically change the questions themselves. (We may call this the *explication fallacy*.) We cannot answer the question, What can we know? by making *know* mean something quite different from what it ordinarily means. For the problems of knowledge, like most, though not all, other philosophical topics, arise in the terms of our common, natural conceptual stock. Fidelity to the latter, and great concern with it, I suggest, are neither necessary nor philosophically desirable. But excessive, and especially inadequately explained, divergence from it is likely to result in incoherence, though perhaps disguised; or such divergence may constitute the establishment of an entirely different concept, which, though not illegitimate, would probably be irrelevant to the philosophical topics which occasioned its creation. Indeed, the proper philosophical question, I suggest, is not so much, What *does* such and such a word mean? as, What *should* such and such a word mean? However, if the demands we make on the meaning of the word are excessive, we may well find ourselves no longer concerned with what meaning *that* word should have. We must avoid not only the Scylla of philosophy as a glorified philology but also the Charybdis of philosophy as a conceptual dream world. Throughout our work, we must remain under the firm but gentle control of the everyday uses of the terms expressive of the concepts with which we are concerned. Conceptual criticism is not conceptual analysis. But neither is it conceptual synthesis.

How can we achieve this? What method should we follow? Our critical conceptual activity can, of course, take many forms. First, it may consist in discerning and isolating that of the several ordinary senses of a word which is of philosophical interest and value, and perhaps in a cautious revision of such a sense by means of regarding only some of the occasions of its use as paradigmatic, either to bring out the logical primacy of that sense or to render it more distinctive and the use of the word more illuminating. This, we shall find, is the sort of procedure called for in our account of the concept of knowledge. Second, we may find that what is required is not so much a change in the sorts of situations in which the word is actually employed as a change in the way in which such situations are usually classified, in the way in which they are regarded, in the genus under which they are subsumed, and thus in a corresponding revision of the *place* of the concept in our conceptual framework. We shall find such a procedure particularly suitable in our discussion of the concept of perception. Third, we may find that the concept under investigation is in fact identical with another concept, which is seemingly distinct and less familiar, but philosophically more enlightening. I shall argue that this is the case with the concept of necessary truth.

In general, from the point of view of philosophical conceptual criticism, there are three criteria that a concept must satisfy. First, it must be a *philosophical* concept, that is, it must have the sort of generality, fundamentality, and intrinsic importance that are characteristic of the subject matter of philosophy. It would not have been necessary to emphasize this criterion were it not for some of the excesses of the contemporary interest in ordinary language, which at times lead to conceptual investigations insufficiently general and important to be philosophical. We shall find that the concepts associated with some of the senses of *know* fail this test (e.g., knowledge as social acquaintance). It is more likely, however, that a concept may fail one or both of the other criteria, which, following Descartes, we may call clarity and distinctness. So, second, a concept must be *clear,* that is, its content, and thus the criterion for its applicability, must be intelligible and sufficiently determinate; the content of the concept must be, so to speak, clearly visible intellectually. Examples of concepts that often fail this second test are those of mind, God, infinity, and, in the context of this inquiry, the concepts of knowledge and necessary truth. Third, a concept must be *distinct,* that is, its relations, its similarities and differences, to other concepts must be intellectually visible; its place in conceptual space must be determinate. The concept of sense perception is a prime example of a concept likely to fail this third test, and so probably is the concept of knowledge. Different methods of inquiry correspond to these different criteria. Distinctness is mainly to be achieved by discovering significant analogies, that is, by emphasizing conceptual similarities and differences. Clarity can be achieved by detailed explanation, whether through definitions or examples. Philosophical importance can be achieved through understanding of, and respect for, philosophical tradition. Often a concept may fail two or perhaps all three criteria. The philosophical criticism of it would then be an even more demanding task.

2. *The Senses of Know*

IF A CRITICAL ACCOUNT of the concept of knowledge is to have roots in ordinary, natural thought and thus be relevant to the philosophical problems that occasioned it, it must be guided, though not shackled, by the actual meaning of the word *know.* Thus some consideration of the latter is a necessary preliminary task for our inquiry. However, it is likely that our attention will immediately be drawn to the fact that there is considerable impropriety about speaking of *the* meaning of the word *know.* There are many different senses in which this word is used, some closely related, some quite different, and thus we cannot really speak of *the* actual meaning of *know.* One may even argue that the very notion of an account of the meaning of a word is dangerous. For such an account presumably would consist, if not in actual definition, at least in the specification of various rules and criteria for the use of the word. But a natural language is too rich, too complex, and too intimate a part of our lives to function according to neat rules and criteria. The primary requirement of a natural language is that it be useful in the everyday course of events. But usefulness and logical neatness do not go hand in hand. So, one may conclude, it is likely that, especially in the case of a word such as *know*, we shall fail to find anything that all of the occasions of its use have in common, or even anything that a sufficient number of them have in common to justify our regarding such occasions as exemplifying one sense of the word. And even if we do succeed in roughly identifying and classifying several senses of the word, this is likely to be the result more of a vague linguistic intuition than of the discovery of necessary and sufficient conditions for the applicability of the word in various situations.

Such observations are probably right. But what they really show is the enormous gap between the philosophical and the philological concerns with language, the incapacity of the mere description of the ordinary uses of a word such as *know* to constitute an account of a concept, of a way of classifying, of a place in thought for certain things. To the extent to which the uses of a word are governed by many and very different rules and at times by no identifiable rules at all, and to the extent to which there are no clear, distinct, or even identifiable limits of its applicability, the word has, at most, rudimentary conceptual value and thus can at best play a purely preliminary role in the cognitive enterprise. For instance, it has been said that the word *real* has many uses, governed by quite distinct criteria (as exemplified in distinguishing between real and hallucinatory objects, live ducks and decoy ducks, real diamonds and imitation diamonds, the real color of one's hair and its artificial color), and from this it has been concluded that whoever proclaims that one of these criteria (e.g., that for distinguishing between real and hallucinatory objects) is *the* criterion of reality distorts our concept of reality.[2] But, assuming that the criteria for the use of the word *real* are indeed quite distinct, that they are not species of the same genus, one could not possibly distort the corresponding concept of reality, for there is no such concept. What there is, perhaps, is a *group* of concepts, possibly related in varying ways and degrees. And a philosopher's choice of one of them (presumably because of its special philosophical interest and greater importance) neither constitutes nor leads to conceptual error, unclarity, or confusion. Indeed, it does

2. J. L. Austin, *Sense and Sensibilia* (Oxford: Clarendon Press, 1962), chap. VII,

superficially resemble something which would be erroneous, namely, the view that the word *real* is not used in everyday discourse in accordance with other criteria. But this would be an extraordinarily mistaken philological view that even a philosopher would not have espoused. The faithful account of the actual ways in which a word is employed is not necessarily, or even probably, a good account of a concept.[3]

Philosophers have usually been concerned with the sense of *know* in statements such as (1) "*A* knows that the pike will be biting tonight," "*A* knows that the product of 12 and 15 is 180," "*A* knows that a bachelor is an unmarried man." A useful way of referring to this sense is to speak of *propositional knowledge.* (Whether there are further distinctions to be made among subsenses of this sense is a question to which I shall attend repeatedly in this book.) But there are many other, clearly different, senses in which *know* is used. The philosopher does not usually refer to the sense in which *know* is synonymous with "to have sexual intercourse with." But he is likely to refer, in addition to (1), to the uses of that word (and of *knowledge*) in statements such as the following: (2) "*A* knows several officials in the State Department." (3) "*A* knows his brother better than you do." (4) "I know this feeling well." (5) "*A* knows what a chameleon is." (6) "*A* knows how to swim." (7) "*A* knows how to solve trigonometric problems." (8) "*A* knows how John got here so soon." (9) "*A* knows French." (10) "*A* knows the history of philosophy." (11) "I know that God will never betray me!" (12) "Let me know when you receive this letter." (13) "*A* knows who spilled the milk." (14) "*A* knows the truth about Jones's divorce." (15) "*A*'s knowledge of French is inadequate." (16) "Our knowledge of business conditions in Italy is a valuable asset." (17) "*A*'s knowledge of the fact that Jones is divorced can be explained easily."

It is likely that at least some of the uses of *know* and of *knowledge* in the above statements exemplify different senses of these words, which, though related, perhaps partially overlapping, and probably bearing "family resemblances," are not species of one general sense. If so, then of course it would be useless to attempt an account of the concept of knowledge

---

3. "The basic meaning of an expression is not always, and perhaps not even usually, its normal (most frequent) meaning. It may even happen that an expression never has its basic meaning in ordinary language, at least not outside philosophers' discourse" (Jaako Hintikka, "Epistemic Logic and the Methods of Philosophical Analysis," *Australasian Journal of Philosophy,* XLVI [May, 1968], 43). Hintikka's reasons for holding such a view, however, differ significantly from mine.

that would be faithful to all of them. For there can be no such concept. We can enumerate and describe these uses, but such enumeration and description would not be an account of a concept. It would be at best a series of accounts of distinct, even if related, concepts. Some of these concepts, though philosophically important, may be expressed more precisely and less misleadingly by words other than *know* or *knowledge,* or any other epistemic term. They may belong, so to speak, in a completely different region of conceptual space from that occupied by the typical concepts of epistemological interest, namely, those of evidence, justification, truth, belief, proof, rational action, probability, and certainty. Others may simply be uninteresting philosophically or unimportant conceptually. They occupy, so to speak, remote minor rooms in the conceptual edifice. Still others may be complex notions in part derived from some other member of the cluster and thus only partially epistemic.

As I have already observed, the epistemologist is ordinarily concerned with the use of *know* exemplified in statements such as (1). He would defend his neglect of the remaining sixteen uses by arguing that the corresponding statements are equivalent to statements that either are clearly nonepistemic or employ *know* in a sense reducible to that of (1). Briefly, his defense might run as follows.

"*A* knows several officials in the State Department" (2) probably means what would be expressed more precisely by the statement "*A* has at least minimal social connection with several officials in the State Department." Clearly, this use of *know* is neither irreducibly epistemic nor philosophically important. "*A* knows his brother better than you do" (3) presumably means that *A* knows a greater number of, and/or more important, facts (truths) about his brother than you do. And to know a fact or a truth is to know *that* something is the case. "*A* knows a certain fact about *x*" surely means "There is a fact about *x* such that *A* knows that it is a fact" or, alternatively, "There is a proposition about *x* such that *A* knows that it is true." The epistemic content of statement (3) is thus completely expressible by *know* in the sense of (1).

"I know this feeling well" (4) seems to say nothing more than that I remember this feeling well. If *remember* is an epistemic term at all, its epistemic content would be expressible by *know* in the sense of (1). The topic of memory is too difficult to allow for quick opinions, but I suggest that "I remember this feeling" has as its only epistemic content that I know that I have had this feeling before and that I know that on previous occasions it had the same characteristics it has now. "*A* knows what a chameleon is" (5) means that *A* knows that a certain kind of animal is a chameleon. If he knows this, then probably he can recognize a chameleon when he sees one and can tell us what a chameleon is.

"*A* knows how to swim" (6) is equivalent to "*A* can swim." Clearly, *knowing-how* need not be a capacity of intelligence. Puppies are not classified as dull or bright according to their ability to swim. Nor need *knowing-how* be the result of training or instruction. Puppies know how to swim without having received instruction in the subject. On the other hand, "*A* knows how to solve trigonometric problems" (7), though it means that *A* can solve trigonometric problems, does describe a capacity of intelligence, generally though not necessarily acquired through training and instruction. Moreover, unlike "*A* knows how to swim," it describes a capacity that presupposes and is the result of a number of *knowings-that*. Whether its being a capacity of intelligence consists in this fact is irrelevant to our inquiry. What is relevant, both in the case of knowing how to swim and in knowing how to solve trigonometric problems, is that insofar as *know-how* describes a capacity, however the latter may be acquired and whatever it may presuppose, it is not expressive of an epistemic concept at all. It has no connection with the notions that are characteristic of the subject matter of epistemology, such as truth, belief, evidence, and justification. It belongs to a very different set of concepts, more properly characteristic of the subject matter of psychology, such as habit, capacity, learning, and intelligence. On the other hand, insofar as *know-how* makes at least indirect reference to the *knowings-that* which are causally and perhaps logically necessary for the capacity (as it does in the case of knowing how to solve trigonometric problems), it may be said to have epistemic content. But that content would be expressible in the sense of *know* in (1). This is why epistemologists have generally ignored *knowing-how,* and not because of carelessness, ignorance, or ghostly interests.

"*A* knows how John got here so soon" (8) exemplifies a use of *know* quite different from that in "*A* knows how to swim." Unlike the latter, the former is not at all a description of a capacity. It means, roughly, that *A* knows that a certain way (means, method, procedure) of arriving here soon is the way John employed. Clearly, this use of *know* is derivative from that exemplified in (1).

"*A* knows French" (9) ordinarily would mean that *A* can speak and/or read French. The sense of *know* here is quite similar to that in *know-how* statements. "*A* knows the history of philosophy" (10), on the other hand, is quite different from "*A* knows French," despite the superficial similarity. Little, if anything, of its content is expressible by *know-how* statements. What it means is expressible, roughly, by saying that there are a number of important propositions about the history of philosophy such that *A* knows that they are true.

"I know that God will never betray me!" (11) is likely to mean that I am absolutely sure that God will never betray me, unless in it *know* is used in the sense of (1). "Let me know when you receive this letter" (12) probably means the same as "When you receive this letter tell me or write to me saying that you have received it." "*A* knows who spilled the milk" (13) is more complicated, though the expressibility of its epistemic content by means of *know* in the sense of (1) is unquestionable. It does not mean "*A* can truly answer the question, Who spilled the milk?" for *A* can truly (and perhaps consistently) answer many questions even if he does not know that his answers are true; a pupil finds himself in such a position often. I should be inclined to express its content by saying, "There is a proposition of the form '*x* spilled the milk' such that *A* knows that that proposition is true."[4] "*A* knows the truth about Jones's divorce" (14) would mean, roughly, "There are certain important propositions about Jones's divorce such that *A* knows that they are true."

"*A*'s knowledge of French is inadequate" (15) means that *A* does not (cannot) speak and/or read French adequately. "Our knowledge of business conditions in Italy is a valuable asset" (16) is, of course, very complicated, but surely it means roughly that there are a number of important propositions about business conditions in Italy such that we know that they are true, and the fact that we know that they are true is a valuable asset. "*A*'s knowledge of the fact that Jones is divorced can be explained easily" (17) surely means the same as "The fact that *A* knows that Jones is divorced can be explained easily."

The existence of uses of *know* such as those exemplified in statements (2) through (17) is thus of little, if any, epistemological relevance. Such uses are either philosophically uninteresting (2, 6, 9, 12, 15), or lack distinctively epistemological significance (7, 11), or are based on the propositional use of *know* (3, 4, 5, 8, 10, 13, 14, 16, 17).

---

4. A similar account would be given of the sense of *know* in statements such as "*A* knows when the plane is due to arrive," "*A* knows what Williams said," "*A* knows Williams' views about the election."

Nevertheless, the existence of some of these uses of *know* has stimulated the proposal of certain quite erroneous views about the nature of knowledge. It is plausible to suppose, for example, that the use of *know* in statements like *"A* knows how to swim" and *"A* knows how to solve trigonometric problems" has encouraged philosophers to regard knowledge even in its epistemologically primary sense of (1) as a certain kind of behavioral capacity. It has been argued that " 'Know' is a capacity verb, and a capacity verb of that special sort that is used for signifying that the person described can bring things off, or get things right," [5] that "When we use, as we often do use, the phrase 'can tell' as a paraphrase of 'know,' we mean by 'tell,' 'tell correctly.' " [6] It has also been argued that *knowing-that* is reducible to *knowing-how*—specifically, to the capacity to state what is the case.[7]

Such arguments have been valuable insofar as they have reminded us that *know* is ordinarily used dispositionally. To say that someone knows that something is the case is not to say that a particular mental or physical event is taking place. Indeed, any account according to which knowledge is, at least in part, a certain kind of belief, must acknowledge this fact, for *believe* is also ordinarily used dispositionally. To say that someone believes that something is the case is not to assert that a particular mental or physical occurrence is taking place. These are facts that no epistemologist need deny. The important question concerns the nature of the events in which epistemic and doxastic dispositions are actualized. The behavioral account of knowledge makes a controversial claim because according to it such dispositions are actualized only in behavioral (whether verbal or nonverbal) events. To reject this account need only be to insist that epistemic and doxastic dispositions may be actualized *both* in behavioral events and in certain mental events (e.g., acts of believing or knowing) that are themselves describable as beliefs or knowledge.[8] Indeed, the behavioral account would claim that there are no such mental occurrences, though it may allow that there are other, nonepistemic and nondoxastic, sorts of mental occurrences (e.g., thoughts, images, emotions). But this claim is certainly false.

It is phenomenologically false. We do sometimes find ourselves in

5. Gilbert Ryle, *The Concept of Mind* (London: Hutchinson's University Library, 1949), p. 133.
6. *Ibid.,* p. 130.
7. See John Hartland-Swann, *An Analysis of Knowing* (London: Allen & Unwin, 1958).
8. Cf. Ryle, *Concept of Mind,* pp. 117–18.

conscious states that may quite intelligibly be described as states of believing; and insofar as knowledge is a kind of belief, we also find ourselves sometimes in conscious states that constitute at least part of what we should describe as knowledge. But the claim is also false from the standpoint of ordinary usage. *Believe* and *know* are not purely dispositional verbs. "When I saw his letter I knew that he had deceived me" exemplifies an episodic use of *know*. "When I saw the Gallup poll that morning, I believed for the first time that Nixon would win in November" exemplifies an episodic use of *believe*. (Indeed, one cannot say in English that one is knowing or believing something. But this can no more show that knowledge and belief are not episodes than the fact that one cannot say in English that one is having a headache can show that having a headache is not an episode.) Such episodic uses are not as common as the dispositional uses of *know* and *believe*. Perhaps one reason is our natural interest in knowledge and belief as dispositions rather than as episodes; a person's mental states have no practical importance for us unless they result in behavior. A further reason is that there is another set of terms which can unmistakably refer to episodes of knowledge and belief, for example, *realize, see, grasp,* in the case of knowledge, and *feel sure, be convinced, accept, assent to,* in the case of belief.

That knowledge and belief are not merely behavioral dispositions is also evident from the logical possibility (and, surely, everyday fact) that one may know that one believes, and perhaps that one knows, that something is the case in complete abstraction from one's knowledge, if any, of one's dispositions to act and talk in certain ways.[9] When I found myself believing, as a result of having just read the latest Gallup poll, that Nixon would win in November, or perhaps even that, having considered the evidence, I knew that he would, I did not find that I was then disposed to act and talk in certain new ways; indeed I was not even thinking of any actions or talk in which I might engage. While it is a phenomenological fact that there are occurrent beliefs, and perhaps knowledge, it is a logical fact that one can know that one believes, and perhaps that one knows, something in a way quite unlike the way in which one can know one's tendencies, capacities, and propensities. And should we deny that it makes sense to speak of one's knowing that one believes, there is the logical fact

---

9. Cf. A. Phillips-Griffiths, "On Belief," *Proceedings of the Aristotelian Society,* LXIII (1962–63), 167–86.

that it *does* make sense to speak of one's knowing one's tendencies, capacities, and propensities.

Of course, the behavioral account of knowledge has considerable plausibility with respect to third-person epistemic judgments. Our evidence for such judgments can only be the person's behavior, and impatient philosophers do have the tendency to identify the content of a judgment with the evidence for it. But it is with respect to first-person epistemic judgments that the adequacy of an account of knowledge must primarily be judged. The reason is that first-person epistemic judgments have a certain sort of logical priority over third-person epistemic judgments. I cannot be justified in asserting that *A* knows that *p* unless I would be justified in asserting that I know that *p*, while the converse of this is false. (I will return to this point.) Yet, as we have just seen, the behavioral account of knowledge has no plausibility at all with regard to first-person epistemic judgments. It is here that it manifests its deepest inadequacy. It need make no distinctive claims about the specific problems regarding the concept of knowledge—for example, those of the sort of evidence required for knowledge, whether one must believe what one knows, whether what one knows must be true, and the distinction between primary and derivative knowledge—in fact, almost everything I shall say about these problems in the present inquiry will be compatible with the behavioral account. Where the behavioral account does make a distinctive claim is in its view of the general *place* of the concept of knowledge, not of the concept's *internal* features. And there the account is grossly inadequate. At its best, it is like a map that represents the internal features of New York State quite faithfully but places it in the middle of Europe.

Another account of knowledge that seems to be the result of taking as primary a sense of *know* other than that of propositional knowledge has identified it with awareness or consciousness. This is the traditional conception of knowledge, which was made explicit and rejected by Plato in the *Theaetetus* as the view that knowledge is perception, accepted in the *Republic* as the view that knowledge is the contemplation of Forms, and accepted also by Russell in his claim that there is such a species of knowledge as acquaintance. It seems plausible to regard this conception as due in part to the familiarity of the use of *know* in statements such as "*A* knows several officials in the State Department," and "I know this feeling well," although, as we shall see, in part it is also due to the fundamental role of perception as a *source* of knowledge. The theory is especially appealing to philosophers who are preoccupied with a posteriori knowledge, for it has little initial plausibility regarding our knowledge of necessary truths. Whatever such a truth may be, one's knowledge of it can hardly be described as one's awareness of something. In fact, however, the theory is even less acceptable with respect to a posteriori knowledge, for there we can quite clearly identify something that really is awareness of objects, namely, sense perception. If knowledge were awareness or consciousness, then sense perception would be knowledge. But, quite clearly, it is not. Sense perception may provide a posteriori knowledge with its evidential foundation, but in no sense is it knowledge itself. There is no sense of *know* such that to perceive something is to know it. (None of the senses listed above is one.) The mere fact that I see something does not at all mean that I know it, or that I know what it is, or that I know any truths about it, including the truth that I see it. An infant may enjoy sense perception no less extensive than that of an adult. But the infant is likely to know nothing. If sense perception, which is our paradigm of awareness, can in no way be described as knowledge, then surely no nonparadigmatic kind of awareness, whether it be of necessary facts, Platonic Forms, or God, could be so described. My being aware of something may be a necessary condition of my knowing it. A sufficient condition it is not.[10]

The view that knowledge is consciousness has tended to encourage metaphysical speculations that still constitute a major trend in philosophy. I have in mind the belief that there is a fundamental, ontological separation between the World, on one hand, and the Knower, on the other. It is natural to think of perceiving (especially seeing) as a sort of relation between oneself and the object perceived. And it is natural to think of knowledge as capable of having anything in the world as an object. When these two features of ordinary thought are combined in the theory of knowledge as consciousness they force upon us the picture of knowledge as a beam of light, of the World as whatever may be illuminated by that light, and of the Knower as the source of the beam, never itself illuminated and thus never a part of the World, though tied to the World by the light which too is outside the World.

How could such an identification of knowledge with consciousness

---

10. Locke was sufficiently astute to define knowledge not as the perception of ideas but as the perception of the *agreement* and *disagreement* of ideas.

have been made? The philosophical steps that have led to it are several. One is the careless introduction of technical philosophical uses of such terms as *experience, consciousness,* and *acquaintance.* Such uses derive whatever sense they have from the ordinary notions of seeing, feeling, smelling, and so forth. Yet, by virtue of their very introduction, they pretend to be different. So it appears possible to suppose that to know something is to be conscious of it, while it would not have been supposed that to know something is to see it or feel it or smell it. A second step is the supposition that the sense of *know* in statements such as "*A* knows several officials in the State Department" is both philosophically important and irreducible to the sense of *know* in a statement such as "*A* knows that the pike will be biting tonight"; hence the consequent picture of knowledge as a relation between two entities (e.g., between *A* and an official in the State Department), which is obviously incompatible with the sense of *know* in "*A* knows that the pike will be biting tonight." A third step is a crude conception of what it is to perceive. I have in mind the view that perceiving is a sort of two-term relation. This view is encouraged by certain characteristics specific to visual perception, especially the existence of a spatial distance between one's body and the object seen. (The view fits poorly with tactile, auditory, olfactory, and gustatory perception, let alone with nonsensory states such as one's inner feelings.) It seems that if there is a spatial distance between oneself and what one sees, then one's seeing must be a kind of bridge between oneself and what one sees, something that connects the two. And once the irrelevance of a scientific account in terms of entities actually traveling across this space has been acknowledged, the philosopher finds himself compelled to introduce the notion of a special kind of bridge, namely, a relation—although neither a spatial nor a causal nor a logical nor any other familiar sort of relation. Thus the notion is born of a Consciousness that connects Oneself and the World.

But whatever the proper account of perception may be, it cannot be in terms of any such relation. For such a relation to be even possible there must be entities capable of constituting its relata. One of its relata seems unexceptionable: the object seen. But what of the other? Were the relation spatial or causal, that other relatum would, of course, be one's body. But the relation is not at all the sort that can take bodies as both of its relata, even if it can take a body as one of them. Nor can the required relatum be something mental. The paradigms of a mental entity are mental images, pains, thoughts, emotions. Even if there could be a relation between such an entity and something seen, it would not be at all what the relation of seeing is supposed to be. Thus the philosopher feels forced to produce another conceptual creature: a *Self* which is neither a body nor a characteristic of a body—neither heat nor cold, light nor shade, love nor hatred, pain nor pleasure—but something whose whole function is to be the second peg on which the two-term relation of perceiving can be hung, to be the Perceiver, the Awarer, the Knower.

David Hume was the first major philosopher to declare that he could find no such entity in himself. His commentators have often accused him of looking for it in the wrong place or in the wrong way. But Hume's point was that he could not even understand what such an entity would be, that he had no "idea of self," that the notion of such a self is not clear and intelligible. His commentators have also tended to interpret his argument as just another application of his general rejection of substances, forgetting that what is at stake is not merely the existence of a substantial self but the existence of an entity "to which our several impressions and ideas are suppos'd to have a reference," of an entity that, though radically different from one's body, thoughts, and feelings, can intelligibly be regarded as the referent of a relation of perceiving. For Hume's rejection of the notion of the sort of self that "some metaphysicians" may have was in part due to his inability to understand "After what manner . . . do [all our particular perceptions] belong to self; and how are they connected with it?"[11] And it has as a direct and quite important consequence (though one he perhaps did not see) the rejection of the very intelligibility of the notion of perceiving as a relation, and thus the very intelligibility of the notion of a Consciousness that hovers in the space between Oneself and the World. It seems to me that Hume's negative arguments are quite conclusive, though his positive doctrine (that the self is a collection of perceptions and that to be perceived is to be a member of that collection) is at best in need of drastic reformulation.[12]

11. *Treatise of Human Nature,* ed. L. A. Selby-Bigge, (Oxford: Clarendon Press, 1888), pp. 251–52.

12. I discuss Hume's theory of self in "The Self and Perceptions: A Study in Humean Philosophy," *The Philosophical Quarterly,* IX (April, 1959), 97–115. (Reprinted in the Bobbs-Merrill Reprint Series in Philosophy.)

3. Knowledge as True Belief Based on Sufficient Evidence

THE PHILOSOPHICALLY IMPORTANT and conceptually distinctive sense of *know* is that exemplified in statements such as "*A* knows that the pike will be biting tonight," "*A* knows that the product of 12 and 15 is 180," and "*A* knows that a bachelor is an unmarried man," though, of course, further distinctions within it may be possible. It is the sense in which we speak of one's knowing *that something is the case*. Knowledge, in this sense, has been called propositional, or factual, or of truths.

According to the most widely accepted account, to say that *A* knows that something is the case is to say (1) that it is true that it is the case, (2) that *A* believes that it is the case, and (3) that *A* has sufficient evidence that it is the case. If I were to say that *A* knows that the pike will be biting tonight, I would be taken to be saying that it is true that the pike will be biting tonight, that *A* believes that this is true, and that *A* has sufficient evidence that it is true. And, it would seem, were I to say that it is true that the pike will be biting tonight, that *A* believes that this is true, and that *A* has sufficient evidence that it is true, I would be taken to be saying, somewhat pedantically, that *A* knows that the pike will be biting tonight. Whatever one really knows must be true; for the notion of false knowledge is incoherent, though that of false belief or false theory or false description is not. Whatever one really knows one also believes; for a statement of the form "*x* knows that *p* but does not believe that *p*" seems to be, if not incoherent, puzzling without any redeeming informativeness, though it may be neither puzzling nor uninformative to say that *x* has sufficient evidence for a certain proposition which in fact is true, but does not believe it. And, finally, whatever one really knows, one has sufficient evidence for. One must have evidence because knowledge is not mere true belief. An ignorant man's belief that eating peanut butter causes cancer may turn out to be true, but even if it does the man does not know. And one's evidence must attain a certain standard; it must be sufficient, not merely present or even merely good. The fact that now is December is some evidence that tomorrow the temperature in Minneapolis will be below freezing; it may even be counted as very good evidence, but it does not entitle me to claim to know that tomorrow the temperature in Minneapolis will be below freezing, even if this should turn out to be the case. Knowledge is not mere true rational belief. By sufficient evidence is meant, of course, evidence sufficient for knowledge, that is, such that no additional evidence is required in order that one may know. Whether such evidence would be a sufficient *condition* of the truth of what one knows is a further question that must not be prejudged. Evidence, whether sufficient for knowledge or not, is always evidence that something is true; it is evidence for the truth of something. It is sufficient for knowledge when it is of the sort or magnitude that knowledge requires.

I do not think that the above account is mistaken. There have been objections to it, but I shall try to show that they can be met by relatively straightforward explanation or minor reformulation. However, while the account is not mistaken, it is hopelessly inadequate. It is analogous to an attempted explanation of the nature of a fish that restricts itself to the enumeration of the main organs of the fish and completely ignores, say, the fact that a fish lives in water and swims. An adequate account of the concept of knowledge must display its essential place in the conceptual framework through which we would most perspicuously understand ourselves, our life, and the world in which we live. It must delineate a concept which is *clear, distinctive,* and intellectually *enlightening.* It must address itself to the question of how and why, if our conceptual framework had lacked the concept of knowledge, we would introduce such a concept. What concept would fill the vacuum that would then exist in our thought? Let us imagine that our language did not contain the word *knowledge* or words of similar meaning. What technical term, what new concept, would we then have to invent?

A relatively unimportant but quite clear example of the inadequacy of the above account of knowledge is its inability to even suggest an answer to the question whether someone who knows that p must believe that p *because of* the evidence he has, or whether it is sufficient that he merely possess such evidence. Without a clear conception of the place that the concept of knowledge occupies in thought, we are likely to engage in pointless citations of examples and counterexamples from ordinary usage. And ordinary usage is quite uncertain on this question. If John believes that Mary is brilliant because he loves her, and she is brilliant, does he come to know that she is brilliant when he is given the results of the intelligence tests she took? It may seem that he does. If John has the results of Mary's intelligence tests but does not believe that she is brilliant until he falls in love with her, does he come to know that she is brilliant when he so comes to believe that she is brilliant? It would seem that he does not. If we recognize, however, that the distinctive and intellectually central role of the concept of knowledge has to do with one's appraisal of one's beliefs and the choice of one's actions (I shall, of course, return to this point), it becomes obvious that it is not the accidental conjunction of possession of evidence and the holding of the corresponding true belief that constitutes knowledge, but rather the holding of the true belief *because of,* as a result of, on the basis of, the evidence one possesses. For one to appraise a belief or choose an action, in the relevant sense, is for one to attempt to determine whether something should be believed or done, *in the light of* a certain evidence for its truth or desirability.

Attention to the role of the concept of knowledge in the appraisal of one's beliefs and the choice of one's actions would also provide us with the answer to another vexing question, which otherwise seems answerable only by arbitrary stipulation. If one knows that p, must one know that one's evidence for p *is evidence for p?* Must one *know* that there is an evidential connection between one's evidence and what one knows? Again, ordinary usage is uncertain and uninteresting. But in the context of the appraisal of one's beliefs and the choice of one's actions, the answer is obvious. In determining whether one knows that p, one evaluates one's evidence for p, and, obviously, in concluding that one knows that p, one in part appeals to the fact that one knows that such evidence is evidence for p. Of course, if we include in the definition of knowledge as true belief based on evidence the requirement that one must *know* that one's evidence is evidence, we seem to make the definition circular. In fact, the definition should seem circular in virtue of the very inclusion of the requirement that to know one must *possess* evidence, for to possess evidence may only mean to *know* that certain propositions are true. This is not an error in the definition but rather a sign that as it stands it is applicable literally only to derivative knowledge and must be drastically reinterpreted if it is to apply also to primary knowledge. I will come to this topic in section 6 of this Part.

A third example of the inadequacy of the account of knowledge as true belief based on sufficient evidence is its application to the question whether one must know that one knows that p if one is to know that p. We wish to say that one (e.g., a student being examined) may know the correct answer to a certain question, for example, "What is the capital of Egypt?" yet not know that one knows it. But we also wish to say that one cannot think (or say) that one knows that Cairo is the capital of Egypt and at the same time think (or say) that one does not know that one knows that Cairo is the capital of Egypt.[13] How do we resolve this apparent inconsistency? The account provides us with little guidance. In both cases, let us suppose, what one knows is true, one believes it, and one has sufficient evidence for it. And let us ignore the unproblematic case in which one knows dispositionally but not actually that one knows (i.e., the case in which one does not know that one knows simply in the sense that one has not thought or considered whether one knows), as well as the case in which one does not know that one knows because one has doubts about the applicability of the word *know*, either through ignorance of its meaning or through philosophical doubts about the nature of knowledge. The interesting case is that of one's knowing that p but not knowing that one knows that p because one does not have sufficient evidence that one knows that p. The account of knowledge we are concerned with seems to allow for the possibility of such a case. It contains nothing that should make us unwilling to admit that one may have sufficient evidence that p but not sufficient evidence that one knows that p. Yet such an admission is clearly absurd. Why? Again, the answer is clear if we consider the role of the concept of knowledge in the context of the appraisal of one's beliefs and the choice of one's actions. In this context there is no difference between one's determining that one knows that p and one's determining that one knows that one knows that p; there is no difference between choosing to act in a certain way because one knows that p and choosing to act in that way because one knows that one knows that p. For one to have sufficient evidence for knowing that one knows that p is for one to have sufficient evidence for knowing that p. And for one to have sufficient evidence for knowing that p is for one to have sufficient evidence for knowing that one knows that p.

A fourth and much more important defect, though not error, of the account of knowledge as true belief based on sufficient evidence is the very fact that, in its statement of the third necessary condition of knowledge, it makes use of the concept of evidence. Of course, it is unreasonable to

---

13. I have used the word *say* in parentheses in this sentence in order to suggest that the impossibility in question does not consist in the queer or self-defeating character of a certain use of language but in something much deeper.

demand of a philosophical account of a concept that it make no use of other philosophically interesting concepts. Thus, I suggest, it would be unreasonable to demand of an account of knowledge that it avoid the concepts of truth and belief. But these two concepts are relatively clear and distinct in themselves—their content is for most philosophical purposes intellectually visible, and their places in natural thought and discourse are quite determinate—even though they are important subjects of philosophical discussion. And this is not the case with the concept of evidence. Our notion of evidence (to say nothing of that of the *right* to be sure, or that of a proposition it is *reasonable* to accept) is far less clear and distinct, and has a far less determinate place in natural thought and discourse, than our notion of knowledge. It seems fantastic to suppose that we may learn what knowledge is by appealing, ultimately, to our understanding of what evidence is. A satisfactory account of knowledge, I suggest, must be ultimately stateable independently of the concept of evidence, although, I am afraid, the initial use of this concept in the statement of the third necessary condition of knowledge is dialectically indispensable.

However, the most characteristic symptom of the inadequacy of the account of knowledge as true belief based on sufficient evidence is its complete failure to show why knowledge should have the three features of truth, belief, and sufficient evidence; how these are related to one another; and why all three must be present if knowledge is to be present. Is it a sheer accident that we have a concept that possesses these, just these, and all these features? Is the concept a mere composite of these other concepts? Or could it be that only one of these features is essential, that one of them constitutes the essence of knowledge, the other two being merely aspects or consequences of that one? We must address ourselves to these questions, for it is in them that we will find the key to an adequate account of the concept of knowledge. But before we do so, we must undertake, in this section, the task of showing why the account of knowledge in terms of truth, belief, and sufficient evidence is not mistaken, inadequate though it may be. I will return to our main argument in the following section.

The objections to that account have usually taken the form of denials that one of the three conditions stated above is really necessary. That what one knows must be true has seldom been denied. Any tendency to deny it is probably due to a misunderstanding: either this condition is confused with a requirement that one's evidence must entail what one knows, or the assumption is mistakenly made that if it is necessary that if one knows that p then p is true, then p itself must be necessarily true. This latter assumption is perhaps also one of the sources of the view that one can have knowledge only of necessary truths. We shall see, however, that this view has other, more significant sources.

There are two main objections to the condition that one who knows that p must believe that p. According to the first, to say that one believes that p is to imply, at least in some cases, that one does not know that p. For example, if I am asked whether my wife is faithful and I reply by saying that I believe she is, I would be taken to imply that I do not *know* that she is faithful. However, I would be taken to imply this not because of any incompatibility between the notions of knowledge and belief, but because of the important fact that in reply to such a question I chose to say that I believe rather than that I know. When one is expected to say that one knows but chooses instead to say that one believes, it is natural to take one as implying that one does not know. But this fact seems to me to have no conceptual significance. One who knows does not *merely* believe what one knows, but one believes it nevertheless.[14]

The second objection to the condition of belief is more serious. According to it, there are cases that we may describe as knowledge without belief. A standard example would be the mother officially notified of the death of her son. Surely, she knows that he is dead. Yet she might not be able to bring herself to believe it. Now it is difficult to say how seriously such admittedly special cases should be taken. Nor is it clear that in them *know* is used in a standard sense. Perhaps "She knows that her son is dead but does not believe it" in such a case means "She has all the evidence needed for knowing that her son is dead, yet still does not believe that he is." Or, perhaps the point is merely that, while she knows that her son is dead, she does not (yet) have the *feeling* of conviction that normally goes with belief. And, surely, we must admit that what is necessary for knowledge is not belief in the sense of a certain feeling of conviction but simply belief in the sense of assent or acceptance. Surely, much of our knowledge is quite unaccompanied by any special feelings, though it clearly does involve our *assent* to or *acceptance* of the truths we know, our making the *judgment* or holding the *opinion* or at least *taking*

14. Cf. Keith Lehrer, "Belief and Knowledge," *Philosophical Review*, LXXVII (1968), 491–99.

for granted that they are truths. It is simply false that when I come to know that the sum of 347 and 168 is 515 or that the liquid on the floor is spilled milk I must immediately come to have certain special feelings. But it is equally false that I need not assent to or accept the propositions whose truth I know, that I need not judge or opine or at least take for granted that they are true. I shall use *belief* in this wider sense.

However, the objection can be put in a stronger and deeper version, one which does not rely on the occurrence of certain unusual utterances of *know*. The defender of the account of knowledge as true belief based on sufficient evidence will be asked whether, according to him, one must determine that one believes something in order to determine that one has knowledge of it. If belief is a necessary condition of knowledge in the sense in which sufficient evidence is, then one would be expected to consider, in determining whether one knows, whether one believes, as well as whether one has sufficient evidence. Yet nothing of the sort is the case. And the reason is not the self-evidence of one's believing or not believing a proposition; one can easily, and sometimes does, wonder whether one really believes a certain proposition (e.g., that one's wife loves one, that God exists, that honesty is preferable to wealth). The reason, surely, is that one concerned with knowledge is not concerned with whether one believes but with whether what one does believe or could believe is true. But this does not show that knowledge does not include belief. On the contrary, it serves to explain the manner in which it does.

It is in the context of belief that the distinction between what we know and what we do not know actually arises. It is in the appraisal of beliefs and thus of the rationality of actions that the concept of knowledge has its natural home. One's believing what one knows is not a requirement one must strive to meet but rather one which gives point to one's striving to meet the remaining requirements for knowing. The relationship between belief and knowledge is analogous to that between one's having a certain amount of money and one's investment of the money in a certain enterprise. One cannot make the investment unless one has the money. But in the making of the decision to invest, it is not the possession of the money that is in question. One takes for granted that one possesses it or at least that one will possess it when the investment is to be made. The considerations relevant to the wisdom of the decision are unaffected by one's not having the money. One may still study investment opportunities, evaluate them, and reach conclusions as to which would be best for one having such an amount of money to invest. In a similar fashion, one may collect evidence for various propositions, evaluate it, perhaps even conclude that such evidence renders the relevant proposition impossible to be mistaken about, even if in fact such an activity neither generates nor is stimulated by belief in the proposition. But it would be improper to conclude from this that there is no logical relationship between knowledge and belief, just as it would be improper to conclude from the possibility of merely playing at investing that there is not a logical relationship between the making of an investment and the possession of the money to be invested. Just as playing at investing is not the same as investing, so the mere entertainment of a true proposition for which one has evidence sufficient for knowledge is not the same as knowledge.

It is hardly an accident that one who seeks to know ordinarily adopts such a casual attitude toward, takes for granted without further thought, the fact that one will believe what one seeks to know when one's search is successful. Surely, the explanation of this attitude is not that belief, though a logically necessary condition of knowledge, is in itself unimportant. Were assent usually, or even often, absent where truth and sufficient evidence are present, inquiry would seem a mere form of entertainment and human life would be fundamentally irrational. But it is a fact about human nature that assent or belief almost inevitably accompanies the possession of the sort of evidence required for knowledge (although that this is so would become clearer when we have determined what sort that is), the converse, sadly, not being true, and thus that to one seeking knowledge it seems of no greater concern than the availability of oxygen in ordinary circumstances. It is because of this contingent though lawlike connection between the possession of sufficient evidence and belief that it is possible for both to be logically necessary conditions for knowledge even though we are ordinarily interested in and concerned with only the satisfaction of the former. And, we may now observe, it is this connection that explains why it does not ordinarily occur to us to insist that to know one must believe what one knows *because* of the evidence one possesses and not for other, accidental reasons. We shall see in section 6 of this Part that in fact the tie between evidence and belief is even more intimate.

Several objections to the account of knowledge as true belief based on sufficient evidence concern the inclusion of the condition of evidence. According to the first objection, there are cases in which we would say that someone knows even though he has no evidence for what he knows. If a person suddenly tells me exactly what I was thinking this morning while walking to my office, I would be inclined to say that he knows, even if I am convinced that he has no evidence. Indeed, we distinguish between knowledge and a lucky guess. But sometimes the circumstances are such that it is most implausible to describe one's success as a lucky guess. If the truth one states is quite specific or unusual, we would be disinclined to describe it as a guess at all; and if it is not a guess, then it is not a lucky guess. Let us imagine certain persons (perhaps a whole tribe) who are born with certain true beliefs. Even if they are incapable of justifying these beliefs, should we deny that they have innate *knowledge?* The fact is that there is a sense of *know* in which to know something is to believe it truly, namely, a sense applicable to cases in which the belief is sufficiently unusual not to have been the result of simple chance. But it is a *special sense* of *know,* not an exception to the requirement that in the more usual sense of *know* one who knows must have evidence. And what is more important is that such a sense of *know* cannot be primary, for it presupposes the sense of *know* as true belief based on sufficient evidence. Even if a certain unusual belief of mine happens to be true, even if I happen to be born possessing such a belief, I cannot legitimately express it by saying that I know, unless I *discover* that it is true. And to discover that a belief is true is precisely to find sufficient evidence for it. On the other hand, I can say that another person's unusual or innate belief constitutes, in that special sense, knowledge, because I can *know,* in the standard sense, that his belief is true. So even if there is a sense in which one can know without evidence, it is a sense applicable only in second- and third-person epistemic judgments. This is a significant limitation. It is also a sign that such a sense of *know* would be logically secondary, for, as we have already observed, it is an important fact about the concept of knowledge that second- and third-person epistemic judgments can be made legitimately only if the corresponding first-person judgment can be made legitimately, the converse not being true. The judgment "He knows that *p*" cannot be made legitimately by a person unless he can make the judgment "I know that *p*" legitimately. But the judgment "I know that *p*" can be made legitimately by a person even if he cannot make legitimately any judgment of the form "*x* knows that *p*," where *x* is another person. In this respect, second- and third-person epistemic judgments

33

are logically parasitic on first-person epistemic judgments.[15] Therefore, a sense of *know* in which that word can be used only in the expression of second- and third-person judgments cannot be a primary one.

A second objection to the inclusion of sufficient evidence as a condition of knowledge is important and deserves careful consideration because it makes clear the need for the essential distinction between primary and derivative knowledge. It points out that the occurrence of the word *evidence* in the definition of knowledge suggests that one's evidence that *p* is describable in a statement, say *q*, from which *p* follows, whether deductively or in some other fashion, and thus that unless there is such a statement as *q* and the person who asserts his knowledge that *p* can appeal to it, his assertion of knowledge is worthless. And there are serious reasons why such a notion of evidence should not be incorporated in our definition of knowledge. First, there are many perfectly justified epistemic judgments that require no support from other epistemic judgments. (I will give examples of such judgments shortly.) Second, as Plato pointed out in the *Theaetetus,* nothing can serve as evidence for something else unless the possession of such evidence is itself knowledge. This has the formally unacceptable consequence that the definition of knowledge as true belief based on sufficient evidence must, if what is implicit in it is made explicit, include its definiendum (*know*) in the definiens, and the epistemologically unacceptable consequence that we cannot have any knowledge at all, since an actually infinite process of justification is impossible. It is useless to try to avoid this objection by saying, as several philosophers have done, that in some cases we can have knowledge without evidence. If this means literally what it says, then it is a totally inadequate, indeed frivolous, view. The epistemic judgments that require no support from other epistemic judgments are not at all mere expressions of true belief; they have a ground, a basis, and are thoroughly *justified,* whether or not we like to describe this fact by saying that they are based on evidence. On the other hand, if what is meant is that the condition of evidence must be reformulated, then this is legitimate, but very misleadingly stated. Much of our discussion will be an attempt at just such a reformulation.

If the objection is to be met, we must distinguish between derivative epistemic judgments, which are subject to justification by reference to

15. Perhaps it is this fact that should be understood by the phrase *the egocentric predicament.*

other epistemic judgments, and primary epistemic judgments, which do not require, or perhaps even allow, such justification, but are, so to speak, justified or evident in themselves;[16] we must make a corresponding distinction between derivative and primary knowledge; and we must make clear the nature of primary knowledge. That most of our knowledge is derivative should be obvious. This does not mean that in every case we acquire such knowledge by actual derivation; perhaps only seldom do we go through a process of inference. What is meant is that the legitimacy of most of our epistemic judgments depends on the support they receive from other epistemic judgments. That there *are* primary epistemic judgments, and thus that there is primary knowledge, seems to me equally obvious (I will give examples presently), though much of the rest of this book will consist in the analysis of the notion and the demonstration of the existence of such judgments. That there *must* be primary epistemic judgments if knowledge is to be possible seems to me to be a necessary truth. It follows from the very idea of justification. One cannot be said to have justified a judgment by appealing to the truth of another unless the latter can be said to be justified. Consequently, if an infinite regress is to be avoided, as it must be if the justification is to be genuine, there must be epistemic judgments justified in themselves. The really serious, thoroughgoing coherence theorist of truth is a thoroughgoing skeptic.

An epistemic judgment is a judgment that someone knows that something is the case. In the logically fundamental case, it is one's judgment that one knows that something is the case. Even if such a judgment can be made only in the form of a statement, i.e., in uttering or thinking a sentence assertively, the question whether a certain epistemic judgment is *primary* must not be confused with the question whether a certain epistemic statement is incorrigible. I will consider this question in greater detail in section *8* of Part Three. Suffice it here to acknowledge that all statements are corrigible with respect to linguistic propriety. But a primary epistemic statement is merely one that expresses an epistemic judg-

16. A primary epistemic judgment would, of course, be entailed by numerous other judgments and thus would be the conclusion of many valid and sound arguments. Such an argument, however, would never be *epistemically serious:* it could never have premises that are more deserving of assent than its conclusion. A proof that two and two are four may teach us something about the nature of mathematics, but it would not teach us that two and two are four, for we know the conclusion of the proof at least as well, and probably far better, than we know the premises.

ment that is not in need of support from any other epistemic judgment, one with respect to which the question "How do you know?" would not, and need not, be answered by making another epistemic statement. Even if it contains an error of expression, and even if for that reason it is, in a sense, a false statement, it would still express a primary epistemic judgment because its truth would still not have been regarded as in need of justification by reference to other statements. I may think that *toothache* means headache and, if I do have a headache, say that I know that I have a toothache. But even though my statement would, in a sense, be false, it would still be primary because it would still express a primary epistemic judgment. Its *truth* would not have been regarded as in need of justification, though its *propriety* might have been. The question "How do you know that you have a toothache?" would not cease to be inappropriate just because I might be able to recite dictionary definitions. It is not the same as the question, "How do you know that it is the word *toothache* that describes your state?" which I might quite appropriately attempt to answer by appealing to a dictionary. Failure in justification is one thing; failure in linguistic expression is quite another. A mistake in judgment is not the same as a mistake in statement.

The examples that I might give of primary epistemic judgments are the following: "I know that I have a headache." "I know that three and two are five." "I know that orange is more like yellow than like green." "I know that this looks blue to me now." "I know that a surface cannot be both circular and not circular." All of these examples are *first-person* epistemic judgments. There cannot be second- or third-person primary epistemic judgments, because, as I have already pointed out, any such judgment would require for its justification at least the corresponding first-person epistemic judgment, as well as a number of other judgments about the verbal and nonverbal behavior of the person it is about.

Important philosophical issues can be raised with respect to any one of these examples. It is also of great philosophical importance whether further sorts of judgments should be added, such as "I know that there is a typewriter before me now" and "I know that one ought to pursue the good of others." But such issues constitute specific epistemological concerns and cannot be dealt with here; I will consider some of them in Parts Two and Three. I have listed the above judgments in order to *illustrate* what I mean by a primary epistemic judgment, not in order to take a stand on the myriad issues involving them. I have stated why I think that if knowledge is to be possible and the idea of justification intelligible there must be such judgments. I believe that all of the above are primary, though nothing in our inquiry depends on this belief being true. But there is a general argument to the effect that some of the above are not even intelligible, let alone primary, epistemic judgments, and I shall conclude this section with a discussion of this.

It has been argued that some of the above are not genuine epistemic judgments, on the grounds that it is senseless to suppose that they may be mistaken. For instance, it has been argued that "I know I am in pain" is nonsense, because it is nonsense to say that I doubt whether I am in pain.[17] This may seem a curious argument, for one could say that it is precisely the fact that I cannot doubt, or suppose to be mistaken about, something that entitles me, in the best possible way, to claim to have knowledge of it. We may only seldom make such claims, because the bare assertion of the proposition expressing the content of such knowledge is ordinarily sufficient. Ordinarily, we *say* that we know that p when the truth of p has been questioned or may be questioned by someone. But the fact that seldom, if ever, would one make the statements listed above does not constitute a reason for saying that they are senseless, any more than someone's assertion that he knows that he was born within the solar system is senseless, simply because such assertions are seldom, if ever, made.

However, to make such a reply would be to misunderstand the argument. The latter appeals not to the fact that one never makes statements such as "I know that I am in pain," but to the fact that if the locution "I know that . . ." is to make sense, then the locutions "I do not know that . . . ," "I doubt that . . . ," "I may be mistaken in believing that . . ." must also make sense. And this is nothing other than the fact that if a word is meaningful, then its contradictory and contraries must also be meaningful. The locution *"x is blue"* cannot be meaningful if the locution *"x is not blue"* is not meaningful. Now were the locution "I do not know that I am in pain" literally senseless (like "I do not abrakadabra that I am in pain" or "Pain that know in"), then so would be the locution "I know that I am in pain." But, of course, it is not, and the argument could not possibly claim that it is. If it were literally senseless, then any locution of the form "I know that . . ." or "I do not know that . . ." would be sense-

17. Wittgenstein, *Philosophical Investigations,* tr. G. E. M. Anscombe (Oxford: Basil Blackwell, 1953), § 246 and pp. 221–22.

less; for "I am in pain" is a statement, it is true or false, and not at all a locution that cannot meaningfully complete the form "I know that. . . ." In what other way could "I do not know that I am in pain" be senseless? Clearly, only in that it cannot possibly be true, in that it is a logical false-hood. And from this, of course, it would not follow at all that its contradictory is senseless. "Two and two are not four" is logically false, but "Two and two are four" is perfectly intelligible and indeed necessarily true. But what better reason can there be for regarding one's claim to know that one is in pain as true than that the denial of this claim is logically false?

However, the argument does not establish even that. For it may be true that someone who is in pain does not know that he is in pain in that he has not even considered, thought about, his being in pain. He may be a newborn baby or a hospital patient in an unthinking, but not unfeeling, state, or he may simply not have paid attention to his pain. In the first two cases, of course, he would be unable to *make* the statement "I do not know that I am in pain" because he would be unable to make *any* statements. In the third case it is quite possible that he may make the statement "I do not know whether I am in pain" and that the statement would be true. Cases such as the following are not uncommon. A patient is administered an anesthetic. He begins to feel drowsy. He is asked, "Do you still feel pain?" He replies, "Well, I don't know . . . let me see . . . yes, a little."

There are deeper reasons for denying that the statement "I know that I am in pain" is senseless. Whether a statement is senseless or not depends on whether it is capable of describing a state of affairs. And the above statement does describe a state of affairs. For it is only with this statement that we can describe obvious features of certain familiar activities and inquiries.

One's knowledge that one is in pain is not at all the same as one's being in pain, though of course the former entails the latter. There are actions and inquiries that one performs that cannot be explained by reference to one's being in pain but can be explained by reference to one's knowledge that one is in pain. An infant may be in pain (and, of course, consciously so) and perhaps cry because he is in pain. An adult may also be in pain and perhaps cry because he is in pain. But an adult may, in addition to being in pain, *know* that he is in pain. For he may draw conclusions from the fact that he is in pain; he may reflect on it, attempt to explain it, compare his present pain with *remembered* previous pains, and attempt to eliminate his pain in a certain manner. (Consider the not at all unfamiliar case of a man afflicted with frequent headaches who distinguishes kinds of headaches in terms of their intensity, location, and indeed some other characteristics which he has no words for, remembers previous headaches, and examines his present headache with some care in order to determine what medicine to take for it—he has *learned,* for example, that aspirin is sufficient for some headaches but that for others, such as his present headache whose characteristics he *knows,* only Darvon will do.) None of this is intelligible or explainable solely on the supposition that the man is in pain. It becomes intelligible and explainable only on the supposition that he *knows* that he is in pain and that he knows that his pain has such and such characteristics. Had some contemporary philosophers considered not so much the abstract state of being in pain, but the actual states of being in a certain specific pain (e.g., a specific sort of headache, toothache, sore foot, backache), they would not have been so convinced that one cannot know that one is in pain or that the pain one is in has such and such characteristics. To deny that it is intelligible to speak of one's knowing, reflecting on, drawing conclusions from, remembering, examining the *specific* pains one sometimes suffers would be an absurdity into which a philosopher could only be led by disregard for certain facts of common experience and ordinary language.

4. The Degree of Evidence
Sufficient for Knowledge

WE HAVE CONCLUDED THAT the usual objections to the account of knowledge as true belief based on sufficient evidence are either unsound or can be met by minor reformulation. We can now return to the deeper issues regarding this account, issues that must be dealt with in detail if the account is to become a genuine philosophical contribution. It is generally taken for granted that these issues have to do with the third condition: that to know, one must have sufficient evidence. We shall find that this indeed is so, though we shall also find (which should hardly be surprising) that the notion of evidence sufficient for knowledge cannot be understood in abstraction from the other two conditions of knowledge.

There are two main philosophical questions regarding this notion. The first is the nature of the *sufficiency* of the evidence sufficient for knowledge. The second is the nature of the *evidence* that primary knowledge may be based upon. The first question concerns, so to speak, the *degree* of the evidence that is sufficient for knowledge. The second question concerns the sense in which we may speak of evidence at all in the case of primary knowledge, the nature of *self-evidence*. It is convenient to begin with the first question, for it is not specifically restricted to primary knowledge. We shall find that the answer to it will suggest the proper answer to the second question.

I have urged that the key to an adequate account of the concept of knowledge is the question why knowledge has the three elements of truth, belief, and sufficient evidence and what draws these three elements together into one concept, the existence of which is hardly the result of an accidental combining of three otherwise distinct concepts. To answer this question we must understand the distinctive role of the concept of knowledge, the reason such a concept is intellectually indispensable, the place it occupies in the conceptual framework, and thus to grasp its essence in the only way the essence of a concept can be grasped.

In what context is the concept of knowledge indispensable and at the same time of obvious philosophical importance? We have already hinted at what our answer would be. It has two parts. First, the context required is the appraisal of the truth of beliefs and the choice of actions. Second, it is one's appraisal of the truth of one's own beliefs that is conceptually primary. The second part of the answer indeed follows from the first, for one can choose only one's own actions. We require an appraisal of the truth of a belief most naturally in the context of determining the rationality of a certain action. And we require a determination of the rationality of a certain action most naturally in the context of choosing whether or not to engage in that action. But it is only our own actions that we can choose to engage in. Consequently, the natural and most distinctive application of the concept of knowledge is to the appraisal of the truth of our own beliefs. It is thus not surprising that second- and third-person epistemic judgments ascribe knowledge to others, so to speak, by proxy, and that, as we have repeatedly observed, first-person epistemic judgments are logically primary.

In what other contexts is the concept of knowledge employed? There is that of offering one's word, or guaranteeing, that something is the case.[18] I say to someone that I know that the bank will not foreclose his mortgage. By saying this I make a commitment to the truth of the proposition I say I know. But there is nothing distinctive or philosophically important about this context. At most it is, so to speak, of sociological interest. Insofar as what I do in it by employing the concept of knowledge is indeed nothing but my giving my word or guaranteeing something, I could accomplish the same by saying "I give you my word (or I guarantee) that the bank will not foreclose your mortgage." And insofar as what I do has an epistemic character, as of course it does, its epistemic character is left quite unilluminated by its "performative" character, for I am not giving my word or guaranteeing that I will *do* something (I am not saying that *I* will not foreclose the mortgage), but that a certain proposition is true. And if asked, "Why do you guarantee that the bank will not foreclose my mortgage?" I would reply, "Because I know."

There is a second epistemic context, which can be understood in a similar manner. That is the context of confirming what someone else says, or emphasizing what one says oneself. A person says that the pike will be biting tonight, and I reply, "Yes, I know." Or I wish to emphasize my statement that the pike will be biting tonight and say, instead, "I know that the pike will be biting tonight." But if all I am doing by saying this is to confirm or agree with what the other person has said, or to emphasize what I am saying myself, I could have accomplished it by saying only "Yes," perhaps "Yes, indeed!" or "The pike *will* be biting tonight." On the other hand, if there is a further point to saying "I know," then that point is that I agree with or confirm what the person says or that I emphasize what I say, *because I know* that what he says or I say is true.

A third context is that of saying about *someone else* that he knows that something is the case. I say that my student Jones knows that Wittgenstein had read Schopenhauer. Let us suppose that my statement means that Jones believes this, that it is true, and that he has sufficient evidence that it is true. Here we have a far more important context of the use of *know* than those of issuing guarantees and confirmations. It is conceptually distinctive and irreplaceable. But it is not a self-sufficient, independent epistemic context. The reason, of course, is the logically secondary, para-

---

18. See J. L. Austin, "Other Minds," *Proceedings of the Aristotelian Society*, Supplementary Volume XX (1946), 148–87.

sitic status of second- and third-person epistemic judgments. One can make such a judgment legitimately only if one can make legitimately the corresponding first-person epistemic judgment. But one can make the latter judgment legitimately without being able to make the former judgment legitimately. To recognize this is to recognize that what is distinctive about the use of the concept of knowledge in second- and third-person epistemic judgments is, so to speak, anthropological, or psychological, or social in character and not epistemic. The point of such a judgment is not to claim that a certain proposition is true or that there is sufficient evidence for its truth; that would be done with the corresponding first-person judgment. Its point may only be to claim that a certain other person *too* happens to know what I already know to be true.[19]

A fourth context is that of one's *claiming* to know, of one's staking out a claim to a certain parcel of knowledge. This context must not be confused with that of one's judging, or concluding, that one knows, any more than one's claim to ownership of a certain land is the same as one's judgment or conclusion that one is the owner of that land. One makes claims to knowledge in the hustling, bustling, and chattering of one's everyday dealings with other persons. The typical issues regarding *claims* to knowledge, as distinguished from the epistemic *judgments* such claims sometimes express, concern the social appropriateness of the claim, the moral or prudential reasons for making it, and the circumstances in which the claim would have a point (fortunately, one does not claim to know everything that one knows). The justification of a claim to knowledge qua a claim consists in the justification of a certain kind of social behavior. It is a function of the particular circumstances in which the claim is made, the sort of person who makes it, the sort of person to whom it is made, the consequences to be expected of making it, and the degree of importance of what it is about. The justification of an epistemic judgment, on the other hand, is of a completely different sort. It consists in showing that the judgment is true, in evaluating the evidence for it. Very often, of course, in evaluating a claim to knowledge we evaluate only the epistemic judgment that is expected to lie behind it. But it is only the latter that is of direct epistemological interest, though it is possible that

19. But why should first-person epistemic judgments be philosophically important when their subject matter, namely, myself, is far less general and fundamental? But that is not their only subject matter. Their subject matter also includes the world, the facts which I know, including those which I know that others know.

we may learn something about it from a consideration of the former.

The illuminating, philosophically important, and conceptually primary kind of situation in which the concept of knowledge is employed is not that of issuing guarantees to someone about the truth of a proposition, or confirming what someone says, or describing someone else's intellectual achievements, or making claims to knowledge, but, I suggest, that of wondering about the world, seeking truth, appraising one's beliefs, and deciding how to act. No moments in our lives are more important than those when we consider whether certain propositions are true; when we seek, or try to determine that we possess, knowledge of something; when we need, and make, distinctions among what we know, what we believe with reason though not knowledge, and what we merely believe. The search for truth, the appraisal of beliefs, and the distinctions we draw among knowledge, rational (or probable) belief, and mere belief determine the actions we perform and thus the lives we live. It is the world of inquiry and action rather than that of casual social talk that is the true home of the concept of knowledge.

We are not likely to receive much illumination from the use of the concept of knowledge in the usual sorts of contexts in which we are apt to hear questions such as the following: "Does he know that there will be water in the gorge this afternoon?" "Is there an ink bottle in the house?" "Is that a goldfinch?" "Does he know that I am expecting him for tea?" We are, I suggest, even less likely to learn something from examples such as "I know that this is a hand" or "I know that I have not been on the moon." But we may learn something about the concept of knowledge from contexts in which its use is likely to have considerable import, in which our choice of an epistemic term really matters. Such, for example, would be the contexts that probably would provide the setting for questions like these: "But do I really know that Jones will honor his commitment or should I demand that he sign a contract?" "Are you sure that you turned off the oven before leaving for Florida?" "Is it certain that divorce is not a sin?" "Should I buy an extension on my fire insurance even though I am selling my home next week?" "Do I really know that I shall live through the day?" I do not mean, of course, that the concept of knowledge is applicable only, or even mainly, in such somber contexts. But, as we would expect, its essential features are particularly visible in the cases where it is of great practical importance whether we really know or not.

The requirement that for knowledge we must have, in addition to belief and truth, evidence or reasons or a basis is what distinguishes knowledge from *true belief*. The requirement that the evidence we so have must be sufficient, that is, must come up to a certain standard, is what distinguishes knowledge from *rational belief*. All three concepts— knowledge, true belief, and rational belief—are intimately related and yet sharply distinguishable. This is not merely an accidental fact about our language. It is a fact about human life which is of the utmost importance. Our decisions, and thus our lives, are largely determined, insofar as we are reflective, rational beings, by our estimates of the truth of our beliefs, assumptions, expectations, and convictions. And these estimates are made in a framework to which each of the above three concepts is essential. If I believe that *p,* then I have at least a tendency to act in certain specific ways rather than in other ways, though the actual account of the relationship between belief and action is notoriously difficult to provide. But insofar as I am reflecting on the wisdom of so acting, insofar as I am a rational agent, I am concerned not with the fact that I do or do not hold certain beliefs but with the question whether the beliefs I hold are true and what beliefs that I *might* hold would be true. Belief is what determines, at least in part, conscious, intentional action. But is is *true belief* that a rational person wishes to have determine his actions. And the truth of a belief is precisely what lends itself to, and intellectually requires, appraisal. In trying to determine what (actual or possible) beliefs are true, the rational agent is trying to determine what beliefs can be supported with reasons, what beliefs have a basis, for what beliefs there is evidence. In appraising the truth of a belief he is, and may only be, appraising the evidence for, the basis of, the belief. But not all beliefs are equally well supported by evidence or have an equally solid basis. The rational agent is one who not only tends to act in accordance with supported beliefs but also tends to act in accordance with the better-supported beliefs. Here the third concept, that of knowledge, becomes crucial. For many of our decisions in life, and perhaps for *all* of the most important ones, it is not enough that the relevant beliefs be supported by evidence or even that they be better supported than their opposites are. The decisions may be too important; they may concern happiness or misery, life or death, salvation or damnation. In order to make such decisions we seek to provide the relevant beliefs with support that comes up to a certain standard, with evidence sufficient for knowledge.

The crucial task of an inquiry into the concept of knowledge is to account for the requirement that if one knows, one must have sufficient evidence. And the crucial task for the account of this requirement is to preserve the distinction between true rational belief and knowledge. Rational belief is simply belief based on evidence, or, at most, on evidence stronger than the evidence, if any, for the opposite belief. There is no sense of *know* in which such a belief, even if it is true, automatically constitutes knowledge. A gambler is sometimes right, and his expectations are usually based on some evidence, often a precise degree of probability. But, although the evidence may be very strong, neither he nor we should say that he knows, even if he turns out to be right. To be knowledge, one's true belief must be rational, based on evidence; but it must be based on evidence that comes up to a certain standard, on sufficient evidence.

What is meant by the sufficiency of such evidence? Let us keep in mind what we actually mean by *knowledge* and not just when and where we utter the word. (In this case it is better to ask for the meaning, rather than for the use.) We would then easily see the inadequacy of the following, very familiar answers to this question.

Clearly, if I am to know that *p,* then my evidence that *p* is true must be sufficient in more than the sense that it is stronger than my evidence, if any, that *p* is false. Someone's evidence that he will not draw a pair in a game of poker is stronger than his evidence that he will draw a pair, but even if he believes that he will not draw a pair, and indeed does not draw a pair, he still does not know, according to any established criterion for the use of *know,* that he will not draw a pair.

Nor can the evidence required be sufficient in the sense of being the best possible evidence. An expert's evidence that the stock market will be down tomorrow may be the best possible, though he may not know that the market will be down. Nor is sufficient evidence the best that is *logically* possible. The evidence to which the argument from design appeals may well be the best evidence for the existence of God that is logically possible, but it is not obvious that such evidence is sufficient for knowledge of the existence of God. The best possible may not be good enough. (Therefore, one cannot refute the skeptic regarding some species of derivative knowledge, for example, of other persons' thoughts and feelings, by showing that it is logically impossible for us to have grounds for such knowledge that are better than those we do have. The skeptic would regard such an argument as a confirmation of his thesis.)

Nor can sufficient evidence be such that no evidence we have for anything else is greater. We might be woefully ignorant. Nor can it be evidence sufficient to justify the belief that what it is evidence for is true. A man may have evidence sufficient to justify his believing that his wife is faithful even if, though she is faithful, he does not know that she is. Hence, knowledge cannot possibly be *justified* true belief, though it may be true belief supported with sufficient evidence, evidence sufficient for knowledge, not for justified belief.

Nor can sufficient evidence be one that would justify *action* in accordance with the proposition it supports. A man may be perfectly justified in gambling even though he does not know that he will win. Nor is sufficient evidence one that would justify one's *saying* that one knows. A man may be justified in offering encouragement by saying that he knows that success is near, even if he does not know that success is near. Nor should we say that evidence sufficient for knowledge is the evidence a person must have in order to say *legitimately* that he knows. If by "legitimately" we mean "in accordance with the conditions necessary for knowledge," then we have received no illumination, since one of these conditions is that one have sufficient evidence. And if by "legitimately" we mean "without showing ignorance of the meaning of *know*," then a man can legitimately say that he knows even when he does not, because a man can exaggerate and even lie without showing ignorance of the meanings of the words he uses.

Nor can evidence sufficient for knowledge be one that makes doubt unreasonable. It is unreasonable that I should doubt that I will be alive one year from now, but I do not know that I will be alive one year from now. Nor can sufficient evidence be one that makes doubt impossible. For then the believer's credulity might suffice to transform his true beliefs into knowledge.

It has been suggested that there is a "weak" sense of *know* in which the only difference between rational belief and knowledge is that one can believe rationally that *p* even if *p* is false, but one cannot know that *p* if *p* is false.[20] This would suggest that if any of the above cases of rational belief turned out to be true they would be cases of knowledge. And this, of course, is false. The reason it is false is not that in these cases the evidence is too weak. The probability that a belief is true may be 99 per

---

20. See Norman Malcolm, "Knowledge and Belief," in *Knowledge and Certainty* (Englewood Cliffs, N. J.: Prentice-Hall, 1963), pp. 58–72.

cent, but the belief still would not be knowledge, in any standard sense of *know,* even if it were true. One who is asked to draw a marble out of a bag containing ninety-nine white marbles and one black marble may believe (quite justifiably) that he will draw a white marble, and he may turn out to be right, but, if at all thoughtful, neither he nor we would say, whether before or after the drawing, that he knew. Of course, we very many times do say that we know, even when the probability is much lower. But the fact that we say this so often does not show that there is a *sense* of *know* applicable to such cases, a sense in which knowledge is mere true rational belief, a sense in which to say that one knows is to say that one has good reasons for believing something that in fact happens to be true. To show that there is such a sense we must show what about these cases distinguishes them from the many cases in which we would not say that we know even though we have equally strong evidence and do turn out to be right. We must show that one who uses *know* in such cases would insist that he knows even when conscious of the limited degree of his evidence. Otherwise, the mere appeal to what we say is of no conceptual importance. The prevalence of the use of *know* in cases of true rational belief can be explained not only as a result of the existence of a special sense of *know* but also as a result of people's natural tendency to exaggerate, to others as well as to themselves, the support of their beliefs. The discovery of a sense of a word requires more than assembling reminders of its use. I will return to this topic in section 5 of this Part.

All the aforementioned alternatives regarding the nature of evidence sufficient for knowledge, and the conception of knowledge as true rational belief that they encourage, fail for the reason that none of them does justice to the intimate connection between the first and the third condition of knowledge, between the truth of what one knows and one's evidence for it. They treat as separate and equal the requirement that one must have sufficient evidence and the requirement that what one knows must be true, and the corresponding conception of knowledge is the result of a mechanical, lifeless addition of the one requirement to the other, something that can only be described as a conceptual monstrosity. They ignore the all-important fact that the satisfaction of the requirement of truth cannot be determined independently of the satisfaction of the requirement of evidence. Even in retrospective appraisals of one's own epistemic judgments there is no such thing as determining that what one knew was true which is not the same as determining that there is a certain sort of evidence that it was true. And in the primary case, that of one's own *present-tense* epistemic judgment, there is not even the illusion of a distinction between determining that the condition of sufficient evidence is satisfied and determining that the condition of truth is satisfied. Nevertheless, the truth of what I hope to know *is* part of the criterion for legitimately judging that I know. To suppose otherwise would be to render the listing of all three conditions senseless. Consequently, the truth of what I hope to know is one of my reasons for regarding my epistemic judgment in a certain situation as legitimate. But how could it function as such a reason? The impression that the two conditions of truth and sufficient evidence are separate and independent is fostered by our preoccupation with third-person and first-person *past-tense* epistemic judgments. With respect to these, one can indeed determine independently the satisfaction of the condition of truth, namely, by appealing to *one's own present knowledge*. But it is first-person *present-tense* epistemic judgments that are logically primary, precisely because one must appeal to *them* in appraising both third-person and first-person past-tense epistemic judgments. And with respect to first-person present-tense epistemic judgments, such an independent determination of the satisfaction of the condition of truth is impossible.

If I am to use the truth of a proposition as part of my criterion for judging that I know it, then it would seem that in a certain sense I must *have the truth* of what I hope to know, and that if I do not then I simply have no knowledge but at best rational belief, which I hope is true. But, clearly, we do not *have* truth in the sense in which we have belief or in the sense in which we have reasons for thinking that something is true. To say that we have the truth about some matter is to say that we know, that we have discovered, the truth about it. To say that we have discovered the truth may only be to say that we now have evidence sufficient for knowing the truth we seek. We may be tempted to distinguish between judging that a proposition is true and judging that we have sufficient evidence for knowing that it is true because of the important difference in the case of empirical propositions between the observation of the situation described by the proposition as a ground for judging the proposition to be true and other possible grounds for making such a judgment, for example, inference from another observed situation or someone's testimony. We are tempted to say that in the former case we do not merely have grounds or evidence for the truth of the proposition but that we have the truth of the proposition itself. And as long as saying this is a way of pointing out the primacy of observation as a means of discovering the truth of propositions describing observable situations, it is legitimate and illuminating. But when it becomes a way of dealing with the concept of knowledge itself, it is misleading. In some situations, observation may constitute absolutely sufficient evidence for knowing the truth of the proposition. But such observation would not be some mysterious possession of the situation described by the proposition, or of the truth of the proposition, but simply sufficient evidence for knowing that the proposition is true. If we do not like the word *evidence,* we can use equivalently a word such as *grounds, basis,* or *reason.* But the fact remains that we know the situation we observe *because* we observe it; if asked, "How do you know that there is a typewriter before you now?" I would reply not by saying, "There is a typewriter before me now," but by saying, "I *see* that there is a typewriter before me now." And if asked, "How do you know that you see this?" I would hardly appeal to my seeing the fact that I see this. I will return to this point in section 2 of Part Three.

Nevertheless, we continue to feel that one who knows that p does not merely have evidence, however good, that p, or reasons for believing that p, but somehow has the truth of p itself. The reason for this feeling is, of course, the requirement that what one knows must be true. Yet, as we have seen, to determine that this requirement is met one may only appeal to the evidence one has. Thus we seem faced with a paradox. On one hand, we regard the truth of what we know as separate from the evidence we have for it and as equally necessary for knowledge. On the other hand, it does not even make sense to attempt to determine that what we hope to know is true independently of determining what sort of evidence we have that it is true. But we seem to be faced with this paradox only because we have no clear understanding of the sort of evidence one must have in order to know. At the same time, the fact that we are faced with the paradox suggests the proper account of such evidence. It suggests that the condition that what one knows must be true is not a requirement which is additional to that of sufficient evidence but is a more explicit specification of the latter requirement. It is really redundant. But its inclusion performs a useful function, for it is a kind of insurance that we will not completely misunderstand the concept of knowledge. It is a conceptual reminder of what our evidence must be if it is to be sufficient for knowledge. Specifically, it draws our attention to the fact that this evidence must be such that if one has it, then one "has" the truth of the proposition known; that if one has satisfied the requirement that one must have sufficient evidence, then one has satisfied the requirement that what one knows must be true; and that the latter requirement is part of, included in, the former. Had we, to begin with, a clear understanding of this fact, we would not have needed to include the condition of truth in our account of knowledge. But, in reality, when we commence such an account we have only a rudimentary notion of the sort of evidence knowledge requires, though we have a fairly adequate everyday notion of what knowledge is, and we make up for this deficiency by demanding separately that if one knows then what one knows must be true.

Now in what sense can it be the case that if one has satisfied the requirement of sufficient evidence, then one has satisfied the requirement of truth? How can the latter be included in the former, rather than being a separate and additional requirement? Clearly, only in the sense that if one is to know that *p,* then one's evidence that *p* must be such that it is *absolutely impossible* that *p* is false, the sense in which one's evidence that *p* makes a mistake about *p* absolutely impossible, the sense in which one's evidence that *p, entails* that *p* is true.[21] Only if we understand the notion of evidence sufficient for knowledge in this way do we avoid the above paradox. Only then do we understand how the truth of what one knows is a necessary condition but not a separate criterion for one's knowing it. And, what is even more important, only then do we understand both the distinction between knowledge and true belief and that between knowledge and rational belief. Only then do we perceive the difference between knowledge and a rational belief that merely happens to be true (e.g., a gambler's belief). Thus, only then can we claim to have rendered the concept of knowledge clear and philosophically enlightening and to have assigned to it a distinctive place in our conceptual framework.

If the condition that to know one must have sufficient evidence is so understood, then the condition that what one knows must be true need

21. I am using Hume's term *absolutely impossible* instead of the more common Kantian term *logically impossible* in order to allow that something may be as impossible as a self-contradictory state of affairs even if it is not a self-contradictory state of affairs, and my use of *entails* should be understood in a correspondingly broad sense. The reasons for allowing this will become plain in Part Two. Further, in sections 7 and 8 of Part Four, I shall consider the question whether there may be other kinds of impossibility. If there are, then our account of sufficient evidence would be far less austere than it now appears to be. But it is with regard to derivative, and not primary, knowledge that the existence of such additional kinds of impossibility becomes relevant or plausible.

not be added. We have also seen that the condition that one who knows must believe what one knows, although logically necessary, is satisfied as a matter of contingent fact whenever the requirement that one possesses sufficient evidence is satisfied, and that for this reason one's believing what one hopes to know is not a criterion one uses in determining whether one knows but rather a description of that which provides the context for, gives point to, and is the natural purpose of, such a determination.[22] Therefore, we have in effect reached the conclusion that knowledge does not have three distinct and independent features, namely, truth, belief, and sufficient evidence. Essentially, to know that p is to have a certain sort of evidence that p, for the possession of that evidence entails that p is true and is naturally accompanied by, perhaps causally implies, the belief that p. This sort of evidence that p is evidence that makes mistake in believing that p absolutely impossible. We may say then, in brief, that knowledge is the absolute impossibility of mistake, and that an epistemic judgment of the form "I know that p" can be regarded as having the same content as one of the form "It is absolutely impossible that I am mistaken in believing that p." Although we must of course remember that the belief regarding which mistake is impossible is a belief that one actually holds, and not merely a possible belief; that the absolute impossibility of mistake is due to the possession of a certain evidence for the truth of the belief, and not, trivially, to the fact that the belief happens to be true (whether contingently or necessarily); that the belief must be held *because of* the evidence that makes mistake regarding it impossible, and not merely coincidentally; and that one must know that the evidence that makes mistake impossible is indeed such evidence.[23] But this is only a provisional conclusion. We will find, in section 7 of this Part, that it must be revised in some very important respects. And most of Part Four will be devoted to the development of another and independent argument for that conclusion.

The above argument may seem excessively abstract and thoroughly implausible. But, contrary to the usual philosophical opinion, there is no alternative explanation of the sort of evidence one must have in order that one know, which is at all in conformity with the ordinary concept of knowledge. Several pages back a number of such alternatives were enumerated, and it was found, with little difficulty, that none accords with

22. See above, pp. 31–32.
23. See above, pp. 26–27.

any standard sense of *know*. This, perhaps, should not matter. Perhaps we should *introduce* a sense of *know* that would include a standard of sufficient evidence weaker than the absolute impossibility of mistake. But the fact is that there is no conceptual room for such a sense of *know* because there is no room for such a conception of sufficient evidence. At most we can just *rename* the concept of a rational belief that happens to be true and call it *knowledge*. But renaming is no more the filling of an empty place in our conceptual framework than renaming of a horse is the acquisition of a second horse.

However, there are reasons in favor of our account of sufficient evidence that are deeper than the actual meaning of *know* or the fact that there is room in conceptual space for a concept of knowledge distinguishable from the concept of true rational belief. If our account is false, then the concept of knowledge may only be identified with the concept of true rational belief. (It makes no difference what specific account of the rationality of a belief we adopt, as long as it does not coincide with our account of sufficient evidence.) But there could not be a concept of true rational belief (although perhaps there could be a concept of rational belief) if there were not another, and stronger, concept of knowledge. For the very applicability of the concept of true rational belief presupposes the applicability of another concept that can only be described as a concept of knowledge. In judging that someone else holds, or oneself in the past held, a certain true rational belief, one must determine, among other things, that the belief is true; merely to determine that it is based on reasons is, obviously, not to determine that it is a *true* rational belief. Could such a determination of truth consist in one's coming to hold a true rational belief that has the same content? If so, one must be able to determine that the belief one so comes to hold is indeed rational and true. There is no difficulty in determining that it is rational; one may possess evidence supporting it. But how would one determine that the belief is true? By hypothesis, not through the possession of evidence entailing the truth of the belief. But there is no other way.

The fact is that the conception of knowledge as rational belief that happens to be true makes inexplicable the really distinctive function of the concept of knowledge. When we seek knowledge and distinguish it from mere rational belief we are employing a criterion for making such a distinction *now* and with respect to our *own* knowledge. The distinction between knowledge and rational belief is only secondarily one that is made retroactively, after we have discovered the truth, or with respect to other persons. It is now that I want to determine whether I know that the limb on which I find myself will hold me or merely have good reasons for believing that it will. The view in question seems to suggest that the discovery of the truth of a proposition is something distinct from and beyond knowledge, that, for example, when I discover that my confident prediction yesterday of rain today turned out to be true and thus, according to this view, I may call it knowledge, I have done something more than, and distinct from, simply *coming to know* that it is raining and thus coming to know that what I said yesterday was true. We have seen that this suggestion must be rejected. But if it is rejected, and if consequently I also know now what I knew yesterday, then the difference between my knowing this yesterday and my knowing it today, since it lies neither in the truth of what I know nor in the firmness of my conviction, would have to be stated in one of the following three ways. It might consist in my now having better evidence than the evidence I had yesterday, which by itself would be to fail to recognize either case as one of knowledge. It might consist in my now having more sufficient evidence than the evidence I had yesterday, which is unintelligible. Or, finally, it might consist in my now having evidence sufficient for knowing that for knowing which yesterday I had insufficient, though perhaps good, evidence, in which case yesterday I did not have knowledge though today I do.

It is the search for truth and the discovery of truth that constitute the chief and most important subject matter of epistemology. We require a concept of knowledge in order that we may understand what it is to seek truth and to discover truth. And the concept of true rational belief is totally inadequate to this task. It is simply nonsense to suppose that to *seek* truth is to aim at holding a rational belief that happens to be true. It is simply nonsense to suppose that to *discover* truth is to come to hold a rational belief that happens to be true. For then there would be no difference between identifying a belief as rational and identifying it as a true rational belief. Only the concept of knowledge as the absolute impossibility of mistake can do justice to the concepts of seeking and discovering truth.

Our account of the notion of evidence sufficient for knowledge allows us to understand why philosophers have usually regarded deductive proof as the paradigm of justification. They have done so not because of some queer fascination with the "deductive mode of reasoning," but because in a deductive proof the premises are such that if they are true then it is absolutely impossible for the conclusion to be false. If one "has" the truth of the premises, then one also "has" the truth of the conclusion. We can also understand why some philosophers have claimed that one can know that one knows by reflection.[24] The entailment of what one claims to know by one's evidence for it is just the sort of thing that can be discovered purely by reflection. And we can understand why there is an analogy between certain uses of *know* and the standard uses of *"promise."* [25] One who has sufficient evidence, in the sense described, that a certain proposition is true can indeed *guarantee* that the proposition is true, for the evidence makes the falsehood of the proposition absolutely impossible.

It is this sense of "sufficient evidence," I submit, that comes closest to expressing the ordinary concept of knowledge. It would be impossible for us, however, to adopt it without drastic reformulation. As it stands, it is quite unsuited for the account of the concept of primary knowledge. Primary epistemic judgments are not justified because they are entailed by certain other judgments. The evidence needed for primary knowledge cannot be some other item of knowledge. But before I attempt the needed reformulation I must consider the major, and of course obvious, objection to the above account of the notion of sufficient evidence.

5. The Usage of Know

WHY IS IT THAT in actual usage *know* usually seems governed by much less stringent criteria? Few of our claims to knowledge are based on evidence that entails that what we claim to know is true. Why is this so? I suggest that the reason is that the word *know* (and related expressions) falls into a class of words that quite naturally lend themselves to habitual yet perfectly justifiable *exaggerated* uses. One subgroup of such words consists of words whose very utterance is likely to have considerable *practical import*. Another subgroup consists of words referring to *standards*. *Know* belongs to both.

In addition to *know,* the first subgroup contains such words as *love,*

24. See H. A. Prichard, *Knowledge and Perception* (Oxford: Clarendon Press, 1950), pp. 85–97.
25. See Austin, "Other Minds."

good, believe, stupid, friend. To a degree far greater than in the case of other words, the members of this subgroup occur in statements that would be appraised not only as true or false, but also as wise or foolish, optimistic or pessimistic, honest or dishonest, trustworthy or misleading, careful or careless, mature or immature, experienced or inexperienced, forceful or weak, effective or ineffective. The reason, of course, is that the use of such a word is likely to produce in the listener important attitudes and perhaps encourage him to act in certain ways. And even in the case of the speaker himself, his actual use of the word may clarify and solidify certain attitudes and lead him to action. A lover's claim to be in love could cause attitudes and actions on the part of his listener that would largely determine the lives of both. And the very making of the claim may actually convince the lover that he is in love, or at least commit him to acting as if he were. If one hopes to become clear about the meaning of the word *love* by assembling reminders of its use, one is likely to reach some rather absurd conclusions. The word is far too often used in cases in which it does not apply, not because of ignorance of its meaning or of the actual circumstances of its use but because of the desire for the consequences uttering it is likely to have, including perhaps a certain pleasure the speaker himself derives from his very utterance of the word. In a similar way, people very often claim to know when they do not, although they are not ignorant of the meaning of *know* or of the circumstances in which they use the word. By using the word, even though illegitimately, one can encourage important actions, gain respect and admiration, cause attitudes one regards as desirable, and even acquire the confidence one needs to achieve some difficult ends. A man who hesitates is lost, we say, and so very often is a man who does not tell himself that he knows. A leader would have few followers if he did not exaggerate, both to others and to himself, the extent of his knowledge of the ways of success. To deplore and attempt to eliminate such exaggerated uses of *know* would be a practical mistake. To regard these uses as paradigms of a *sense* of *know* would be an intellectual mistake.

It is more important, however, that *know* belongs also to the subgroup of words that refer to standards employed in appraisals of qualities of things and of actions and beliefs of persons. Divergence from such a standard is generally a matter of degree, and where the degree is sufficiently small to be unlikely to make a practical difference we honestly, justifiably, and usually unconsciously ignore it. Perhaps the most familiar examples are words such as *circle, white, equal* and *second* (as a noun). One need not be acquainted with the formal definition of the circle in geometry in order to have a precise notion of what a circle is. Children at the age of seven already have such a notion. At the same time, the word is consistently applied to various shapes that unquestionably and obviously fail to be circles, though they resemble circles. (Consider the usual circles drawn on blackboards!) It would be absurd to explain this fact by saying that in such cases different criteria for the application of the word are used, or that the word *circle* has a different sense in such applications. Nor could it be claimed that such uses constitute extensions of the conventional meaning of *circle* for no one, if the difference between the figure to which the word is applied and the standard circle were pointed out to him, would claim that the word is applicable to the former because of an additional rule of language. The obvious explanation of such consistent exaggerated uses of the word *circle* is that the objects of its application in such cases are sufficiently like circles to make the application of the notion to them quite convenient, and usually harmless. For practical purposes one sometimes can regard an ellipse as a circle, knowing perfectly well that in no sense of the word *circle* is an ellipse a circle.

A person can also say, with justification, "I will be back in a second," knowing that he will be back in a minute. Only a child would think that such a statement is false. Yet it would be absurd to suppose that there is a criterion for applying the notion of a second to periods of one minute. Very much the same can be said about many of the uses of the words *equal* and *white*. And, in a similar fashion, for practical purposes a man may justifiably say that a certain case is a case of knowledge, even if he recognizes or could be made to recognize that in fact it is nothing of the sort. For practical purposes a man may justifiably claim to have knowledge of something even if he does not. This fact may have psychological and sociological importance. But it is relevant to the theory of knowledge only insofar as it engenders the mistaken view that there are genuine criteria of knowledge much less stringent than the impossibility of mistake. Let us consider some examples.

If on going to bed at midnight I notice that there is snow on the ground and that the temperature is about 30° F., I may say that I know that there will be snow on the ground in the morning. And yet, of course, it is possible (not merely because it is not self-contradictory) that there will not be snow on the ground tomorrow (a warm spell may come overnight and melt the snow). So, it may be said, I must be using *know* in its "weak" sense,[26] in a sense in which knowledge need be nothing more than true rational belief. Now such a case can be understood as exemplifying at least three very different sorts of situations: (1) I am unacquainted with, or even simply not thinking at the moment of, the possibility that a warm spell will come overnight and melt the snow. If so, then my claim that I know would be neither conceptually incorrect nor loose, but neither would it exemplify the use of a criterion of knowledge other than the impossibility of mistake, for I may still be using, though erroneously, the impossibility of mistake as my criterion for saying that I know. (2) If I am acquainted with, and aware of, that possibility, my claim may still be neither conceptually incorrect nor loose, but neither would it exemplify the use of another criterion of knowledge, for I may not take the possibility of mistake seriously, somewhat as one who is seriously ill may be aware or be made aware of the possibility that he will die and yet not take it seriously; and not to take the possibility of mistake seriously in such cases is simply not to take it as a genuine possibility. Neither of these two alternatives exemplifies a special, "weak" sense of *know*, though they may exemplify ignorance, or intellectual failure to think of relevant facts, or foolishness. (3) I may be aware of, and take as genuine, the possibility that a warm spell may come overnight and melt the snow and yet consider it so remote that I refuse to take it into account in deciding to use the word *know*, though if I were to take it into account I would not use that word. In a similar fashion, an air traveler may claim to know that he will be in New York tomorrow, and then, if pressed, say that of course an accident is possible and thus that he does not really know but that it would be foolish to dwell on such a remote possibility by making it a point to say that he only has excellent reasons for believing that he will be in New York tomorrow. It is this third sort of situation that creates the illusion that there is a "weak" sense of *know*, a sense in which knowledge is true rational belief. But that there is such a sense of *know* is only an illusion. To suppose that it is not would be like supposing that someone who, in a certain context, calls a light grey white and then admits that of course it is not really white, but remarks that it would be foolish, in that context, to insist on calling it only light grey, is using the word *white* in a different sense, a "weak" sense.

26. See above, pp. 46–47.

The kind of situation in the use of *know* that would prove the existence of a weak sense of this word would be that of a man who says (and *means* what he says), "I know that there will be snow on the ground tomorrow," although he is aware of the possibility that the snow may melt overnight, takes that possibility seriously, and regards it as relevant to the legitimacy of his use of *know*. Any such case, however, would clearly be a case of misuse of *know*, in any ordinary sense of this word. The reason is that such a case would violate the admitted requirement that "I know that *p*" entails that *p*. Indeed, the description of such a case does not contain the denial of *p*. But it does contain the assertion of the possibility that *p* is false. To deny that *p* entails *q*, one can assert *p* and deny *q* or assert *p* and assert that *q* may nevertheless be false.

When, instead of indiscriminately listing actual cases of the use of *know*, we consider what the user of the language would say (and does say) in circumstances that require him to speak with care, precision, and dispassion, the facts about the ordinary meaning of *know* are seen to be quite different from what most contemporary philosophers suppose. The air traveler does not and would not say while purchasing air accident insurance that he knows that he will not be the victim of an accident. The businessman, whose career may depend on his judgment of his partner's intentions, would not claim to himself to know his partner's intentions while signing a contract designed to protect him from fraud (despite what recent theorists of our knowledge of other minds may tell him). A person who, departing from his home on a long journey, returns to make sure that the oven has been turned off would not claim to know that he did turn off the oven, even though his memory seems as clear as ever. When asking for another physician's opinion, a patient who has been advised to have his leg amputated does not claim to know that his doctor's advice is right, even if he has no doubt that it is.[27]

Yet are we not led by our insistence on impossibility of mistake as the

27. If knowledge as true rational belief is understood, more specifically, to be the same as true probable belief then, in that sense, "*A* knows that *p* and *A* knows that *q*" would not entail "*A* knows that *p* and *q*." (See Herbert Heidelberger, "Knowledge, Certainty, and Probability," *Inquiry*, VI [1963], 242–50; and Keith Lehrer, "Knowledge and Probability," *Journal of Philosophy*, LXI [1964], 368–72.) Another paradoxical consequence of this conception of knowledge has been pointed out by E. Gettier in "Is Justified True Belief Knowledge?" *Analysis*, XXIII (1963), 121–23. If evidence sufficient for knowledge need not be evidence entailing the truth of what one knows, then one can have sufficient evidence for a false proposition which however entails a true proposition; and if one then believes the latter, one would have satisfied all three conditions of knowledge and still, obviously, not know.

criterion of knowledge to the paradoxical conclusion that most of what is ordinarily called knowledge, in everyday life as well as in the sciences, is not knowledge? We are led to that conclusion, but it is not paradoxical. Indeed, it *seems* paradoxical, but only because of our natural tendency to assume that what is not knowledge is mere belief, bare opinion, and that nothing but knowledge can have intellectual, "cognitive" worth. But such an assumption is false. Knowledge is contrasted not only with mere belief but also with rational belief. Is it paradoxical to assert that most of what is called knowledge is in fact rational belief, a set of judgments whose truth is only probable, even if very highly probable? Such an assertion may be false, but it is hardly paradoxical; it is even generally accepted by nonphilosophers.[28]

This is why it would be a serious, though hardly novel, mistake to interpret the view that knowledge is the absolute impossibility of mistake as equivalent to skepticism. The interesting sort of skeptic is not the one who denies that we know what we think we know but the one who denies that we have good (or even any) reasons for believing what we think we are justified in believing. A philosopher who says that all we can have is "probability" and not "absolute certainty" is likely to be confused, but he would hardly be a skeptic. Consequently, to try to avoid skepticism by tampering with the notion of knowledge would be futile. The skeptic could be satisfied with the identification of knowledge with true rational belief and still raise his question, Are our usual beliefs really rational? We shall consider skepticism in the last part of our inquiry. For our present purposes it is sufficient to remind ourselves that we must not attempt to avoid future problems by present conceptual subterfuges.

But the fact that the view that knowledge is the absolute impossibility of mistake is not equivalent to skepticism should not mislead us into supposing that that view is then mere pedantry. We apply the concept of knowledge to what in reality are only cases of rational belief because such cases are regarded as sufficiently like knowledge to be, for practical purposes, counted as such. And, more generally, the very concept of a

---

28. Another reason for the appearance of paradox is that the role of the word *knowledge* does not always parallel that of *know*. (This is why in this inquiry, as in most other attempts at an elucidation of epistemic concepts, it is the latter that has been of main concern.) In one of its most common senses, *knowledge* is a synonym of *learning* and *erudition*, and there is no corresponding sense of *know*. One can be erudite with respect to scientific cosmology yet admit that such erudition consists almost entirely of opinions, some not even very probable.

rational belief is that of a belief that is *like* knowledge and thus can function, for many purposes, as a substitute for knowledge. But if knowledge is the absolute impossibility of mistake, how can any belief be *like* knowledge without *being* knowledge? How can any belief be rational? How can there be evidence that does not consist in the rendering of mistake absolutely impossible, or, briefly, in the absolute impossibility of mistake?

The real skeptical challenge is the question, How can anything be sufficiently like the absolute impossibility of mistake—which undoubtedly is a kind of evidence or reason for belief—that it may be called evidence without simple and uninteresting equivocation on the word *evidence?* The habitat of the concept of evidence, of reason for belief, is the appraisal of belief and choice of action. It is undeniable that the absolute impossibility of mistake is at least *one* paradigm of the natural concept of evidence. For anything else to be evidence it must be sufficiently like the absolute impossibility of mistake to be regarded as an object of the application of the same concept. For only if it is the latter can it be relevant to the appraisal of belief and the choice of action. Therefore, if rational belief is to be possible, and thus the interesting kind of skepticism false, the application of the word *evidence* both to the basis of rational belief and to the basis of knowledge must not be a case of mere equivocation. The skeptic would argue that this is all that it can be, for he would deny the possibility of any similarity between the absolute impossibility of mistake and whatever we wish to regard as a basis of the general kinds of rational beliefs we hold (e.g., about bodies, other minds, the past, etc.). Indeed, it is generally admitted today that there is no such similarity. And the usual way of attempting to refute the skeptic is not to insist that there is but to argue that the lack of such a similarity does not render the application of the word *evidence* equivocal. I shall call this view the *thesis of nonequivocating multiple criteria of evidence* and will consider it in detail in Part Four.

I have argued in this section that the view that knowledge is the absolute impossibility of mistake does conform to the ordinary meaning of *know.* The supposition that it does not has rested on the failure to recognize that, at least in the case of words such as *knowledge, love, circle,* and *white,* we must determine what people mean not by indiscriminately noting what they say but by learning what they *would* say in carefully prepared and selected, significant cases. But even if the ordinary meaning of *know* were quite different, we would still defend the above account. If there were not the concept of knowledge as the impossibility of mistake, we should invent such a concept. For such a concept is indispensable for our understanding of the cognitive enterprise, of the search for truth and the discovery of truth. It provides us with a yardstick with which we can measure the relative adequacy of beliefs. Even if knowledge so understood constituted only a small part of what we have achieved in our pursuit of truth, indeed even if it were entirely unattainable, it is precisely that which such pursuit necessarily seeks to approximate. It is that which gives direction to our cognitive enterprise. It is that which makes it possible for us to judge the degrees of success in that enterprise. This is why it would be quite false to say regarding an account of knowledge such as ours that it renders the word *knowledge* almost useless and the concept of knowledge unimportant. To say this would be to ignore the fact that the ideal may well have far greater practical significance than the real. Political ideals often have more important consequences than political realities. The notion of a rod that is exactly one meter long is much more useful than any number of actual measuring rods. Few circles in nature or in human artifice may correspond to the definition of the circle. Perhaps none do. But this fact disturbs us not at all. The ideal of perfect circularity, even if unrealized, remains of the greatest practical significance. It is our yardstick for measuring the relative adequacy of the circles we find or create. The circles we draw or manufacture are expressly designed as approximations to that ideal. The latter is what gives direction to our creation of circles. It is that which makes possible our evaluation of the degrees of success in such creation. One need not be a Platonist to recognize this.

6. The Nature of Self-Evidence

THE GENERAL NOTION of evidence sufficient for knowledge is clear enough. Such evidence guarantees the truth of the proposition known; it renders a mistake impossible. In the case of derivative knowledge a paradigm of such evidence (though perhaps only one of several paradigms) is the set of premises of a formally valid argument. The nature of formal entailment is intuitively clear enough to render the *general* nature of evidence sufficient for knowledge also clear. But the application of the notion of such evidence to primary knowledge is obscure. For such knowledge, by definition, is that for which the evidence does not consist in the truth of certain other propositions; consequently, the evidence for it cannot consist of certain true propositions that entail the proposition known. But in what other way can there be evidence sufficient for knowledge? What is the nature of *self-evidence?*

It is important that we recognize that while the applicability of the notion of evidence to primary knowledge is obscure, it is not questionable. It is a fact that sometimes we know certain truths without appealing, or even being able to appeal, to any other truths, and that we regard a claim to such knowledge as justified, as supported, as having a basis, and not at all as an expression of a mere true belief. It is a fact that sometimes what we believe is such that it is impossible that we may be mistaken about it, even though it is not the truth of anything else that renders such mistake impossible. It is absolutely impossible that I may be mistaken in believing that I have a headache, that three and two are five, that I believe that the sun will rise tomorrow. I find such *mistake* unthinkable, inconceivable, even though in the case of the first and third examples, but not the second, I find the *falsehood* of the proposition quite conceivable. And when I say that mistake with regard to these three propositions is unthinkable, I certainly do not mean that each of them is entailed by certain other propositions that I know to be true. Consequently, there can be no question that the notion of evidence sufficient for knowledge is applicable to primary knowledge, that there is primary knowledge, that mistake in believing something can be absolutely impossible even when no relevant inference is or can be performed, and that there is such a thing as self-evidence. The possibility and existence of self-evidently true beliefs should not be questioned. But of course their nature can and must be inquired into.

On the other hand, an inquiry into the nature of self-evidence must not be thought of as aiming at the discovery of a *method* for determining what beliefs are self-evidently true and what are not. For such a method would presumably consist, at least partly, in a set of instructions as to how to prove that such a belief is true. But a self-evidently true belief is precisely one which can be known to be true without proof, one for which a proof could never be epistemically serious but would at best amount to a logical exercise (like proving that Jones is sitting to the left of Williams by appealing to the fact that Williams is sitting to the right of Jones). An inquiry into the nature of self-evidently true beliefs must not, and cannot, aim at the discovery of features of such beliefs from the presence of which we may infer that the belief is self-evidently true. Perhaps such an inference can be performed and perhaps it would be sound, but it can never be epistemically serious.

The most common view is that a primary epistemic judgment is one describing knowledge of what is experienced, that only truths about what is experienced require no justification by appeal to other truths.[29] This view is valuable insofar as it draws attention to the important role of perception in the acquisition of primary knowledge. But it throws no light at all on the nature of primary knowledge, nor does it explain why knowledge of what is experienced should be primary. To say that a certain knowledge has as its object something experienced is not to say that such knowledge is primary, that it neither needs to be nor is capable of being justified by appeal to knowledge of something else. It may be true that knowledge of what is given in experience is always primary. But even if this were true, it would not be an explanation of the concept of primary epistemic judgment or of the concept of a self-evident belief. On the contrary, its truth can be determined only if such an explanation has already been given.

In fact, the view that primary knowledge is knowledge of what is experienced is not only conceptually unilluminating, but, at least as it stands, certainly false. A paradigm of experience is visual perception. But one's claim to see something, and especially to see that something is the case, is a familiar example of a claim that is subject to justification by appeal to other truths (e.g., that the light is good, one's eyes normal, one's mind undisturbed). Consequently, it cannot possibly be primary. This is why, of course, philosophers defending this view are dissatisfied with the notion of experience and require that the notion of *immediate experience* be introduced. But *how* is this done? If one introduces the notion of immediate experience by saying that one has immediate experience only of what one neither does nor needs to infer,[30] then of course one cannot define primary knowledge in terms of immediate experience. But if the notion of immediate experience is introduced in some other way, then the question *on what grounds* one supposes that what one immediately

29. The most recent theory of knowledge based on this view is that offered by A. C. Danto in *Analytical Philosophy of Knowledge* (Cambridge: At the University Press, 1968).
30. See H. H. Price's introduction of the terms *sense-datum* and *sensing* in *Perception* (London: Methuen, 1932), p. 3.

experiences is really there and has the qualities it is experienced to have, could be raised; and thus the fact that what one knows is immediately experienced could not be identified with the fact that one's knowledge of it is primary.

The identification of primary knowledge with knowledge of what is experienced has another, perhaps even greater, defect. It fails to even *seem* to be an account of the primary nature of our knowledge of some necessary, a priori, truths, of such truths as that three and two are five and that a surface cannot be both circular and not circular.[31] For what we know a priori is not given to us in immediate experience in the way in which headaches and the looks of things can be said to be. In entertaining a priori truths we may have introspective experiences of images, ideas, even concepts, of numbers, of surfaces, and of shapes. But it is not these mental entities that we know a priori, even if their occurrence is a necessary condition of a priori knowledge, while the headache one experiences is precisely what one knows when one knows that one has a headache.

According to a second view of the nature of self-evidence, what justifies, constitutes sufficient evidence for, a primary epistemic judgment is the fact itself that is judged to be known.[32] Indeed, it is plausible to say that what justifies my judgment that I know that I have a headache is simply the very fact that I have a headache and that the possibility of an infinite regress of justification arises only if we assume, unwarrantedly, that a judgment can be justified only by another *judgment*. Plausible though such an argument may be, it is radically wrong. Indeed, if knowledge is to be possible and the idea of justification intelligible, we must agree, as we have already done, that it is false that only a judgment can justify another judgment. But we must not agree that, for this reason, a judgment may be justified by the fact it is about. A fact may make a judgment *true*. But no fact as such can *justify* a judgment. Only a fact that is known, that is, only our knowledge of such a fact, can serve such a justificatory function. And we certainly should not attempt to account for the primacy of certain epistemic judgments by saying that they are justified by our knowledge of

31. It is significant that Danto denies that the notion of truth is applicable to "analytic sentences" and claims that " 'm knows that r' is nonsense where r is analytical" (*Analytical Philosophy of Knowledge*, pp. 178–81).

32. See R. M. Chisholm, *Theory of Knowledge* (Englewood Cliffs, N.J.: Prentice-Hall, 1966), pp. 26–29.

the facts which are judged to be known. A fact may justify a judgment in the sense of rendering it *true*. But this is not the same as justifying it in the sense of rendering it *known* to be true. The view under discussion tacitly commits the error of confusing truth with knowledge and trades on an equivocation in the word *justification*.

In the case of some proposition p, one tempted to suppose that the fact that p is what justifies one's judgment that one knows that p should ask oneself why some facts would have this extraordinary justificatory function and others would not? If a fact may by itself justify one's judgment that one knows that fact, then why are not all true beliefs knowledge? Why should it be that the fact that I have a headache justifies my judgment that I know that I have a headache, while the fact that the earth is round does not justify my judgment that I know that the earth is round? Obviously, an explanation is required. To provide such an explanation, one must mention something other than the fact that p, in virtue of which a primary epistemic judgment about p is justified. Consequently, a primary epistemic judgment about p is never justified by the mere fact that p.

Should we revise the view by saying that only facts of which we are directly aware justify primary epistemic judgments? But then we would be back at the previous view. Moreoever, we would have to admit that it is not "I know that p" that would be the primary epistemic judgment but "I know that I am directly aware of the fact that p." Even if for some values of p (e.g., "I have a headache") these two judgments are equivalent, still the revised view would require us to regard the latter as the primary epistemic judgment. But then what justifies *this* judgment? The fact that I am directly aware of the fact that p? Perhaps so, but we must then explain (see the previous pargaraph) why *this* sort of fact should justify the corresponding epistemic judgment while other sorts of fact would not. If our explanation were that we are directly aware of this fact, then obviously we would be involved in an infinite regress, at least one step in which would be simply false (I may be directly aware that I am directly aware of the fact that I have a headache, but I am not directly aware of the fact that I am directly aware of the fact that I am directly aware that I have a headache). On the other hand, to simply say that facts of which we are directly aware just happen to be the only ones that justify the corresponding epistemic judgments would be to offer neither explanation nor illumination. Why are the facts of direct awareness so special? We have seen that we should not answer this question by talking about knowledge by acquaintance.

In some sense, a primary epistemic judgment must be justified in itself: it must be self-evident—the sufficient evidence supporting it must be, so to speak, an internal feature of the knowledge itself. But the knowledge itself is nothing but a belief which is true and is supported with evidence that guarantees its truth. So it would seem that the evidence itself would have to be, in some sense, a feature either of the *belief* or of the *truth* of the proposition that expresses the content of the belief. The two other major theories about the nature of the evidence sufficient for primary knowledge correspond to these two alternatives.

In what sense can one's sufficient evidence that p consist in a certain feature of the *truth* of p? It would seem that the only characteristic of the truth of a proposition that would be even remotely relevant to our question is its necessity. Hence the venerable Platonic view that one can have knowledge only of necessary truths. For, it would seem, if the evidence required is one that would make a mistake absolutely impossible, then only the necessary truth of the proposition known could do so. If it is impossible that p is false, then necessarily it is impossible for anyone to be mistaken in believing that p. And if it is impossible for anyone to be mistaken in believing that p, then it must be impossible for p to be false; for if it were possible for p to be false, then precisely because of this possibility it must also be possible for anyone believing that p to be mistaken.

But this argument, of course, is fallacious. One's evidence that p could not consist in the truth of p, whether that truth be necessary or contingent, for if it did, then every true belief would be knowledge. The truth of p is that for which one needs evidence, that which one determines by appealing to one's evidence, and not the evidence itself. Indeed, if p is true then, in a sense, no one could be mistaken in believing that p, but from this it would not follow that anyone knows that p. For no one may believe that p, or if someone does he might believe that p without evidence, or, if with evidence, not *because* of that evidence. That the truth of p may be necessary would not affect this point. It is a confusion to suppose that if p is necessarily true then mistake in believing that p would be impossible in a sense different from that in which it would be impossible if p were contingently true. Mistake in believing that p would be impossible not because of the necessity of the truth of p but simply because of the truth of p. Otherwise there would be no difference between believing that p is true and believing that p is necessarily true. Impossibility of mistake is one thing, impossibility of falsehood quite another.

In any case, what value could there be in a conception of evidence sufficient for primary knowledge that requires us to admit, for example, that one cannot know that one has a headache, not on the grounds of special and questionable considerations about the nature of language or of the mind but precisely on the grounds that it is possible for one to be mistaken in believing that one has a headache? Even if there are legitimate theoretical reasons for denying that one can say properly that one knows that one has a headache, surely there are no reasons that would require us to say that one can always be mistaken in believing that one has a headache.

In what sense can one's sufficient evidence that p consist in some feature of one's *belief* that p? Presumably, the likely such feature would be the impossibility of questioning this belief, the impossibility of both entertaining the proposition expressing its content and not believing that it is true (not assenting to its truth), that is, the impossibility of doubt. What would be meant here by "impossibility" is, of course, absolute impossibility. For the psychological impossibility of doubting something is largely the effect of a person's individual characteristics, which need have nothing to do with his possessing or lacking knowledge; the possession of knowledge cannot consist in credulity. Hence we have a second venerable view of the nature of evidence sufficient for primary knowledge. According to Descartes, we have primary knowledge of that of which doubt is absolutely impossible, inconceivable. In this view the foundations of knowledge consist of the indubitable.

It is, however, precisely the use of the notion of absolute impossibility that renders the Cartesian view inadequate. For how could something like a belief or a disbelief or a doubt be absolutely impossible? In what sense could one's assent or nonassent to a proposition be absolutely, and not just psychologically, impossible? We know very little about the nature of assent or belief. And we know even less about any feature of it to which we could intelligibly appeal in explaining what may be meant by the absolute impossibility of doubt. Of course, we may agree that as a matter of fact we are psychologically incapable of not assenting to those propositions of which we have primary knowledge. We may even agree that a satisfactory theory of the nature of assent would show that this is not a mere matter of fact but a logical necessity. What we cannot admit is that the view that sufficient evidence for primary knowledge is the absolute impossibility of doubt illuminates the nature of such evidence.

Sometimes the Platonic and the Cartesian views are combined into the view that evidence sufficient for primary knowledge consists in the absolute impossibility of *counterevidence, of grounds for doubt.* Descartes himself seems to subscribe to this notion when he argues that even if God were to deceive him into believing that he exists, he still must exist in order to be deceived. This seems to be also the view of Norman Malcolm with respect to what he calls "the strong sense" of knowing.[33] But such a theory is quite useless as an elucidation of the nature of primary knowledge, and in this respect, I suggest, would at best amount to a case of *obscurum per obscurius.* The main task of an account of primary knowledge is to explain how a primary epistemic judgment can be said to be justified even if not justified by another epistemic judgment, how such a judgment can be self-evident. To say that its self-evidence consists in the absolute impossibility that anything would be *counterevidence* with regard to it is at best to obscure the issue even further. If we are unclear about what could be meant by evidence *for* such a judgment, we shall be even less clear about what could be meant by evidence *against* it. At worst, it is to violate the very notion of self-evidence, for do we *infer* that the judgment is true from the fact that there cannot be counterevidence for it?

Nevertheless, the attempt to solve the problem by combining elements of the Platonic theory with elements of the Cartesian theory is promising. Each theory seems to contain a part, though only a part, of what is needed. The Platonic theory draws attention to the undeniable fact that the notion of the absolute impossibility of mistake must have some relationship to the notion of necessary truth, and away from the temptation to look for a solution in the realm of the purely psychological. The Cartesian theory draws attention to the equally undeniable fact that knowledge is a kind of belief and that mistake is something the knower does, and away from the temptation to look for a solution in the realm of the purely logical. What both ignore is that a belief as well as a doubt arises in a *context* of certain things that one perceives, thinks, imagines, a context of certain experiences and concepts. It is in terms of the role of

33. "Knowledge and Belief" in *Knowledge and Certainty.*

this context, I suggest, that the absolute impossibility of mistake in the case of primary knowledge must be understood.

A belief is not a brute phenomenon such as pain, even though it is not only a disposition but also an occurrence. A belief has a content; it is necessarily a belief *that* something is the case. It is identified as this, rather than another belief, in part, by reference to the person by whom it is held and the time at which it is held. But the specific criterion of its identity is its content, what it is about, its "objective reality." And what a belief is about is determined, at least in part, by its context, by a certain set of concepts and perhaps experiences. That the identity of a belief is dependent, at least in part, on the conceptual elements in its context has usually been taken for granted, though perhaps not explicitly. A belief, insofar as it involves concepts, is the particular belief it is, at least partly, because of the content of the concepts it involves. One's belief that a table is round would cease to be the particular belief it is if one's concept of round were changed. But the identity of some, though not all, beliefs is also dependent on certain experiential elements in their contexts. My belief that I now see these black marks on this white background would cease to be the particular belief it is if instead I came to see yellow marks on this background. Even if I were to believe that the color of the marks has not really changed, that what I see is really still black marks, *this* belief would not be the same as the previous belief. For I would not still believe that I see *these* black marks on a white background, though I might still believe that I see marks that are really black but look yellow. I would not have the *particular* belief I do have now that there is a typewriter before me if I did not have certain visual and tactile experiences now, though I could still have *a* belief that there is a typewriter before me now. For, despite their similarity, the two beliefs would be different. There is a difference between what I believe when I believe that there is a typewriter before me that I see and touch and what I believe when I believe that there is a typewriter before me that I neither see nor touch. Once way of expressing the difference is to say that the former belief has as its content the proposition that there is *this* typewriter before me now, while the latter has as its content the proposition that there is *a* certain typewriter before me now. Another, clearer, but philosophically more controversial, way of expressing it is to say that the former is a belief that there is before me now a typewriter seen and touched by me now, while the latter is a belief that there is before me now a certain typewriter that is not seen and touched by me now. I will return to this sort of distinction in section *8* of Part Three.

How does the notion of the context of a belief help illuminate the nature of the absolute impossibility of mistake in the case of primary knowledge? To say that a proposition is necessarily true is to say that it cannot be false. To say that it is impossible for one to be mistaken in believing that a certain proposition is true is again to say, though only in part, that the proposition cannot be false. In the case of derivative knowledge, this is so in the sense that, given the truth of the propositions constituting the evidence, the proposition known cannot be false. There is nothing puzzling about this sense. In the case of primary knowledge, however, the proposition known cannot be false unconditionally, in itself, independently of the truth of any other propositions. It is this sense of "cannot be false" that is puzzling. Obviously, this sense is quite different from the sense of "cannot be false" that is relevant to derivative knowledge. But it is also quite different from the sense in which a necessarily true proposition cannot be false.

A necessarily true proposition cannot be false in the sense that it *could* not have been false, that it would be true at *any* time and in *any* circumstances. A proposition of which one has primary knowledge cannot be false in the sense that *it is impossible for it to be false in the present circumstances;* even though (if it is contingent) it *could* have been false, it *can* be false at other times and in other circumstances. For example, there is a clear sense in which someone who has a headache may say that it is unthinkable, inconceivable, absolutely impossible, that he does not have a headache *now,* though of course it is perfectly thinkable that he *might* not have had a headache. In the sense of "cannot be false" relevant to necessary propositions, it *can* be false that he has a headache, for he might not have had a headache. Yet in the sense relevant to primary knowledge, it *cannot* be false that he has a headache, for it is unthinkable, impossible, that he does not have a headache in the present circumstances. On the other hand, a necessarily true proposition (e.g., that three and two are five) of which one has primary knowledge cannot be false, in both senses.

But what is meant here by "the present circumstances"? If this phrase referred merely to whatever is now the case, then the second sense of "cannot be false" would collapse into the first. For what I have primary knowledge of is of course part of what is the case now, and it cannot be false in the present circumstances simply because it is true. Nor can "the present circumstances" refer to my total present *conscious* life, that is, to everything that I perceive or think or imagine or feel. For then impossibility of mistake in the present circumstances would consist in the conditional impossibility of something's not being the case *if* the facts of my present conscious life were such and such. And such a conception of impossibility of mistake obviously would be inapplicable to *primary* epistemic judgments.

I suggest that the "present circumstances" that would render the notion of the absolute impossibility of mistake in the present circumstances readily intelligible when applied to primary epistemic judgments are what I have called the context of a belief. The impossibility of *p*'s being false in the present circumstances consists in the impossibility of a state of affairs such that *p* is false and yet such that the context of the belief that *p* remains the same. The context of a belief is the set of concepts and experiences that provide, at least in part, the belief with content and thus identity. Mistake is impossible when the proposition believed cannot be false unless the content, the identity, of the belief, that is, the belief itself, is changed. Insofar as we think of the context of a belief as a certain set of *facts* about one's conscious life, the impossibility of mistake seems to be very much a case of ordinary logical impossibility, and the Platonic theory of self-evidence constitutes an emphasis on this aspect of the truth. Insofar as we think of the context of a belief as the fact of the occurrence of the belief itself, the impossibility of mistake seems to be the impossibility of doubt, and the Cartesian theory of self-evidence constitutes an emphasis on this second aspect of the truth. But neither theory is satisfactory by itself. The first makes the impossibility of mistake conditional on the fact that certain propositions about one's conscious life are true and thus ceases to apply to *primary* knowledge. The second, in effect, explains only the impossibility of a certain *nonbelief,* while what has to be explained is the impossibility of the *falsehood* of a certain belief. In reality, the crucial fact about the context of a belief is that it determines the content of the belief, and thus that it provides the materials for our conception of what is believed. The falsehood of what is believed then would be impossible in the sense that it is incompatible with the very conception of what is believed.

That this is the case with primary knowledge of *necessary truths* has usually been recognized. It is often said that the falsehood of three and two being five is impossible in that it is impossible that our concepts of these numbers, in terms of which we understand the proposition that three and two are five, remain the same and yet that three and two would not be five. And since the falsehood of the proposition would have to be understood in terms of a change in the *conceptual* part of the context of the belief, we also find it impossible that three and two *might* not have been five. But the falsehood of certain contingent propositions is also impossible in the first sense, though not in the second. When I believe (take for granted, accept as a matter of course the fact) that I have a headache, I identify *what* I believe, namely that it is *this* specific headache that I have, in terms of the context of the belief, and this context includes a certain experience, the having of the headache. To conceive of my not having a headache now would be to suppose that I do not have that experience which is part of what provides my belief that I have a headache now with a content, that is, that which makes it the particular belief it is. It *seems* that the case here is different from that of knowledge of a necessary truth because we tend to identify the conception of what I believe with the understanding of the statement describing what I believe. In the case of a truth such as that three and two are five, such an identification is quite legitimate. But in the case of a truth such as that I have a headache, it is misleading. The *statement* that I have a headache does not at all have the specificity of what I believe when I believe that I have a headache; this is why I have expressed the latter belief by saying that I believe that I have *this* specific headache. The belief that I have a headache is far more specific than the statement that I have a headache. The difference between them is analogous to that between the statement "John is in the room" and the statement "There is a man in the room." The specificity of the content of primary a posteriori knowledge, unlike that of primary a priori knowledge, can seldom, if ever, be reflected in language. Consequently, the unthinkability of the belief's being false must not be confused with the unthinkability of the statement's being false; the latter would entail the former, but may well be incapable of being determined in itself. This is presumably why philosophers have insisted on the inexpressibility of immediate experience, on the necessity of using "logically proper names" in describing the content of immediate experience, on the fact that the foundations of empirical knowledge are incorrigible but cannot be expressed adequately in language.[34] But precisely because the contextual element that would be incompatible with the falsehood of my belief that I have a headache is an *experience* and not a *concept,* it is unthinkable that I do not have a headache in the present circumstances, now, but not at all unthinkable that I might not have had a headache, that I will not have a headache, or that I have not had a headache.

This account of self-evidence may become clearer if it is recognized that to believe that something is the case is at least to think that it is the case, that a belief is at least a *thought-that.* For the dependence of *thinking-that* on the context in which it occurs is a more familiar notion. My thought that I have this headache would be impossible if there were not *this* headache, and my thought that there are these black marks before me would be impossible if there were not *these* black marks before me. The dependence of a *thinking-that* on the conceptual elements in its context is an even more familiar notion. It is a standard sort of claim to say that one cannot think of an *x* which is *F* but not *G* because of the very content of one's concepts of *F* and *G.*

But are we not simply adopting here the view that self-evidence lies in immediate experience? We are doing justice to the truth contained in this view (no account of knowledge can be legitimate if it entails that this view is simply false), yet we are not adopting it as constitutive of our account of self-evidence but rather as a welcome consequence of that account. For we are now able to *explain* why (at least some) propositions describing our conscious life are known in a primary way, rather than simply take this as a brute fact. Moreover, our account does not (and ought not to) entail that all propositions of which we have primary knowledge describe facts about our conscious life. For we also have primary knowledge of necessary truths, such as those of elementary school arithmetic, that do not describe any facts about conscious life ("three and two are five" is a statement about numbers, not about concepts or meanings or uses of words). We have such primary knowledge not because the proposition whose truth we know describes a fact about our conscious life but because its falsehood would be incompatible with certain elements of the context of the belief that render the belief intelligible, namely, certain conceptual, rather than experiential, elements.

34. Cf. C. I. Lewis, "The Given Element in Empirical Knowledge," *Philosophical Review,* LXI (1952), 168–75.

We can now also understand the nature of *indubitability*, in the epistemologically relevant sense of a doubt that is absolutely, and not only psychologically, impossible, and we can understand the reason philosophers have tended to identify the self-evident with the indubitable. To doubt that a certain belief is true is, at least, to suppose that the belief is false. But if the belief is such that its falsehood would be incompatible with the context that determines the identity of the belief, then to doubt that the belief is true would be in effect to suppose that the belief has a content other than the one with respect to which the doubt was intended. Such a doubt would be unintelligible. And so would be the belief that the proposition doubted is false. It is unintelligible to me that I should doubt the proposition that I am not now in excruciating pain. For my belief (assent, taking-for-granted) that I am not now in excruciating pain derives its content, its "objective reality," from a context that is quite incompatible with my being now in excruciating pain. That I should assent to the proposition that I am in excruciating pain now is also unintelligible to me and not merely psychologically impossible (as perhaps would be my assent to the proposition that I will not live through the day). Even if I were to be seized now by a peculiar "feeling of conviction," I would not at all be inclined to describe such a feeling as one of conviction that *I am now in excruciating pain*. It is also unintelligible to me now that I would doubt that three and two are five. And the reason for this is not that the proposition that three and two are five is necessarily true; so is the proposition that 79 and 176 are 255, but I find nothing unintelligible about doubting it. The reason is that while both the concepts of 3, 2, and 5 and the concepts of 79, 176, and 255 are elements in the contexts of the respective beliefs and thus in part determinant of the identity of these beliefs, the falsehood of the first belief would be incompatible with the presence of those concepts in its context, while the falsehood of the second belief would not.[35] For the same reason, it is unintelligible to me now that I would believe that three and two are six. And it is unintelligible to me now that, while sitting in front of a

---

35. I shall not attempt to determine the reason for this difference. That there is such a difference is a familiar fact, usually acknowledged by philosophers by saying that we have "intuitive knowledge" of the truth that 3 and 2 are 5 and only inferential knowledge of the truth that 79 and 176 are 255. Perhaps the difference is due to the fact that for most of us the content of the concepts of 3, 2, and 5 is far more perspicuous than that of the concepts of 79, 176, and 255.

typewriter in my office and looking at the type on this page, I would doubt that I see black marks on a white background or that I would believe that I see yellow marks on this white background.

It should be noted that I *find* the ideas of such doubts and beliefs unintelligible, that I *find* mistake in certain beliefs unintelligible, and not that I *infer* this unintelligibility from my knowledge of the constitution of the contexts of the beliefs. Were I to do the latter, an appeal to the notion of the context of a belief would be useless for my purposes. But I do not. That the constitution of the context of a certain belief is such and such may *explain* why I find mistake regarding that belief unintelligible but would not *justify* my so finding it. As I pointed out at the beginning of this section, the account of the nature of self-evidence must not be confused with an account of a method for determining what beliefs are self-evident. That mistake regarding a certain belief is unintelligible is a fact. My purpose in this section has been to explain how such a fact is possible, not to prove that it is a fact.

Our account of self-evidence allows us now to understand and endorse the familiar philosophical claim that one can have primary knowledge only of one's "immediate experiences" (of what one is "presented with") and of simple necessary truths. It is plausible to suppose that one's immediate experiences are inevitably elements in the contexts of one's beliefs regarding their occurrence or characteristics. And a simple necessary truth is precisely one whose falsehood would be incompatible with the very concepts that make one's belief in that truth possible. And insofar as the context of a belief can contain nothing but immediate experiences and concepts, we can have primary knowledge of nothing other than truths about our immediate experiences and simple necessary truths.

Our account of self-evidence also allows us to see that, contrary to common assumption, our knowledge of necessary truths, a priori knowledge, does not have a privileged status. A necessary truth may be very different from a contingent truth. But primary knowledge of the former is of the same nature as primary knowledge of the latter. Both consist in the absolute impossibility of mistake. And with regard to both, mistake is absolutely impossible because of the incompatibility of the falsehood of the belief with the constitution of its context. Our account thus seems to have the merit of grounding a posteriori knowledge in no less firm foundations than those of a priori knowledge—and it is generally admitted that a priori knowledge has very firm foundations.

7. The Principle of Unthinkability

I HAVE ARGUED that knowledge is the absolute impossibility of mistake in belief. But how is the absolute impossibility of mistake determined? What *reason,* what *grounds,* do we have for regarding mistake, in a particular case, as impossible? As long as we were not specifically concerned with primary knowledge, these questions did not seem to require a revision in our account of knowledge. For in the case of derivative knowledge, such impossibility is a function of one's knowledge of something else, namely, whatever constitutes one's evidence. Strictly speaking, what is absolutely impossible there is not so much that one is mistaken in believing what one is said to know, as that what one is said to know is false while the propositions constituting one's evidence are true; were these propositions not true, mistake in believing what one is said to know would be quite possible, and thus one would not know at all. So our reason for regarding mistake in the case of derivative knowledge as impossible is simply our knowledge of our evidence. In the case of primary knowledge, however, knowledge consists in the absolute impossibility of mistake in believing what one is said to know, regardless of anything else one may know. How, then, do we determine, in that case, that mistake is absolutely impossible? What reason does one have, in respect to a particular primary epistemic judgment, for regarding mistake as absolutely impossible? Certainly, not one's knowledge of anything else, not any inference one may perform. Yet a reason there must be, for the absolute impossibility of something is precisely the sort of thing that requires *determination,* that one needs a *reason* for regarding as the case; it is a standard example of something that must be proved, argued for, inferred. The only such reason in the case of primary knowledge, I suggest, is our finding mistake in what we believe *unthinkable, inconceivable, unintelligible.* (The reader may have noted the frequency with which I have had to use these three terms in the account of self-evidence offered in the previous section. There is nothing unthinkable about mistake regarding what one knows derivatively, as long as one ignores one's evidence. That this is so in the case of derivative a posteriori knowldege is obvious. But it is so also in the case of derivative a priori knowledge; it is perfectly thinkable for most people that 15 multiplied by 15 is 250.)

The direct, immediate, unconditional *unthinkability* of mistake is our only possible reason for regarding mistake in the case of primary knowledge as absolutely impossible. For even if the sort of incompatibility between the falsehood of a belief and its context, in terms of which we have explained the absolute impossibility of mistake in primary knowledge, were a *logical* incompatibility, even if the belief's having that context and also being false would constitute a self-contradictory state of affairs, such an incompatibility could not itself be our reason for regarding mistake to be absolutely impossible. At most, our *knowledge* of that incompatibility would be such a reason. And then, of course, what we originally took to be primary knowledge would no longer be primary. On the other hand, neither would our knowledge of the logical incompatibility be itself primary. We can have such knowledge only if we first know (1) that the context of the belief does include those elements in virtue of which it would be incompatible with the falsehood of the belief, and (2) that there cannot be self-contradictory states of affairs—that the principle of noncontradiction is true. So even our knowledge of the incompatibility would not be primary. If any knowledge in this case would be primary, this would be our knowledge of (1) and our knowledge of (2). But, on pain of an infinite regress of justification, we must admit then that our reason for regarding *these* as knowledge cannot be the logical incompatibility of the falsehood of the respective belief and its context.

Of course, the above argument also shows, though indirectly, that even in the case of *derivative* knowledge the only reason for regarding mistake as absolutely impossible is the unthinkability, inconceivability, unintelligibility of something. For, ultimately, one's only reason for regarding as absolutely impossible that what one hopes to know is false while the propositions constituting one's evidence for it are true, is that one finds such a state of affairs unthinkable. Even if such a state of affairs would be self-contradictory, the mere fact that it would be so cannot be one's reason for regarding it as impossible. One must *know* that it is self-contradictory and also that whatever is self-contradictory is impossible. And one's reason for supposing that one knows this could not itself be the mere fact of the self-contradiction of a certain state of affairs—unless we accept an infinite regress and thus in effect acknowledge that there is no primary knowledge. That whatever is our reason for regarding something as primary knowledge is ultimately also our only reason for regarding something as derivative knowledge should not be surprising. It follows from the very distinction between primary and derivative knowledge.

To say that the only reason for regarding mistake in the case of primary knowledge as absolutely impossible is that we find such a mistake unthinkable is in effect to say that, strictly speaking, primary knowledge consists not in the absolute impossibility of mistake but in the *unthinkability* of mistake. The absolute impossibility of something requires determination, and in the case of primary knowledge, we can determine the absolute impossibility of mistake only by appealing to the unthinkability of mistake. But we cannot both acknowledge that our *reason* for regarding mistake in a certain belief as absolutely impossible is the unthinkability of such a mistake and still insist that the judgment that mistake in that belief is absolutely impossible is primary, one not in need of justification by reference to another judgment. Therefore, we must say that the primary epistemic judgment "I know that *p*" must be equivalent to "I find it unthinkable that I am mistaken in believing that *p*," not to "It is absolutely impossible that I am mistaken in believing that *p*." And since, ultimately, derivative knowledge is grounded in primary knowledge, we must now, as I have hinted we would,[36] revise our account of the concept of knowledge as the absolute impossibility of mistake by saying that knowledge is the unthinkability of mistake.

But how should we understand the unthinkability of mistake? While mistake in a certain belief may be unthinkable *because* of a logical incompatibility between the falsehood of the belief and its context, we have seen that it is not to this logical incompatibility that one can appeal ultimately in defending one's epistemic judgment, but to the brute fact that one *finds* mistake in the belief unthinkable, inconceivable, unintelligible. Indeed, according to our account of self-evidence, it may even be logically necessary that certain mistakes are unthinkable. But it would not be the *logical necessity* of their unthinkability, but the *fact* that one finds them unthinkable that constitutes primary knowledge. One may appeal, as we have done, to such logical necessity in *explaining* why certain mistakes should be unthinkable, but not in *defending* one's primary epistemic judgments; the logical necessity can be appealed to only if its presence is known, and this can be known only in the sense that mistake regarding it is found to be unthinkable.

That knowledge ultimately is grounded in the brute fact that we simply cannot think of mistake in certain beliefs has an important and very welcome consequence. We can now understand the concept of knowledge

36. See above, p. 51.

in terms of concepts which are not in themselves philosophically problematic. The concept of the unthinkability of mistake is not an epistemic concept. It does not belong to that gloomy circle of notions such as evidence, justification, probability, certainty, and rationality, to break out of which has been the major epistemological challenge. Nor is it a normative concept. It does not belong to the even gloomier circle of notions such as right-to-be-sure, worthy-of-belief, and being-more-reasonable-to-believe-than, which epistemologists sometimes enter when trying to leave the previous circle. That we find mistake in certain of our beliefs unthinkable, that we simply cannot think of such mistakes, is in itself a philosophically quite unobjectionable (though most interesting) sort of fact, whether we describe it as one about the world or as one about ourselves. It should be noted that while we have employed epistemic terms such as *evidence* and *justification* on the dialectical way to the account of the concept of knowledge, we have now left them behind and have no need for them in the final statement of that account. The notion of the unthinkability of mistake presupposes the notions of truth, belief, and inability-to-think-something, but not those of evidence and justification. But this very important advantage of our account goes hand in hand with a major disadvantage. By defining knowledge as the unthinkability, rather than the absolute impossibility, of mistake, we have made our account more desirable but also less plausible.

It may seem that we should have simply identified the concept of absolute impossibility of mistake with the concept of unthinkability of mistake. But to have done so would have been, of course, an error. They are two different concepts. The proposition "It is absolutely impossible that p" entails that p is false, but the proposition "It is unthinkable that p" does not. And this fact introduces us to two very important and very difficult questions that our account of primary knowledge must now answer.

The first question is whether that account satisfies the requirement that what one knows must be true. Why should we suppose that if mistake in a certain belief is unthinkable, then it is impossible and thus the belief true? The second question is whether our account satisfies the requirement that if one knows, then one must have evidence for what one knows. Are we justified in believing (do we have evidence) that what we take to be unthinkable is really unthinkable? The first question casts doubt on the success of our distinction between primary knowledge and rational belief. The second question casts doubt on the success of our distinction between primary knowledge and true belief. I will consider the first in this section, and the second in the next section.

The first question is likely to be raised for two reasons. One is the philosophical illusion, currently widespread, that there are more "objective," more solid, more reliable grounds for judging something to be impossible than its unthinkability. The examples usually given are the principle of noncontradiction, the contents of our concepts, the meanings of words, and the conventions of our language.[37] What makes this view plausible is that indeed such grounds as the above, in the order they have been given, do seem far more acceptable than any other *specific* grounds we could appeal to in claiming something to be impossible. What makes the view false, and I would have thought obviously so, is that none of these is the ultimate ground for such a claim, that each of them is such a ground only because of the support it receives from the *general* ground for claiming something to be impossible, namely, its being unthinkable. I shall call the proposition that ultimately our only ground for regarding something as absolutely impossible is our finding it unthinkable, the *principle of unthinkability.*

To begin with, there is much that we know to be necessarily false without appealing to its being self-contradictory. Examples would be the propositions "Three and two are six" and "Something is both round and square." Perhaps we can derive a formal contradiction from each of these propositions. But we might not know this fact (very few people do) and still know that the propositions are necessarily false. Indeed, the definitions and axioms that would allow us to derive a contradiction from such a proposition are selected in the light of the latter's *known* necessary falsehood.

But even in the case of obviously self-contradictory propositions, we can still be asked why we should regard them as necessarily false. And the fact is that we should reply that we so regard them simply because we find the states of affairs they purport to describe unthinkable, unintelligible, inconceivable. If we are urged to admit that self-contradictory states of affairs might be possible (e.g., that there might be a square that is not a square), our response would be that we simply do not *understand* how this might

---

37. The actual connection between these and the notion of necessary truth will be discussed in detail in Part Two. In this section I am concerned only with the question of their self-sufficiency as grounds of our knowledge of necessary truths.

be the case. And even if we were to say that to admit such a possibility would be incompatible with the contents of our concepts, or would make communication impossible, or would violate the rules of language, we would ultimately still have to appeal to the principle of unthinkability. For, if asked, why could not our concepts only appear to demand what we take them to demand, or why could we not communicate with self-contradictory statements, or why could not the linguistic conventions (e.g., that if one says that p one must not say that q) be compatible with one's breaking them (e.g., with one's saying both that p and that q), we would again reply that we simply cannot understand these suppositions, that we find them unintelligible.

By saying that we do not or cannot understand such suppositions, we can only mean that we find what they suppose unthinkable, inconceivable. For, of course, we do not literally mean that we do not or that we cannot understand them; what we mean is that we cannot *think* what we do understand them to suppose. If we did mean the former, our reply would be irrelevant. It would be like telling a foreigner that we do not or cannot understand what he is saying. Nothing follows from this regarding the truth-value of what he is saying. Inability to understand, in the sense in which philosophers appeal to it when determining the absolute impossibility of something, is the *unthinkability* of what, in a sense, is *understood* to be described by the proposition, not the literal nonunderstanding of that proposition.

The principle of unthinkability has sometimes been rejected on the grounds that it has proved to be unreliable. We are all familiar with the timeworn example of people's finding the sphericity of the earth unthinkable. But the appeal to such an example is a case of *ignoratio elenchi*. The terms *unthinkable, inconceivable,* and *unintelligible* have established and easily taught strict uses in philosophy, and the fact that in ordinary discourse they are used loosely, chiefly as synonyms of *unbelievable,* is of no more significance for epistemology than the similarly loose ordinary use of *implies* is for logic. Indeed, philosophers and mathematicians have disagreed about the unthinkability of certain things. Usually, these disagreements have had to do with the necessary truth of certain propositions, such as the principle of causality and Euclid's parallel postulate. I have no explanation of such disagreements. But we must not suppose that they have been, or can be, resolved by appealing to a more fundamental principle, that is, that we do, or could, possess a method for resolving such disagreements. The demonstration that the denial of the principle of causality or of the parallel postulate is neither self-contradictory nor inconsistent with certain other evident propositions does not refute one who regards such a denial as necessarily false on the grounds that what it describes is unthinkable. The fact is not that the principle of unthinkability is reliable or capable of resolving disagreements but that we have no alternative to it since any other proposed criterion of absolute impossibility presupposes it. That a square's being round is a self-contradictory state of affairs seems to us a more solid reason for regarding it as impossible than the mere fact that we cannot think of such a state of affairs. But what is our reason for regarding self-contradictory states of affairs as impossible if not our inability to think, conceive, of such states of affairs? We may liken the relationship between our finding something unthinkable and its being impossible to that between our perceiving a body and the existence of such a body. The existence of a body is not the same as its being perceived, and our finding something unthinkable is not the same as its impossibility. Nevertheless, our ultimate source of knowledge of the existence of bodies is perception, however unreliable this source may be. Similarly, our ultimate source of knowledge of the absolute impossibility of a state of affairs is our finding such a state of affairs unthinkable, even if this source were unreliable. And the illusion that the principle of noncontradiction, or the contents of our concepts, or the conventions of our language are more reliable and independent sources of such knowledge is quite similar to the less common illusion that the readings of scientific instruments are a source of knowledge of the existence of bodies that is more reliable than, and independent of, perception.

A more important reason for the rejection of the principle of unthinkability has been the assumption that by "unthinkability" is meant unimaginability, together with the understandable unwillingness of philosophers to deny the possibility of everything for which a mental image is lacking. But this assumption should not be made. Indeed, unthinkability and unimaginability do seem to coincide in the case of states of affairs that, were they possible, would be perceivable. For it seems true that we can imagine only what we can perceive. The unthinkability of something that is both red and green all over seems to be the same as its unimaginability, for the color of something is just the sort of thing that one can perceive and thus imagine. And if whatever is unimaginable is unperceivable, then something that would be perceivable, if at all possible, must be imaginable in order to be possible. But nothing follows from this regarding thought of what is not a perceivable sort of thing. For such a thing would be unimaginable only in the trivial and irrelevant sense that there is no mental image of it. What is unimaginable in this sense need not be unthinkable at all. In the relevant sense of *unimaginable,* a state of affairs is unimaginable if, although it may contain no element of which one does not have a mental image, a mental image of the whole state of affairs is impossible. A ball that is both red and green all over is unimaginable because a mental image of such a ball is impossible even though one has mental images of a ball, of something red, and of something green. Only what is unimaginable in this sense would also be unthinkable. But the states of affairs that usually make the empiricist unhappy are unimaginable in the first, irrelevant sense. The actual infinity of space is unimaginable not because we would be unable to combine our images of actual infinity and of space into one image but because we lack at least one of the required images, that of actual infinity. The distinction between the two senses can be made also in the following way. A state of affairs is unimaginable in the sense in which unimaginability entails unthinkability only if the contradictory state of affairs is not unimaginable. A state of affairs is unimaginable in the sense in which unimaginability does not entail unthinkability only if the contradictory state of affairs is also unimaginable.

The belief that there are genuine alternatives to the principle of unthinkability is an illusion. But from the fact that there is nothing better than it we cannot infer that it is good enough. And this leads us to a second, far deeper reason for objecting to our appeal to that principle in the account of primary knowledge. That is the fact that the unthinkability of mistake does not entail truth, while knowledge does. Can this objection be met?

Let us begin by observing that, although the unthinkability of mistake in a certain belief that one holds does not entail that the belief is true, it does entail something else: that one cannot understand what it would be for the belief to be false, that one cannot understand how one may discover that the belief is false, that one cannot understand how one might go wrong in acting in accordance with the belief. (Although, of course, one can easily understand what it would be for the proposition believed to be false, if that proposition is not necessary.) I have argued that to seek knowledge is to seek truth and that to have knowledge is to have truth; to have anything less than that is to have, at best, rational belief that happens to be true. But, as we have seen, the expression "to have the truth of *p*" cannot be understood literally. How it should be understood in the case of derivative knowledge has been made clear: to have the truth of *p* is to have evidence that entails it. But how should it be understood in the present case, that of primary knowledge? The truth of a proposition is not something that one *possesses*. Yet we continue to feel that even in primary knowledge there must be something *like* the possession of truth and that only when one does so possess truth can one be said to know. What could be so much *like* the possession of truth without *being* the possession of truth? I suggest that it can only be the unthinkability, inconceivability, unintelligibility of one's not possessing truth; the unthinkability of one's being mistaken in believing such a truth. I suggest that in the case of primary knowledge the phrase "having the truth" is a natural but misleading description of the unthinkability of mistake. For even if there were a genuine notion of literal possession of truth, it would function, in life and in thought, in the way in which the notion of unthinkability of mistake does. If I cannot think how my belief may be false, then the question whether it is false can play no role for me. The requirement that what one knows must be true can play no role distinct from that played by the requirement that if one knows, then mistake in believing what one knows must be unthinkable.

It is the fact that one's evidence sufficient for primary knowledge does not entail that what one knows is true that generates the fanciful conception of a chasm between the Ego and the Non-Ego, stimulates the Cartesian metaphysical doubt, and leads either to complete skepticism (if one admits that there is such a chasm and regards it as unbridgeable) or to absolute idealism (if one denies that there is such a chasm by identifying absolute impossibility with unthinkability and thus being able to claim that unthinkability does entail truth). But the above fact is merely the fact that we cannot literally *have* truth. It is not a symptom of a tragic condition of the human intellect. The reason we cannot have truth is that it is not the sort of thing that one can be said to have. It is not that truth is always beyond our grasp but that it is not the sort of thing that one grasps. Or, rather, one "grasps" truth only in the sense of finding error regarding it unthinkable. But to lament this fact would be like a lover's lamenting his inability to become fused with his beloved into one person; if they were not distinct, one could not love the other. The fact that we

84

can have truth, ultimately, only in the sense of finding mistake regarding it unthinkable amounts to the tautology that we can know only by knowing.

There is thus both truth and falsehood behind the view that knowledge cannot be a state of mind because no state of mind can guarantee its veridicality.[38] The quest for certainty is indeed a hopeless task, if understood as this view suggests. But there is another possibility: that while no state or act of the mind can guarantee its veridicality, some states of mind are such that their nonveridicality is unthinkable.

There are, however, even more fundamental grounds on which we can deal with the claim that the unthinkability of mistake does not constitute knowledge because it does not entail truth. These grounds have to do with the nature of self-evidence, as it was described in the previous section. The plausibility of the above claim depends on the conception of a belief as an entity or state *separate* from what it is a belief about. This conception suggests that the unthinkability of mistake in believing something is a property of the belief, while the truth of the belief consists in there being the fact, external to the belief, that the belief is about. It would not be surprising then if it seemed to one that the unthinkability of mistake could have no real connection with the truth of the belief and thus could not possibly constitute knowledge. The chasm between the Ego and the Non-Ego would then appear in all of its unbridgeable horror. But there is no reason for regarding beliefs constituting primary knowledge as states separate from their objects, though to be sure they cannot be simply identical with the latter. There is no reason for supposing that the Ego and the Non-Ego cannot overlap or partly coincide, insofar as the Ego is something that has, or consists of, beliefs. We must not take seriously metaphorical expressions such as "in the mind" and "outside the mind" and picture the mind as a place; we would do far better to agree with Locke that to be in the mind is to be perceived or understood,[39] for then at least we would find it easier to resist the temptation to point at our heads when we speak of our minds. And we might be less inclined to regard the unthinkability of mistake in a certain belief as something separate from the truth of the belief.

I have argued that what determines, at least in part, the identity of a

38. See A. J. Ayer, *The Problem of Knowledge* (London: Macmillan & Co., 1958), pp. 15–28.

39. *An Essay Concerning Human Understanding*, bk. I, chap. II, 5.

belief, and endows it with content and "objective reality," is its context. But its context may well include what the belief is about. For it may include one's awareness of the fact which is the object of the belief, and, at least in some cases, one's awareness of something includes the something itself: it is what it is, partly, but necessarily, because there is this something. For example, my belief that I now have this particular headache derives its content and identity in part from my feeling this headache. *What* that belief is may be said to include my feeling this headache and thus my headache itself. In a similar manner, my seeing certain black marks before me now, and thus the black marks themselves, are part of the context, and thus determine the identity, of my belief that there are *these* particular black marks before me now. The headache and the black marks are constituents of the contexts of my respective beliefs and thus are in a certain sense constituents of the beliefs themselves. If so, then the incompatibility of the falsehood of the belief with its context, because of which mistake in the belief is unthinkable, would not be a *sign* (whether fallible or infallible) of the truth of the belief, but, so to speak, an *aspect* of that truth, something that includes at least in part the actuality of what is believed. Insofar as what is believed is, at least in part, in the belief, the unthinkability of mistake in the belief would be a fact not only about the belief but also about what is believed. And there would be no separation of, and thus no need for a bridge to connect, the belief and its object. We will find, in section *8* of Part Two, that this would be so even in the case of beliefs that constitute primary knowledge of necessary, a priori truths. And in sections *7* and *8* of Part Three the nature of the entities whose presence in the contexts of certain beliefs render these beliefs primary a posteriori knowledge will be made clearer.

The partial overlap of the beliefs constituting primary knowledge with their objects should not, however, be taken as a proof that, after all, the unthinkability of mistake does entail truth. Even if there were such entailment, we cannot *appeal* to it as justification for a claim that what we find unthinkable to be mistaken about is true, for only a known such entailment can be appealed to; and to *know* that there is such entailment would, directly or indirectly, itself be to find a certain mistake unthinkable. As I have observed above, to explain the self-evidence of certain judgments is not to justify these judgments. On the other hand, we are now in a position to give a final answer to the objection that primary knowledge cannot consist in the unthinkability of mistake because unthinkability of mistake does not entail truth, while knowledge does. Indeed, the mere fact that we find mistake in a certain belief unthinkable does not entail that the belief is true. But the reason for this is not the general reason for denying that a certain entailment holds, namely, the thinkability of the conjunction of the truth of the antecedent and the falsehood of the consequent. For it is precisely the falsehood of the consequent in this case that is unthinkable. To find mistake in a certain belief unthinkable is precisely to find the falsehood of that belief (though perhaps only in the present circumstances) unthinkable. Rather, the reason is that the entailment of the truth of the belief by the unthinkability of mistake cannot itself be determined by appealing to the unthinkability of mistake and, more generally, that the principle of unthinkability cannot itself be appealed to in defending the legitimacy of the principle of unthinkability.

The objection began by pointing out that while the *impossibility* of mistake does entail truth, the *unthinkability* of mistake does not. But while this is true, it is also grossly misleading. The reason we say that the *impossibility* of mistake entails truth is that we find it unthinkable that mistake in a certain belief may be impossible and the belief nevertheless false. As we have seen, there is, ultimately, no other way of judging that an entailment holds or, generally, that something is absolutely impossible. But, now, the reason we say that the *unthinkability* of mistake does not entail truth is not that we find both mistake in a certain belief unthinkable and the falsehood of the belief in the present circumstances thinkable (this would be self-contradictory) but that we cannot, so to speak, go outside thought and determine that whenever mistake is unthinkable there really is no mistake. Once again, the lament that the unthinkability of mistake does not entail truth is merely the lament that we can "have" truth only by knowing it, that we can know only by knowing. The unthinkability of my being mistaken in believing that I have a headache cannot be said to entail that I do have a headache, but only because I cannot apply the method for determining that something entails something else to that method itself. But I do find the falsehood of what might have been entailed, namely, that I do have a headache, unthinkable and thus am in a position regarding it that is no worse than my position regarding the consequent of any genuine case of entailment. There can never be more reason for doubting the entailment of truth by the unthinkability of mistake than there is for doubting that *anything* is really a case of entailment. So, after all, we might say that, contrary to appearances, the unthinkability of mistake does entail truth, though only as much as the absolute impossibility of mistake, or anything else, entails truth. If mistake in believing that *p* is unthinkable, then the falsehood of *p* is indeed unthinkable (at least in the present circumstances). It is just that in the case of the unthinkability of mistake we have hit rock bottom and can no longer hope to descend deeper into thought. To suppose that this is not sufficient is merely to indulge in the picturesque conception of a necessary separation between a belief and its object and in the no less picturesque conception of the human mind as imprisoned in the human skull and tragically incapable of reaching out into the world.

8. Knowing That One Knows

WE MUST NOW COME to the second crucial question regarding a primary epistemic judgment: in what sense can such a judgment be said to be justified at all? For we seem once again to be faced with the following dilemma: if a primary epistemic judgment is to be justified by some other epistemic judgment, then it cannot be primary at all; but if it is not justified by some other epistemic judgment, then it does not differ from mere true belief. Even if primary knowledge consists in the unthinkability of mistake in a certain belief, why can we not still ask for a justification of the judgment that such mistake is unthinkable? One may argue that even if a judgment of the form "I know that *p*" should be understood as equivalent to "I find it unthinkable that I am mistaken in believing that *p*," the judgment must itself be justified if it is to be an expression of knowledge and not of mere belief. But if it is justified, then it is not primary; and whatever the judgment to which one would appeal in such a justification, this judgment itself would have to be justified, and so on ad infinitum. The argument is not pointless. It does draw attention to a certain important fact about knowledge, one to which Descartes alluded. But that fact is very different from what the argument is intended to prove.

According to the argument, a justification, and the possible infinite regress in which it is involved, of what we would regard as a primary epistemic judgment differ in no significant way from the justification, and the possible infinite regress in which it is involved, of an ordinary nonprimary epistemic judgment. Let us see if this is true. The following would be an example of the justificatory process in the case of an ordinary nonprimary epistemic judgment as this process would be conceived by the argument. *F:* I know that Mary will marry John. Because, *G:* I know that she loves him. Because, *H:* I know that she writes to him every day. And so it could go, perhaps ad infinitum. This series of justificatory steps has two noteworthy features. The first is that all steps constitute first-order epistemic judgments; that is, none of them is a judgment that one knows that one knows. The second, and crucially important, feature is that each successive step can be—and if the justification were at all legitimate would be—regarded as more reliable, more deserving of confidence, in itself, independently of any argument, than the previous step would be. Were this second feature absent, the process would not be genuinely justificatory. If *G* is not regarded as by itself more reliable than *F* is by itself, and *H* more reliable than *G*, then the justification of *F* in terms of *G* and of *G* in terms of *H* would be a sham. The criteria of a *logically sound* argument are validity and true premises. But the criterion of an *epistemically serious* argument is that the premises be regarded as more reliable, more deserving of confidence, than the conclusion already is.

Let us now compare the above series *F, G, H . . .* with an example of the series of justificatory steps that according to the argument would be required for what we would regard as a primary epistemic judgment. Let us suppose that "I know that I exist" is such a judgment. According to our account, it is equivalent to *P:* "I find it unthinkable that I am mistaken in believing that I exist." *P*, because of what? What *could* serve as sufficient evidence for *P*? Clearly, only the unthinkability of mistake in my believing that *P*, that is, *my knowledge that I know that P.*[40] Thus, if there is to be a series of justificatory steps with respect to *P*, the second and third steps would be the following. *Q:* I find it unthinkable that I am mistaken in believing that I find it unthinkable that I am mistaken in believing that I exist. *R:* I find it unthinkable that I am mistaken in believing that I find it unthinkable that I am mistaken in believing that I

40. There is of course another sense in which one can speak of knowing that one knows that *p*, namely, knowing that one's state, given that its specific characteristics are as one takes them to be, is properly classified as knowledge. On a lower level, such knowledge mainly consists in knowing the meaning of the word *know*. On a higher level, it consists in the possession of an adequate philosophical account of the concept of knowledge. In neither case is the possession or lack of such knowledge relevant to the question of the justification of one's belief that *p* is true. It is only relevant to the everyday or philosophical propriety of classifying that belief as knowledge.

find it unthinkable that I am mistaken in believing that I exist. The series P, Q, R . . . is fundamentally different from the series $F, G, H.$ . . . The former has neither of the two noteworthy features we found the latter to have. First, P, Q, and R are not all first-order epistemic judgments. P is, but Q is in effect a judgment that one knows that one knows, and R is a judgment that one knows that one knows that one knows.[41] Second, no step in this series can be regarded as less reliable than the *next*. In fact the opposite might be true: each step but the first might be regarded as less reliable than the *preceding* step. Q cannot be more reliable than P, and R cannot be more reliable than Q. For *on the assumption that they require support by something else*, all three would require as their support the satisfaction of the same two conditions, since all three have the same kind of content, that is, that something is unthinkable. The two conditions would be the following: (1) that the *kind* of evidence one employs for judging that one finds something to be unthinkable is legitimate (that one's method for determining that one finds something to be unthinkable is the right method) and (2) that one recognizes or identifies correctly something about one's state as constituting such evidence (that one is right in supposing that one's method is applicable in this particular case).

Now to suppose that P needs to be justified is to suppose that it may be erroneous. To suppose that it may be erroneous is to suppose that there really are such two conditions as the above and that one or both of them might not be met. But if they might not be met in the case of P, they might at least as easily not be met in the case of Q or R. For, with respect to the first condition, all three judgments obviously stand or fall together. And with respect to the second condition, P seems to be in the best position. The likelihood that the second condition would not be met in the case of Q seems greater than the likelihood that it would not be met in the case of P, and the likelihood that it would not be met in the case of R seems greater than the likelihood that it would not be met in the case of Q. For what Q asserts is a more complex, and thus probably harder to identify, instance of finding something to be unthinkable than is what P asserts, and what R asserts is a more complex, and perhaps harder to identify, instance of finding something to be unthinkable than is what Q asserts. But to say this is to say that what alone would even seem to be a justification of what we would regard as a primary epistemic judgment

41. Compare the P, Q, R . . . series with the not unrelated series "it is true that p," "it is true that it is true that p," "it is true that it is true that it is true that p. . . ."

cannot be intelligibly regarded as a justification, that the only argument that may even seem to have such a judgment as its conclusion cannot be epistemically serious. *An epistemic judgment cannot be intelligibly regarded as subject to justification if what alone would even seem to be such justification would involve an appeal to what is not more, indeed is probably less, certain.* At best, that I find it unthinkable that I am mistaken in believing that I find it unthinkable that I am mistaken in believing that *p* is no more certain than that I find it unthinkable that I am mistaken in believing that *p*. In fact, it is rather clearly less certain, because it is considerably more complicated. There is no intelligible sense in which a judgment can be said to require such justification. Therefore, since there is no other sort of justification that what we would regard as a primary epistemic judgment can intelligibly be said to require, such a judgment cannot be intelligibly said to require justification. So, whatever defects our account of the concept of knowledge may have, at least it frees us from the main scourge of other accounts: the seeming need for an infinite process of justification.

But is not the account impaled on the other horn of the dilemma? If a primary epistemic judgment is not subject to justification, then is it not simply not justified, is it not the expression of a mere true belief? But we must not confuse the sense in which, according to our account, a primary epistemic judgment would not be justified and the ordinary sense in which it would be said that a certain epistemic judgment is not justified. In the latter case what is meant is that something could be intelligibly said to justify the judgment, but in fact nothing does. According to the account, a primary epistemic judgment is not justified not only because nothing in fact justifies it but because nothing whatever could be intelligibly said to justify it.

This, however, is not sufficient to show that we have escaped the second horn of the dilemma. Perhaps nothing could be intelligibly said to justify certain theological or moral or metaphysical epistemic judgments. Perhaps they are stated and explained in such a way that nothing can intelligibly be regarded as a set of premises supporting them. To conclude from this that they are legitimate would be preposterous. On the contrary, precisely for that reason we should conclude that they are illegitimate, that they at best express mere beliefs and at worst are senseless. If our account is to show that primary epistemic judgments are, though literally not justifiable, nevertheless *legitimate* and not mere expressions of belief, it must provide a positive reason for so treating them. Such a reason can be provided. It would not consist, of course, in a justification of such judgments. It would consist in showing that there is a difference between the nonjustifiability of primary epistemic judgments and that of certain theological, moral, and metaphysical epistemic judgments, namely, that unlike the latter, the former are not justifiable only in the sense that the reliability of human thought in general is not justifiable.

To suppose that a primary epistemic judgment, that is, a judgment that I find it unthinkable that I am mistaken in believing that something is the case, may be illegitimate is to suppose that our reliance on our capacity to distinguish between what we can think and what we cannot think may be illegitimate. It is, in effect, to cast doubt on our capacity to *even employ* what I have called the principle of unthinkability. This would be a more fundamental sort of doubt regarding the principle than that concerning its validity, which was considered in the preceding section. And our defense of the validity of the principle suggests the sort of defense that our capacity to employ it legitimately, and thus the legitimacy of primary epistemic judgments, can be given. The principle of unthinkability, I have argued, is the foundation of all discrimination between possibility and impossibility, of all principles of reasoning, even of the principle of noncontradiction itself. Indeed, I may add, it is the foundation of any recognition and thought of truth, for such recognition and thought are possible only if one finds unthinkable the truth's being also a falsehood. And it is a necessary condition of the actual entertainment of any doubt, for one cannot doubt something unless one can recognize its being otherwise as thinkable. To question the legitimacy of the principle of unthinkability (as in the preceding section) or the legitimacy of our identification of something as an object of the applicability of this principle, that is, as unthinkable, would, in effect, be to question the legitimacy of human thought itself, the legitimacy of utilizing human thought in the search for knowledge. Indeed, such a question cannot be answered by offering anything resembling a proof of the legitimacy of human thought. On the other hand, it is clear that since the lack of justification of primary epistemic judgments consists only in the lack of justification of the legitimacy of human thought in general, it is not at all like the lack of justification of certain theological, moral, or metaphysical judgments. The latter cannot be grounded in anything at all. The former are grounded in the capacity of the human mind to distinguish between what it can think and what it cannot think and are ungrounded only in the sense that there cannot be a ground for the judgment that the human mind does have such a capacity. And this is an extraordinary "ungroundedness." To regard it as a reason for doubt is to engage in Descartes' metaphysical doubt, in his supposition that our mental faculties themselves may be defective or that an omnipotent being may be constantly deceiving us. To attempt to remove such doubt by argument is to enter the Cartesian circle. This does not mean that there is something ridiculous, logically improper, or absurd about metaphysical doubt. On the contrary, such doubt is logically possible; Descartes engaged in it briefly, and I have just described it. The logical possibility of such doubt is perhaps the most significant fact that one can learn about human thought and knowledge. But, I suggest, to have shown that the question of the legitimacy of primary epistemic judgments reduces to the question of the significance of Cartesian metaphysical doubt is to have shown that primary epistemic judgments are not illegitimate, that they are not ungrounded.

9. A Priori and A Posteriori Knowledge

WE HAVE REACHED the conclusion that primary knowledge consists in the unthinkability of mistake in believing, and that this unthinkability is due to the incompatibility of the falsehood of the belief with the context that renders the belief intelligible, endows it with content, and is a necessary condition of its identity. In the case of primary knowledge of contingent truths, the falsehood of the belief would be incompatible with experiential elements in the context of the belief, and thus while it is unthinkable "in the present circumstances," there is nothing unthinkable about it "in other circumstances." In the case of primary knowledge of necessary truths, the falsehood of the belief would be incompatible with conceptual elements in the context of the belief, and thus it would be unthinkable in *any* circumstances. I can think of a time when I do not have a headache, but not of a time when a triangle does not have three angles.

An important virtue of our account of primary knowledge, if it is true at all, is that it requires, and at the same time accounts for, the traditional division of knowledge into a priori and a posteriori. For the generally accepted formulation of this division is woefully unsatisfactory. *A poste-riori knowledge* is generally defined as knowledge based on empirical (experiential) evidence, and *a priori knowledge* is defined as knowledge which is *not* based on empirical evidence. The unilluminating character of these definitions is obvious as soon as one considers the conceptual disparity between the two. The first definition does determine, at least in general, a concept with intellectually visible content. We have a determinate notion of empirical evidence, even if we do not have a satisfactory account of it. But we have no determinate notion of nonempirical evidence, or of knowledge which is just *not* based on (is "independent of") empirical evidence. The definition of a priori knowledge does not determine a concept, though it suggests a wildly general direction in which to look for such a concept. Nonempirical evidence is not a certain *kind* of evidence, and knowledge which is not based on, or is "independent of," experience is not a certain kind of knowledge, any more than non-red is a certain kind of color.

Some of our knowledge is dependent on experience, and some of our knowledge is not dependent on experience. This is true regardless of the particular theory of a priori knowledge that we hold. Even if an a priori proposition is merely a consequence of "the benign redundancy of our notation," [42] it is still independent of experience, for it is not *about* the benign redundancy of our notation but a consequence of it. But a theory of knowledge cannot be satisfied with the mere admission of the fact of the division of knowledge into a priori and a posteriori. It ought to be able to account for this fact. First, it must make clear how it is possible that both are kinds of *knowledge,* why (contrary to hasty philosophical suppositions) we in fact do not mean different things by "knowledge" when we speak of a priori and of a posteriori knowledge. And, second, it must explain why knowledge should fall into these two kinds. It is not obvious why both what we call our knowledge of contingent truths and what we call our knowledge of necessary truths should be classified together as knowledge. But neither is it obvious why there should be two, rather than just one or perhaps three or more, kinds of knowledge.

Our account seems to resolve both puzzles. Both primary a priori and primary a posteriori knowledge consist in the unthinkability of mistake in belief, and this unthinkability is due, in both cases, to the incompatibility

42. Max Black, *Models and Metaphors* (Ithaca, N.Y.: Cornell University Press, 1962), p. 86.

of the falsehood of the belief with the context of the belief. And knowledge falls into two kinds, for the context of a belief consists of two kinds of elements: experiences and concepts, or of *what* one perceives, feels, and imagines when one believes that something is the case and *how* one thinks of, grasps, or classifies what one believes. The difference between these two kinds of elements in the context of a belief is obvious and fundamental. It is natural that knowledge itself would fall into two equally obviously and fundamentally different kinds, depending on whether the falsehood of one's belief would be incompatible with an *experience* or with a *concept* in the context of the belief. In the case of derivative knowledge, of course, there may be special or additional differences and similarities between a priori and a posteriori knowledge. We may say in general that a derivative epistemic judgment is a priori or a posteriori depending on whether *all* of the primary epistemic judgments from which it is ultimately derived are a priori, or whether at least one of them is a posteriori. And the derivation in both cases may well be of the same kind; the demonstrative ("a priori") inference of one a posteriori proposition from another does not render the former proposition a priori.

But while the adequacy of a general account of the nature of knowledge depends, in part, on its ability to provide an account of the division of knowledge into a priori and a posteriori, the adequacy of this latter account depends mainly on its ability to answer two fundamental questions. Regarding a priori knowledge, there is the question of the nature of the objects of such knowledge. What, if anything, is such knowledge about? This question must be answered if we are to regard our account of the general concept of knowledge as adequate. For this account, in common with most, makes a distinction between the truth of what one is said to know and one's evidence that it is true. Now, the natural conception of the truth of a belief is that of a certain sort of agreement of the belief with the world. Even if, as philosophers, we were to adopt a theory of truth other than the correspondence theory, we would have to allow, on pain of being unintelligible, that a true belief is one which is about something that is as it is believed to be. This, it seems to me, is the indispensable core of any concept of truth that has roots in ordinary discourse and thought. But then does our account of knowledge as a certain kind of true belief apply to a priori knowledge? If it does not, then either our account is unacceptable or we must show in detail why what is called a priori knowledge should not be knowledge at all. But if it does, then our account presupposes an affirmative answer to the question, Are the beliefs whose truth we know a priori *about* something? and an adequate answer to the question, *What* are they about? In either case, a full-scale investigation into the nature of a priori knowledge is required.

Second, there is the question of the applicability of the distinction between primary and derivative knowledge to the major kind of a posteriori knowledge, namely, perceptual knowledge. It is generally supposed that our perceptual knowledge of bodies is derivative. But there is no agreement what, then, we have primary perceptual knowledge about. The fact is that the very distinction between primary and derivative knowledge is quite unclear, indeed perhaps inapplicable, in the case of perceptual knowledge. Yet that distinction is essential to our account of knowledge, for only by means of it do we avoid an infinite regress of justification. Consequently, our account of the concept of knowledge cannot be accepted until its applicability to the most important kind of knowledge human beings have is seen to be warranted and has been made clear.

We have a fairly clear idea of the difference between primary and derivative a priori knowledge but virtually no idea of what the objects of such knowledge may be, or indeed whether it has objects at all. We have a fairly clear idea of what are at least the typical objects of a posteriori knowledge, namely, bodies, but only the vaguest idea of what in such knowledge is primary and what derivative. Our investigations in Parts Two and Three will attempt to make clear the nature of the objects of a priori knowledge and the nature of primary perceptual knowledge and thus to fill out what so far is a purely formal account of the general concept of knowledge.

We shall consider first the question of the objects of a priori knowledge. This is really the question of the nature of necessary truth, for it is necessary truths, and only necessary truths, that we know a priori. The reason for this lies not in the definition of a priori ("independent of experience") knowledge, but in the fact that, in addition to experiences, the contexts of our beliefs include only concepts. If they also included a third something, we might have knowledge that is independent of experience but also independent of our concepts and that thus would perhaps still be knowledge of contingent truths. But they do not, and for this reason a priori knowledge is knowledge of necessary truths, and to determine the nature of the objects of a priori knowledge is to determine the nature of necessary truth. On the other hand, even if we ignore the possibility of a third element in the contexts of our beliefs, we shall see that we ought not to suppose that the *concept* of a necessarily true proposition is identical with the concept of an a priori proposition, nor even that necessary truth can be defined in terms of a priori knowledge. The notion of the a priori, being negative, is in need of elucidation in terms of the positive content of another notion, namely, that of the necessarily true; it has no content of its own in terms of which another notion can usefully be understood.

PART TWO

The Objects of
A Priori Knowledge

1. The A Priori and the Necessary

IT MAY SEEM THAT what I have already said about our knowledge of necessary truths constitutes a theory of the nature of necessary truth. But it does not. From the fact that the unthinkability of mistaken belief in the sort of necessary truth of which we have primary knowledge is due to the incompatibility of its falsehood with certain conceptual elements in the context of the belief, it does not follow that *what* we know when we know a necessary truth is something that has to do, directly or indirectly, with concepts. (Hence both the propriety and the danger of describing necessary truths as conceptual.) Of course, neither does the opposite conclusion follow. To reach either conclusion, independent investigations in considerable detail are required. In a similar fashion, from the fact that we know what other people think and feel on the basis of observation of their bodily behavior, it does not follow, without further argument, that what we so know are patterns of other people's bodily behavior. This is why our account of our knowledge of necessary truths is really not controversial; it would appear controversial only if confused with an account of the

99

nature of necessary truth. For, whatever our views about this latter topic may be, surely we all must admit that we discover that a proposition is necessarily true (except when deriving it from other necessarily true propositions) by simply finding the state of affairs its denial purports to describe unthinkable in terms of the concepts that would be required for thinking it. That this is so is not a matter of philosophical theory, but of everyday fact.

Of course, the way in which we come to know that a proposition is necessarily true may *suggest* a certain account of the nature of necessary truth. For example, insofar as a concept is the meaning of a word, the unthinkability of what a necessarily false proposition purports to describe may be due to a violation of the meanings of words employed in such a proposition. Or one might simply be tempted to identify the necessary truth of a proposition with the unthinkability of what its denial purports to describe. But any such conclusions must be argued for in detail. They do not follow at all obviously from the way in which we come to know that a proposition is necessarily true. Moreover, we want to discover *why* we come to know necessary truths in the way in which we do. And such a discovery would depend in part on an independent account of the nature of necessary truth.

There is a philosophical topic of the nature of necessary truth because there is a prima facie distinction, which has great philosophical importance, between two groups of propositions. One group of propositions, in addition to being undisputably true and known to be true with complete certainty, are also such that one cannot intelligibly suppose that they might have been false. And this fact about them can be expressed by saying that they are necessarily true. Examples of such propositions would be the following: "Three and two are five." "All black cats are black." "If John is sitting to the left of Peter, then Peter is sitting to the right of John." "Either it is raining outside or it is not." Another group of propositions, though perhaps also undisputably true and known to be true with complete certainty, are such that it makes perfectly good sense to suppose that they might nevertheless have been false. And it is natural to describe them, for this reason, as contingently true. Examples of such propositions would be the following: "The earth is round." "I have a headache." "It is raining now." "The sun will rise tomorrow." That there is a prima facie distinction between two such groups of propositions would seem unquestionable, although there may be philosophical questions about the propriety of classifying some particular proposition (including those mentioned above) as necessarily true (or as contingently true). I shall not attempt to prove that there really are necessarily true propositions, though I think this obvious, for the topic I wish to consider is logically prior to any such attempt. I shall be concerned with the *nature* of necessary truth, with the very *concept* of necessary truth. One cannot ask whether there really are necessarily true propositions unless one is clear about the concept of necessary truth. Even if, in fact, there are no necessary truths, surely there are contingent truths, and thus it should be possible to explain what would be a noncontingent, a necessary, truth. Moreover, we must not forget that ordinarily doubts about the existence of necessarily true propositions are motivated by philosophical considerations which are largely based on the adoption of a particular account of the concept of necessary truth. Consequently, we must not *begin* by taking such doubts seriously.

Some of the difficulties in dealing with the question of the nature of necessary truth are due to the failure to distinguish it sharply from some other questions about necessarily true propositions, which are quite distinct, though of course not unrelated. In addition to (1) the nature of necessary truth, that is, the content of the very concept of a necessarily true proposition, we can be concerned with (2) the ways of determining that a given proposition is necessarily true, that is, with the "source" or nature of our knowledge of necessary truths, or with (3) the kinds of propositions that are necessarily true, meaning, of course, the kinds of propositions that can be identified independently of the distinction between necessary and contingent truth, or with (4) the subject matter, if any, of necessarily true propositions, that is, with the sorts of entities, facts, relations, and situations they are *about*. Most of the familiar theories of necessary truth are concerned with topics (2), (3), or (4) and not with (1). For instance, as we have seen, to say that a necessarily true proposition is one whose falsehood is unthinkable or inconceivable is probably to offer a view about topic (2), not about (1). The necessary truth of a proposition may only be known on the basis of the unthinkability of its falsehood. Yet to say that a proposition is necessarily true is not the same as saying that its falsehood is unthinkable; these two statements are not synonymous. To take another example, it seems obvious that logical principles and their substitution-instances are necessarily true, and it can at least be argued that such propositions alone are necessarily true. But this is an observation regarding topic (3), not (1). To say that a proposition is necessarily true is not the same as saying that it is a principle of logic or a substitution-instance of such a principle. It may also be true that all necessary propositions are propositions about universals. But this would be a discovery about topic (4), not (1), for to say that a proposition is necessary is not the same as saying that it is about universals. In this Part, I shall be concerned chiefly with topic (1), although the account I shall offer will also constitute an account of topic (4) and will suggest views on the other two topics.

The familiar theories about the nature of necessary truth employ certain technical philosophical terms without which they probably cannot even be stated. I have in mind the terms *a priori, a posteriori, empirical, factual, logical, analytic, synthetic, formal, material, self-contradictory, essential,* and *transcendental,* and the corresponding theories that to say that a proposition is necessarily true is to say that it is a priori, or nonempirical, or nonfactual, or logically true, or analytic, or formally true, or one the denial of which is self-contradictory, or one describing either the essential structure of reality or the transcendental structure of thought or of language. I shall try to show that, despite their obvious importance for other issues, none of these theories throws light on the nature of necessary truth, that is, on the content of the very concept of a necessarily true proposition. In so doing I shall presuppose specific senses of the above technical terms, although I shall try to explain these senses at the beginning of my argument. My conclusions, of course, will follow, if they follow at all, partly because of the senses of such technical terms that I have adopted. But it will be seen that these senses are not at all arbitrary. I believe that any explanations of these technical terms other than those I suggest would either be irrelevant to the issue before us or would lead to the same conclusion, for it is with the senses of *technical* terms that we are concerned.

The terms *a priori* and *a posteriori* are applied to knowledge as well as to truths or propositions. Their application to knowledge has already been discussed. Here we are interested in their application to propositions and, specifically, in the possible identification of the concept of a necessary proposition with the concept of an a priori proposition. But serious difficulties with the notions of the a priori and the a posteriori arise precisely with respect to their application to propositions. It may seem that this cannot be the case. For can we not simply define an a priori proposition as one knowable a priori and an a posteriori proposition as one knowable a posteriori? Of course we can, but if we do, then the concept of an a priori proposition and the concept of an a posteriori proposition become thoroughly useless. The reason is that there is nothing in such definitions that would suggest that a proposition cannot be both a priori and a posteriori, that we cannot have both a priori and a posteriori knowledge of one and the same proposition. And this is a consequence not of our specific elucidations of a priori and of a posteriori knowledge but of any reasonable conception of what it is for knowledge to be dependent on experience. To begin with, let us recognize that there is nothing self-contradictory about the supposition that a certain paradigm of an a priori proposition, e.g., a simple arithmetical proposition, may also be known to be true by appeal to experience. Surely one can treat the proposition "Three and two are five" as an empirical generalization. One would look for pairs of collections of objects, one three in number, the other two; count their members together (whether by actually assembling them or not); and happily discover each time that indeed there are five objects. To deny that one can *know* that three and two are five as a result of such a procedure would be merely to deny that one can know any inductive generalization. On the other hand, to say that what one would know is not that three and two are five but some empirical generalization about actual collections would be to beg the question.

Nor is it obviously self-contradictory to suppose that a certain paradigm of an a posteriori proposition, e.g., that there is a typewriter before me now, may also be known a priori. Indeed, I do not have primary a priori knowledge that there is a typewriter before me now, even though perhaps I have primary a posteriori knowledge of this fact. But why should I not be able to have derivative a priori knowledge of it? Is there an obvious contradiction in the supposition that I may derive such knowledge with formal validity solely from premises of which I have primary a priori knowledge? For example, these premises may constitute the foundations of a theology, whose theorems will include not only the proposition that God exists but also propositions describing everything that an omniscient, omnipotent, and omnibenevolent God would create. The fact that we do not have such a theology is completely irrelevant.

Of course, we can (and for other purposes will) continue to regard the notions of a priori and a posteriori propositions as contradictories by saying that an a priori proposition is one that *can* be known independently of experience and an a posteriori proposition is one that cannot. An a priori proposition would be one of which we can have a priori knowledge, though perhaps also a posteriori knowledge. An a posteriori proposition would be one of which we can have only a posteriori knowledge. But such definitions would render the notions of a priori and a posteriori propositions even less illuminating; and, as we have just seen, perhaps they would allow for the possibility that there are no a posteriori propositions at all.

It is at this point that one is tempted to introduce the term *empirical* and assert that a posteriori propositions are empirical while a priori propositions are not. But the word *empirical* is ambiguous. In one sense, it means a proposition describing an observable or experienceable state of affairs. In another sense, it simply means a proposition which is an object of a posteriori knowledge. These two senses must not be confused. The distinction between them is philosophically important and probably essential to a philosopher such as Hume who asserts that only propositions about experienceable entities are intelligible and yet argues in effect that some relations of such entities are necessary and thus presumably knowable a priori. (The relations of ideas that Hume regarded as necessary must also hold between the corresponding impressions; for example, if the idea of pink necessarily resembles the idea of crimson, then any impression of pink must resemble any impression of crimson.) Now the introduction of the term *empirical* would be useful only if it is intended in the first sense, for in the second sense the term is merely a trivial synonym of "a posteriori proposition." But if so understood, it would still not help us in giving useful content to the concept of an a posteriori proposition, for there are propositions describing experienceable states of affairs which nevertheless can be known a priori. "Crimson is darker than pink," "Nothing is both red and green all over," and "All black cats are black" describe experienceable, observable states of affairs, at least as much as "Ice is cold," "Nothing is both metal and lighter than air," and "All cats have fur" do. Thus, there would be a priori empirical propositions. But there would also be a posteriori nonempirical propositions, that is, propositions knowable a posteriori but not describing observable states of affairs. Some of the theoretical propositions in physics would be plausible examples. Consequently, we would learn nothing about the nature of a priori or a posteriori propositions by saying that the former are nonempirical and the latter empirical.

But, the Theory of the A Priori, according to which the concept of a necessary proposition is identical with that of an a priori proposition, can be rejected on more direct grounds. Indeed, it seems true that all necessary propositions are knowable (if at all) a priori, and thus that all propositions knowable (if at all) only a posteriori are contingent. But this only seems to be the case; whether it really is the case has to be argued, and such an argument would have to employ the concept of necessary proposition without identifying it with the concept of a priori proposition. It seems to us that all necessary propositions are knowable (if at all) a priori because we are confident that all propositions describing the occurrence of experiences and observations are contingent, and that knowledge of necessary truth cannot be based on, dependent on, knowledge of contingent truth. Even if such confidence is justified, we understand what we are so confident about only if we already understand the distinction between necessary and contingent truth, specifically, only if we understand what it is for a proposition describing an experience to be contingent. But it is not clear that we should be confident that it is impossible for a proposition to be both knowable only on the basis of contingent experience and yet necessarily true. Is it impossible that there are mathematical truths that we can know only by experiment but that in reality are necessarily true? If we were to say that while one can have a posteriori knowledge of the truth of such a necessarily true proposition one cannot have a posteriori knowledge of the necessity of its truth, we would presuppose the concept of necessary truth and thus would not elucidate it. The Theory of the A Priori is a possible theory because it identifies the notion of a necessarily true proposition with that of a proposition knowable a priori. It is not even a possible theory if it identifies the notion of a necessarily true proposition with the notion of a proposition the *necessity* of whose truth can be known only a priori.

2. The Standard Logico-Linguistic Theories of Necessary Truth

THE MOST WIDELY HELD recent theories of necessary truth have been logico-linguistic. They have claimed, in general, that the necessary truth of a proposition is nothing but a feature of the language in which the proposition is expressed, a feature moreover that is ultimately conventional in character. Of course, the claim becomes significant only when made more specific. Then actual theories of necessary truth are put forward, such as that a necessarily true proposition is one true in virtue of the conventional meanings of the words in it, or one true in virtue of its logical form, or one whose denial is self-contradictory, or one true in virtue of the rules of language. The exposition of these theories has generally depended on the introduction and use of the technical term *analytic*. Our discussion of them must therefore begin with a definition of that term.

The phrase *analytic proposition* has been used in many senses, ranging from the excessively obscure, but important, sense of a proposition true solely in virtue of the meanings of the words in it to the relatively precise and clear, but question-begging and quite unilluminating, sense of a necessarily true proposition. Some of the theories regarding analyticity seem to consider the term *analytic* sacrosanct, they seem to consider its application to all necessary, or a priori, propositions an article of philosophical faith, whatever the term may mean.[1] I shall treat it, however, as I would any other technical term. While I shall attempt to use it in a sense generally recognized by philosophers, my main concern is that this sense be unambiguous, clear, and philosophically useful. I define an analytic proposition as one which, by substitution of synonyms for words occurring in it, is reducible to a logical proposition. And I define a synthetic proposition as one which is not analytic. Thus "All bachelors are unmarried men" would be an analytic proposition while "All bachelors are bachelors" would not. I am using the term *logical proposition* in the generally accepted and, at least for our purposes, sufficiently clear sense that would allow us to say that the principles of logic (e.g., "No proposition is both true and false"; "If one proposition implies a second one, and the second implies a third, then the first implies the third"; "If no individuals that have a certain property also have a certain second property, then no individuals that have this second property also have the first property") as well as their substitution-instances (e.g., "It is false that Jones is tall and that Jones is not tall"; "If it is true that if Jones is tall then he is heavy and that if he is heavy then he is strong, then it is true

---

1. The most distinguished example of such a theory is C. I. Lewis' theory of the a priori in *An Analysis of Knowledge and Valuation* (LaSalle, Ill.: Open Court Publishing Co., 1947).

that if Jones is tall then he is strong"; "If no men are angels then no angels are men") are logical propositions.

According to the Analyticity Theory, the concept of necessary truth is identical with the concept of analytic truth. Clearly, on the basis of our definition of the term *analytic,* the theory is false. If the terms *analytic, synthetic,* and *logical* are understood in the manner I have explained, and if we make the natural assumptions that all necessary propositions are (knowable) a priori and that all logical propositions are necessary, it follows that (1) all analytic propositions are necessary, (2) all logical propositions are synthetic, necessary, and a priori, thus (3) there are synthetic a priori propositions if there are analytic propositions, for (4) analytic propositions are necessary only because of their reducibility, by substitution of synonyms, to certain necessary synthetic propositions, namely, logical propositions. If some of these consequences of my definition of analytic proposition seem paradoxical and question-begging, the reason is not that the definition is eccentric but that this technical term has been brandished in philosophical debates much too long and with far too little care.

Indeed, we could easily stipulate that an analytic proposition is one that is either a logical proposition or reducible to a logical proposition by substitution of synonyms and thus placate some vigorous philosophical spirits. But such a stipulation would only disguise, and not eliminate, the above philosophical consequences. It would be not only etymologically inaccurate but philosophically misleading. It would fail to preserve the original connotation of the phrase "analytic proposition," that of a proposition which analyzes, or is true in virtue of the analysis of, one or more of the concepts employed in it.[2] It would disguise the fact that the ultimate ground of the truth of a proposition that is reducible to a logical proposition is not the relations of synonymy that make such a reduction legitimate but the truth of the logical proposition itself. What the meanings of "bachelor" and "unmarried man" in "All bachelors are unmarried men" do is *not to make this proposition true* but *to allow its reduction* to the proposition "All unmarried men are unmarried men," the truth of which is a necessary condition of the truth of the former proposition. If we do

---

2. "Analytic judgments . . . as adding nothing through the predicate to the concept of the subject, but merely breaking it up into those constituent concepts that have all along been thought in it, although confusedly, can also be entitled explicative" (Kant, *Critique of Pure Reason,* tr. Norman Kemp Smith, A7).

not ignore this fact, then the plausibility of the general claim of any logico-linguistic theory, that there are propositions the truth of which has a purely verbal origin—that is, propositions that are true solely because of facts about language or are peculiar indicative shadows of imperatives about linguistic usage—decreases considerably and one who wishes to make this claim must make it good with respect to logical propositions themselves.[3]

Our definition of analytic proposition, and consequent refutation of the view that a necessarily true proposition is one that is analytic, thus has the virtue of stressing that the main task of any logico-linguistic theory of necessary truth is to provide an account of the concept of necessary truth as it is applied to logical propositions. Such propositions may be trifling, as Locke would have said. But that there are such trifling propositions is not at all a trifling matter. For should we discover that the grounds of the truth of logical propositions are in no sense linguistic or conventional, then the main concern of theorists of necessary truth in the past two centuries—namely, whether nontrifling necessary propositions, the alleged "synthetic a priori" truths, are reducible to logical propositions—would lose most of its philosophical interest. We shall now consider several accounts of logical truth, though we will leave the most important one, what I shall call the Game Theory, for section 3 of this Part. All of these accounts (often confusingly lumped together as analyticity theories) may be understood as attempts to show that logical propositions themselves are true solely because of facts about language. All are theories about the nature of logical truth.

We shall begin with the account that would be presented by the Analyticity Theory itself. According to it, the truth of logical propositions is the direct result of the definitions of the words in them. But what definitions? Suppose we define implication and conjunction in terms of negation and alternation. Then what are the definitions of negation and alternation that would justify, for example, the principle (p) $(p \text{ v} \sim p)$? Clearly, they must be a radically different kind of definition, for otherwise negation and alternation would not be our primitive connectives. The theory is likely to appeal to truth-tables here. The truth-tables of $\sim p$ and of $p \text{ v} q$ are such that the truth-table of $p \text{ v} \sim p$ shows that the latter is true in all possible circumstances, that is, is necessarily true. But the very

---

3. Cf. Arthur Pap, *Semantics and Necessary Truth* (New Haven and London: Yale University Press, 1958), chaps. 5, 6, and 7.

construction of a truth-table for the purpose of demonstrating the necessary truth of a proposition depends on the observance of fundamental logical principles. We make sure that we assign only two truth-values to every constituent of a compound proposition. And we make sure that in each of its occurrences on the same row of the truth-table a constituent proposition is assigned the same truth-value. (The reason the truth-tables of the principles of noncontradiction and excluded middle "prove" them to be necessarily true is that we have made sure that they will do so in abiding by the principles of noncontradiction and excluded middle in the very construction of these truth-tables.) Thus the truth-tabular definitions of the primitive connectives are possible only if constructed in accordance with necessarily true propositions that would themselves be stated with the use of these connectives or their synonyms. This fact renders the sense in which a truth-table can be said to be a *definition* quite obscure and of very doubtful value. But, what is more significant for our purposes, this fact also shows that the appeal to truth-tables can throw no light on the concept of necessary truth.

Of course, the truth-tables could be regarded as purely syntactical rules for assigning the signs T and F to molecular sentences. But they would be relevant to the account of the notion of necessary truth only if the signs T and F are interpreted to mean, respectively, true and false. And when they are given such an interpretation, the assignment of one and only one of these two signs to each constituent, and the nonassignment of both T and F to one and the same constituent, in the same row of the table, would not be merely a matter of syntactical rules; and the consequence that the molecular sentence is true for all possible truth-values of its constituents would not be a consequence merely of syntactical rules.

Could it be, however, that logical propositions (as well as any other recalcitrant necessary propositions) are true in virtue of *implicit* definitions of words in them?[4] The point of using the word "implicit" is to deter us from insisting that a proposition can be true in virtue of definitions (meanings) of words in it only in the sense that the substitution of synonyms for such words reduces the proposition to some other, perhaps less questionable, proposition. So an implicit definition is not a definition that *can* be made explicit. The notion of such a definition is sometimes introduced in order to explain the meaningfulness of the uninterpreted

4. Cf. Anthony Quinton, "The *A Priori* and the Analytic," *Proceedings of the Aristotelian Society*, LXIV (1963–64), 31–54.

primitive terms in an axiomatic system. The axioms of such a system are said to implicitly define the uninterpreted primitive terms in the sense that the assertion of the truth of the axioms determines the possible interpretations (preferably only one) of, or meaning-assignments to, these terms. What has made saying this plausible is that such axioms are in effect propositional functions. And a propositional *function* (or a set of such functions) can be said to determine the values of its variables in the sense that only for some such values would it become a true *proposition*. The notion of implicit definition is also introduced in the explanation of the meaningfulness of those terms in a scientific system that can be neither directly interpreted in terms of familiar empirical predicates nor defined solely in terms of such predicates. We say then that such terms are implicitly defined in the sense that the set of propositions in which they occur entails propositions in which only empirical predicates occur. I would be inclined to regard the notion of implicit definition as useful in this latter context and as only obfuscating in the former. But even if it is perfectly clear and legitimate in both contexts, it fails to render the notion of *truth* in virtue of implicit definitions clear or legitimate. The reason is quite simple. In both contexts, by "implicit definition" we mean the endowment of a word with meaning by the assumption or assertion of the truth of certain propositions in which the word occurs. It immediately follows that it is nonsense to then turn around and say that the truth of such propositions can itself be the result of the implicit definition of the word. It is difficult enough to understand how the truth of a proposition may determine the meaning of one or more of its terms and thus the meaning of the proposition itself, for, it would seem, the proposition cannot be true or false except insofar as it already has a fully determinate meaning. But surely it is impossible to understand how a proposition may be true in virtue of what a word in it means if what that word means is itself determined by the proposition's being true.

Of course, the defender of the Analyticity Theory may simply claim that all that he intends to say in appealing to implicit definitions in the case of logical propositions themselves is that such propositions are true directly in virtue of their meaning and not in virtue of their reducibility to some other propositions. To say this, however, is not to present a theory of necessary truth but at best to suggest the direction in which such a theory should be sought. If it is to have a point, the claim must be made far more specific. *Ex hypothesi*, it cannot be specified in the way in which the claim can be specified that propositions such as "All bachelors are unmarried men" are true in virtue of their meaning. I suggest that if the former is usefully specified, it will turn out to be the claim of the Game Theory, to which we will turn our attention in section 3 of this Part.

According to a second logico-linguistic theory, the concept of a necessarily true proposition is identical with the concept of a proposition the denial of which is self-contradictory. Let us ignore the familiar, embarrassing to the theory, questions (1) whether it allows us to regard all logical propositions as necessarily true (the self-contradictoriness of the denials of most logical propositions cannot be shown without appealing to other logical propositions) and (2) whether there are necessarily true propositions the denial of which is not self-contradictory (the "synthetic a priori"). But let us insist that by a self-contradictory proposition the theory mean a proposition of the form "*p* and not-*p*" or a proposition reducible to one of this form. For the theory would be utterly spurious if by self-contradiction it meant necessary falsehood. And it would be reducible to other theories of necessary truth if by self-contradiction it meant unthinkability, or violation of a rule of language, or incompatibility with the essential features of reality.

Now, indeed, all propositions the denial of which is self-contradictory are necessarily true. But the obvious explanation of this is that the principle of noncontradiction itself is necessarily true, and the theory does not even purport to throw light on the necessary truth of *that* necessarily true proposition or to explain why all propositions the denial of which is *not* self-contradictory should be contingent. There is nothing about the formal notion of self-contradiction that would even suggest that a self-contradictory proposition is necessarily false or that a proposition the denial of which is self-contradictory is necessarily true. The basis of the theory is the natural belief that the principle of noncontradiction is necessarily true and also the important fact that at least a very large number of necessarily false propositions are substitution-instances, or are reducible to substitution-instances, of the denial of the principle of noncontradiction. The theory under discussion derives its philosophical importance from this latter fact, which it indirectly tends to emphasize. But it collapses because of its failure to give an account of the principle of noncontradiction itself and because of its inability to explain the relation between the concept of necessary truth and the concept of a proposition the denial of which is self-contradictory. Needless to say, to point this out is not to question the truth of the principle of noncontradiction. It is merely to draw attention to the fact that, since that principle is necessarily true, an account of the nature of necessary truth must also account for the nature of the necessary truth of that principle. A demand for a demonstration of the necessary truth of the principle of noncontradiction would be silly, but the demand for an account of what is meant by saying that it is necessarily true is not.

One does not explain (though perhaps one renders obvious, were this needed) the necessary truth of the principle of noncontradiction by saying that, when a man contradicts himself, "from the point of view of imparting information, of communicating facts (or falsehoods), it is as if he had never opened his mouth. He utters words, but does not say anything. . . . A contradiction cancels itself and leaves nothing"; [5] or by saying that "the difference between a language and a practice of making arbitrary noises is that the former embodies a concept of negation. And the law of contradiction is an essential part of all definitions of negation, even if the law of excluded middle is not. But this primacy does not show the law of contradiction to be non-conventional. To choose to speak rather than babble is, amongst other things, to accept the law of contradiction. But to speak is still a choice and the law of contradiction still a convention . . ." [6] *Why* is it that contradicting oneself has all these consequences? Surely, not because it really is a case of not saying anything or a case of just babbling. There is a world of difference between uttering words but not saying anything, and contradicting oneself. To say that something is both blue and not blue is neither to simply utter meaningless sounds nor to utter meaningful sounds but in a meaningless order. The notion of falsehood is simply inapplicable to either of the latter two cases, yet it obviously is applicable to someone's saying that something is both blue and not blue. Surely, the natural explanation of what is wrong with contradicting oneself is that what one says in contradicting oneself is *necessarily* (and, what perhaps is even more important, *obviously*) false. A contradictory statement fails to communicate simply because it is necessarily and obviously false. A language in which all statements are self-contradictory would not be a language only if a language in which all statements are necessarily false would not be a language.

It may be observed here that it is a mistake to suppose that if the

5. P. F. Strawson, *Introduction to Logical Theory* (London: Methuen, 1952), pp. 2–3.
6. Quinton, "The *A Priori* and the Analytic," p. 42.

principle of noncontradiction were false, then language, thought, and argument would be impossible. To deny that no propositions are both true and false is to assert not that *all* propositions are both true and false but that *some* propositions are both true and false. The principle of noncontradiction may be false even if no propositions that we have ever entertained are both true and false. For, the exceptions to it may be quite limited and unknown to us, though perhaps we shall learn about them in the future (perhaps from visitors from outer space). In such a situation, it would be the case both that our language, thought, and reasoning are safe and that the principle of noncontradiction is false.

The thesis that all necessary propositions are, or are reducible to, logical propositions, which is the root both of the Analyticity Theory and of the Theory of Contradiction of Denial, is sometimes defended in a different and more fundamental manner. The distinction between formal and material truth is introduced. It is argued that the truth of at least some necessary propositions depends entirely on their "logical form" while the truth of all contingent propositions depends in part on their "matter" or "content." And the claim is made not only that all necessary propositions are true solely because of their (explicit or implicit) logical form but also that the very concept of necessary truth is adequately accounted for as identical with the concept of formal truth.

What is meant by the logical form of a proposition? How is the logical form of a proposition identified? And how and why would the logical form of a proposition, in some cases, make the proposition true? If these questions can be answered without presupposing the notion of necessary truth, then at least we would have a possible theory of necessary truth, even if one that eventually turns out to be false. But if they cannot, then we would have a theory which may be of relevance for other philosophical topics (e.g., for the classification of the various kinds of necessary propositions) but of no relevance at all for the topic of the nature of necessary truth. Unfortunately, the latter is the case. Consider the claim that the ground of the truth of the necessary proposition "If John is a bachelor then John is a bachelor" is that it has the logical form "if p then p." How do we discover that this is the logical form of the proposition? One explanation is that we discover this by substituting blanks or variables for the "inessential elements" in the proposition. But what is an inessential element of a proposition? We are told that it is such that the substitution for it of any other expression of the same grammatical kind would yield a true proposition. But surely to recognize an element in a proposition as inessential in this sense is simply to recognize the necessary truth of a certain more general proposition, e.g., (p) $(p \supset p)$, "Every proposition implies itself."

Indeed, we could say that an *essential* element in a logical proposition, that is, a "logical word," is one of supreme generality, one that can be employed in discourse about any subject matter. Then we would have offered a description, independent of the notion of necessary truth, of the only words that can occur in the principles of logic or that can occur essentially in the substitution-instances of these principles. But with such a description we would have succeeded only in emphasizing the supreme generality of the principles of logic and not at all in elucidating their necessary truth. Talk about the "formal character" of a logical principle is simply a muddled way of referring to its supreme generality. For a logical principle may be defined as a necessary truth of supreme generality, that is, one in which no reference is made to anything other than all (or any) individuals, all (or any) properties, all (or any) classes, all (or any) propositions. But supreme generality, and thus "formality," is not at all the same as necessary truth.[7] The distinction between supreme and limited generality is quite unconnected with that between necessary and contingent truth. They cut across each other. For example, the following proposition is of supreme generality and is quite *formal,* but *contingent,* and is in fact *false:* (x) (F) (G) $[(Fx \supset Gx) \supset (Gx \supset Fx)]$.

Let us suppose that we discover the logical form of a proposition without employing the notion of necessary truth, perhaps by identifying it with the grammatical syntactical structure of the proposition or by appealing to a list of "logical words" prepared without reference to the necessary truth of some propositions containing such words. (I shall ignore the familiar dangers of doing the former and the equally familiar difficulties of doing the latter.) For example, we may appeal to an intuitive distinction between "descriptive" and "nondescriptive" words and label the latter "logical." That there is such an adequate distinction seems to me quite doubtful. To be sure, *green* can be said to be descriptive in a fairly clear sense in which *if . . . then* would not be descriptive. But is *to the left of* descriptive, in that sense? And are *property, individual,* and *proposition* nondescriptive? However, the issue can be dealt with on a more funda-

---

7. The confusion of the two is encouraged by speaking of a logical principle as "true in all possible worlds."

mental level. Let us assume that we have identified, in some manner, the logical form of a proposition. We are immediately faced with the question, how and why should the so-identified form have anything to do with the truth of the propositions that have it? I submit that the answer to this question is perfectly clear, though the use of bound variables to express general propositions has tempted philosophers to ignore it. The form "if *p* then *p*" renders all propositions which have it necessarily true not because it possesses a mysterious truth-making virtue but simply because it is necessarily true that every proposition implies itself, that is, that if a proposition is true then it is true, that $(p) (p \supset p)$. For $(p) (p \supset p)$ means absolutely nothing more or less than what "Every proposition implies itself" means. And this latter proposition is not "formal" in any sense of the word; it does not even *appear* to have anything to do with the "form" of a proposition.

Of course, there is a point to saying that "If John is a bachelor then John is a bachelor" is true in virtue of its having the form "if —— then ——." But to say this is simply to say that the proposition is true because any proposition of the form it has is true. And this latter proposition, namely, "Any proposition of the form 'if —— then ——' is true," is in no sense itself describable as true in virtue of its form. The substitution-instances of logical principles may be described, though I believe misleadingly, as true in virtue of their form. But the logical principles themselves cannot then be true in virtue of their form. For if we must describe them in terms of the notion of form at all, they amount to assertions that all propositions of a certain form are true, that the possession of a certain form guarantees the truth of a proposition. And such a statement *about* a form cannot itself be true in virtue of that form.

The Theory of Formal Truth has another, though related, source. There is a sense in which the *assertion* of a necessarily true proposition is uninformative. A necessary truth, being a priori, cannot be regarded as confirmed or disconfirmed by observation or experiment, and thus the assertion of it would not be a way of informing one of the occurrence of a certain observation or of the success of a certain experiment. For this reason, a person with positivistic tendencies is likely to conclude that a necessarily true proposition is only vacuously true, has no content, is not factual, is really not about anything. But what is the warrant for such a conclusion? Of course, a necessarily true proposition does not describe something that might not be the case and thus is not subject to empirical disconfirmation. Otherwise it would not have been necessarily true, and it would not have been knowable a priori. To conclude from this that it is uninformative or vacuous would be either to say once again that it is indeed necessarily true and knowable a priori or to avow one's allegiance to a rather crude empiricism. But there is a second, philosophically more significant reason for holding that a necessarily true proposition is uninformative. Consider a substitution-instance of a logical principle, e.g., "All black cats are black." It may be argued that whatever the nature of its necessary truth, it can have nothing to do with what the proposition is about, namely, black cats. For the proposition would be true whatever the adjective *black* and the noun *cat* meant, and one would know it to be true regardless of what one meant by these words. But how can the truth of a proposition have nothing to do with what the proposition is *about*? How could its truth remain unchanged even when we transform the proposition into one about completely different entities, for example, blue elephants? And how could such a proposition inform anyone about anything if what it is about is irrelevant to its truth? The only plausible answer to these questions might seem to be that such a proposition is really not about anything at all, that it is purely formal, that it is completely uninformative.

Despite its plausibility, this answer is false. To begin with, it is significant that it is plausible only for *substitution-instances* of logical principles and not for logical principles themselves. There is nothing plausible about the view that, for example, the truth of the principles of propositional logic has nothing to do with what they are about, namely, propositions (or possible facts, states of affairs, etc.). It would be equally implausible to suggest that they are not about anything, that they have no content. Surely they are about propositions, just as "All cats have fur" is about cats, and thus they have content. Are they informative? One would not be surprised by such a proposition. But then one would not be surprised by many contingent propositions, for example, "You were born within the solar system" or "London is farther than five inches from New York." On the other hand, one who knows the principles of propositional logic knows something, one is informed about something, namely, a number of truths about propositions. So, *of course,* a logical principle has a content, for it is *about* something, even though this fact is disguised by the use of bound variables in the current symbolic notation. In quantificational logic a principle is a proposition about all individuals, or all properties, or both.

In propositional logic a principle is a proposition about all propositions (or possible facts, states of affairs). And since such principles are necessarily true, it may be said that they are also about all *possible* individuals or properties or propositions. This supreme generality of logical principles is what generates the desire to say that they are uninformative and formal in nature. There is no harm in saying this as long as we do not mean by it anything more than that logical principles are on the highest level of generality.

Nevertheless, it is plausible to say that the substitution-instances of logical principles are uninformative, have no content, are purely formal, are not about anything. But what is the source of this plausibility? Surely, it is the fact that they are substitution-instances of universal necessarily true propositions which ordinarily are completely obvious to everyone, quite self-evident, quite unquestionable, and the fact that ordinarily they are known to be true on the basis of our knowledge of these universal propositions. I know that all black cats are black because I know that all individuals that have a certain property do have that property and I know this latter proposition with certainty far greater than that with which I might have known the former inductively by observing that a number of individual black cats are indeed black. No wonder then that the truth of "All black cats are black" seems to have nothing to do with what it is about.

In fact the case of some contingent propositions is quite similar. Consider "All books fall when not supported" and "All bodies fall when not supported." One could learn the truth of the former without learning the truth of the latter. But as soon as one knows that all bodies fall when not supported, one's knowledge that all books (which of course one takes as paradigms of bodies) fall when not supported may *appear* to be vacuous, trivial, formal, since one would recognize that the proposition's being about books rather than about any other kind of body is inessential to its truth. Yet we would hardly take this appearance as a sign that the proposition "All books fall when not supported" is vacuous, uninformative, or true in virtue of its form.

Not only do logical propositions have a content—are about something and contain information—but at least some of them also describe—are about—empirical, observable facts, even though the latter are known a priori. Ordinarily, a proposition is about what its subject terms refer to. It is an assertion of a fact, if it is true. If the fact it asserts about what its subject terms refer to is observable, experienceable, then the proposition has empirical content, even though, if it can be known independently of experience, it is a priori.[8] A proposition such as "All black cats are black" is clearly about something; since it is true, it asserts a fact, and what it asserts is no more separated from the empirical world by a logical curtain than is the fact that all cats have fur. It is quite appropriate to ask what this proposition is about, and obviously the answer can only be that it is about black cats. It is also perfectly appropriate to ask what it says about black cats, and again the answer would be that it says that they are all black. That black cats are observable and that so is their being black should not need even mention. There is no mystery here at all. There is no mystery regarding the further question, whether that proposition is true or false, or in the answer that it is true. And, I suggest, there is just as little mystery regarding a final question of what is meant by saying that it is true, or in the reply that what is meant is nothing special or unusual but simply that all black cats are indeed black.[9]

The reason a nonphilosopher would find nothing peculiar about calling the proposition "All black cats are black" true (though he would find the proposition itself peculiar and perhaps the way in which he knows its truth mysterious) is that he knows that if he were to examine a black cat, any black cat, he would find that it is black. The reason he would call the proposition "Some black cats are not black" false is that he knows that he could never find a black cat that is not black. The way in which he knows this, of course, is very different from the way in which he might know that the proposition "All cats have fur" is true or that the proposition "Some cats do not have fur" is false. But the reason he would designate these latter as, respectively, true and false is the same: he believes that if he were to examine a cat, any cat, he would find that it had fur and that he could never find a cat that does not have fur. While one's knowledge that all black cats are black need have nothing to do with what one has observed about cats or black things, it would be simply false to say that one does not, or cannot, observe that a certain black cat is black. What is true is that one could *know* the results of such an observation before, independently of, the observation, not that one cannot observe that a black

8. Cf. above, p. 104.
9. My point here, of course, is not that there is no *general* problem of the nature of truth but that the sense in which a logical proposition is said to be true is not a special or unusual one.

cat is black. Thus, in this sense, the proposition "All black cats are black" is as empirical as any universal proposition could be, though it would still be knowable a priori. I suggest that the thesis of classical empiricism, as exemplified in the works of the philosopher who distinguished between matters of fact and relations of ideas, is merely that all propositions are empirical, in the sense I have explained, and not that all (informative, nonvacuous) propositions are contingent. But this is a historical claim that I cannot defend here.

So much for the Theory of Formal Truth. Another logico-linguistic theory would attempt to explain the nature of logical truth (and thus of necessary truth since it would assume that all necessary propositions are, or are reducible to, logical propositions) by denying the assumption we have made all along that logical propositions are propositions at all. This Nonpropositional Theory of Logic would argue that our criticisms of the other logico-linguistic theories of necessary truth have really depended on this assumption. For instance, only if this assumption is made, may we demand of the accounts of necessary truth in terms of analyticity, contradiction of denial, and formal truth that they also explain the necessary truth of logical principles themselves. But is this assumption really true? It may be argued that the assumption is false because so-called logical propositions lack the essential characteristic of a proposition, namely, the capacity to provide differential information about the situations in which they are used.[10] And the provision of such information is the only distinctive function of a proposition, a use to which only a proposition, and neither a rule of inference nor a stipulation of meaning nor a mere consequence of such a rule or stipulation, can be put. Obviously, the denial of a logical proposition does not have a genuine use in language, as a proposition,[11] for there can be no situation which it would describe. But then the logical proposition itself would not have a genuine use as a proposition, for there is no proposition *in use* with which it can be contrasted. To recognize this is, in substance, to recognize that such a proposition can really say nothing, that it cannot describe or express either a truth or a falsehood, and thus that it ought not to be regarded as a proposition at all.

10. See Max Black, *Models and Metaphors* (Ithaca, N.Y.: Cornell University Press, 1962), p. 86.

11. It can and does, of course, have other uses, e.g., for illustrating a certain syntactical structure, for making a joke, etc., but none of these can be regarded as distinctively propositional.

Before I consider this much more sophisticated view, I want to point out that even if justified it only tells us what the so-called logical propositions are not and not what they are. It may be true that a sentence such as "All unmarried men are unmarried" does *not* express a genuine proposition. What *is* it then, what *does* it do? A sentence such as "All bachelors are unmarried," which would usually be said to express an ordinary analytic proposition, may well be accounted for as merely a consequence of the sometimes excessive terminological wealth of language. But this cannot be the account of the nature and role of the sentence "All unmarried men are unmarried," which clearly is the more fundamental of the two. The theory before us has nothing to say about this. Nevertheless, it deserves careful consideration. For if it is true, then the whole question of the nature of necessary truth must be drastically restated. That the so-called logical propositions are not really propositions would be a discovery of the utmost importance, even if it would not be a solution of the problem of their nature.

Now it may appear that the claim that a proposition such as "All black cats are black" has no use is obviously false. Is not its use precisely to assert the fact that all black cats are black? And on what grounds would one refuse to classify this as a fact? Surely not on the grounds that it is not a contingent fact, for the purpose of the discussion is precisely to answer questions such as, Are all facts contingent? But the theory avoids such an objection. For it would point out that the use of a proposition cannot be explained by merely repeating the proposition and prefacing it with the expression "the fact that." Were such an explanation the only one possible, then the notion of fact becomes merely a shadow of the notion of proposition and thus has no explanatory power with respect to the latter. The use of a proposition can be explained only by referring to the kinds of situations in which the utterance of the corresponding sentence would have a point, would make a difference. For instance, the sentence "If there is a cat here then it is black" has a genuine use, there is a fact or truth for it to describe, because there are situations in which its utterance would have a point, would make a difference, and thus would have a genuine, actual function. If I am looking for my white cat and a man tells me that if there is a cat here then it is black, his statement at least *could* produce a change in what I do. The reason it could do so is that what it says can be said correctly only in some situations and not in others. The statement classifies the situation in which it is made, distinguishes it sharply from other possible situations, and on the basis of this classification and distinction I can act in ways in which I might not have acted had that statement not been made. But nothing like this is true with respect to the proposition "If there is a black cat here then it is black." Indeed, the corresponding sentence can be uttered. But its utterance can make no difference; it would not classify any situation in a way that distinguishes it from other possible situations and thus would not induce me to act in ways in which I might not have acted otherwise; it would not have an actual function. Such an utterance would be vacuous, and for this reason it would not actually constitute a *use* of language, any more than hitting a nail with a hammer in the air would constitute a use of the nail. The utterance would merely appear to be a use of a proposition, and sentences that are capable only of such utterances merely appear to express propositions.

Now one could argue that logical propositions do have a use, though a rather complicated one. They have a use only in conjunction with other propositions—in particular, only in the context of the use of other propositions in a process of inference. Certain contingent propositions, the utterance of which could make a difference, are as a matter of fact uttered only by being explicitly inferred from other propositions by means of logical propositions. Thus the use of the latter *can* make a difference. Nevertheless, it can be retorted that even if logical propositions do have such a use, that use is so fundamentally different from the use of contingent propositions that it should not be classified as a use for the assertion of a truth or a fact, any more than the use of a proposition for the purpose of illustrating a point in syntax should be so classified. While a contingent proposition has a genuine use both in isolation and in the process of inference, a logical proposition does not. And it may be thought that this fact is sufficient for the claim that logical propositions do not have a genuine, actual use. For, obviously, to make this claim is not to claim to have made an empirical discovery of a special and difficult-to-discern property of logical propositions. It is merely to claim that there is a fundamental difference between a logical proposition and a contingent proposition, namely, that while the use of the latter could make a difference in an actual situation, regardless of whether it occurs in a process of inference, the use of the former could not. Is it true, however, that if the use of a proposition makes no difference, in this sense, then the proposition does not describe a fact or a truth and thus is not really a proposition?

How does one answer such a question? Let us assume that logical propositions do not have an actual use, in the above sense. The problem is whether they are propositions at all. Now I suggest that there would be an excellent reason for saying that they are not, if the notion itself of necessary proposition were independent of what is meant by saying that a proposition has no actual use. For then the conclusion that logical propositions do not have an actual use would disclose a certain fact about them which is not only extremely important—so important indeed that it may serve as a justification for refusing to classify logical propositions as propositions at all—but which can also legitimately be appealed to in an explanation of what is meant by the necessary truth of such propositions. But, in reality, the discovery that logical propositions do not have an actual use is nothing but the "discovery" that they are necessarily true. It may be illuminating to say that logical propositions are not propositions at all because they lack a very important, perhaps the most important, characteristic of all other propositions. But it would not be illuminating at all to say this if the characteristic that they lack turns out to be merely their noncontingency. Indeed, were the fact that some propositions lack this characteristic unknown or insufficiently recognized, its obviously enormous importance could be illuminatingly stressed by asserting that such propositions are not propositions at all. But there is nothing unknown or insufficiently recognized about the fact that logical propositions are not contingent. To refuse to classify them as propositions merely on the ground that they are noncontingent is to make no philosophical point at all, although to have refused to classify them as propositions because they lack some other characteristics that all other propositions have could have been interesting philosophically.

We have seen that to say that a logical proposition (e.g., the principle of identity or a substitution-instance of it) has no actual use is not to say that the sentence expressing it cannot be uttered or that its utterance can never serve any kind of function. What is meant is that such an utterance would not serve to classify the situation in which it is made, it would not distinguish it from other situations, it would make no difference in this respect to the listener. But why is this so? Why, for example, does the utterance of "If there is a black cat here then it is black" make no difference? Clearly, because it is *impossible* for a black cat not to be black; it *goes without saying* that a black cat is black. To say that a logical principle or a substitution-instance of it conveys no differential information may only be understood as meaning that it cannot fail to be true. Its denial can describe no fact, and thus its assertion is vacuous, only because *there can be no fact* such as that which its denial would describe. But to recognize this is to recognize that the alleged reason for regarding logical propositions as incapable of having an actual use, as failing to be genuine propositions, has turned out to be simply their necessary truth. One does not illuminate the notion of necessary truth by *stipulating* that necessarily true propositions are not propositions.

It may be supposed that our dissatisfaction with the familiar logico-linguistic theories of necessary truth should be a sufficient reason for embracing a traditional theory, such as the Essentialist Theory or the Transcendental Theory, which sets up the ontological distinction between essence and accident and explains the necessity-contingency distinction in terms of the former. For example, it can be claimed that the principles of logic are truths about the essence of the world or that they describe the essential features of all thought (or, one may add, of all language). Less general necessary propositions would describe the essence of their respective subject matter, whether it be men or colors, or of specific modes of thought (or discourse). Such claims may have value as an antidote to a serious consideration of a theory such as that of analyticity or of formal truth, but they have little intrinsic worth as accounts of the concept of necessary truth. For once we recognize that, at least in part, they amount to the assertion that necessary propositions describe the *necessary* features of reality or of thought (or discourse), or the necessary features of men and of colors, or the necessary features of thought (or discourse) about men and about colors, they are immediately seen to be thoroughly unenlightening. At least the theories of formal truth and of analyticity *appeared* to be promising. The above mentioned traditional theories do not even do that.

It may also be tempting to appeal to the Conceivability Theory. According to it, to say that a proposition is necessarily true is to say that its falsehood is inconceivable, unthinkable. (We are concerned here with the view that necessary truth *is* unthinkability-of-falsehood, and not with the view, which I have already discussed and defended, that unthinkability-of-falsehood is our only way of knowing the necessary truth of necessarily true propositions.) The strength and plausibility of the theory lie in the analogy it draws between the distinction between necessary and contingent truths and the much more familiar distinction between what one cannot do, try as one might, and what one can do, though perhaps only with great effort. Coupled with a subjectivist inclination in philosophy, the analogy appears not only illuminating but thoroughly plausible. Yet it fails for the same reason for which most other analogies designed to elucidate the concept of necessary truth fail. The distinction between what one can and what one cannot conceive presupposes the distinction between necessary and contingent truths. For a necessarily true proposition could not be one the falsehood of which is inconceivable as a matter of contingent psychological fact. It would have to be one the falsehood of which absolutely, "logically," *cannot* be conceived. Thus the force of the "cannot" here is not that of a difficulty which has not yet been overcome but may be overcome in the future, nor even that of a difficulty which for accidental reasons (e.g., one's education or one's intelligence) will never be overcome, but that of a difficulty which cannot be overcome, regardless of the circumstances, places, and times in which it may be faced. But to say this is simply to say that a necessarily true proposition is one for which it is necessarily true that its falsehood is not conceived. Thus the Conceivability Theory cannot even purport to throw light on the nature of necessary truth. On the other hand, this should not be regarded as a defect of the theory insofar as the latter is concerned merely with the way in which we know that a given proposition is necessarily true. For, as we have observed above,[12] unthinkability, whether of falsehood "in the present circumstances" or of falsehood in general, is a brute fact, whatever the proper explanation of it may be. Even if it is necessarily true that the falsehood of a certain proposition cannot be thought, it is not to this necessary truth that we appeal in judging the proposition to be necessarily true but to the fact that we simply cannot think of its being false.

3. The Appeal to Rules of Language

I HAVE EXAMINED several theories and found them all wanting as accounts of the nature of necessary truth, though they have obvious merits as accounts of the means of discovering that a proposition is necessarily true (e.g., the inconceivability or self-contradictoriness of its denial), or of the kinds of propositions that are necessarily true (e.g., logical and analytic propositions), or of the subject matter of necessarily true propositions (e.g., the essences of things). But there is another theory that does attempt to solve precisely the problem of the nature of necessary truth and which,

12. See pp. 78–79.

because of its resemblance to the Analyticity Theory and the Theory of Formal Truth, has probably lent these whatever plausibility they have. I shall call it the Game Theory. It does not haplessly attempt to identify necessarily true propositions with those that are logical, or reducible, in virtue of substitution of synonyms, to logical propositions, or that have self-contradictory negations, or that are true in virtue of their "logical form." Indeed, it refuses to simply identify necessarily true propositions with any other kind of proposition. But neither does it deny, as does the Nonpropositional Theory, that they are propositions. Instead, it attempts to explain, to illuminate, the nature of such propositions by comparing them with something else which is obviously distinct from them.

The logico-linguistic theories that we have examined have shared the same general defect. They have attempted to explain the necessary truth of a proposition in terms of a certain internal feature of the proposition, whether it be the meaning of the words in it or its syntactical structure. In each case the explanation has been insufficient unless, in addition to these features, an appeal was also made to the necessary truth of some *other* proposition. And once this is evident, the conclusion may only be that the theory is either circular or is involved in an infinite regress. For example, the proposition "All bachelors are unmarried men" is true not only in virtue of the definition of "bachelor" but also, unavoidably, in virtue of the necessary truth of the proposition "All unmarried men are unmarried men." And the proposition "All unmarried men are unmarried men" is true not only in virtue of the fact that it has the logical form "All———— are————" but also, unavoidably, in virtue of the necessary truth of the proposition that all propositions of that form are true. The appeals to implicit definitions, to the distinction between descriptive and logical terms, and to the principle of noncontradiction merely disguise this defect of the theories. They do nothing to repair it.

But while any linguistic theory of necessary truth must claim that the truth of a necessarily true proposition is the result solely of facts about language, these facts about language need not be internal features of the proposition. There is another possibility, which appears far more promising. The facts about language that render a proposition necessarily true may be rules about what we must say, or about what we may but need not say, or about what we must not say. They would not be rules about the meanings of individual words, and thus the appeal to them would not be open to the objections to which the Analyticity Theory is open. They would be rules about the propriety or impropriety of whole sentences, rules which are not regarded as justifiable by appeal to rules about the meanings of individual words in such sentences or to the syntactical forms of such sentences. For example, the necessary truth of the proposition "Nothing is both red and green all over" would be accounted for by saying that there is a rule of language forbidding our saying of anything that it is both red and green all over, or, equivalently, that in our language there is no use for the phrase "red and green all over." [13] The necessary truth of the principle of noncontradiction would be accounted for by saying that it is a rule of language that one not contradict oneself, that there is no use for sentences of the form "*p* and not-*p*." And in neither case would one attempt to justify the rule by appealing to the meanings of individual words.

Were this all there is to this novel suggestion, it need hardly be taken seriously. For one could gladly admit that the sort of rules it appeals to are indeed present in language, explicitly or implicitly, and then one would point out that the obvious reason such rules are in fact adopted is the necessary truth of the corresponding propositions. For example, one would admit that there is the rule "Don't say of anything that it is both red and green all over!" but would point out that the reason the rule is accepted is the necessary truth of the proposition "Nothing is both red and green all over"; one would admit that there is the rule "Don't contradict yourself!" but would point out that the rule is accepted only because of the necessary truth of the principle of noncontradiction. To be at all interesting, the suggestion must include the claim that the question of the legitimacy of the rules in question cannot be raised—that the acceptance of such a rule is a mere convention, an essentially arbitrary human decision—and that there can be no sense to the attempt to justify the rule by appealing to any facts or truths. For only if this claim is true would the appeal to rules of language in accounting for the necessary truth of propositions be of use to a linguistic theory of necessary truth, one according to which a necessarily true proposition is true solely in virtue of facts about language.

But how can such a claim be defended? For one thing, it is not at all obvious that there are in fact such rules of language as the claim requires.

13. See Wittgenstein, *The Blue and Brown Books* (Oxford: Basil Blackwell, 1960), p. 56. But there is not sufficient evidence in Wittgenstein's works for ascribing to him the Game Theory, or, it seems to me, any other specific theory of necessary truth.

That there are rules regarding the meanings of individual words or phrases may be clear, for it is clear that the meaning of a particular word is not a natural phenomenon but a human convention. But that there are rules such as "Don't contradict yourself!" and "Don't say of anything that it has each of two colors all over!" is not at all clear. A rule of language cannot simply be manufactured whenever we are faced with a necessarily true proposition. It must be independently identifiable, as presumably the rules determining the meanings of individual words are. If it is not actually stated in grammar books or in dictionaries, at least it should be actually stated as a rule by parents teaching their children how to talk. If there are such rules, it must be possible to study the ways in which they are established and enforced, the approximate dates of their adoption or appearance in linguistic practice, their histories, and the effects of their adoption. We can do all this with regard to the rules of chess, of poker, and of the meanings of individual words, but it is not at all clear that we can do it with regard to a rule such as "Don't say of anything that it has each of two colors all over!" let alone a rule such as "Don't contradict yourself!" (Imagine a discovery of the time at which such a rule was adopted!) But even if it were plausible that there are such rules, it would still have to be shown that they are mere *conventions,* ultimately arbitrary human decisions, rather than unexciting prudential rules such as "Don't say of anything that it has each of two colors all over, because if you say this you would have said what is false." What possible discovery about language could show this? What possible investigations would lead to such a discovery?

It is only through a complete rethinking of the nature of language as a whole that the above appeal to rules of language could be made plausible. We could see the possibility, and perhaps actuality, of such rules of language only if we conceive of language in a drastically different way. To achieve such a conception, we must see language in a different light, we must see it as falling in a different classification from the one in which it has been supposed to fall, we must understand it in terms of a novel, powerful, and illuminating *analogy.* Indeed, this is exactly the basis of what I have called the Game Theory of necessary truth. It is the view of language as being, in some very important respects, like a game such as poker or chess. Language is supposed to be like a game in that it is an autonomous, self-sufficient human activity, the specific characteristics of which are not dictated by any facts about the world; it is neither a premeditated, artificial picture of the world nor a mere tool for expressing our thoughts. Hence, not surprisingly, it is also like a game in being purely conventional and thus not subject to appraisal regarding legitimacy. Just as the rules of a game are ultimately arbitrary decisions, about which the question of legitimacy cannot be raised, so what we say in what circumstances is a matter ultimately of human convention and not of any facts about the world. And just as in a game certain moves are required by the rules, others forbidden, and still others neither required nor forbidden but allowed, so in language we have necessarily true, necessarily false, and contingent statements.[14]

A major advantage of the Game Theory is the sophisticated methodological basis on which it rests. The problem of the nature of necessary truth, it would argue, is a typical philosophical issue. It is a mistake to think that we do not really know what is meant by "necessary truth." The fact is that, in a sense, there is no obscurity whatever in the notions of necessarily true proposition and contingently true proposition. We can immediately say that the former is a proposition which cannot, under any circumstances, be false, while the latter is one which, in some identifiable circumstances, would be false. There is nothing difficult to understand or theoretically puzzling about this; it seems obvious that this is exactly what in fact philosophers mean by the terms *necessarily true proposition* and *contingently true proposition*. Nor should it be supposed that the proper solution of the problem of the nature of necessary truth could consist in the discovery of a certain *feature* or *element* of necessarily true propositions that those that are contingently true do not have. For one thing, as we have seen, even if there were such a feature or element, it would probably still not represent what in fact we *mean* by necessary truth. For another, in a rather obvious sense the nature of necessarily true propositions is completely laid out before us; it is not the sort of object of inquiry that may really have hidden features or elements which can be *discovered*. The nature of necessary truth is not an object of study in the way in

---

14. In fact the analogy between necessarily true statements and moves in a game required by the rules is doubtful. Except in the case of extremely simple games, to every forbidden move there is not a corresponding required move, as in language there is for every necessarily false statement a necessarily true statement. And in the case of simple games where this part of the analogy would hold, there would not be moves that would be analogous to contingent statements. But I shall ignore this difficulty of the Game Theory. It might be enough if there is an enlightening analogy between necessarily false statements and forbidden moves. Indeed, we might then learn that it is the concept of necessary falsehood that "wears the trousers."

which the natures of cats and dogs are. If it were, it would not have been studied by philosophers.

What then is the problem of the nature of necessary truth? It demands an enlightening analogy between the distinction between necessary and contingent propositions and some other, more familiar, more definitely identifiable, less philosophically charged distinction. It demands an account of the similarities and differences between this distinction and other distinctions of comparable generality. The useful philosophical theories of the nature of necessary truth, it would be argued, are attempts to draw and defend such analogies. The Game Theory insists on the analogy of the distinction between necessary and contingent statements to the distinction between moves in a game that are either required or prohibited by the rules and moves that are allowed but not required by the rules. And its case is strengthened by the familiarity of the notion of a rule of language; by the fact that, even if language were not at all like a game, it would still be quite proper to speak of rules of language and rather easy to give examples of such rules; by the ease with which we can construct extremely plausible rules about what one may or may not say that would correspond to each necessarily true proposition.

On the other hand, by appealing to an analogy between necessary propositions and rule-determined *moves* in a game, the Game Theory appears to avoid the obvious defects of two other, quite familiar, views. According to the first, a necessary proposition is itself a rule of language: to say that nothing can be both red and green all over is merely to say "Do not say of anything that it is both red and green all over!" And the obvious defect of this view is that, unlike any rules, a necessary proposition (e.g., that nothing can be both red and green all over) is a standard example of something of which it makes sense to predicate truth or falsehood. If the view is to be defensible at all, it must be regarded as a primitive version of the far more sophisticated Nonpropositional Theory of necessary truth, which we have already considered. According to the second view, a necessary proposition is true *in virtue of* rules of language. And this, of course, is nothing but the Analyticity Theory, which we have also considered, for the rules in question may only be rules regarding the meaning or use of words. The Game Theory achieves methodological sophistication, obvious superiority over the above two views, and thus considerable importance by acknowledging the propositional status of necessary propositions and by claiming that necessary propositions are *analogous* to certain rule-determined actions in a game; it does *not* claim that they are true in virtue of the rules of language, or that they are themselves such rules. On the other hand, the Game Theory must still appeal to something that can plausibly be described as rules of language, for the analogy in question would not hold if there were no rules of language whose relationship to necessary propositions would be analogous to that holding between the rules of a game and the required or forbidden moves in that game.

In its simplest version, the Game Theory defends this analogy merely by pointing out two basic similarities: (1) that just as a move in a game that violates a rule is counted as incorrect, so the serious denial of a (sufficiently simple) necessary proposition is usually counted as a case of linguistic mistake or at least of misunderstanding of the sense of the proposition; and (2) that just as a move which is required by the rules of the game does not have *strategic* value and thus cannot be said to make a contribution to a person's winning the game, so a necessary proposition has no informative value and thus makes no contribution to our knowledge of the world. I have already discussed (2) in connection with the Theory of Formal Truth, and here shall consider only (1). The Game Theory simply argues that the fact that the denial of a necessary proposition would generally be regarded as a linguistic mistake is a sufficient reason for concluding that what is wrong with such a denial is that it constitutes a violation of the rules of language. Since, ordinarily, if a man were to seriously deny a necessary proposition he would be taken to be making a linguistic mistake, it follows that it is a sufficient explanation of the concept of necessary truth to say that a necessarily true proposition is one the denial of which violates a rule of language.

Now, were there no other explanation of why such a denial is generally regarded as a linguistic mistake, the argument would be plausible and perhaps conclusive. But there is such an explanation, a perfectly obvious one, and in fact one precisely in terms of that which the Game Theory attempts to explain. A necessarily true proposition is not merely one that is always true. It is one that may only be true, not because of some special scientific law but in general, independently of any particular information or evidence. But to say this is to say that such a proposition, if sufficiently simple, is one that no rational person can seriously and understandingly deny. Suppose then that a person does deny such a proposition and that we have independent evidence that he is rational and that his denial is serious. What possible explanation can we give of the fact that he denies the proposition? Surely, simply that he does not understand what he is saying, that his mistake is a linguistic one. However, this is not an explanation of the necessary truth of the proposition but merely of a person's willingness to deny the proposition. That this is so becomes even clearer if we recognize that exactly the same explanation would be given of a rational person's serious denial of an obviously true contingent proposition, for example, that he was born within the solar system. Of course, in the latter case we can at least suppose that he might not be making a mistake, while in the former we cannot. But the reason for this is that while we can at least suppose that a person might have been born outside the solar system, we cannot even suppose, e.g., that a person is both a bachelor and not a bachelor.

As we have seen, our knowledge of necessary truths is such that there is an intimate connection between the necessity of a proposition and the meanings of the words used in it or the concepts in terms of which it is entertained. A person's serious denial of such a proposition is usually a sufficient reason for supposing that he is misusing certain words. Conversely, the correct explanation of the meanings of the words in a necessary proposition must conform to the latter's necessary truth. If *all* and *are* are understood in a certain manner, then it is necessarily true that all bachelors are bachelors. And if it is necessarily true that all bachelors are bachelors, then *all* and *are* must be understood in a certain way. The simple version of the Game Theory emphasizes the former fact. The Conceivability Theory emphasizes the latter. Each fails to recognize that both facts are *consequences* of the necessary truth of the proposition and not *constitutive* of it.

The Game Theory becomes interesting when it ceases to offer arguments and simply insists on its major insight—the possibility of an analogy between necessary propositions and moves in a game required or forbidden by the rules. For then, if one is to reject the theory, one must show crucial places at which the analogy breaks down. And this may not be easy. On the other hand, no special defense of the analogy is required. It is not one of several competing and equally plausible familiar analogies. On the contrary, it seems to be the last straw that a theorist of necessary truth can grasp.

There are a number of well-known objections to the analogy between necessarily true propositions and moves required by rules (not between necessarily true propositions and rules). It may be asked, why should the rules that determine necessary propositions be accepted or followed? Because there can be no language in which the violations of such rules are allowed? Or because assertions violating such rules are self-canceling? Or because, through some mysterious reason, whenever one violates such a rule one says what is false? But why should all these be so? Other rules of language can be changed without such fatal consequences. Why can these not? To say that such a rule is essential to language would merely be to say that it is necessarily true that language incorporate it or conform to it. And, in any case, why is, for example, the rule determining the principle of noncontradiction essential to language while some other rule of language, for example, one governing the formation of the third-person singular of English verbs, is not essential? The evident difference between a move in chess required by the rules and a necessary proposition is that while it is perfectly easy to suggest changes in the rules of chess (even if the game were to become so different as to cease to be plausibly called chess) so that such moves would no longer be required, it is not even intelligible to revise the rules of language in such a way that contradictory propositions are allowed.

But such arguments against the Game Theory are insufficient. First, they ignore the distinction between fundamental and relatively minor rules. Second, they fail to note that the analogy the Game Theory proposes is not that between *particular* languages and games, but between language *as such* and games. In a game there may be rules which if changed would only modify the game without affecting its nature. Examples would be the numerous rules that poker players adopt and abandon, sometimes in one evening, and to which the endless varieties of poker correspond. Whether deuces or jacks are wild may determine a distinction between two kinds of poker, but if it does, the distinction would be of little significance to the nature of the game played, to its being poker. But there are rules that are essential to the game, without which it would no longer be the same game and perhaps not a game at all. An example would be the rule in poker that one may not raise one's own bet. To abandon this rule would be to destroy the game. Now, necessarily true propositions would be analogous to moves in a game that are required by the rules fundamental to the game. What would be analogous to moves required by superficial rules of a game would be, perhaps, the rules of the grammatical etiquette of a particular language. The rejection of a rule of grammatical etiquette would be like the refusal to play with deuces wild. It may be socially unpleasant but not fatal to language. The rejection of the rules determining necessarily true propositions, however, would constitute a rejection of the fundamental rules of *all* languages, of language as such. Thus it would be like one's being allowed in poker to raise one's own bet. Just as the rule in poker that prohibits one's raising one's own bet is essential to any game that is poker, the rules that prohibit necessarily false propositions are essential to any activity that is a language.

There are, however, other objections to the Game Theory. The appeal to the fundamental nature of the rules that determine necessarily true propositions is uncomfortably close to an appeal to the *necessary truth* that a language has such rules. But perhaps the theory can avoid this objection by refusing to allow that this closeness amounts to identity. Certain rules of poker can be recognized as fundamental, in the sense that without their observance the game would *in fact* lose its point, and not in the sense that it is necessarily true of poker that it be played in accordance with them. Perhaps the Game Theory would achieve its purpose by drawing an analogy between necessary propositions and moves required or forbidden by *such* rules. But there is another, much more serious objection. According to it, there is indeed an analogy between language and a game such as poker or chess. But there are other analogies that are even closer and that have exactly the opposite effect with respect to our understanding of the nature of necessary truth.

The Game Theory appeals to an analogy between language and a game such as poker or chess because it must argue that just as there can be no question about the legitimacy or illegitimacy of the rules of such a game, so there can be no question about the legitimacy or illegitimacy of the rules of language that would correspond to necessarily true and necessarily false propositions. But there are many rule-determined activities whose rules, unlike those of games, are subject to appraisal as legitimate or illegitimate, by appeal to facts external to the activity. For instance, there are rules of fire-fighting, drilling for oil, constitutional reform, artificial respiration, successful teaching, and open-heart surgery. There are moves in these activities that are forbidden by the rules, moves that are required, and moves that are neither forbidden nor required. But the crucial fact about the rules of such activities is that, typically, they are not arbitrary conventions. Their legitimacy is subject to appraisal, and we appraise it by appeal to objective facts about fires, oil fields, political institutions, respiration, education, and hearts. There may be some analogy between language and games such as chess and poker. But isn't the analogy between language and activities such as fire-fighting and drilling for oil far closer? If it is, then we should expect the question about the legitimacy of the rules of language that determine necessary propositions to be one that can be raised. And if it can be raised, then we no longer can hold a Game Theory of necessary truth. Indeed, it should be obvious that language is far more like fire-fighting than it is like chess, and thus that the Game Theory of necessary truth is unacceptable.

In any rule-determined activity, whether it be chess, language, or fire-fighting, the correctness or incorrectness of an action is a function not only of the appropriate rule but also of the context, the circumstances, in which the action takes place. For the rule determines the correctness or incorrectness of the action only if the rule is applicable to the action. And it is applicable to the action only if the context in which the action takes place has certain characteristics. (Indeed, the identity of the action, *what* sort of action it is, may well be determined by the context in which it takes place.) And either the rule itself contains some specification of the needed context, or, more likely, such a specification is provided by the remaining rules in the activity. For example, for a certain two-places move of a particular pawn to be correct, there must not only be the rule allowing such a move but also it must take place on a standard chessboard, the other pieces must have certain positions, and the move must be the first move the player makes with that pawn. For the statement "That book is blue" to be correct, there must be a rule regarding the applicability of the word *blue* to any object of a certain color but also there must be a book, it must have that color (or at least the speaker must be under the impression that it does), the speaker must be in a position to use the demonstrative pronoun, etc. For a certain chemical to be used on a certain fire, there must not only be, let us suppose, the rule that such a chemical is to be used on that sort of fire, but also the fire in question must be of that sort, what one uses must indeed be that chemical, no unacceptable destruction of the property must follow from its use, etc. So far chess, language, and fire-fighting seem quite similar. But the fundamental difference between chess, on the one hand, and language and fire-fighting, on the other, is already evident.

The context in which a move in chess takes place, and by reference to which the correctness of the move is partly determined, is itself purely conventional; it is itself the result of ultimately arbitrary human decisions. The chessboard, the number and kinds of other pieces, their arrangement, and the stage at which the game is at any given moment, are determined by the other conventional rules of chess. This is the point of saying that chess is just a game. This is the point of saying that chess is a self-sufficient, autonomous, purely conventional activity. But the context in which a typical statement is made, e.g., "That book is blue," is not determined by rules of language, it is not the result of linguistic conventions. That there is a book and that it is, or at least appears to be, blue are in no sense conventions or the result of conventions, any more than fires, chemicals, and the causal properties of such chemicals are conventions or the result of conventions. And this is the point of saying that language is *about the world,* in a sense in which chess is not about the world, and that the correctness or incorrectness of a statement is in part a function of the nature of the world, in a sense in which no move in chess is so. Hence the fundamental difference between the purposes for which we play chess and the purposes for which we talk. In the case of chess we take the context of a move for granted, we have no interest in it as such, and we make the move for its own sake or for the sake of subsequent moves. In the case of language, it is the context, the situation in the world, in which we make the statement that we are usually interested in. It is simply false that language has the autonomy, self-sufficiency, and complete conventionality of a game such as chess. Language is far more like fire-fighting, whose rules generally are required by facts about the world, than it is like chess, whose rules are mere conventions.

The above should not be misunderstood. I am not proposing a proof that necessarily true statements are true, at least in part, because of facts about the world, nor am I offering any theory about the relationship between such a statement and the context in which it is made. I am demonstrating that the analogy of language with games, once it is qualified with the obvious observation that, unlike moves in games, statements are made in nonconventional contexts, is seen to be much less plausible than the analogy of language with rule-determined activities such as fire-fighting, whose actions take place in nonconventional contexts and whose rules can be judged as legitimate or illegitimate by appealing to facts about the world. If this is so, then the Game Theory can no longer claim to explain the nature of necessary truth by appealing to the analogy of language with games. Of course, it may still insist that the truth of necessary propositions is due entirely to purely conventional rules of language, and nothing that I have said shows that this is not so. But this would be just an insistence, not a reasoned conclusion from an initially not implausible analogy. This insistence may be justified in some other way. It is probable, however, that such a way would be one of those we have already considered and rejected.

Indeed, it is likely that the reason for the Game Theorist's surprising confidence that there is an important analogy between necessarily true propositions and required moves in a game such as chess is his not unnatural tendency to revert to the Analyticity Theory. Unlike any rules determining the propriety or impropriety of entire statements (e.g., the rules of logic), the rules determining the synonymity of expressions are indeed purely conventional and quite like the rules of ordinary games. Were it possible to claim that the necessary truth of a proposition is *entirely* the result of such rules, then the Game Theory would be invulnerable. But we have seen that this is not possible. It may seem possible, but only because of a failure to recognize that while conventions of synonymity are the sole reason for the *reducibility* of an analytic proposition to a logical proposition, it is the necessary truth of the logical proposition itself that is the source of the *necessary truth* of the analytic proposition. It is this confusion that makes it appear plausible to describe necessarily true propositions as empty, trivial, purely verbal—as mere consequences of the terminological wealth of language.

It would be a matter of linguistic convention and thus of "rules" that the term "*a*" denotes this quality and the term "*b*" denotes that quality. And if it is true that nothing can be both *a* and *b* (e.g., nothing can be both red and green all over), it can be said that this is so because of the rules we have established for the use of "*a*" and "*b*." For, obviously, had we established certain other rules, it might not have been true that nothing can be both *a* and *b*. So far the linguistic theorist is right. However, when he draws the conclusion that the necessary truth of the proposition that nothing can be both *a* and *b* is due to the fact that by our rules "*a*" denotes this quality and "*b*" denotes that quality, he is faced with disaster. For in addition to asserting that it is necessarily true that nothing can be both *a* and *b*, we should be able to assert that it is necessarily true that *if* "*a*" denotes this quality and "*b*" denotes that quality, then nothing can be both *a* and *b*. But the necessary truth of this *hypothetical* proposition is no longer accounted for by the rules for the use of the terms *"a"* and *"b."*

Another example would be the proposition that crimson is darker than pink. It is inevitably possible to offer plausible definitions of the terms *crimson, pink,* and *darker than* that would allow the reduction of the proposition to a logical proposition. For instance, it is plausible to define *crimson* as a certain one of the darker reds, and *pink* as a certain one of the lighter reds. There is nothing surprising about the plausibility of such definitions. For the proposition in question is necessarily true, one such that the relata referred to in it cannot be even conceived as not related in the way asserted by the proposition. But the terms *crimson* and *pink,* whatever their actual meanings may be, are obviously capable of ostensive definition. Suppose that I am faced with two shades of red, which would ordinarily be identified, respectively, as crimson and pink, although I do not know this. I perform then the following ostensive stipulations of meaning: I shall mean by the word *pink* this and only this exact shade, and by the word *crimson* that and only that exact shade.[15] I can now immediately conclude that crimson is necessarily darker than pink. Of course, I could not conclude this if it were not for my stipulations of the meanings of *crimson* and *pink.* But neither could I conclude this if it were not for my realization of the necessary truth of the *hypothetical* proposition that *if "crimson" means this particular shade and "pink" means that particular shade then crimson is darker than pink.* And the truth of *this* proposition is no more dependent on linguistic rules (e.g., for the use of *crimson* and *pink*) than is the truth of any contingent proposition. In reality, the proposition is true because of the truth of a certain far more basic proposition that can be expressed in language, though with obvious inadequacy, by the sentence "This shade is darker than that." Such a proposition can be used quite successfully, for example, in the context of comparing samples of wall paint. Clearly, it would be necessary; there would be no possibility of its being false. The supposition that the relation asserted does not hold would require the supposition that, *per impossibile,* the relata, that is, the shades, are not what they are. Yet the necessary truth of the proposition cannot be due to any linguistic conventions, for there are no relevant such conventions in its case.

15. I am here intentionally stipulating that *crimson* and *pink* mean absolutely specific shades of color in order to avoid unnecessary complications.

The case with a logical proposition such as "All black cats are black" would not be different from that of "Nothing can be both red and green all over" or "Crimson is darker than pink," although it is more difficult to make clear because of the nonostensive character of the explanations of the meanings of *all* and *are*. Indeed, the proposition could not be false unless the meaning of one or both of these words is changed. And, given the meanings they do have, the proposition is true. But, as we have seen, none of these facts should even suggest that the proposition is true because of the meanings of *all* and *are*. For we would expect these facts precisely because the proposition is necessarily true. The question is whether the necessary truth of the proposition is the result of an explicit or even implicit rule regarding the use of these words. And it seems quite clear that it is not. Conceivably, some children are told never to deny a proposition of that form. But even if this were so, it would hardly explain their conformity to this rule—children as well as adults are notoriously lax in conforming to rules they have been given. The fact, of course, is that we do not undergo such early instructions in the rules of logic. We learn the meanings of *all* and *are* by reference to ordinary situations, such as those in which we are told to pick up *all* of our toys or that our friends *are* downstairs. Later we can utilize what we have so learned for the making of statements such as "All cats have fur." If we ever contemplate a proposition such as "All black cats are black," which certainly would happen seldom, if ever, we may recognize it as necessarily true. And our recognition would depend on the truth of the hypothetical proposition *that if the words "all" and "are" have the meanings that we have learned, then all black cats are black.* And *this* proposition clearly cannot be true because of the meanings of *all* and *are*.

The above arguments, including the one used against the Analyticity Theory in section 2 above, can be regarded as specific instances of the following general argument against any theory according to which necessarily true propositions are true because of their meaning. Let *p* be a necessarily true proposition. To say that it is true because of what it means is to say that it is true because of the (necessary) truth of the hypothetical proposition "If '*p*' is understood to mean *x*, then *p*." But this hypothetical proposition is necessarily true not because of the fact that it is "*p*" (rather than, say, "*q*") that is understood to mean *x*, but because of *x* itself, because of its characteristics, nature, content, etc. The hypothetical would be necessarily true regardless of what we put in place of "*p*."

138

The argument does not depend on any particular philosophical view regarding the nature of meaning, that is, of what it is for "p" to mean x. Indeed, if we state x as a proposition, then we could say that x itself is true because of what it means. But, first, we would still have demonstrated that p is necessarily true, not because of what *it* means but rather because it is equivalent, in virtue of what it means, to the necessarily true proposition x; and were we to assert that x itself is necessarily true because of what it means, the same analysis would have to be given of *this* assertion, and so on ad infinitum. And, second, it is false that to understand what a proposition means is to understand that it is synonymous with some other proposition. There must be some propositions whose meaning we understand without the benefit of translation. Consequently, one can know what "p" means without being able to *describe* what it means in a sentence other than "p." Nevertheless, one could still refer to what "p" means with a demonstrative pronoun. Then the above hypothetical would read, "If 'p' means this, then p." (Compare "If 'being a good American' means this, then Jones is a good American.") And the necessary truth of this hypothetical (if p is necessarily true) would not be the result of the fact that "p" is assigned such-and-such a meaning but of the nature of the referent of "this." [16] The use of *this* in "If 'p' means this, then p" is not more puzzling or improper than its use in "He thought of this earlier," "I like this," "This is a queer objection."

The reasoning in the last few paragraphs suggests an even more general argument against any linguistic theory of necessary truth. If its premises were granted, this would be an absolutely conclusive argument. But some of these premises would usually be questioned, and their defense would require far-reaching investigations into the nature of thought and belief that cannot be attempted here. The premises in question are that the notion of thought is logically independent of the notion of language; that thoughts, beliefs, and judgments are quite distinct from sentences and statements; and that the notion of truth, in all of its species, is applicable to thoughts, beliefs, and judgments far more clearly and more fundamentally than it is applicable to sentences and statements. If these premises were granted, then it would follow conclusively that the notion of neces-

---

16. But not of the meaning of "this," if by "the meaning of 'this' " is meant the conventions regarding the use of "this." I could use "this" in the above hypothetical both in perfect accordance with the conventions of language and with such a reference that the hypothetical is false.

sary truth cannot be accounted for in terms of features of language, for judgments, thoughts, and beliefs would be necessarily true, regardless of whether or not they are expressed in sentences or statements. And we would also understand how it is possible that even one who is not in possession of relevant linguistic skills (e.g., a small child) may well believe and think and know, for example, that the top of a table cannot be both round and square, or that if one thing is bigger than a second and the second bigger than a third, then the first must be bigger than the third.

4. *The Synthetic A Priori*

WE BEGAN OUR DISCUSSION of the logico-linguistic theories of necessary truth with the most plausible case in which a proposition may be said to be necessarily true because of the meanings of the words in it: that of an analytic proposition, one reducible to a logically true proposition by substitution of synonyms for words in it. We immediately concluded that such a proposition is *true* because the synonymous logical proposition is true, the meanings of the words in it being responsible merely for its reducibility to that logical proposition. And, clearly, a logical proposition itself cannot be analytic in this sense. We then considered several other theories that have attempted to show that logical propositions themselves are true solely because of certain features of language, whether these features be the logical form of the proposition or invisible rules governing its use. We have found none of these theories satisfactory. We have found no satisfactory defense of the view that logical propositions are true because of purely linguistic facts.

An important conclusion to be drawn from this is that the relentless campaign of many recent philosophers to show that all necessary propositions are either logical propositions or reducible to logical propositions, that is, to show that there are no "synthetic a priori" truths, is misguided. The motive behind this campaign has been the belief that logical propositions are philosophically unembarrassing because they are purely verbally determined. Success in showing that all necessarily true propositions are, or are reducible to, logical propositions would have been success in showing that all necessary propositions are philosophically unembarrassing to those who would be embarrassed by the existence of necessary propositions that are not of purely verbal origin. But if logical propositions themselves cannot be explained solely by reference to features of language, then there seems to be no reason for insisting that there cannot be *several* fundamental and mutually irreducible kinds of necessary propositions. One would consist of those on the highest level of generality, of universal applicability, namely, logical principles. Another might consist of mathematical propositions, such as "Seven plus five is twelve," and probably some geometrical propositions. A third would consist of propositions such as "Nothing can be both red and green all over," "Whatever has color has shape," "Whatever is red is colored." A fourth might contain certain moral propositions.

The heart of the theory that all necessary propositions are analytic has been the unwillingness to admit that there can be such additional, nonlogical and nonanalytic kinds of necessary propositions. Our discussion, if correct, has shown that this unwillingness is baseless. For, of course, it has been motivated by general metaphysical and epistemological convictions, and not by any self-evident reducibility of apparently nonlogical and nonanalytic necessary propositions to logical ones. Such reducibility would be possible only if certain expressions are synonymous even though they do not seem to be synonymous. And the synonymity of expressions is hardly the sort of thing that should be decided on the basis of philosophical considerations and through heated argument.

Consider Kant's example of the proposition "Seven plus five is twelve." His claim that this is a synthetic proposition depends on the assumption that the concept of the sum of seven and five does not include its equality to twelve, that is, that for "seven plus five" there is no synonym that if substituted would render the proposition an identical truth. The point is not that we could not plausibly propose such a synonym. As I have pointed out repeatedly, *of course* we could, since the proposition in question is necessary. The point is that we know that the proposition is necessarily true even though the expression "seven plus five" as *understood by us* does not *in fact* mean something equal to twelve. One can understand the meaning of "seven plus five" and of "twelve" without knowing that the sum of seven and five is equal to twelve. (Must one, in order to understand the meaning of "seven plus five," also know that seven plus five is equal to nineteen minus seven, to twenty minus eight, to twenty-one minus nine, and so on ad infinitum?) There is, therefore, no relation of synonymy that renders the proposition true; consequently, it is not analytic. This seems to be the point of Kant's claim that the concept of the sum of seven and five does not include its equality to the number twelve and of his consequent claim that mathematical propositions are synthetic. For what could be meant by saying that two expressions are synonymous if not that they are *understood* to have the same meaning, to express the same concept? A proposition is analytic if it is reducible to a logical proposition in virtue of the concepts we actually employ, not in virtue of concepts we could have employed. Equality to twelve is not part of the content of the actual concept of the sum of seven and five, although it is necessarily connected with that content and can be known to be so a priori. As Kant asserted, "the question is not what we *ought* to join in thought to the given concept, but what we *actually* think in it, even if only obscurely. . . ."[17]

5. The Concept of Necessary Truth and Ordinary Thought

EVEN THE GAME THEORY has turned out to be unsatisfactory. Could we nevertheless preserve its methodological basis? Could we seek some other, more satisfactory, analogy with which to illuminate the nature of necessary truth? Unfortunately, the methodological basis of the Game Theory is no more promising than the theory itself. There are topics in philosophy with respect to which the method of analogy may be the most appropriate. They are those concerned with concepts whose content is indeed completely clear and entirely laid out before us, the only philosophical task being the most proper, most illuminating categorization of such concepts. But there are other topics in philosophy that are concerned with what is really unclear, implicit, perhaps entirely hidden. An example familiar to us would be the sense in which a proposition such as "All bachelors are unmarried men" is true because of the meanings of the words in it. That the meanings of the words in such a proposition do not render it true but only show that it is synonymous with a true logical proposition is something which is not entirely obvious and requires actual bringing out, actual discovery, though hardly a particularly difficult one. Some concepts

17. *Critique of Pure Reason*, B17, tr. Norman Kemp Smith.

are puzzling in their own right. They seem unclear, incoherent, perhaps self-contradictory. Other concepts are puzzling only in the sense that their classification, categorization, their relations of similarity and difference to other concepts, are puzzling; in themselves they are completely clear and unquestionable. The method of the Game Theory is applicable to the account of the latter sort of concept. But the concept of necessary truth falls in the former sort. It is puzzling in itself. We may say that a necessarily true proposition is one that cannot be false, and we may think that this is quite clear and unobjectionable. But, as we shall see presently, it is not.

There is an assumption that has underlain all of the theories of necessary truth which we have examined, in the case of the Game Theory explicitly and in that of the other theories implicitly; namely, that the concept of necessary truth is not a technical philosophical concept, though perhaps it should be analyzed in terms of technical concepts. Therefore, the *nominal* account or definition of the concept, that is, that a proposition is necessarily true if and only if it cannot be false (nominal because, of course, it does not elucidate the concept—if anything, it presupposes it in the use of "cannot"), has been thought to be quite unobjectionable. And the attempts at a philosophical account have consisted either in the claim to a discovery of some hidden element in this concept (e.g., the contradictoriness of the denial of the proposition or its formal character) or in the defense of an illuminating analogy between it and some other, clearer concept. The former have generally presupposed that the concept of necessary truth is complex. The latter have assumed that it is a fundamental concept, incapable of analysis in itself but bearing to other notions similarities and differences, which deserve bringing out. Both have taken for granted that the concept is not a philosophical creation and thus that the account of it *could* be a matter of discovery. But if in reality the concept is a technical one, then, while we should try to discover the content of the associated notions in ordinary thought and discourse, our main task would be to determine a content for it that would most faithfully and most clearly serve the purposes for which the concept has been introduced.

The fact is that the concept of necessary truth is a technical one. It is *taught* to the philosophical novice, not simply appealed to. It is a philosophical creation designed to elucidate the prima facie differences between two familiar classes of propositions and to offer a distinction that corresponds to the difference. For while the *difference* between necessarily true and contingently true propositions is a fact, it is not one reflected in ordinary language; the *distinction* is not one naturally made. We attempt to understand this difference by introducing the concept of necessary truth as applying to that feature which all members of the one class and none of the other have. The value of the concept is not merely that of notational convenience. By expressing it in ordinary terms such as *necessity* and *truth,* we also attempt to describe, to understand, that feature. Specifically, we suggest that the feature in question is the possession of a certain *kind* of truth. And we describe the differentia of that kind by using the adjective *necessary*. But, as we saw in section 2 above, it is most unlikely that one could speak of *kinds* of truth in the sense required for an elucidation of the difference between necessary and contingent propositions. The only such sense could be that in which the truth of some propositions would consist in their agreement with a fact, while the truth of other propositions would consist in their having certain internal, perhaps purely formal, properties. We have seen that such a sense can neither be made clear nor does it take into account the all-important fact that we predicate truth of necessary propositions without making such drastic distinctions between senses of the word *truth* and that if asked to explain the sense in which a certain necessary proposition is true we would offer the same kind of explanation as that which we would offer of the truth of a contingent proposition.

The use of the term *necessary* in introducing the technical concept of necessary truth is even more obscure and objectionable. It may seem that the notion of the necessity of a necessary truth is conveyed quite precisely in ordinary discourse by saying that a proposition is necessarily true if it cannot be false, and thus that the concept of necessary truth is, after all, an ordinary concept, though of course one very much in need of elucidation. Indeed, philosophers have usually introduced it in just this way: in terms of what I called the nominal philosophical conception or definition of necessary truth. They have appealed to the perfectly ordinary words *can* or *may* and have thought it sufficient to say that p is necessarily true if and only if p is true and it is false that p may be false. But there is no ordinary sense of the phrase "it is false that p may be false" that would come even close to elucidating the difference between necessary and contingent propositions.

To begin with, in at least one fairly obvious sense of that phrase, it would be applicable to all true propositions, and thus, if seriously used in the definition of "*p* is necessarily true," it would require us to conclude that all true propositions are necessarily true. If a proposition is true, then, in an obvious sense, it is not possible for it to be false, because of the principle of noncontradiction. The sentence "*p* is true but may be false" would ordinarily appear absurd. It is not absurd to say "*x* is blue but it is possible for *x* to be red," for this could mean that while *x* is blue it can *become* or be *made* red. But usually it is absurd to say "*x* is blue but it is possible *that x* is red (that it is not blue)." If a proposition is true, then not only is it not false but it is not possible for it to be false. The principle of noncontradiction is not only true but necessarily true!

In addition to the sense of "it is false that *p* may be false" (or of "*p* cannot be false") in which this locution is equivalent to "*p* is true," there is another, no less ordinary, sense in which it is equivalent to "*p* is absolutely certain." Thus, despite frequent warnings, we may be tempted to identify the notion of a necessarily true proposition with that of a proposition known with absolute certainty. But this would be a mistake. The two notions are quite independent of one another. I know with equal certainty that three and two are five and that I have a headache. Yet a fundamental difference remains between the two, which a philosopher would describe by saying that while it is necessarily true that three and two are five, it is only contingently, though absolutely certainly, true that I have a headache. The clearest demonstration of the nonidentity of the two notions lies in the fact that with respect to some propositions (e.g., in mathematics) it would be true that such a proposition is either necessarily true or necessarily false but false that it is either known to be true with absolute certainty or known to be false with absolute certainty.

There is a third ordinary sense of the locution "it is false that *p* may be false," which in fact is the one usually employed in explanations of the concept of necessary truth. Strictly speaking, it is a sense of the locution "it is false that *p* might (could) have been false." A proposition, we may say, is necessarily true if and only if it is true and it is false that it might have been false. The corresponding definition of contingent truth may seem even clearer: a proposition is contingently true if and only if it is true but might have been false. Unfortunately, the clarity and plausibility of these definitions are achieved by identifying the notion of necessary truth with that of causal necessity. For the ordinary sense of saying that something might have been otherwise is that it is not *causally* necessary, that it is *accidental*. The reason the above definition of necessarily true proposition is plausible is that the notions of necessity, contingency, and impossibility that one does find in ordinary language are the notions of *causal*, and perhaps more specifically even *physical*, necessity, contingency, and impossibility.[18] The ordinary, natural notions of necessity, contingency, and impossibility are applicable to events, not to truths or propositions. Thus any definition of necessary truth in terms suitable for a definition of causal necessity would appear attractive. Yet it would be quite unsatisfactory. Even if we could speak of the causes of facts, of what true propositions assert, and thus of the truth of certain propositions as being, in a corresponding sense, causally necessary, there would be no connection between such a notion of causally necessary truth and the philosophical concept of necessary truth.

For one thing, the standard examples of necessary propositions have been mathematical and logical, and whatever such propositions may be said to describe or assert, it can hardly be regarded as the sort of thing or fact that has causes; it would hardly be an event. For another, the very idea of a causally necessary event seems to presuppose the idea of necessary truth. Let us asume that, given the present state of the solar system, the rising of the sun tomorrow is causally necessary, that in a certain sense it *must* take place. Whatever analysis of the nature of causality we may adopt, it seems to me that the following *general* account of what is meant by saying that such an event is causally necessary is indisputable. The proposition "If the solar system, on a certain day, is in such-and-such a state, then the sun will rise on the next day" is true; it is certainly true that the solar system is in such a state today; therefore, the sun will rise tomorrow. If the *conclusion* of this argument is said to be necessarily *true*, all that this could mean is that it is obtained by valid argument. On the other hand, the ascription of *causal* necessity to the *event* it describes may only mean, I suggest, that the first, hypothetical premise is not only true but in some sense *necessarily* true. The problem of the nature of causality concerns this predication of necessary truth of certain hypothetical propositions, not the predication of causal necessity of certain events. The latter, being entirely derivative from the former, presents no mystery at all. The former does. It should be noted that what the hypothetical proposition "If

18. I shall ignore here the very different notions of moral necessity (obligation), moral contingency (indifference), and moral impossibility (prohibition), which one also finds in ordinary language.

today the solar system is in such-and-such a state, then tomorrow the sun will rise" itself describes is not a causally necessary *event,* in the sense in which the rising of the sun might be such an event; if what it describes is necessarily the case at all, it is not so because of being the product of a cause.

I conclude that there is no ordinary sense in which the definiens of the nominal philosophical definition of necessarily true proposition can be understood, and thus that the conception of necessary truth this definition determines is not an ordinary, natural conception. But it would be a mistake to suppose that perhaps there is an error in the very definition: "*p* is necessarily true if and only if *p* is true and it is false that *p* may be false." This definition, though purely nominal and philosophically unenlightening, is nevertheless quite unquestionable. To give it up would be to deprive the concept of necessary truth of the last shreds of its root in ordinary discourse, namely, the familiar logical connections between the notions of necessity, possibility, and impossibility, and the expressibility of these notions in sentences by the use of the verbs *can* and *may.* On the other hand, that there is conceptual room for such a philosophical concept of necessary truth seems obvious. There is an obvious difference between the propositions paradigmatically described by philosophers as necessarily true and the propositions paradigmatically described as contingently true. We require a concept for the elucidation, for our understanding, of this difference. But this concept must be constructed; it cannot be acquired from the conceptual store of the race. The required construction involves several conceptual jumps away from the ordinary notion of necessity, that of causal necessity. Yet if it is to be intelligible at all, if it is to be the construction of a concept of *necessary* truth, it must remain in some connection, however indirect, with that notion.

The first step of the construction is the suggestion that "*p* is true and it is false that *p* may be false" should be taken to mean that *p* is *always* true, that there is no time at which *p* is false. The suggestion is plausible and useful. It draws attention to the fact that the notion of necessary truth does seem to have a connection with the notion of time. And, surely, this is so for the reason that the notion of causality involves intimately the notion of time, and the natural, ordinary notion of necessity is that of causal necessity. Moreover, it is a fact that all necessarily true propositions are always true. Nevertheless, the suggestion, though a step in the right direction, is only the first such step. Is it also a fact that all propositions that are always true are necessarily true? And is it at all proper to speak of propositions as *always* or *sometimes* true, to assign a temporal location to the truth of a proposition? Indeed, even if we were to answer both of these questions affirmatively, the concept of a necessarily true proposition would still not be identical with the concept of a proposition that is always true. For we would want to distinguish between propositions that *just happen* to be always true and propositions that are *necessarily* always true. And this distinction would be a species of the usual distinction between contingent and necessary propositions.

Nevertheless, the supposition that a necessarily true proposition is one that is always true is suggestive and leads to the second step of the construction. There is a sense in which a proposition may be said to be always true not by just happening to be always true but by necessity: that is the sense in which a proposition describes something which *can* never be otherwise, *can* never change, is *immutable*. The second step of the construction consists in the suggestion that a necessarily true proposition is one that describes something that not only is always the case but can never be otherwise. It benefits from its intimate and quite visible reliance on the natural notion of causal necessity, as change, whether it be locomotion or alteration, generation or corruption, is precisely what is subject to causal explanation. A thing does not change where causes for its change are absent or where causes for its not-changing are present. And to the extent to which change and nonchange are subject to causal explanation, they are also describable as necessary. Now the notion of causal necessity allows for the conception of something that not only could not have been otherwise, is causally necessary, but that can *never* change, can never be otherwise, because either causes for its changing are never present or because causes for its not-changing are always present. Thus a description of such an entity as necessarily existing and necessarily remaining the same is quite natural. But, of course, it is still a causal necessity and thus a conditional necessity: the entity exists or remains the same only *because*, only *if*, certain causes are present (or absent). This sort of conception of eternal though conditional necessity is the closest that the philosophical conception of necessary truth comes to the natural, causal conception of necessity. But it is not close enough for regarding the former as a mere extension of the latter.

At the third step in the construction of the concept of necessary truth, we take for granted the notion of conditional eternal necessity and raise what now would be a typically philosophical question: Can there be *unconditional* eternal necessity? Of course, the answer is no, for the necessity in question is causal and the description of something as unconditioned and yet caused is self-contradictory. But the question suggests a second, equally typical, philosophical question: Why can't something be immutable, incapable of ever changing, not because of causes but in itself? The asking of this question constitutes the birth of the philosophical concept of necessary truth. Corresponding to the sense in which the existence or characteristics of something may be immutable and yet not because of causes, there would now be a sense in which the propositions describing these characteristics may be said to be necessary and yet not because of causes. A necessarily true proposition, we can now say, is one that describes what is immutable, incapable of ever changing, in itself and not because of causes.

The conception of necessary truth that we have now reached is indeed philosophical. But its obscurity requires little comment. How is it possible for something to be immutable and yet not because of causes? What is so immutable, and what is not? And what is the sense of the modal term *immutability?* If this term is not to be understood causally, can it be understood at all? These questions can be answered. But their answers constitute the fourth and final step in the construction of a philosophically *adequate* concept of necessary truth. The answer to the first question is that something can be immutable, and yet not because of causes, in the sense that it is not in time at all; for the notions of change and causality are both applicable only to the temporal. The answer to the second question is that whatever is nontemporal is noncausally immutable and that whatever is temporal is either not immutable at all or immutable because of causes. The answer to the third question is that the notion of noncausal immutability is not a modal notion at all but simply the descriptive notion of the nontemporal. A necessarily true proposition is one that is true and has as its subject matter nontemporal entities. It is always true because what it is about is not in time at all. It is necessarily always true because what it is about is immutable in that it is not subject to change at all, that is, is not in time. If we call a proposition about nontemporal entities a "nontemporal proposition," then we may say that the concept of a necessarily true proposition is identical with the concept of a true nontemporal proposition.

A convenient, though superficial, test of the nontemporality, and thus necessity, of a proposition is the senselessness of prefixing it with the phrase "At time t" or the phrase "During the period from t_1 to t_2." It is nonsense to speak of the time at which or during which the sum of the angles of a triangle is equal to two right angles, three and two are five, crimson is darker than pink, and no proposition can be true or false. However, the fundamental test of the nontemporality, and necessity, of a proposition would be the fact that the entities it is about are nontemporal, that is, have no location in time and thus do not enter in temporal relations such as earlier-than, simultaneous-with, or later-than. A convenient test of the nontemporality of a certain entity is that it is senseless to assign a date to its existence or to its having certain characteristics, that is, that it is senseless to assign to it a location in time or a time-predicate such as earlier-than-x, somewhat in the way in which it is senseless to assign a color-predicate to a taste. It is nonsense to speak of the time during which triangularity, the number five, and the color crimson exist, or occur, or have certain characteristics.

I shall consider the very difficult question of what precisely is meant by saying that a proposition is *about* (has as its *subject matter*) nontemporal entities in section 6 of this Part. It suffices for our purposes here to say that a proposition is about those entities that must exist and must have certain characteristics if the proposition is to be true and to disclaim any semantical views about which words in a sentence refer to entities and which do not. I should also observe that nothing that I have said is intended to be an argument for the existence of nontemporal entities. Any such argument must appeal to considerations deeper and more general than any specific analysis of the concept of necessary truth. What I have said is intended to be an argument regarding the content of the concept of necessary truth, and, more specifically, one regarding the intimate connection between this concept and that of nontemporal entity. But the question whether there are nontemporal entities, which as we shall see amounts to the question whether there are universals, must be answered quite independently. I will return to this point in section 7 of this Part. At the moment, however, we have a more pressing task.

Is not the account of the concept of necessary truth that I have offered bought at the high price of circularity? For is not the notion of the nontemporal simply the notion of that which *cannot* be in time, that for which it is necessarily true that it is not in time? The objection is clearer in the case of the notion of a nontemporal proposition, and of course the notion of necessary truth is applicable to propositions and not to entities. I have said that a nontemporal proposition is one that cannot be intelligibly prefixed with a date. For example, "Three and two are five" is a nontemporal proposition because it would be nonsense to say that today three and two are five. According to the objection, if it is nonsense to say that three and two are five today, the reason is that to say this would have a point only if, say, yesterday three and two might not have been five. So the unintelligibility of the statement "Three and two are five today" is simply the result of the necessary truth of the statement "Three and two are five." But this argument is unsound. It may do justice to the nonsense of the proposition that three and two are *not* five today, but hardly to the nonsense of the proposition that three and two *are* five today. The argument amounts to the claim that it is nonsense to say that three and two are five today because it is necessarily the case that three and two are five today. And this claim is clearly false. It is necessarily the case also that red is a color, but not nonsense, or even extremely unusual, to say that red is a color. We are never in doubt that red is a color. Nevertheless, at least in the context of classifying properties, we could say that red is a color without drawing blank gazes. There are no circumstances in which we would say that three and two are five today.

In any case, the more fundamental definition of a nontemporal proposition refers to the nature of its subject matter. A nontemporal proposition is one whose subject matter consists only of nontemporal entities. The charge of circularity must be directed against this formulation. And when it is, it appears more convincing, though still refutable. Our account of necessary truth would be circular if it must appeal to the necessary truth of propositions to the effect that something is, or is not, a temporal entity. And the objector may claim that this is just what it does do. For are we not saying that a nontemporal entity is one that *cannot* be in time, that is, cannot be assigned a date and cannot enter in temporal relations? But we are not. Indeed, it may be a necessary truth that a certain kind of entity is nontemporal, but from this it does not follow that the notion of nontemporal entity presupposes the notion of necessary truth. In this respect, the distinction between the temporal and the nontemporal is like the distinction between colors and sounds, shapes and pains, numbers and smells. If something's being in time is a necessary truth, then probably so is something's being a color (or a sound). But, clearly, it would be an error to infer from this that the notion of color (or the notion of sound) presupposes the notion of necessary truth. Just as one can distinguish between colors and sounds without employing the notion of necessary truth, without appealing to the *necessity* of something's being a color rather than a sound, so can one distinguish between temporal and nontemporal entities without employing the notion of necessary truth, without appealing to the necessity of something's being a temporal rather than a nontemporal entity. Just as a child can acquire the notion of color and the notion of sound without learning that it is *necessarily* true that something is a color and something else a sound, so can a philosopher propose the notions of temporal entity and of nontemporal entity (by giving examples or by offering definitions such as "a nontemporal entity is one that has no location in time") without employing the notion of necessary truth or appealing to the necessity of something's being a temporal (or nontemporal) entity.

6. The Subject Matter
of Necessary Propositions

EVEN IF NOT CIRCULAR, our account of the nature of necessary truth may still be false. There are at least four serious objections to it, and we must attempt to meet them. The first is that many necessary propositions are *not* about nontemporal entities at all. The second is that one can offer plausible examples of *contingently* true propositions that are about nontemporal entities. The third is that there is no reason why the nontemporal cannot be thought to be otherwise, and thus, since the unthinkability-of-falsehood is the test of necessary truth, that the necessary truth of a proposition cannot be identified with its nontemporality. The fourth is that in fact we do not mean by a necessarily true proposition one about nontemporal entities and thus that our account of the content of the concept of necessary truth is simply false.

The first and second objections are closely connected and may be considered together. The proposition "All black cats are black" is necessarily true. It is about black cats. But black cats are not nontemporal entities. Therefore, there are necessary propositions that are about temporal entities. On the other hand, take the proposition "If anything is a cat then it has fur." What is it about? It would be wrong to say, one may argue, that it is about *anything,* or about *all things.* Or, if we were to say this, then we must recognize that the nature of what all propositions of this form are about has nothing to do with the truth-value of the proposition. It is not a *property* of all things that if they are cats then they have fur. Consider "If anything is triangular then it has angles equal to two right angles." Obviously, the proposition is true not because of some property of all things that it, luckily, happens to disclose but because of a certain connection between the properties of being triangular and having angles equal to two right angles. In a similar fashion, it may be argued, "If anything is a cat then it has fur" is true not because of some fact about *anything* or about *all things* but because of a certain connection between what it is to be a cat and what it is to have fur. For this reason it would be better to say that it is about only the properties of being-a-cat and having-fur. These, like all properties, are nontemporal. But the proposition is clearly contingent.

Both objections rest on a confusion, made plausible but hardly legitimate by contemporary logic, between what H. W. B. Joseph called true universal judgments and collective judgments.[19] Let me illustrate this distinction with, respectively, the following extreme examples: "All triangles have angles equal to two right angles" and "All presidents of the United States are male." The difference is obvious. Yet it does not consist in one of these propositions having existential import and the other being purely hypothetical. Both could be stated as hypotheticals. Nor does it consist, as Joseph seemed to think, in that the latter sort of proposition is really enumerative, that it is really the conjunction of singular propositions and thus, to use Joseph's term, collective. The reference to presidents of the United States need not be restricted to any particular, determinate collection of such presidents. Indeed, the first proposition is necessary, the second contingent; but this is the difference to be elucidated. Is there another difference, a difference between the kinds of entities the propositions are about? Clearly, there is. The first proposition is, so to speak, only incidentally, only derivatively, about particular triangular things. It is clearly intended to be an assertion of a relation between two properties and thus, equally clearly, it is about properties. Whether what it says is necessary or contingent is beside the point here. What is to the point is *what it is intended to be about,* an intention discernible in our readiness to

19. *An Introduction to Logic* (Oxford: Clarendon Press, 1916), pp. 177 ff.

153

state the proposition as "The triangle has angles the sum of which is equal to two right angles." This becomes clearer if we consider a proposition such as "All triangles are scalene." Is it true or false? If we say, as we ordinarily would, that it is false, then, I suggest, we are taking it to be about properties and not about individual things, for, surely, we do not decide that it is false because we believe that a triangular surface of at least one thing in nature has at least two really equal sides. On the other hand, if we say that probably it is true (presumably because of doubts that any triangular surface of a thing really has two equal sides), then it is clear that we are taking the proposition to be about individual triangular things and not about the properties of being triangular and being scalene.

Now, similarly, that "All presidents of the United States are male" is intended as a statement about individual things and not about the properties of being president of the United States and being male, should be obvious. Were it the latter, it would be false. It is not at all equivalent to the statement "The president of the United States is male," which might have been part of the Constitution. Using Joseph's terminology, though without understanding a collective judgment to be enumerative, we could say that both the hypothetical and categorical forms of a universal proposition disguise a distinction between truly universal and collectively universal propositions. Only the former are about nontemporal entities. And only the former can be necessarily true. Whether we say that all cats have fur or that if anything is a cat then it has fur, we are talking about individual things in space and in time, and not about properties. It is not at all nonsense to speak about the time during which the proposition is true, that is, the time during which if anything is a cat then it has fur. (For example, this may be so only when certain levels of radiation are not exceeded.) It is nonsense, however, to speak about the time during which triangles have angles the sum of which is equal to two right angles.

But now what should we say about a proposition such as "All black cats are black?" Is it not in fact intended to be about black cats? Yet is it not necessarily true, even though black cats are in time? The answer to these questions is yes. But this is a derivative proposition. It is a substitution-instance of a much more general proposition, if not "Whatever is, is," then at least of "Whatever is black is black." "All black cats are black" is indeed about individual things, for it is intended to be an application of a more general proposition to certain specific individual things. To this extent we must qualify our definition of a necessary proposition by saying that it is a proposition about nontemporal entities or is derivable from a proposition about nontemporal entities.

But the above have been merely the initial skirmishes with the first two objectors. What lies behind their objections is the fact that most necessary propositions, including some of those I have already mentioned, make irreducible reference to individual, and thus temporal, entities. All truths of the first-order functional logic belong to this category. So does a proposition such as "Nothing is both red and green all over." The latter has sometimes been regarded as equivalent to, or at least as entailed by, some such proposition as "Being red excludes being green." [20] But there is no two-term relation such as exclusion or incompatibility between the properties red and green. If there were such a relation as their incompatibility, it would be a three-term relation, holding between red, green, and *something that can be red or green.* This is why it is more plausible to speak of a relation of exclusion between the "properties" of *being* red and *being* green. But, if at all distinguishable from red and green themselves, these are not properties at all but incomplete states of affairs. To speak of their mutual exclusion is merely to speak of the impossibility of the same individual, *temporal* thing's being both red and green all over.

Nevertheless, while "Nothing is both red and green all over" does not refer merely to the properties red and green, it does not follow that its additional reference is to individual, temporal entities. May we not regard it as making reference to red, to green, and to the characteristic of being an individual, that is, to individuality as such? For surely the truth of the statement is not grounded in any actual individual things, of each of which it is true that it is not both red and green all over, but *in what it is to be an individual thing,* or an entity that may have a color, and in what it is to be red and what it is to be green. It would be misleading to call such a characteristic as individuality a property, for it is not at all in the same category as colors, shapes, relations, etc. But there can be no reason for not applying to it the technical philosophical term *universal,* which is generally intended to refer to any *recurrent entity,* whether the latter be a property or not. We could then distinguish between *property-universals,* such as green and square, and what we may call *formal universals,* such as individuality. A formal universal would as obviously be a nontemporal entity as a property-universal would usually be regarded to be. It makes

20. See R. M. Chisholm, *Theory of Knowledge* (Englewood Cliffs, N.J.: Prentice-Hall, 1966), p. 71 ff.

no more sense to assign temporal relations, such as later-than, to individuality than to colors and shapes. On the other hand, if there are sufficient reasons for accepting the existence of property-universals, these should also be reasons for accepting the existence of formal universals. We argue in favor of property-universals in attempting to account for the similarities or samenesses we find in the world (e.g., that between two green things). But there is a sameness or similarity between any two individual things that there is not between individual things and properties. This sameness or similarity would demand the existence of the formal universal individuality as much or as little as the sameness or similarity between two green things would demand the existence of the property-universal green.[21]

The introduction of the notion of a nontemporal entity such as the formal universal can be immediately seen to facilitate the claim that even the truths of first-order functional logic are truths about nontemporal entities. "Whatever has a certain property does have that property" does not even appear to be about specific properties. But surely what it is about are the formal universals individuality and being-a-property? Indeed, that this is so seems clearer in the formal statement of this proposition, namely, "For any x and any F, if x is F then x is F." What determines the truth of this proposition is not any fact about certain particular individuals and certain specific properties but the general nature of what it is to be an individual and what it is to be a property.

But even the introduction of formal universals does not allow us to meet the first two objections. For even if we allow that, in addition to nontemporal entities such as property-universals, there are nontemporal entities such as formal universals, the fact remains that in most necessary propositions reference is made to individual, and thus temporal, entities. It is completely obvious that, whatever else they may be about, propositions such as "Whatever has a certain property does have that property" and "Nothing is both red and green all over" are also about individual things. Were this not so, we would be able to reduce such propositions to ones explicitly mentioning only nontemporal entities, as indeed we can reduce "Whatever is blue is colored" to "Blue is a color." But we cannot perform such a reduction. We have no idea what statement that mentions only individuality, red, and green would be equivalent to "Nothing is both red and green." But if we cannot omit from many, if not most, necessary propositions their reference to temporal entities, then we cannot simply claim that all necessary propositions are about nontemporal entities. Clearly, what we must do is to offer a more precise account of what would be meant by saying that a necessary proposition is one about nontemporal entities.

The sort of account I have in mind may be stated initially and only propaedeutically in terms of the notion of a fact, or facts, *in virtue of which* a proposition is true. To say that a proposition is about nontemporal entities would be then to say that it is true in virtue of certain facts about nontemporal entities. For example, "Nothing is both red and green all over" is true in virtue of certain facts about colors and individuality. But "Nothing is both a cat and furless" is true in virtue of the fact about cats that each of them has fur. Hence, according to our definition, the former would be about nontemporal entities, while the latter would not. But the expression "in virtue of" is excessively vague. It is also misleading, for its use above suggests that if a proposition is true in virtue of one fact (or set of facts), it is not also true in virtue of another fact (or set of facts). But we should be allowed by our theory to say that while "Nothing is both red and green all over" is true in virtue of certain facts about colors and individuality it is also true in virtue of the fact about individuals that none is both red and green all over. So I shall avoid the expression "in virtue of" and attempt to make the notion of a proposition which is about nontemporal entities more precise by introducing the notion of *truth-sufficient reference.*

The reference in a proposition to certain entities is truth-sufficient if, and only if, the nature or characteristics of these entities (what they are in themselves) is a *sufficient* (though perhaps also necessary) condition of the truth of the proposition, that is, if the nature of the entities requires that the proposition be true, if nothing else is needed for the proposition to be true than that the entities referred to be what they are. A reference to entities is *truth-insufficient* if and only if the nature or characteristics of the entities is not a sufficient condition (though perhaps it is a necessary condition) of the truth of the proposition, that is, if it does not require the truth of the proposition. For example, in the proposition "Nothing is both red and green all over," the reference to the colors red and green, and presumably to individuality (to what it is to be an entity that can have color), is truth-sufficient. For the nature of the colors and of individuality are sufficient for the truth of the proposition. All one need consider in considering whether the proposition is true is what the colors and individuality are, since the truth of the proposition is required by the nature of the colors and of individuality. One need not, and ordinarily would not, consider any individual things. Indeed, the question of the truth of the proposition could be raised intelligibly even if no red or green object existed, even if there were no individual things at all.

On the other hand, the reference to the properties of being-a-cat and having-fur in the proposition "All cats have fur" would not be truth-sufficient. For, presumably, the nature of these properties, what they are, would not be sufficient for the truth of the proposition. The only reference in it that would be truth-sufficient is that to individual cats or, we may wish to say, that to individual things; if the proposition is true at all, it is so because of a characteristic of individual cats, namely, that all of them have fur, or, if we wish, of individual things, namely, that none of them is a furless cat. In considering whether the proposition is true, one must consider individual cats or individual things in general. There is nothing in the nature of the properties of being-a-cat and having-fur that requires the proposition to be true, and if anything does require it to be true it is some characteristic of individual things. Indeed, the question of the truth of the proposition would not even arise if there were no cats, except in the contemporary logician's sense in which the proposition would be true precisely because there are no cats (a sense in which it would be true that all centaurs have fur and also true that no centaurs have fur). And if there were no individual things at all, then the question could not arise even in that sense.

I specify now the definitions of necessary and contingent propostitions by saying that a necessary proposition is one that is about nontemporal entities in the sense that it makes truth-sufficient reference to nontemporal entities, even if there is reference in it to temporal entities which perhaps is also truth-sufficient. A contingent proposition is one that is about temporal entities in the sense that it makes truth-sufficient reference *only* to temporal entities, though presumably it also contains reference, *though not truth-sufficient,* to nontemporal entities (e.g., properties). It is legitimate to so specify the sense in which a proposition is *about* nontemporal entities because it is natural to say that a proposition is about those entities the nature or characteristics of which are a sufficient condition of the truth of the proposition. The definitions would be much sharper, of course, if we denied that, in addition to a truth-sufficient reference to nontemporal entities, a proposition may also contain a truth-sufficient reference to temporal entities. The reason our definitions expressly allow for this possibility is that to allow it does not really affect our account of necessary truth, while to disallow it would involve that account in the difficult question of the meaning of universal propositions in general. For if the reference to temporal entities in a necessary universal proposition cannot be truth-sufficient, then presumably such a reference in a contingent universal proposition would also not be truth-sufficient. Perhaps this is the conclusion that an analysis of the nature of universal propositions ought to reach. One can argue with plausibility that it follows from the fact that no number of true instances of a universal proposition constitute a sufficient condition of the truth of the proposition. One may argue that if the reference in a certain universal proposition to individuals were truth-sufficient, then the proposition would not be a true *universal* proposition but a mere conjunction, even if infinite, of singular propositions, an *enumerative* proposition. And, if a genuine proposition must be true or false and thus must contain a truth-sufficient reference to some entities, it would follow that all genuine universal propositions must be either necessarily true or necessarily false. This is probably the sort of reasoning that led Joseph to the views mentioned above. But it is not required by our account of the nature of necessary truth.

It is important that we do not confuse the distinction between truth-sufficient and truth-insufficient reference with some other distinction. For example, it is not the familiar distinction between essential and inessential elements in a proposition; we must not confuse what is sufficient with what is necessary for the truth of a proposition. A truth-*insufficient* reference may be necessary for the truth of a proposition (that is, it cannot be replaced with a reference to just any other entity without a change in the truth-value of the proposition). For example, this would be the case with the reference to being-a-cat and having-fur in "All cats have fur." Nor is the distinction intended to be the same as the epistemic distinction between sufficient and insufficient evidence. A truth-sufficient reference in a proposition is not defined as one that would be sufficient for our knowledge of the truth of the proposition. At least, it is not to be so understood, and if it turns out to have this added characteristic this would be the result of additional, epistemological considerations. Indeed, so far as our inquiry in this Part is concerned, a truth-insufficient reference may well be epistemically sufficient, that is, sufficient for knowledge of the truth of the proposition. I have not denied the possibility that one may come to know that all cats have fur by appealing to one's observation of a certain number of cats that have fur.[22]

Nor should the notion of truth-sufficient reference be confused with the notion of meaning-sufficient reference. To say that in a proposition the reference to certain nontemporal entities is sufficient for the truth of the proposition is not to say that everything else in the proposition can be changed without changing the latter's meaning. For these other elements in the proposition may partly determine the meaning of the proposition, and no reference to entities is sufficient for the truth of a proposition except with respect to a certain meaning of that proposition.

Finally, our distinction is not only not the same as, but in fact is quite independent of, the distinction between necessarily true and contingently true propositions. To recognize that a proposition makes truth-sufficient reference to nontemporal entities is not the same as to recognize that the proposition is necessary. It is merely to recognize that the existence and characteristics of these nontemporal entities are sufficient for the truth of the proposition. But we give an account of the concept of necessary truth by asserting that a proposition is necessarily true if and only if it makes truth-sufficient reference to nontemporal entities.

I have found it necessary to offer a rather elaborate explanation of my

---

22. Bertrand Russell was aware of the difficulties that have led us to introduce the notion of truth-sufficient reference. *"All* a priori *knowledge deals exclusively with the relations of universals. . . .* The only case in which it might seem, at first sight, as if our proposition were untrue, is the case in which an *a priori* proposition states that *all* of one class of particulars belong to some other class. . . . In this case it might seem as though we were dealing with the particulars that have the property rather than with the property" (*The Problems of Philosophy* [London: Oxford University Press, 1946], pp. 103–4). He suggests that "the difference between an *a priori* general proposition and an empirical generalization . . . comes in the nature of the *evidence* for it. In the empirical case, the evidence consists in the particular instances" (*ibid.*, p. 106), while in the other case it consists in "a knowledge of the relations of universals" (*ibid.*, p. 108). We might say that truth-sufficient reference in a proposition to certain entities is reference to entities our knowledge of which would be sufficient evidence for our knowledge of the proposition. But such an explanation in terms of knowledge and evidence would contribute nothing, for the reason our knowledge of such entities is sufficient evidence for the truth of the proposition is simply that the existence and characteristics of such entities are sufficient to render the proposition true. And, at least in the context of our inquiry, such an explanation would be obscurantist, for we are concerned with the nature of necessary truth in order to grasp more clearly certain features of the nature of knowledge.

original simple proposal that a necessary proposition is one that is about nontemporal entities. What has forced me to do so has been the important fact that most necessary propositions make reference to individual, temporal things. This is true of the principles of first-order functional logic and of many propositions such as "Nothing is both red and green all over," "Whatever is colored is extended," "If equals are added to equals then the result is equals." Were all such propositions reducible to singular propositions in which reference is made only to nontemporal entities (as "Whatever is blue is colored" is reducible to "Blue is a color"), there would have been no difficulty in our account. But it is impossible to construct such singular propositions for all cases. In the case of logical principles it is obvious that the attempt cannot even be made. In other cases, we may be tempted to construct propositions such as "Red and green are incompatible" or "Color is extended," but, as we have seen, when we do so it becomes clear that the constructions are quite forced and implausible. It is not the universal Color that is extended but the individual thing that is colored. And the incompatibility of Red and Green is not a two-term relation between Red and Green: it clearly and necessarily makes reference to the individuals exemplifying color. It is for reasons such as these that the traditional view, argued by Plato as well as by Russell, that necessary propositions describe the relations of universals has seemed indefensible.[23] It has been interpreted as meaning that all necessary propositions either are or can be translated into singular propositions whose subject-terms refer only to universals. It has seemed plausible because of the existence of singular necessarily true propositions such as "Blue is a color" and "Middle C is higher than Middle E." But most necessarily true propositions are not singular and cannot be reduced to singular propositions.

I believe that the traditional theory need not be rejected for such reasons. It must, however, be restated and made much more precise. I have tried to do so with the help of the notion of truth-sufficient reference. Why is it, however, that the truth-sufficient reference to universals in most necessarily true propositions is unavoidably accompanied by a reference to individuals? Why is it that most necessarily true propositions are not singular in form and are not reducible to singular propositions? The reason does not seem hard to find. Indeed, I suggest, the reference in

23. See Pap, *Semantics and Necessary Truth*, pp. 47–53.

necessary propositions to individuals is just what should have been expected. What is surprising is, rather, that there are singular necessary propositions such as "Blue is a color." For universals are necessarily qualities of individual things, even if there is a sense in which they may be said to exist uninstantiated. (I shall consider this in section 7 of this Part.) Thus it is natural that we should be unable to talk about universals except by talking also about individuals. That most talk about universals involves, unavoidably, reference also to individuals should be no more surprising than the fact that most talk about individuals involves, unavoidably, reference to universals. But just as the latter fact should not make us unwilling to admit that in certain propositions we are essentially concerned with individuals, so the former fact should not make us unwilling to admit that in other propositions, namely, necessary ones, we are essentially concerned with universals and only incidentally with individuals.

Of course, we could indicate the sort of singular propositions we cannot in fact state by introducing suitable notational devices. For example, if we interpret "For any x and any F, if x is F then x is F" as making truth-sufficient reference to individuality and to being-a-property, that is, as true in virtue of what individuality and being-a-property are, then we could introduce the locution $R\ (I, P)$ and make believe, so to speak, that it expresses a singular proposition, one asserting a certain relationship between individuality and being-a-property, to which the universal proposition is reducible. In doing this we may be guided by the analogy provided by the pair of propositions "Everything crimson is darker than pink" and "Darker than (crimson, pink)." But this analogy would be deceptive, though not unilluminating. For we do not actually have a predicate "R" that is analogous to the predicate "darker than" and, more importantly, we seem to have no way of introducing it that would be at all similar to the way in which "darker than" would be introduced if our language did not contain it.

We can now consider the third and fourth objections to our account of necessary truth.[24] They can be dealt with more briefly. According to the third, our account of necessary truth fails to do justice to the fact that the unthinkability-of-falsehood is the test of necessary truth. For there seems to be no reason why the nontemporal cannot be thought to be otherwise

24. See above, p. 152.

than it is. The mere nontemporality of something does not seem to explain the unthinkability of its being otherwise.

To think of any state of affairs, whether involving temporal or nontemporal entities, as being otherwise than one knows it to be, presumably one must think of it as being the case *and also* as not being the case. (If one cannot think of it as being otherwise, then its being otherwise is not a possible state of affairs and the proposition asserting that it is otherwise is necessarily false.) Yet one cannot think of both without making some distinction, for such a thought would be self-contradictory. I cannot think that the chair before me is brown and also that it is not brown by thinking of the chair as both brown and not brown. Consequently, if ordinary contradiction is to be avoided, there must be a difference between the thought of the state of affairs as being the case and the thought of it as not being the case. But the only such difference that would be relevant is a difference between the temporal location of the object of the one thought and the temporal location of the object of the other thought. To think of a state of affairs one knows to be the case as being otherwise may only be to think of it as being otherwise *at a different time*. To think of the chair that one knows to be brown as not being brown is simply to think of the chair as not being brown *at some other time*. In other words, the thinkability of something's being otherwise, which is our reason for regarding this something as contingent, is simply the thinkability of its *changing*. And only temporal entities can intelligibly be regarded as capable of change. I can think of the chair's being brown and I can also think of the chair's not being brown, while I cannot think of three and two as being five and also think of three and two as not being five. The reason for this difference is that I can, so to speak, separate in my thought a chair's not being brown from that chair's being brown by making a temporal distinction. No such distinction is possible in the case of three and two being five and three and two not being five. If I know that three and two are five, then I can think of their not being five only if I can think of their being both five and not five; this would be self-contradictory, for I could not appeal to a temporal distinction in the case of nontemporal entities such as numbers.

The fourth objection to our account of necessary truth is that in fact we do not mean by necessary truth, truth about nontemporal entities. This objection rests on a misunderstanding of our approach to this topic. It is intended to be an accusation that we have committed something analogous to the naturalistic fallacy. But even if there were a naturalistic fallacy in explaining the nature of the good, or perhaps even of knowledge, there can be no such fallacy in an account of a concept such as that of necessary truth. For the concept of necessary truth is a technical one. We have no primitive, common-sense, *natural* understanding of it.[25] It is a philosophical creation, though not a philosophical fantasy. Its function is to elucidate certain fundamental similarities and differences among propositions. It may be clear or unclear, distinct or indistinct, philosophically significant or insignificant, but it cannot be mistaken. Of course, this does not mean that our account of the concept of necessary truth has not been guided by an actual content of such a concept. It has, for if it is to count as an account of *that* and not of *another* concept it must remain to some extent faithful to the *established* nominal notion of necessary truth in philosophy. Its fidelity must not, however, exceed its usefulness. I suggest that our account of the concept of necessary truth not only corresponds closely to, and to some degree is identical with, the usual philosophical notion of necessary truth but also clarifies the distinction between the two classes of propositions for the clarification of which that notion was originally introduced.

The above claim may appear better supported if we draw attention to the light our account of necessary truth throws on certain connections traditionally made between the topic of necessary truth and other philosophical topics. For example, we can understand now why the principle of unthinkability (inconceivability) has provided the usual test for the necessity of a proposition. As an account of the concept of necessary truth, the Conceivability Theory is, as we have seen, woefully inadequate. It is circular, for the notion of inconceivability includes that of necessity. However, as a theory of the only way in which ultimately we determine the necessity of a truth it is not inadequate at all. For, as we have seen, the thinkability of something's being otherwise is the thinkability of its changing. And the thinkability of something's changing is our usual reason for regarding this something as temporal, as having location in time.

We can now also see more clearly the really fundamental reason for rejecting the logico-linguistic theories of necessary truth which we considered above. All of these theories are committed to the view that necessary truth is a peculiar internal property of a proposition, one generated by the

25. See section 5 above.

meanings of the words in it, or by its syntactical structure, or by the linguistic rules governing its use. But this is not possible. If we were to describe necessary propositions as true in a sense of this word totally different from that in which we describe contingent propositions as true—were the application of the word *true* to both an ordinary case of equivocation—then this view might be acceptable, for we would then simply think of necessary truth as a peculiar logico-linguistic property of some propositions, almost as if we meant by the word *truth* in the case of these propositions something like the grammaticality of a sentence. But of course necessary propositions are not said to be true in such a different sense of *true*. I have argued that the ordinary explanation of what is meant by saying, for example, that it is true that all black cats are black would be quite similar to the ordinary explanation of what is meant by saying that it is true that all cats have fur. In the case of substitution-instances of the principles of noncontradiction and excluded middle this is even more obvious. It is true that a cat cannot be both black and not black all over at the same time, or that it is either black or not black, in a sense quite similar to that in which it is true that a cat cannot fly or that it is either male or female. Our account of the concept of necessary truth does justice to this natural understanding of the *truth* of necessarily true propositions. The ordinary conception of truth is that of some sort of agreement between what is true and the world, though perhaps not one of the sorts of agreement described by the correspondence theorists of truth. According to our account, a necessarily true proposition is true because it agrees with the world, namely, with facts regarding the entities it is about. It agrees with facts about the nontemporal entities to which it contains truth-sufficient reference. And it agrees with facts about any temporal entities to which it also contains truth-sufficient reference. "Nothing is both red and green all over" is true because it agrees with a certain fact about individual things, namely, that none is both red and green all over. But it is true also because it agrees with a certain fact regarding the colors red and green themselves, as well as individuality, even though we have no better way of expressing it in ordinary language than by saying something like "Red and green are incompatible."

The connection between the necessary-contingent distinction and the a priori–a posteriori distinction also becomes clearer now. An a priori proposition is one that can be known to be true independently of experience. An a posteriori proposition is one that cannot be known to be true independently of experience. Now the experience or observation which is the best (the paradigm of) evidence for an a posteriori proposition is the experience or observation of the fact itself that is described by that proposition. And usually it is taken for granted that one can experience or observe only temporal facts. On the other hand, whatever our grounds for knowledge of a priori propositions may be, the very fact that they are other than experience or observation *suggests* that such propositions are about entities that are unobservable and thus probably nontemporal. But this suggestion is misleading, and we will consider the connection between the necessary-contingent distinction and the a priori–a posteriori distinction in detail in section 8 of this Part.

It is also clearer now why propositions about the relations of universals have been regarded as necessary and why necessary truth has often been identified with truth about universals. Universals have been supposed to be nontemporal and so have their relations. Indeed, a universal is our paradigm of a nontemporal entity.

Our conclusion then is as follows. The philosophical distinction between necessary and contingent truths may only be understood as a distinction between truths about nontemporal entities and truths about entities located in time. It is a distinction that rests ultimately not on the epistemological notions of truth and knowledge but on the ontological notions of time and universal. And the distinction itself is, if thus understood, not puzzling at all. What is philosophically puzzling is the question whether in fact there is a difference that corresponds to the distinction, whether in fact there are necessary truths, in the sense described. For it seems probable that if there is a mystery corresponding to the original mystery of the necessary-contingent distinction between propositions, it is that of the distinction between universals and individuals, since universals are the obvious objects of application of the notion of the nontemporal and individuals, of that of the temporal. We thus conclude that the traditional theory that necessary truth is truth about universals is indeed correct. But now we see *why* it is so. For we have reached our conclusion, so to speak, by deduction from the very concept of necessary truth.

166

7. *Necessary Truth and the Problem of Universals*

A NECESSARY PROPOSITION is one that describes nontemporal entities. There is nothing in the notion of necessary truth to suggest that all necessary propositions describe universals. It is not self-evident that only universals are nontemporal entities. Nevertheless, in fact it is only of such nontemporal entities as universals that we have anything approaching a sufficiently clear and distinct conception to allow us a genuine understanding of the nature of necessary truth. God and angels may be other proposed candidates. But to attempt to elucidate the notion of nontemporal entity by giving as examples God and angels would, at best, be bad philosophical strategy. Much more promising candidates are perhaps space and time themselves. The seeming necessity of such propositions as that space and time are infinite, that they are infinitely divisible, that time has one direction, that space has three dimensions, etc., may seem to be due precisely to the nontemporality of space and of time, that is, their possession of no temporal location or relations. But space and time can be counted as nontemporal individual entities only if they can be counted as individual entities at all. If they are relational in nature, then necessary propositions about them would describe universals, since a relation would be a prime example of a universal. The stronger the relational theory of space and time, the weaker the suggestion that space and time are entities that are not universals but are described by necessary propositions. And the relational theory of space and time is very strong.

But even if, at least for the purposes of the elucidation of the concept of necessary truth, we must assume that only universals are nontemporal entities, it does not follow that there are universals and thus it does not follow that there are nontemporal entities. What does follow, given that assumption, is that if there are not universals then there are not necessary propositions (or, at least, not *true* necessary propositions). If our inquiry in this Part has been successful, we can be certain about what a necessary proposition would be if there were such propositions. We can be confident in our refutation of other accounts of the concept of necessary truth. Yet there are theories which are consistent with our account but which in effect would claim that there are no necessary propositions, that there are no propositions which if true could not have been false or if false could not have been true.

Such theories fall into two sorts. The members of the first deny that what are usually given as examples of necessary propositions are propositions at all, that they are true or false. The most important theory of this sort is the Rules Theory, according to which so-called necessary propositions are really rules for speaking or for thinking. It must not be confused with the Game Theory, according to which necessary propositions are indeed genuine propositions, that is, they are really true or false, though their truth or falsehood is a *consequence* of rules of language. The members of the second sort agree that so-called necessary propositions are genuine propositions, that is, that they are true or false, but deny that they are necessarily true or necessarily false—that if true they could not have been false and that if false they could not have been true. The most important theory of this sort is the Inductivist Theory, according to which so-called necessary propositions are really the most reliable, though still contingent, inductive generalizations.

To be sure, both the Rules Theory and the Inductivist Theory are quite implausible. What could be less believable than the view that even the principles of logic, even the principle of noncontradiction, are contingent, that they could have been false? And most of our arguments against the Game Theory would also apply to the Rules Theory. Even if so-called necessary propositions were merely rules of language, we must still recognize the fundamental disanalogy between such rules and other essentially arbitrary, purely conventional rules (like the Game Theory, the Rules Theory requires arbitrary, conventional rules, not rules which are merely imperative reflections of truths about means and ends), a disanalogy so great as to render the description of such rules as rules quite misleading. Nevertheless, when nothing better is available, one cannot be blamed for clutching at straws. If there could be no entities that necessary propositions would describe, then we should be prepared to deny that there are necessary propositions, either by denying that what are usually supposed to be such propositions are really propositions or by denying that they are necessary. But if our arguments have been sound we would still not be prepared to admit that there are necessary propositions whose truth is a consequence of their linguistic features.

I shall not attempt to prove here that there are universals,[26] and thus I shall not attempt to prove that there are necessary propositions. For it is with the concept of necessary truth that I am concerned, not with the question whether there are necessary propositions. But what I must prove, if my account of the concept of necessary truth is to be defensible, is (1) that the (technical) notion of universal can be introduced independently of the notion of necessary truth and (2) that the so-introduced notion of universal at least allows for the possibility that universals are nontemporal entities.

It is clear that if the notion of universal is introduced for the purpose of reaching certain conclusions concerning the nature and possibility of necessary truth it must be introduced independently from considerations regarding these topics. For example, it would be quite useless to define universals as constituting the subject matter of necessary propositions. But what other explanation of the notion of universal is there? We must look to the history of philosophy for guidance.

If the notion of universal is to be distinctive, and thus philosophically useful, it must not be simply identified with that of a non-spatiotemporal, nonphysical, otherworldly entity. God, angels, and disembodied souls have been supposed to be such entities, but they have not been supposed to be universals by the philosophers who have employed the term *universal*. Nor should the notion of universal be identified with the notion of abstract entity. For an abstract entity is one which is essentially an aspect, or part, or element, or property, or quality, or relation of something else, yet is considered, and perhaps even supposed to exist, independently of that something else; hence the notion of considering-something-in-abstraction-from-something-else, or of considering-something-abstractly, or of something's-being-a-product-of-abstraction. But the mere fact that something is considered abstractly, in this sense, does not mean that it is considered to be a universal. One may consider the color of a hat abstractly—that is, in itself, independently of the fact that it is the color of that hat—without necessarily supposing that it is a universal. One may even consider the triangularity of a certain shape independently of the fact that it is isosceles without necessarily supposing that it is a universal. Berkeley allowed for abstraction in this sense, though he denied that one

---

26. I have made such an attempt in *Resemblance and Identity: An Examination of the Problem of Universals* (Bloomington & London: Indiana University Press, 1966).

can form a separate idea of such an abstract element.[27] One may even suppose, however extravagantly, that the color of a hat (or the triangularity of a shape) may continue to exist even if the hat (or the shape) no longer does and yet still deny that it is a universal. For one may still deny that the color of the hat can be identical with the color of some other object, e.g., a coat (or that the triangularity of that shape can be identical with the triangularity of some other shape). One may think of such an abstraction as the color of a hat or the triangularity of a shape as a *particular* quality capable of existence even if it does not in fact constitute the quality of any individual thing without thinking that it is possible for it to be the quality of more than one individual thing at any one time, without thinking that it is possible for it to be a color or shape *common* to several things at the same time.

Nor can the notion of universal be identical with that of an ideal, perfect, particular thing, such as Aristotle supposed a Platonic Form to be. For, as the supposition itself entails, such a universal would be a particular, and the technical philosophical terms *universal* and *particular,* whatever their meanings, have been introduced in philosophy expressly as contradictories. If Plato's Forms were perfect particulars, then they were not universals. In fact, there is no difficulty in combining the view that there are ideal, perfect entities which spatiotemporal things may only approximate and which constitute the standards of our thought about such things with the view that such entities are universals. The perfect triangle, which the shapes of triangular things in nature may only resemble but never fully exemplify, can most easily be thought of as an uninstantiated universal. For it seems mere fantasy to suppose that it can be a particular either in the sense of being the shape of a particular non-spatiotemporal thing or in the sense of being a particular quality that is not a quality of any individual thing. But in addition to the universal perfect triangle, there would be other universals, some of them instantiated, such as the shapes that the imperfect triangular things in nature have. All ideal, perfect entities, in this sense, would thus be universals, though not all universals would be ideal or perfect.

I have already employed the term *universal* in its traditional and, I believe, uniquely distinctive and philosophically useful sense. The universal is a common characteristic (or relation, or quality, or property). To

27. See *Principles of Human Knowledge,* Introduction, § 16.

say that there can be universals is to say that a characteristic of one individual can be identical with a quality of another individual. To say that there are universals is to say that in fact there are such common, identical qualities. What is at stake is the proper description of the sort of relationship that exists, for example, between the shape of one penny and the shape of another penny. Are we to say that the two shapes are one and the same shape? Or are we to say that they are two distinct shapes which resemble each other? Or only that the same word, for example, *circular,* is applicable to both shapes? If we adopt the first alternative, we are affirming the existence of universals by accepting the Identity Theory. If we adopt the second alternative, we are denying the existence of universals by accepting the Resemblance Theory. If we adopt the third alternative we are denying the existence of universals by accepting the Nominalist Theory. Which of these three theories provides the philosophically preferable, intellectually illuminating description of the above relationship is a difficult problem that cannot be dealt with in this book. It is sufficient for our present purposes to have indicated how the concept of universal would be introduced independently of the concept of necessary truth.

But would universals, so understood, be nontemporal entities? The existence of universals, however important a fact for other philosophical topics, would be relevant to the topic of necessary truth only if universals were nontemporal. And here a complication arises. In the standard sense of the word *nontemporal,* a nontemporal entity is one which does not enter in relations such as earlier-than and simultaneous-with, one for which it would be senseless to say that it is earlier than or simultaneous with any other entity. The applicability or inapplicability of the word *nontemporal* to individual things, whether tables and chairs, or God and angels, is relatively straightforward. Clearly, a table or a chair (or the event of its existence) can be said to be later than, or earlier than, or simultaneous with some other object (or event). And there is no particular difficulty in the general conception of an individual entity that is neither later than, nor earlier than, nor simultaneous with any other entity, any more than there is a difficulty in the conception of an entity that is neither higher than, nor lower than, nor equal in pitch with another entity; and, if the notions of God and angel are clear on other grounds, they would not be unclear because God and angels are nontemporal in this sense.

Now it seems obvious that a universal, e.g., a color or a shape, cannot enter in temporal relations. It seems senseless to assert that Blue is later than Yellow or that Circularity is simultaneous with Squareness. But the appearance of senselessness in such an assertion is due to our taking for granted that it is senseless to assert that Blue would cease to exist if all blue things were to cease to exist, and that it came into existence when (if ever) the first blue thing came into existence. If we did not take this for granted, then of course universals would be temporal entities. To say that Blue is later than Yellow would be simply to say that the first blue thing came into existence later than the first yellow thing did. And there is nothing senseless about this latter assertion, false and pointless though it may be. Consequently, the nontemporality of universals can be taken for granted only if the existence of *uninstantiated universals* can be taken for granted. To suppose that a universal is nontemporal is to suppose that it would exist even if uninstantiated. For there is nothing timeless about the *instances* of a universal. It makes perfectly good sense to speak of a time when there are instances of a certain universal and of a time when there are not. If a universal may exist only if instantiated, then there would be a perfectly good sense in saying that it does not exist when not instantiated and thus that it has a location in time. On the other hand, there seems to be no sense in which an uninstantiated universal could be said to be in time.

It will not do to suggest that even if universals exist only if instantiated, and thus are in time, they would be subject merely to generation and corruption and not to alteration and locomotion, and that what is relevant to the necessity of a necessarily true proposition is not the *existence* of the entities it is about (although this may be relevant to its having reference and thus perhaps sense) but the immutability of those entities. For how would we then understand the immutability of universals? We can no longer say that it consists in their being nontemporal entities. Nor can we regard it as causal in nature. But then the only alternative left is to say that the immutability of a universal consists in the necessary truth of all propositions about it and thus to render the account of necessary truth circular. It should be recalled that we avoided the charge of circularity only by pointing out that the notion of the nontemporality of an entity can be grasped directly without an appeal to the necessary truth of any propositions.[28] But we can hardly say that a notion of immutability that is distinct from that of nontemporality or causality can be so grasped.

28. See above, pp. 150–52.

The question about the existence of uninstantiated universals is primarily a question about the concept of existence. There are two extreme tendencies in reflections on this latter topic. One may treat the concept of existence as one would, in general, any other concept. Then one would be likely to propose hard and fast criteria for its application and thus would often reach startling conclusions about what does and what does not exist. To be is to be perceived. Therefore, unperceived objects do not exist. Or, to be is to be located in space and time. Therefore, God, angels, disembodied souls, and uninstantiated universals do not exist. Or, to be is to be material. Therefore, minds do not exist. But such a procedure is not likely to do justice to the exceptional generality of the notion of existence. Such criteria of existence inevitably *seem* justified, for indeed there is an enormous difference between what they are intended to distinguish; and the purpose of conceptual investigation, as we have argued, is precisely to reflect in our concepts the similarities and differences among the various kinds of entities. For instance, there is an enormous difference between the spatiotemporal and the non-spatiotemporal. The notion of existence is usually applied to entities that are spatiotemporal. Are we not justified then to reflect these two facts by regarding the non-spatiotemporal as nonexistent? For if we do not are we not rendering the notion of existence so general as to be vacuous? This might be the defense of the first kind of tendency.[29] But such a defense ignores the fact that with a concept as supremely general as that of existence, the similarities and differences to be reflected in its delineation must also be supremely general. What grounds do we have for supposing, for example, that the differences between the spatiotemporal and the non-spatiotemporal, however great they may be, are indeed sufficiently great to justify identifying them with the most fundamental difference possible, that between the existent and the nonexistent?

The second tendency is usually a reaction to the first. Aware of the conceptual crudeness and philosophical fanaticism that usually characterize the proposals of explicit criteria of existence one is determined to be

---

29. But there is little doubt that what *motivates* the views expressive of this tendency is the feeling that one *knows* what it is for something to exist, that the *existence* of something cannot be a matter of what a word means, let alone of what it is illuminating or philosophically useful to say, even if everything else were. But this feeling, though doubtless it is present in all of us, must be resisted. *Existence* is a *word*. Its meaning is purely conventional, like that of any other word. Consequently, the criteria for its use must be subject to philosophical inquiry and perhaps revision, as the criteria for the use of any other word are.

ontologically liberal and unprejudiced. As far as the concept of existence is concerned, one would say, anything may exist: sense-data and material things, electrons and fields of force, the finite and the actually infinite, uninstantiated universals and God. For existence is not a property, one may add, and thus there can be no conceptual limitations to the sorts of entity that may be said to exist (as there are, say, to the sorts of entity that may be said to be red). The concept of existence has now ceased to be a genuine concept. It no longer serves as a way of grasping the similarities and differences in the world. Its application to something no longer tells us anything about that something.

Yet the defender of a view exemplifying the second tendency does not wish to *assert* the existence of every sort of entity that can be mentioned. He does not wish to say, for example, that centaurs exist. He admits that there are existential statements and that some of them are true and others false. This would seem now to suggest that there are criteria for the application of the term *existence*. For how else can the truth-value of existential statements be determined? But if there are such criteria, then the concept of existence does have a determinate content (even if we do not classify existence as a property), and that content must place some limitations on the sorts of entity to which the concept may be applied.[30]

Such are the two extreme tendencies in philsophical inquiries into the concept of existence. The proper way to conduct such an inquiry should now be obvious. We must preserve the concept of existence as a genuine concept and thus insist on its descriptive character and on the possibility of stating criteria for its applicability. But our delineation of its descriptive character and the criteria we state for its applicability must do justice to its supreme generality. They themselves must be sufficiently general to be legitimate. This does not mean that we could not argue that, for example, only the spatiotemporal or only the perceivable exists. But such arguments would have to depend on the discovery that the non-spatiotemporal or nonperceivable fails to satisfy the supremely general criteria of existence and not on a bare claim that it is self-contradictory or unintelligible to say that the non-spatiotemporal or nonperceivable exists, that is, that the criterion of existence *is* spatiotemporality or perceivability.

30. There is considerable similarity between the trials and tribulations of the concept of existence and the trials and tribulations of the concept of meaning. We seem to be, depending on the philosophical fashion of the day, also blown back and forth between the Scylla of razor-thin sectarian criteria of meaning and the Charybdis of anarchic semantical permissiveness.

A supremely general concept such as existence does not lend itself to the usual ways of conceptual elucidation. For example, it would be useless to seek illuminating analogies with other concepts. Such analogies are illuminating insofar as they allow us to see something that the concepts in question have in common, that is, to grasp at least the *possibility* of a more general concept whose species they would be, even if no attempt need be made to actually establish such a more general concept. But there is no natural, nontechnical concept more general than that of existence. Indeed, we may note the fact that there are other concepts on the same level of generality, for example, the concept of being one. But the similarity between such a concept and that of existence would consist merely in the level of their generality and not in any internal content which would be the object of a genuine elucidation.

It would be equally useless to attempt an elucidation of the concept of existence by removing ambiguity and disclosing (and perhaps codifying) the central and philosophically most significant sense of the word *existence*. For, at least prima facie, this word is not ambiguous. Indeed, it applies to fundamentally different sorts of entity and thus seemingly in accordance with fundamentally different criteria. But this is to be expected from a concept of supreme generality, and the different criteria can be expected to be different species of the same genus. Of course, we may suppose that *existence,* despite appearances, is an ambiguous word and that the criteria for its application are not species of the same genus, that they do not have anything in common. But such a supposition may only be the result of a philosophical inquiry into the concept of existence, and not what occasions such an inquiry, not what initially renders the concept puzzling.

Finally, the elucidation of the concept of existence can hardly consist in describing its essential characteristics, or in defining it. It seems false that any such characteristics of existence would be equally general, that is, that the concept of existence is simply a composite notion, a mere logical product of two or more characteristics. No such complexity is evident. Nor can such characteristics be on different levels of generality, as, for example, a generic characteristic and its differentia would be, for there is no concept more general than that of existence, that is, there is no genus of which existence would be a species.

One could give examples of entities to which the notion of existence is applicable and examples of entities to which it is not. (The supposition that the latter sort of example is logically impossible is merely a case of a crude logicism. Any fictional character or imaginary object can be given a proper name and would thus constitute such an example.) But we have already urged that one does not grasp a concept merely because one is provided reminders of its use. One must find a rule, a criterion for such a use; one must discover the sense behind the use. It is unlikely that we can state such a criterion nonredundantly. On this level of generality, the conceptual material at our disposal is necessarily limited. It is likely that any term offered in describing such a criterion would either be roughly synonymous with *existence* (e.g., *reality, actuality, being*) or would be far too narrow, since at best it would refer to a species of the criterion of existence (e.g., *perceivable, causally efficacious*).

To draw attention to the concept of existence in its full generality, to bring explicitly to mind, though probably not state, the general criterion of its application, we have to adopt an indirect, roundabout approach. We have to appeal, so to speak, to propria and universal accidents of existence rather than to the essence of existence. We have to appeal to something that all objects of the application of the concept of existence have in common and yet that is distinct from existence itself, though perhaps in some way necessarily connected with it. I have in mind the sort of relation that exists between something's being a sound and its being capable of being heard, or between something's being good and its being desirable, or between something's being a man and its being capable of laughter. It would be an error to identify the members of such a pair of concepts. Perhaps they are not even necessarily related, though we may believe that they are constantly conjoined. Nevertheless, we can render either concept in such a pair intellectually more visible by appealing to the other.

I suggest that such an illuminating accident, or perhaps proprium, of existence is that we regard the existent as that which we should take into account, that which makes a difference, that which cannot be ignored, that which confronts us—forces itself before us, whether physically, perceptually, or intellectually. Perhaps it is this feature of existence that prompted Plato's dictum that being is power. If this meant that only that which has causal efficacy exists, it would be merely another example of an excessively narrow conception of existence. But if it meant that only that has being which has power over our bodies or our perception or our thought—which can make a difference to what we are, to what we perceive, and to what we think, which constrains us into affirming or denying something and is independent of our fancy and caprice—then the dictum does seem to provide us with the sort of illuminating accident or proprium of existence that we seek.

What is that which could have *no* power over us? First, the absolutely impossible, the unthinkable. The power of that which is unthinkable is itself unthinkable. It is a prime example of what need not be taken into account, for it cannot even be thought. Second, the figments of the imagination, the mere creatures of fancy. They are, we are inclined to say, entirely dependent for their existence and characteristics on our thought of them and on our pleasure of continuing to think of them as such and such. And this is why we also say that they have no existence or genuine characteristics at all. But when we find that we lose our complete control over the creatures of the imagination—that they force themselves upon us and acquire power over us, that they must be taken into account—they begin to acquire existence, reality. When we hallucinate we no longer contemplate voluntarily produced mental images but something we have no control over. And for that reason we are inclined to (and usually do) take what we are so contemplating to be real.

The role of this accident or proprium of existence is especially evident in certain cases where we are inclined to describe something as existent and also as nonexistent. They are the cases of what might be called conditional existence. We create a mere figment of the imagination which would be a prime example of what does not exist. But the logical consequences of what is so created are, *relative to it,* not at all figments of the imagination. The plot of a novel or a mythological story is a mere figment of the imagination. But relative to it the various characters and events depicted are no longer mere products of thought: they have a place in the plot that cannot be denied them by a capricious act of the will, for then the novel or story would be changed. Thus such characters and events acquire a peculiar power of their own, a peculiar resistance to the caprices of our thought, and consequently allow us to apply the notion of existence to them, to speak of them as existent, though not "really" but only conditionally existent; they lead us to introduce the concept of what has been called fictional existence. If arithmetic were nothing more than a possible axiomatic system, then the existence of numbers would be conditional, in the same way and for the same reason as are the characters of a novel.

Let us ask again, can uninstantiated universals exist? The answer now is easy and can be brief. To say that uninstantiated universals exist would be to say that they have control over our thought, that they are not mere figments of the imagination, that they are not creatures of mere caprice. Now, if there are uninstantiated universals, the specific criterion of their existence can only be the logical possibility of their instantiation. To say that there is a certain universal characteristic would be to say that it is logically possible for something to have that characteristic. But what grounds do we have for thinking that this use of *existence* would be legitimate? The answer is clear. The logical possibility of the instantiation of a universal is the logical possibility of a certain kind of individual entity. And that is a hard, objective fact that has power over us, constrains us in our thinking, and is completely independent of our wishes and caprices. Such facts constitute the subject matter of any inquiry into the logically possible, the logically necessary, and the logically impossible, as in mathematics, logic, and much of philosophy. They constitute a *reality*, to which we must adjust ourselves and by whose demands we must abide, that is in some ways far more "objective" and independent than individual things themselves. Therefore, the concept of existence is applicable to uninstantiated universals. A universal does not cease to exist when its instances cease to exist. Thus, a universal is a nontemporal entity.

8. Intuition

OUR ACCOUNT of the nature of necessary truth can now be seen as completing our account of the nature of a priori knowledge. We have a priori knowledge when we hold a belief the falsehood of which would be incompatible with conceptual elements in the context of the belief. We can now, in virtue of the way in which we have introduced the concept of universal, become clearer about the manner in which concepts are involved in the context of a belief in a necessarily true proposition, the manner in which we come to know certain truths by mere thought. We shall find that there is considerable truth in the traditional view that a priori knowledge is based on a certain kind of awareness, on intuition. And, given the traditional view that a posteriori knowledge is also based on a kind of awareness, we will be able to grasp the point of the picture of knowledge as a kind of vision, as Consciousness, as a relation of the Ego and the Non-Ego, and we will be able to do whatever justice can be done to this picture.

The point of using the word *intuitive* in describing primary knowledge of necessary truths has been to emphasize that such knowledge is like primary knowledge of contingent truths in one important respect: that while necessary and contingent truths have fundamentally different objects, in both cases such objects are, in a very general sense, *perceived*. Indeed, something of this sort would have to be true. The mere fact that primary knowledge of necessary truths and primary knowledge of contingent truths both satisfy the general criterion of knowledge, namely, the unthinkability of mistake, is not a sufficient explanation. It can hardly be an accident that men have both knowledge of what they perceive through the senses *and* also of facts about universals. A plausible theory of knowledge must render intelligible how these two species of knowledge belong to the same genus. The traditional view attempts to do just that. In both cases, it would claim, a necessary, though not sufficient,[31] condition of knowledge is the occurrence of the perception of what is known. If the term *perception* is reserved for sense-perception, then we may use the term *intuition* to describe our perception of universals.

As probably is the case with every major philosophical theory that pervades the thinking of philosophers of different periods and convictions, this traditional view is of the utmost importance. There can be little doubt that when we determine *without inference* whether a certain proposition is necessarily true, what we do is not unlike attending to what we *see*. The commonness of both the philosophic and the everyday appeal to what one can *conceive* or *think* or *imagine* in such cases is significant testimony that this is so. There can be even less doubt that some such theory must be true if we are to understand how it is possible for us to have a priori knowledge. But the view cannot be accepted as it stands. It is exposed to numerous objections, most stemming from the fact that our paradigm of perception is sense-perception. More specifically, the view is faced with a dilemma. If intuition is quite unlike sense-perception, then it seems false that we are capable of it. If, on the other hand, intuition is significantly like sense-perception, then it seems false that it can have eternal truths, that is, truths about universals, as its objects. The difficulties of Platonism exemplify the first horn of the dilemma. According to Platonism, primary knowledge of necessary truths is the perception of nontemporal entities, where the entities are fundamentally different from the objects of sense-perception and the perception is fundamentally different from sense-per-

31. Not sufficient, for as we have seen (pp. 21–24), mere perception cannot be knowledge.

ception. But few philosophers have believed such perception possible. The difficulties of Locke's theory exemplify the second horn. According to that theory, knowledge of necessary truths is the perception of certain relations of individual mental entities, of ideas. But while such perception seems perfectly commonplace (it is, presumably, ordinary introspection), it is now inexplicable why it should yield knowledge of necessary truths. Why should certain relations of ideas be necessary? As Locke admitted, there are relations between ideas (e.g., coexistence) that are not necessary.

The manner in which we have introduced the notion of a universal allows us to avoid this dilemma and to get hold of the specific nature of primary knowledge of necessary truths. Universals are common qualities: the qualitative natures that may, though need not, be repeated in a number of individual things at the same time. To perceive a quality (characteristic, relation) of an individual thing is to perceive a universal. To perceive a relation between a quality of an individual thing and a quality of another individual thing is to perceive a relation between universals. To think of a certain quality of an individual thing is to think of a universal. Therefore, to perceive or think about universals one need not perceive or think about uninstantiated universals, or, even less, perceive or think about certain peculiar emaciated mental images.[32] We are aware of the relations of universals, whether by perception or by thought, through our awareness of the relations of qualities of individual things. Thus the first horn of the dilemma, on which Plato's theory is impaled, is avoided. Nevertheless, our awareness has universals as its objects, namely, the universals instantiated in the qualities of individual things, and not individual things as such, whether physical or mental. Thus we avoid the second horn of the dilemma, on which Locke's theory is impaled.[33]

There is ample independent support for our explanation. It is a commonplace that we determine the truth of simple necessary propositions by thinking about or, less often, perceiving individual things (e.g., figures on blackboards and collections of fingers), though not qua individuals but qua representatives of all facts of a certain kind. The appeal to imagina-

---

32. Berkeley was the first to make this point clearly in allowing for the kind of abstractive perception and thought that alone are necessary for primary a priori knowledge. See § 16 of the Introduction to the *Principles of Human Knowledge*. What Berkeley says there amounts to the admission that there is no limit to the generality of the universal one can think about, and thus to a kind of reconciliation between empiricism and Platonism.

33. Cf. also Aristotle, *Posterior Analytics*, 99b15–100b18. In 71a8 he describes induction as "exhibiting the universal as implicit in the clearly known particular."

tion, which is the most obvious form of such thought, is further evidence.

But how could mere thought provide us with knowledge? It seems clear that knowledge of universals obtained through perception of individual things (e.g., figures on a blackboard) would be no more questionable than the knowledge of individuals that is so obtained. But we do not regard mere thought of individuals as providing us with knowledge of individuals. Why should we regard it as providing us with knowledge of universals? There could be two answers to this question. First, to the extent that such thought takes the form of the entertainment of mental images, one might claim that it involves actual perception of universals on the grounds that mental images really do instantiate at least some of the qualities of the things they image. In contemplating the image of a certain blue coat, is not one aware of something that is actually blue itself, though it certainly is not the coat?

The second answer is more general and, I believe, conclusive. Thought of individuals qua individuals cannot provide us with knowledge because it can distort its object and even have as its object something that in fact does not exist. But no such distortion is possible in the case of thought of the *qualities* of individuals and of their relations qua universals.[34] The sufficient and necessary condition of the existence of a universal is the logical possibility of its being instantiated. We determine such a logical possibility, ultimately, by thinking of an individual that contains such an instance. The relations of universals, of which we can think by thinking of the relations between instances of such universals, are necessary. And, again, we determine that they are necessary by finding ourselves unable to think of them as being otherwise. What can be otherwise than it is, can also be thought to be otherwise than it is, and of such entities mere thought can provide us with no knowledge. Therefore we cannot have knowledge of the temporal, the contingent, through mere thought; we cannot know it a priori. But what cannot be otherwise than it is, cannot even be thought to be otherwise than it is, and of such entities we can have knowledge by mere thought. Therefore we can have knowledge of the nontemporal, the necessary, through mere thought; we can know it a priori.

We can now also answer one of the most vexing questions of the intuitive theory of our knowledge of necessary truths: why do we have

---

34. Cf. Descartes' "general things" (*Meditations*, I) regarding which we cannot be mistaken even in a dream.

intuitive, that is, primary, knowledge of only some necessary truths? If all necessary propositions describe the relations of universals, why do we have primary knowledge of only a few such relations? Why must I *prove* that a triangle has angles whose sum equals two right angles, while I need not prove that a triangle has angles only one of which can be right or obtuse? The answer is that the relations of universals, like their relata, are themselves universals. We have intuitive, primary, knowledge of them only when we in fact can perceive them or can think about them as perceived. We (or at least most of us) simply cannot perceive or think about as perceived the relation of equality between the angles of a triangle and the sum of two right angles, but we can perceive or think about as perceived the incompatibility of a figure's being triangular and its having more than one right or obtuse angle. Thus we draw the analogy between intuition and perception even further. Just as we have primary knowledge only of contingent facts that we *actually* perceive, so we have primary knowledge only of necessary facts that we *can* perceive, that is, only of universals and their relations whose instances we can perceive.

If the above reasoning is correct, it has not only the virtue of accounting for the traditional claim that our knowledge of necessary truth is intuitive but also the virtue of completing our account of the nature of knowledge by explaining and incorporating the view, dominant both in common sense thought and in traditional philosophy, that knowledge *is* a kind of perception. The conception of knowledge as awareness or consciousness is intellectually much too appealing to be an ordinary error. We can see now in what ways it is true and in what ways it is false.

I have already argued that the identification of knowledge with perception must be rejected. Knowledge cannot be the perception (awareness, consciousness, intuition) of what one knows. Perception often, in fact usually, occurs without corresponding knowledge, for knowledge is a certain kind of belief. Moreover, there is nothing unintelligible about the possibility of knowledge which is not, in any sense, based on perception. It is not impossible that we should find ourselves holding beliefs, mistake regarding which is unthinkable, even if such beliefs are neither derived from any state of awareness nor have as their objects anything that could be an object of awareness. Some accounts of knowledge by divine revelation purport to be accounts of just such knowledge. Some notions of faith purport to be notions of such knowledge. Nor is the mere occurrence of perception an explanation of why it should yield knowledge or why the knowledge it yields should be primary.

At the same time, while Locke felt no compulsion to define knowledge as the perception of our ideas, he evidently did feel a compulsion, as I believe we all do, to regard knowledge as a perception of something. I suggest that his reason was the recognition that perception, in the general Lockean sense of awareness, is in fact the standard, and perhaps only *source* of human knowledge. The criterion of knowledge, the nature of knowledge, is the unthinkability of mistake. This suggests nothing regarding the *sources* of knowledge, of the ways in which we come to have knowledge. Yet it is a fact about human beings that primary knowledge is obtained solely from perception. That this is the case with what has been called a posteriori knowledge is, of course, true by definition. Our purpose has been to show that this is also the case with what has been called a priori knowledge, yet not by adopting the usual empiricist account that leads to a denial of the necessary character of the truths we know a priori. If we have been successful, we should have achieved not only a fuller understanding of the nature of a priori knowledge but, even more important, a fuller understanding of the *unity* of a posteriori and a priori knowledge. We come to hold beliefs about which we cannot be mistaken by perception. By perception of the facts regarding the existence of certain particular things possessing certain characteristics we come to have a posteriori knowledge. By perception, which as we have seen could take the form of imagination, of the relationships between the qualitative natures of qualities of samples of particular things we come to have a priori knowledge. There does not seem to be a third kind of object of human perception. So human knowledge is derived from perception and falls naturally into two kinds. The recognition of this fact has been the basis of the plausible though erroneous view that knowledge is a kind of awareness. Knowledge itself is the holding of a belief about which mistake is unthinkable. One might acquire such a belief in all sorts of ways. The context of such a belief might contain all sorts of elements. In fact, however, men seem to acquire their primary beliefs only through perception, and the contexts of their beliefs contain only experiential and conceptual (universal) elements.

————————PART THREE————————

Primary

Perceptual Knowledge

1. The Argument from Illusion

PART TWO OF THIS BOOK was devoted to the account of the nature of the objects of a priori knowledge. More specifically, it was concerned with the concept of necessary truth, for necessary truths constitute our standard, and probably only, examples of such objects. Primary knowledge of necessary truths is due to the incompatibility of their denial with conceptual elements in the contexts of the corresponding beliefs. And, in addition to conceptual elements, all we can find in the contexts of our beliefs is experiential elements. But, of course, it does not follow that there cannot be a third kind of element, and thus it does not follow that all a priori knowledge (that is, all knowledge which is due to, or is reducible to one due to, an incompatibility of the denial of the truth known with non-experiential elements in the context of the belief) has necessary truths as its objects.

In the case of a posteriori knowledge such a multiplicity of kinds of objects is not only a possibility but a fact. In virtue of experiential elements in the contexts of our beliefs we can have knowledge, whether primary or derivative, of objects as diverse as our pains, the bodies around us, other persons' thoughts and feelings, electrons and mesons. Nevertheless, the standard and intellectually most significant object of a posteriori knowledge is the "external" world, the universe, the system of bodies that constitutes virtually the whole of our ordinary conception of reality. Most other objects of a posteriori knowledge are known derivatively from knowledge of bodies. Obviously, this is the case with our knowledge of the theoretical entities of physics and of the thoughts and feelings of other persons. It is not the case with our knowledge of our own thoughts and feelings. I do not infer my being in pain from observed facts about my body, and my pain is not a body or a part of a body even if it has location in a body. But a posteriori knowledge of something other than bodies is the exception, not the rule. The standard object of a posteriori knowledge is a body, a material thing, a physical object. The nature and possibility of such knowledge is one of the major problems of philosophy. At least the manner in which the problem should be understood, if not its solution, is crucial for an adequate account of the nature of knowledge.

The major question regarding our knowledge of necessary truths was that of the nature of the subject matter of such knowledge, of the nature of the entities, if any, about which we have such knowledge. The major question regarding our knowledge of bodies is quite different. There are important philosophical issues regarding the nature of bodies. But the importance of these issues is due almost entirely to their connection with the general issue of the possibility and nature of our knowing bodies. And the heart of this issue is the question, What is the primary knowledge from which knowledge of bodies may be derived? It is our answer to this question that largely determines what we say about the possibility and nature of our knowledge of bodies. The *general* answer to it has not been controversial. It is that we know bodies on the basis of sense-perception and thus that we have primary knowledge not of bodies but of our perceivings (even if only "direct" perceivings *of bodies*).[1] What has been controversial is the question of what, precisely, we do know when we know that we perceive something, what is the nature of perceiving something. Obviously, the fundamental concept that requires elucidation

---

1. Conceivably, our knowledge of bodies may require for its derivation, in addition to primary perceptual knowledge, also some sort of primary nonperceptual knowledge. For example, we might have to know certain necessary truths that would serve as principles validating the derivation. I am concerned in this Part only with the perceptual foundations of our knowledge of bodies.

if this question is to be answered is that of sense-perception.[2] This is the topic of this Part.

There has not been a problem of greater interest to modern philosophers, from Descartes and Locke to Kant and Schopenhauer, than that of the possibility and nature of our knowledge of bodies through perception, that is, the problem of the external world. It has been convenient to refer to it briefly as the problem of perception. But brevity has seemed to encourage misunderstanding. Perceiving—that is, seeing, touching, hearing, tasting, smelling—is not only the basis of our knowledge of bodies but also a physiological, psychological, and phenomenological fact. For that reason one may suppose that the traditional philosophical problem of perception is mainly an issue in physiology, or in psychology, or in phenomenology. But it is not. It is mainly an epistemological issue. It concerns mainly the evidential relation, if any, between the occurrence of perception and the existence and nature of bodies. The experimental sciences of physiology and psychology and the philosophical discipline of phenomenology may make a contribution to the solution of this issue, perhaps by clarifying the content of the perceptual basis of our knowledge of bodies. But the epistemological relevance and worth of any such contribution must be appraised separately and not merely taken for granted.

For example, when we are told that the fact that the proximate cause of a perceiving (e.g., of someone's seeing something) is an electrochemical event in the brain is a reason for a degree of skepticism regarding our knowledge of bodies, we must demand a clear explanation of why the neurological causation of perception should affect its evidential status. If mathematical knowledge is based on certain basic mathematical intuitions, and if such intuitions have neurological causes (as, surely, they would), would this latter fact affect the content and certainty of mathematical knowledge? We are also told that the actual characteristics of any perceiving are, to a large degree, due to the beliefs, attitudes, and emotions of the percipient. But exactly how does this change the evidential status of these characteristics? We are told that, in addition to the front surface of a large body, we are also, in some sense, conscious of its back surface. But is

---

2. Henceforth, for the sake of brevity, I shall use the term *perception* as a synonym of *sense-perception*, and my use of the terms *perceptual, perceive*, and *a perceiving* should be understood accordingly. Of course, they are not in fact synonymous; we can speak, for example, of intellectual and of extrasensory perception.

such consciousness relevant to the justifiability of our beliefs about the qualities of back surfaces? We are also told that the objects of perception exhibit characteristics that are not reducible to the distinguishable elements in the object and yet are inexplicable in terms of the contributions of memory and learning. But even if such a rejection of phenomenological atomism is legitimate, how does it affect the question of the legitimacy of our belief that there are bodies that have these characteristics?

The genuinely epistemological discussions of perception have usually taken the form of expositions and defenses of what is called the Argument from Illusion, or of refutations of this argument. For the Argument from Illusion is an attempt to answer precisely the central question regarding our knowledge of an external world: What is the nature of the primary knowledge from which our knowledge of bodies is derived, what is the evidence or basis that our knowledge of bodies may have? It leads to a conclusion about this evidence that seems to require us to regard our possession of knowledge of bodies as questionable. Briefly, the conclusion of the argument is that in perception we are aware not of bodies but of certain other entities, although it is of bodies that we seek knowledge through perception. Consequently, if we are to have knowledge of bodies, we must infer truths about them from truths about those other entities. It will be useful to begin our inquiry with a consideration of this argument.

Before the premises and conclusion of the Argument from Illusion are stated, it is important to introduce and explain certain crucial terms in such a way that their use in the argument does not beg the question either in favor of or against the conclusion of the argument. The first term is *perceptual illusion*. I propose to explain it by giving examples of standard cases to which it would apply. These cases are hallucinations, double vision, dreams, and bodies' appearing sometimes to have qualities that in fact they do not have. That such cases deserve to be grouped together can be shown by pointing out (1) that all of them are perceptual in character, at least insofar as their description would ordinarily include terms such as *perceive, see,* or *touch,* hence the use of *perceptual* in *perceptual illusion;* and (2) that all of them might be intelligibly, though mistakenly, appealed to as grounds or reasons for the making of judgments about bodies that in fact are false, even when such judgments are not actually made (perceptual illusion need not be perceptual deception), hence the use of *illusion* in *perceptual illusion*. The second term is *veridical perception*. Again, if we are to avoid begging the question, we must explain this term by examples of standard cases to which it would apply. These cases are the ordinary situations in which we would say that someone sees or feels a body (or a surface or part of the surface of a body) or sees or feels that a body (or a surface or part of the surface of a body) has a certain quality, where indeed there is such a body and the body does have that quality.[3]

It is important to note that the explanation I have given of each term is merely intended to draw attention to the kinds of situations (which of course are quite familiar to us) by reference to which the term is to be understood, and not as a *definition* of the term. Thus my explanation of the term *veridical perception* does not commit me to any particular account of the cases to which it is to be applied, not even to the view that our ordinary description of them as cases of seeing or touching bodies (that do exist) is true. Nor am I *defining* a perceptual illusion as a situation that might intelligibly be appealed to as a ground or reason for making what in fact would be a false judgment about a body, and that would be naturally described with perceptual terms. The definiens in such a definition would perhaps mention the genus under which perceptual illusions fall but not their differentia. A case of veridical perception may also be intelligibly regarded as a reason, though indirect, for making a false judgment about a body, but we cannot explain, without begging the question, in what sense such a reason would be indirect while that provided by a perceptual illusion would be direct.

A third term is *being sensorily aware of*. I explain first the sense of "being aware of" by listing cases such as one's touching a cat, seeing a mirage, feeling pain, being conscious of one's rising anger, and sensing the tension in the air. That all of these deserve to be grouped together becomes evident when we contrast them with such cases as one's walking, scoring a goal, digesting food, investing money. But not all cases of being aware of something are equally alike. Touching a cat is, in at least one respect, much more like seeing a mirage than it is like feeling pain or being conscious of one's rising anger. I explain "being sensorily aware of" by giving as standard examples of its application one's touching a cat, seeing a mirage, seeing a cat, and feeling pressure on one's foot, which I then explicitly contrast with one's feeling pain or being conscious of one's rising anger.

---

3. I ignore auditory, gustatory, and olfactory cases of perceptual illusion or of veridical perception for reasons to be explained later. Such cases have not been the chief concern of the Argument from Illusion.

The Argument from Illusion can now be stated as follows: (1) There are cases of perceptual illusion. (2) A case of perceptual illusion is always a case of someone's being sensorily aware of at least one entity which is neither a body nor a surface or part of the surface of a body. Such an entity is given the technical label *sense-datum,* and the Sense-Datum Theory is the view that the conclusion of the Argument from Illusion is true. (3) Sense-data are in themselves, though perhaps not in their relations to other entities, indistinguishable from any entities of which one may be sensorily aware in cases of veridical perception. (4) Sense-data and bodies (or the surfaces or parts of the surfaces of bodies) cannot be in themselves indistinguishable, for a sense-datum has been defined as an object of sensory awareness that is neither a body nor a surface or part of the surface of a body. (5) Therefore, even in veridical perception one is sensorily aware of sense-data and not of bodies (or the surfaces or parts of the surfaces of bodies).

The recent history of the philosophy of perception has consisted mainly of elaborate discussions of the relations of sense-data to bodies and of interminable wrangling about the soundness of the Argument from Illusion. It has been argued, for example, that premise (2) need not be accepted, that, in a very clear sense, in cases of perceptual illusion there are no entities of which one is sensorily aware that are neither bodies nor surfaces of bodies, that is, that the notion of "sensory awareness of sense-data" is either without genuine content or is a misleading equivalent of "seeming to oneself to perceive something though perhaps there is nothing so perceived." Premise (3) has also been rejected, either on the general grounds that the notion of "indistinguishable in themselves" is unclear and that what really matters is that sense-data *are* in some way distinguishable from bodies, or on the specific grounds that the premise, though clear and intelligible, is simply false because, for example, dreams do have a dreamlike quality and round coins do not look elliptical in the way in which elliptical coins look elliptical. Premise (4) has been rejected as false on the grounds that two things can be indistinguishable in themselves and still be fundamentally different.[4]

I shall not employ the Argument from Illusion, for reasons to be explained shortly. But it will be important to show that the familiar criticisms of the argument, such as the above, though not without value,

---

4. For some of these criticisms of the Argument from Illusion, see J. L. Austin, *Sense and Sensibilia* (Oxford: Clarendon Press, 1962).

are quite inconclusive. They all rest on a familiar assumption which I believe must be rejected if any productive philosophical inquiry is to be undertaken. This assumption is that a philosophical argument such as the Argument from Illusion must be formally valid and its premises unquestionably true. It is a contribution to philosophy to show that a certain argument is not logically sound, especially to point out the hidden assumptions which must be included as premises if the argument is to be formally valid and to identify the reasons that may be given for questioning one or more of its premises. It has been valuable to show that some of the premises of the Argument from Illusion are not unquestionably true and that if it is to be formally valid the especially doubtful premise (4), which is usually left out, must be included. Indeed, it would be worthwhile to inquire whether the argument is formally valid even as stated above. But it is a serious mistake to conclude from the fact that some of the premises can be questioned or denied without obvious absurdity, or from the fact that if some of the more questionable premises are left out then the argument becomes formally invalid, that the argument is unacceptable or unworthy as a basis for a theory of perception.

Philosophy is not mathematics. To suppose that a philosophical argument must be both formally valid and based on unquestionable premises is to misunderstand the very character of the philosophical enterprise. Were a philosopher to present us with such an argument he would have offered us a triviality that would neither excite our curiosity nor deserve our attention. What is interesting about philosophical concepts, unlike the concepts of mathematics, is not their long-range deductive consequences but their actual, immediate content and the direct and immediately obvious logical consequences of that content. If a philosophical argument is made formally valid, then its formal structure is likely to be of such simplicity that our attention would center entirely on its premises. And if the latter are unquestionably true and their meaning unmistakable, then it is unlikely that the concepts employed would have the sort of generality and problematic character that are definitory of the philosophically interesting concept; and the argument probably would not have been regarded by any philosopher as worth mentioning, let alone as constituting a philosophical contribution. Indeed, one may speculate that self-evident philosophical principles can be discovered which, jointly or severally, would entail either the truth or falsehood of all philosophical propositions. This was Spinoza's ideal. It remains true, however, that what we find important in Spinoza's philosophy is neither the self-evidence of his definitions and axioms (they are the main object of commentaries) nor the formal validity of his proofs (few of them have it).

One cannot reject the Argument from Illusion simply by showing that it is possible to deny some of its premises, that they are not unquestionable, that they are not like simple arithmetical propositions which command our assent with absolute authority. The interesting premises of an interesting version of the argument are precisely those that are not self-evident, that can be questioned, yet that after discussion and careful consideration seem plausible, important, and illuminating. Consider the claim made in premise (3). Of course, in one sense, there is an absolutely fundamental difference between veridical and illusory perception and between their objects. Most sense-datum theorists would describe this difference by saying that the objects of the former are associated with bodies and have characteristics that the bodies themselves have, while the objects of the latter either are not at all associated with bodies or, if they are, have characteristics that the bodies do not have. But merely to admit this is to leave out another, equally important, fact about the objects of veridical and illusory perception: that, *in another sense,* they are quite alike. We describe the latter in the language with which we describe the former. And at least sometimes we have the tendency to mistake the one for the other. How are we to understand this peculiar combination of fundamental differences as well as fundamental similarities? Are we to understand it on the analogy of the differences between snakes and some kinds of eels, differences that are fundamental although the two species really are quite alike superficially? Or on the analogy of the differences between the tastes of different kinds of tea, which seem indistinguishable to the novice but are quite different to the tea-taster? Or on the analogy of the differences between a man who is a United States congressman and a man who is a United States senator, whose distinguishing characteristics must be sought not in the two men as such but in their relations to other men and to institutions? The sense-datum theorist finds this last analogy much more appropriate and argues that both in veridical and in illusory perception we are aware of the same kind of entities, sense-data, though the sense-data of which we are aware in veridical perception have relations to bodies (or perhaps to other sense-data) that the sense-data of illusory perception do not have. And he will defend his choice by pointing out that we learn to distinguish between oases and mirages, real rats and hallucinatory ones, dreams and reality, not by concentrating on, examining, and revealing their intrinsic features, their *monadic qualities,* as we do in learning to distinguish between snakes and eels or between the tastes of different kinds of tea, but by considering their *relations* to other kinds of experiences and the objects of other acts of perception, that is, somewhat as we do in learning to distinguish between a United States congressman and a United States senator.

Similar considerations would be appropriate to premise (2). Of course, in a sense, hallucinating a rat is not a perceiving of something, for it is a crucial fact about a hallucination that its prima facie object is something that does not in fact exist. There is a clear sense, therefore, in which a hallucinatory perception can be said to have no object. Yet, to say just this is to ignore another, equally crucial fact about hallucinations (and dreams, double vision, etc.). Hallucination is not merely nonperception. There is a difference between seeing a rat on the table and hallucinating a rat on the table, but there is also a difference between hallucinating a rat on the table and simply not seeing a rat on the table when looking at and seeing the table. What is this latter difference? It is not that one's hallucinating a rat on the table is the same as one's not seeing a rat on the table but believing that there is a rat on the table. One can not-see something and yet believe that there is such a thing without hallucinating. Philosophers have often been satisfied to explain the difference in question by employing some such word as *appear, seem,* or *look.* They have claimed that to hallucinate that there is a rat on the table is simply to seem to oneself to see a rat on the table when there is no rat on the table. But the explanation so achieved is of doubtful value. For once it is made clear that the use here of such a word as *seem* is not that associated with uncertainty or caution (a hallucinator "seems" to see a rat on the table but not in the sense that he is not sure that he sees a rat on the table or does not wish to commit himself to the existence of a rat on the table), it becomes obvious that the expression "seeming to oneself to see a rat that is not there" now requires just as much (and probably more) explanation as the expression "hallucinating a rat." Like what other situations is the situation described by that expression? Is it like one's perceiving a rat? Is it like one's believing that there is a rat though one does not see one? Suppose we say that "to seem to oneself to see a rat when there isn't one" means the same as "to see a seeming-rat."[5] If the latter expression is intended merely as a technical synonym for the former, then the introduction of such a synonym would explain and illuminate nothing. On the other hand, if this is not the intention, if the latter expression makes clear a feature of the situation in which both could be used that the former leaves obscure, then what is that feature, what exactly is the difference between the two expressions? Surely, the only difference is that while the former expression leaves obscure the question whether when one seems to see a rat that is not there one nevertheless does see something else which *is* there, the use of the latter expression is intended precisely to make clear that in such a situation one does indeed see *something,* though only a seeming-rat, not a real rat. Thus we have come back to the Sense-Datum Theory.

Finally, consider premise (4), namely, that if two things are indistinguishable in themselves, intrinsically, then they cannot be different in kind. Of course, the premise is not unquestionably true. Much depends on the force we give to the use of the word *intrinsically* or its frequent substitute in statements of this premise, *qualitatively.* One could say that while a congressman and a senator are, in a sense, different in kind, they are, in another sense, in themselves, intrinsically or qualitatively indistinguishable, for one cannot identify them, respectively, as a congressman and a senator merely by considering the persons themselves. But one could also say that they are not intrinsically or qualitatively but only superficially indistinguishable, for their offices, their relations to other men and institutions, are facts about them which are at least as important as are their physical or mental characteristics. And a snake and an eel may, in a sense, be said to be qualitatively indistinguishable, though we could immediately recognize that they are fundamentally different in kind. The crucial question is whether the objects of veridical perception and the objects of illusory perception are distinguishable only in virtue of their relations to some other objects or also in virtue of certain characteristics which involve no reference to something else. If the former, the sense-datum theorist would have obtained the admission that he wanted; he could then ignore the question whether the two are of the same kind or not. If the latter, he would probably have lost the ground that he wanted to keep, even if, magnanimously, one granted him that the differences still allow for saying that the two are of the same kind—for such differences are

5. See A. J. Ayer, *The Problem of Knowledge* (London: Macmillan & Co., 1958), p. 106.

likely to constitute an immediate and obvious criterion of veridicality of perception and thus the philosophical wonder that gives rise to the Sense-Datum Theory would not occur.

I want to conclude, therefore, that the Argument from Illusion and the Sense-Datum Theory are far from having been refuted by recent criticisms. Their importance is undiminished. The Argument from Illusion remains one of the more significant philosophical contributions. It constitutes the philosophical recognition of the extremely important similarities between veridical and illusory perception. And the Sense-Datum Theory is an admirable attempt to explain these similarities as well as the accompanying differences in a comprehensive manner. They are a philosophical expression of the fundamental insight which finds striking everyday expression in quite familiar, quite common questions such as whether one is merely imagining what one sees, and which makes intelligible one's occasional hope that one's misery is merely a dream and one's occasional dread that one's joy is merely a dream. They constitute a recognition and account of the similarity between reality and appearance, and between truth and falsehood. It is unlikely that any other fact about us and the world can be of greater importance.[6]

Our problem, however, concerns the foundations of a posteriori knowledge, and the Argument from Illusion is irrelevant to the solution of this problem. The reason is fundamental. It is an argument explicitly dependent on a contingent, though extremely important, matter of fact, namely, the occurrence of perceptual illusions. It has as its premises propositions asserting the occurrence of illusions and describing the characteristics of cases of illusion. There are, as we have seen, excellent reasons for believing that these premises are true. But they are not the appropriate ground on which to build a philosophical account of the possibility and nature of a posteriori knowledge. Are we to say that if illusions did not occur no such account would be needed? Are we to say that if illusory perception did indeed have a special characteristic that distinguished it from veridical perception, then we would need no account of the justification of our beliefs about the existence and nature of bodies? If a race of intelligent

6. Should one doubt that such a question as "Am I dreaming or awake now?" makes sense or has a point, one might consider that the answer to the question involves a prediction that the questioner may verify. If I assert that I am now awake, I imply that I will not have a certain specific experience of waking and finding that my present experiences have been just a dream. If I assert that I am dreaming now, I imply that I may, perhaps even that I will, have this experience.

beings on another planet are, for some physiological reason, not subject to perceptual illusion, would they be incapable of inquiring into the foundations of their knowledge of bodies? To answer these questions affirmatively would be to deprive the theory of a posteriori knowledge of the crucial characteristics of philosophy—independence of contingent empirical fact and utmost generality—and to reduce it to a queer offshoot of empirical anthropology. Moreover, it is only on the basis of perception that we can come to know the contingent premises of the Argument from Illusion. But the purpose of the argument is to teach us something about what can be known on the basis of perception. The account of the foundations of a posteriori knowledge cannot rest on a part of a posteriori knowledge. To recognize this is not to doubt that such a part of knowledge is genuine. It is only to free the account from obvious incongruity and perhaps circularity.

The fact is that the problem of perception, and the more specific question of the nature of primary perceptual knowledge which is our topic in this Part, arise out of purely logical, conceptual considerations. If our knowledge of bodies is not primary, then this is not a matter of empirical fact but a consequence of the concepts of body, knowledge, and perception. If we are to have knowledge of bodies, then we must have another sort of knowledge from which it may be derived. This would be so even if perceptual illusions never occurred. And the characteristics of the knowledge from which our knowledge of bodies may be derived would be determined, if not solely by appeal to conceptual considerations, then by appeal to facts about all perceptual situations, whether veridical or illusory.

This inadequacy of the Argument from Illusion has received implicit recognition by philosophers who have argued that all that is necessary for the admissibility of the argument and for the acceptance of the Sense-Datum Theory is that perceptual illusion and complete intrinsic similarity between the objects of illusory perception and the objects of veridical perception be *logically possible* and not that they be known empirical facts.[7] But it is a mistake to suppose that one merely reformulates the Argument from Illusion if one prefixes some of its premises with the expression "it is logically possible that." For how do we determine that the so-revised premises are true? How do we know that perceptual illusion is logically possible? The logical possibility of perceptual illusion and of a

7. See, for example, Ayer, *Problem of Knowledge,* p. 95.

similarity between real and illusory objects can itself be determined only on the basis of an account of the nature of perception, of its objects, and of our knowledge of these objects through perception. But then it is just such an account that is the avowed goal of the Argument from Illusion! If we must have such an account in order to establish the premises of the argument, then we should have no need for the argument itself. We must therefore begin at the very beginning.

2. *Bodies and Perception*

A VERY LARGE PART of our thought and discourse is concerned with entities such as cats, human bodies, oranges, flowers, rocks, and planets. It is convenient to regard such entities as belonging to one kind, for they are clearly distinguishable from certain other objects of thought and discourse: for example, emotions, desires, and thoughts; or God, angels, and disembodied souls; or actions, relations, and states; or colors, shapes, and numbers. Philosophers have usually referred to such entities as material things, physical objects, or bodies. The first two of these terms have already acquired connotations connecting them with philosophical theories in which they have been employed. I shall therefore use the term *body* as the generic term for entities such as cats, rocks, and flowers but not for emotions, or angels, or relations, or colors.

I shall also use the term *perceive* as the generic term to which correspond the specific terms *see, touch, hear, smell,* and *taste.* The situations described with such terms, whether they be situations of action, or achievement, or relation, or state, would be referred to as *perceptual,* or as *perceivings,* and their essential generic feature as *perception.*

There is an intimate connection between the concepts of body and perception. We acquire the concept of perception by reference, primarily, to situations in which words for bodies would also be applicable. We learn what it is to perceive primarily by learning that what we perceive are entities such as cats, rocks, and flowers and not entities such as emotions, desires, angels, or numbers. Indeed, and this is why I have used the adverb "primarily," we do say that we perceive (i.e., see, touch, feel, smell, taste) colors, shapes, warmth, sounds, and odors. But this is not a primary use of perception-verbs, and it is far less common. We identify perceived colors and shapes, for instance, by reference to the bodies to which they belong. We regard them as essentially and necessarily qualities of bodies, at least insofar as they are perceived. We do not perceive the color blue or the shape triangularity unless we perceive *something* that is blue or triangular. And it is just such a something that we also describe as a cat, rock, or flower. Perhaps this is not entirely true in the case of sounds and odors. But there can be no question that it is true regarding visual and tactile qualities, and it is visual and tactile qualities that are constitutive of our conception of body, if any perceptual qualities are.

But do we perhaps perceive not bodies but sense-data, or the appearances of bodies, or the representations of bodies? Yet, it should be obvious that, in terms of the ordinary concepts of seeing and touching, and of cat and rock and flower, it is cats, rocks, and flowers that we see and touch, not the appearances or representations of cats, rocks, and flowers. We learn what it is to see and touch by learning that we see and touch entities such as cats, rocks, and flowers. And we learn what a cat or a rock or a flower is by learning that it is a certain sort of entity that we see or touch. Cats, rocks, and flowers may in some sense be representations or appearances of certain more fundamental entities, but it is the former and not the latter that we see and touch. And it is the existence and nature of entities such as cats, rocks, and flowers that constitute the problem of perception. The insufficient attention to this fact is an important defect of most *idealist* theories.[8]

What I have said above is not to be interpreted as the espousal of one of the familiar quick and easy solutions of the problem of perception. We shall see, when we consider the requirements for a philosophically illuminating account of the concept of perception, that the usual theories of perception can all be stated and defended despite our admission that the objects of perception are bodies. We shall also see that the question, How and why are statements about bodies justified? is not at all answered by direct appeal to this admission. For example, our account has left open the option (which we will *not* take) of regarding the perception of bodies as analogous to the imagination of bodies. One may, perhaps, perceive a cat

8. Sometimes it is argued that we cannot ("directly") perceive bodies because we cannot perceive all of the necessary characteristics of a body, for example, having a back and insides, being causally efficacious, or being capable of existence unperceived. This is like arguing that we cannot see a triangular surface if we cannot see the equality of the sum of its angles to two right angles. A similar answer may be given to another surprising but not uncommon assumption: that terms for bodies cannot be ostensively explained because not all of the necessary characteristics of a body can be perceived in any one perceptual act. Can *triangle* then be ostensively explained?

even if there is no cat before one, just as one may imagine a unicorn even though there are no unicorns. Our point has been that when one perceives, one, typically and paradigmatically, perceives bodies, rather than sense-data or representations of bodies, even if sense-data or representations are in some way present; just as when one imagines, one imagines, typically and paradigmatically, bodies such as horses or unicorns, and not mental images of horses and unicorns, even though such images are present whenever one imagines. It is important, however, to state the problem of perception in its natural setting, in terms of ordinary, natural concepts, even if eventually we were to revise these concepts in order to achieve philosophical understanding. Assertions such as "We perceive sense-data or appearances of bodies directly and bodies only indirectly," or "We sense sense-data and perceive bodies," or "What we are actually aware of in perception is not entities such as cats, rocks, and flowers but appearances of such entities," or "What we know directly is how we are appeared-to and not what bodies really are" may be defensible at the conclusion of an examination of the problem of perception. They have no value, however, in the statement of that problem.

So the natural concept of perception requires us to say that we do perceive bodies, that is, that we do see and touch entities such as cats, rocks, and flowers. But it is also true that the natural concept of body requires us to say that a body is necessarily an object of perception. We acquire the concept of body by reference to perceptual situations just as we acquire the concept of perception by reference to bodies. The concept of body is inseparable from the concept of perception just as the concept of perception is inseparable from the concept of body.

One can learn what a table is without perceiving a table, because it can be explained to one that a table is a *body* which has such-and-such characteristics. But it seems obvious that one could not have acquired the concept of body itself independently of perception.[9] Can one not happen to have images of bodies, without prior perception, *pace* Hume? Perhaps one can. But even if one could thus acquire the concept of body from images of bodies, when one imagines a body one would also imagine that one perceives that body. If one can acquire the concept of body by pure

---

9. Even if the concept of body is a priori, as H. H. Price argues, in the sense that it could not have been derived from any one or any finite number of perceptual situations, it cannot be a priori in the sense that it could have been acquired without reference to perceptual situations. See *Perception* (London: Methuen, 1932), p. 102.

imagination, to that extent one would also acquire the concept of perception by pure imagination. The concept of body—of entities such as cats, rocks, and flowers—is unintelligible apart from the concept of perception, i.e., of a situation such as seeing or touching. As Berkeley saw, the insufficient attention to this fact is an important defect of most *realist* theories.

It is in the intimate connection between the concept of body and the concept of perception, and specifically in the fact that it is bodies that are the typical, paradigmatic, objects of perception, that lies the explanation of the conceptual fact that perception is a prima facie evidence for the existence of bodies. It is a conceptual fact that one's perceiving something blue is a prima facie evidence for the existence of a blue body before one. No theory of perception can be adequate that renders *unintelligible* the provision by perception of knowledge of bodies. This should not be misunderstood. I am not suggesting that it is a conceptual truth that perception does provide us with evidence for, let alone knowledge of, the existence and characteristics of bodies. Whether it does or not can be determined only after the concept of evidence that would make this true has been given, or shown to have, a clear and distinct content. It is possible that perception never provides us with evidence for the existence of bodies. But what is not possible is that it does not even appear to do so, that it cannot be intelligibly supposed to do so. For this would violate even the most rudimentary requirements of the ordinary concept of evidence and thus could never be the conclusion of an adequate philosophical account of the concept of *evidence*.

Not only is it intelligible to regard perception as a source of knowledge of the existence and characteristics of bodies: it can also be said that if we have such knowledge at all it is *only* from perception that we have it, even if its derivation from perception requires the aid of some kind of nonperceptual knowledge. But this, now, is a matter of contingent fact. Even God could not endow us with a *concept* of body that is independent of the concept of perception. But it is not clear that God could not endow us with *knowledge* of bodies that is not based on perception (assuming that we already have the concept of body), perhaps by special revelation or, in Descartes' fashion, by providing us with a nonperceptual guarantee of specific beliefs we hold regarding the existence and characteristics of bodies. It may be that one could not acquire the concept of body unless one knew on the basis of perception at least those bodies through one's perception of which one acquired that concept. But it does not follow that one could not then acquire knowledge of the existence of all other bodies, quite independently, by entirely nonperceptual means. Nevertheless, while a nonperceptual basis of our knowledge of bodies seems logically possible, there are neither philosophical nor theological grounds for supposing that it is in fact available. The universal assumption, which seems to require no defense whatever, is that if knowledge of bodies is available at all, it is so only through perception.

It is a mistake to suppose that this assumption has been denied by philosophers who have claimed that in certain circumstances a statement such as "That is a pig" requires no evidence and is incorrigible. J. L. Austin has said that "If the animal . . . stands there plainly in view, there is no longer any question of collecting evidence; its coming into view doesn't provide me with more *evidence* that it's a pig, I can now just *see* that it is, the question is settled." [10] And he also has claimed, in the same discussion, that "if I watch for some time an animal a few feet in front of me, in a good light, if I prod it perhaps, sniff, and take note of the noises it makes, I may say, 'That's a pig'; and this too will be 'incorrigible,' nothing could be produced that would show that I had made a mistake." [11] But whatever Austin's intentions may have been in making these assertions, they could not have been to show that one's knowledge, in such circumstances, that something is a pig is not based on something else that one knows to be the case. For he clearly implies that there is something else, and actually explains what it is, by saying that the animal "stands there plainly in view," that "I see that it is [a pig]," and by allowing for the relevance of facts such as that the animal is only a few feet from one, that the light is good, and that one has prodded it, sniffed, and taken note of the noises it makes.

The question before us is not whether the statement "That's a pig" can express knowledge (whether "corrigible" or "incorrigible") but whether it can express *primary* knowledge, that is, knowledge in support of one's claim to which one would not need to appeal to anything else that one knows. And it is obvious that it does not express primary knowledge. If I am asked how I know that that is a pig, the question (unlike the question "How do you know that you have a headache, or that two and two are four?") would be intelligible (even if unreasonable); I would have to be

10. *Sense and Sensibilia*, p. 115.
11. *Ibid.*, p. 114.

able to answer it, and indeed I could answer it immediately by saying, "Because it is plainly in view, I see it, the light is good, it makes such-and-such noises." The "circumstances" in which I would say that I know that there is a pig before me are precisely facts of perception. It may be true that when the animal stands plainly in view I would not ordinarily say that I have *evidence* that it is a pig, but that I just *see* that it is. But this is not to say that my knowledge that it is a pig is not dependent on something else, namely on the fact that I see that it is a pig. One may say that something is a pig either because one sees that it is a pig, or because one has been told that it is a pig, or because one has seen pig-like marks on the ground, etc. But what one asserts in each of these cases is one and the same: simply that the thing is a pig. And there is nothing self-evidently true about this assertion in itself. In no sense is it not in need of support. Consequently the assertion cannot express primary knowledge, even if sometimes it would be *unquestionably* true. And if a statement such as "That's a pig" would not express primary knowledge, even in circumstances such as those described above, then it seems certain that no statement about bodies would express primary knowledge.

What Austin is likely to have had in mind is that one's seeing the pig *includes,* and thus *presupposes,* the fact that there is a pig before one and for that reason cannot intelligibly be said to constitute evidence for that fact. But if this is so, the conclusion to be drawn is not that the proposition asserting that there is a pig before one needs no support and that our knowledge of its truth is not in need of justification or evidence, but that what we thought provided the proposition with support does not really do so, at least not unless we revise our conception of it. For, as we have seen, the statement "That's a pig," unless one misleadingly and illegitimately includes in its actual content also one's grounds for asserting it, is just the sort of statement that does require support. We shall return to this question in sections 5 and 6 of this Part.

We may conclude, therefore, that our knowledge of bodies is indeed derivative, and that it is derived from our knowledge of our perceivings. Someone's unwillingness to admit this may only be due to his unwarranted assumption that by "knowledge of our perceivings" is meant something like knowledge of sense-data, or of appearances, or of ways of being appeared-to. Knowledge of bodies is knowledge of the existence, characteristics, and relations of bodies. Knowledge of perceivings is knowledge that someone perceives something, or that someone perceives that something has certain characteristics and relations. In speaking about knowledge of bodies I mean to exclude any reference to perception. I shall refer to statements which may express knowledge of bodies as body-statements, and statements which may express knowledge of perceivings as perceptual statements. Examples of body-statements would be "There is a penny in the palm of my hand," "The penny in the palm of my hand is circular," "The penny in the palm of my hand is not as shiny as the penny on the table." Examples of perceptual statements would be "I see a penny on the table," "I feel a penny in the palm of my hand," "I see that the penny in the palm of my hand is shiny," "He sees that the penny in the palm of my hand is not as shiny as the penny on the table," but also "I see something shiny," and "I see that this is shiny." To each of these perceptual statements, except perhaps the last two, there corresponds a particular body-statement: "There is a penny on the table," "There is a penny in the palm of my hand," "The penny in the palm of my hand is shiny," "The penny in the palm of my hand is not as shiny as the penny on the table," and perhaps "There is something shiny (before me)" and "This is shiny." I shall sometimes refer to such statements, in relation to certain perceptual statements, as the *corresponding* body-statements.

It should go without saying that one can have knowledge of bodies and knowledge of perceivings even if one makes no statements and even if one is unable to make any statements. A dog may know that a certain bronze cat is not a real cat. A child knows a number of facts about the world around him, and he knows sometimes that he sees or feels a certain thing even before he has learned to speak. An adult deaf-mute can have much of the normal adult's knowledge of bodies, of the ways they appear, and of perceptual illusions, even if he is ignorant of any language. And dogs, small children, and deaf-mutes show that they have such knowledge in a number of ways, some of which are more eloquent than anything that might have been said. To deny these facts can be the result only of philosophical prejudice. But it is convenient to speak of statements and of the logical relations of statements when we are really speaking of knowledge and of the logical relations between various kinds or items of knowledge, although we must not allow the desire for convenience to lead us into philosophical error.

We are able now to provide a schedule of the questions that fall under the general heading of the problem of perception—the problem about the possibility and nature of our perceptual knowledge of the existence and characteristics of bodies. The first question demands an account of the primary perceptual knowledge from which knowledge of bodies may be derived. What is the nature of perception? How are we to understand the meaning of perceptual statements? Should we agree with *Naïve Realism* that such statements are quite unproblematic, that they neither require nor lend themselves to any special interpretation or analysis, and that they support the corresponding body-statements directly and unquestionably simply by entailing them? Or should we agree with the *Sense-Datum Theory* that such statements make reference, at least in part, to entities of which we are aware in perception but which are not bodies at all, yet from whose existence and nature we may infer the corresponding body-statements? Or should we agree with the *Theory of Appearing* and interpret perceptual statements as being, at least in part, assertions to the effect that the perceiver is appeared-to in a certain way? Or is there some fourth interpretation of perceptual statements?

The second question concerns the content of our knowledge of bodies. What is the content of the statements that are to be justified by perceptual statements? What is the meaning of a body-statement? What is a body? Should we agree with *common sense* that a body is a spatially unified, temporally persistent, causally efficacious, mind-independent, publicly observable entity that is filled with stuff? Or with the *Causal Theory* that bodies are not themselves perceived but are the causes of the actual objects of perceptual awareness, namely, sense-data? Or with the *Theory of Sensibilia* that a body is a (probably infinite) collection consisting entirely or mostly of unsensed sense-data? Or with *Phenomenalism* that a body is essentially the permanent possibility of perceivings of a certain kind?

The third question demands an explanation and justification of the derivation of knowledge of bodies from knowledge of perceivings, of the inference of body-statements from the relevant perceptual statements. Should we agree with the *skeptic* that no such inference can be valid? Or with the *causal theorist* that the inference is one based on the principle that everything has a cause? Or with one of the many varieties of *Inductivism* that the inference is inductive? Or could the inference be after all *deductive,* perhaps even (as common sense would suggest) one based on a direct entailment by the perceptual statement of the corresponding body-statement? Or is it based on a *synthetic a priori* connection between the premises and the conclusion? Or is it an *independent para-*

digm of legitimate inference, one that neither can nor need be reduced to some other kind of valid inference?

It is the first question, that about the nature of primary perceptual knowledge, about the nature of perception, that is of special interest to us. We will touch upon the third in Part Four, although it goes beyond the limits of this inquiry. But it is the second question, that of the content of our concept of body, that must be discussed first, for neither perception, which as we have seen must at least initially be understood as perception of bodies, nor the derivation of knowledge of bodies can be understood except on the basis of a prior account of the concept of body.

3. The Publicity and Mind-Independence of Bodies

Discussions of the problem of perception have been bedeviled by the tendency to suppose that the main question is whether or not it is bodies that we perceive. (The question has sometimes been complicated by the technical distinction between direct and indirect perception or between sensing and perceiving. But such a distinction itself has had to be explained by appeal either to differences in the objects of perception or to facts about our knowledge of bodies, and thus it can throw no light on such differences and facts.) This supposition has tended to lead to the adoption of either of two extreme positions. One is that we do not perceive bodies at all, but merely certain peculiar, momentary, private, mind-dependent, two-dimensional entities, usually called sense-data. The second is that we perceive three-dimensional, causally efficacious, mind-independent, publicly observable, persistent through time, and filled-with-stuff entities, which are then identified with bodies. Neither answer is conducive to anything more than the adoption of a dogmatic stand on the problem of perception. The first deprives the notion of perception of its very heart: that it is entities such as cats, rocks, and flowers that we perceive. The second packs into the very concept of body all the general facts we wish to know about bodies and thus either makes one skeptical about the perceivability of bodies (I do not perceive the publicity and mind-independence of a body even if I do perceive its color and shape) or blurs important differences between the various characteristics of what we think we perceive (e.g., between those characteristics that one can intelligibly be said to perceive, such as color, and those that one cannot intelligibly be said to perceive, such as mind-independence) and thus confuses steps that must be kept distinct in the inquiry into our knowledge of bodies. For the various characteristics so packed into the notion of body are logically independent and quite different from one another. The way in which we determine that what we perceive has a certain one of these characteristics is likely to be very different from the way in which we determine that it has another one. Consequently, the question, What do we perceive? can be answered in many more than two ways. And the significance of this fact is not that one of these additional answers is more likely to be true but that the solution of the problem of perception must be understood as consisting of a number of distinct steps, each far clearer and more manageable than the schizophrenic worry whether it is bodies or sense-data that we perceive.

In this section I want to make clear the logical distinctness of the various characteristics we believe bodies to have and to argue that the ordinary, natural concept of body is not at all as gorged with essential attributes as is the philosophical concept of a three-dimensional, mind-independent, publicly observable, persistent through time, causally efficacious, filled-with-stuff entity. Bodies may (perhaps even must) have all of these, and still other, characteristics. But not all of them are constitutive of the concept of body. And thus not all of them need be taken into account in determining the nature of our perception of bodies and the nature of primary perceptual knowledge. Only by making this clear can we, I believe, render consistent two important facts about perception that must be acknowledged. The first is that it is bodies that we perceive, and, consequently, (1) that a perceiving constitutes prima facie evidence for the existence and nature of a body perceived, that a perceiving at least seems to provide, that is, can be intelligibly regarded as providing, one with evidence about a body, even if in fact it does not do so. It is this fact that endows *realism* with plausibility. The second is that we do not, indeed cannot, perceive an object's existence when it is not perceived, nor can we perceive its being perceivable by other persons, and, consequently, (2) that a perceiving does not constitute prima facie evidence for the existence of a mind-independent and public entity. It is this fact that endows *idealism* with plausibility. Berkeley and Hume argued that one's senses can never inform one of the continued and distinct, that is, unperceived, existence of their objects. They probably would also have argued that neither can one's senses tell one that their objects can also be objects of someone else's senses. Now fact (1) and fact (2) seem incompatible because we generally assume (3) that a body is necessarily, as part of its very concept, mind-independent and public.

Clearly, these three numbered propositions cannot all be true. The history of the philosophy of perception has been a series of proposals to sacrifice one of these propositions in order to save the remaining two. The skeptic and the idealist deny (1). But such a denial flies in the face of an obvious conceptual fact. We may deny that we know, or even have any evidence for, the existence and nature of bodies through perception, but we may not deny that it is at least intelligible to suppose that we do, for such a denial would amount to the denial that it is bodies that we perceive. The realist and the common-sense philosopher deny (2). But such a denial also flies in the face of an obvious conceptual fact. We may be able to prove, beyond all possible doubt, that what we perceive is mind-independent and public. But such a proof will have to rely on, in addition to the occurrence of the perceiving, principles whose truth is in no sense learned directly through perception. By itself, a perceiving does not even appear to constitute evidence for the mind-independence and publicity of its object.

I suggest that, rather than (1) or (2), proposition (3), that publicity and mind-independence are parts of the concept of body, should be rejected. If it is, we would be able to accept both (1) and (2) and thus do justice both to the conceptual fact that it is bodies we perceive and that a perceiving constitutes prima facie evidence for the existence of a body that is its object, and to the conceptual fact that perception does not even seem to tell us that its objects exist unperceived and can be perceived by others. But (3) cannot be rejected solely to preserve (1) and (2). Philosophy is not mathematical physics. There must be powerful independent reasons for such a rejection. I shall now try to provide such reasons.

It has been assumed by philosophers of perception that publicity is an essential characteristic of a body and thus that it is part of the very concept of body; that nothing can count as a body unless it is logically possible for it to be perceived by more than one person. For it is precisely the most familiar and unquestionable entities with which we contrast bodies—namely, mental images, pains, thoughts, and feelings—that are generally thought to be, again as a matter of conceptual fact, experienceable by only one person. But there can be no justification for making this assumption. It may be true that bodies are public (and there is no doubt that *one* crucial kind of evidence in support of a body-statement is another person's testimony), but it is impossible that publicity be a part of the very concept of body. For we must already have the concept of body in order to understand sufficiently clearly the very distinction between privacy and publicity, and, more specifically, the notion of something's being perceived by more than one person. To insist that publicity is part of the concept of body is to make the problem of perception not only insoluble, but unintelligible.

Whatever our views on the relationship between mind and body, surely we must admit that our paradigm of another mind is an *embodied* other mind. We acquire the concept of other minds by dealing with other human bodies. Even if we have genuine, comprehensible notions of nonembodied soul and of angel, such notions surely could not be explained without utilizing the notion of an embodied other mind. This is not to say that the concept of *mind* presupposes the concept of body. Nothing that I have said is an argument against solipsism and idealism; perhaps one can conceive of oneself as a nonembodied soul or angel. What I am saying is that the concept of *another* mind presupposes the concept of body. For even if one could imagine *oneself* as a nonembodied mind, one could not generate the notion of *another* nonembodied mind unless one were guided by the notion of another *embodied* mind. It is perhaps a matter of contingent fact that we are not in contact with nonembodied minds or capable of extrabodily (telepathic) awareness of embodied other minds. Nevertheless, our concept of *another mind* presupposes the concept of an *embodied other mind* and thus presupposes the concept of body.

I have stated the above argument in a more general and weaker form than it could have been given. It becomes stronger when we recognize that what has to be shown, if one is to claim that public perceivability is part of the notion of body, is not merely that the concept of another *mind* is independent of the concept of body but that the concept of another *percipient* is independent of the concept of body. The revision of the natural, everyday concept of another mind so that it would make the notion of nonembodied other minds intelligible is difficult enough. Its revision so that it would make the notion of a *nonembodied other percipient* (a nonembodied other mind that can see and feel bodies) intelligible is even more difficult. Whatever the notion of one's own seeing or tactilely feeling something may be, the notion of someone else's seeing or tactilely feeling something seems to me inseparable from the notion of the *body* of such a someone else.

Indeed, it is possible that if the concept of another mind presupposes that of body, then so does, though indirectly, the concept of one's own mind. For it can be argued that the concept of one's own mind cannot be understood except in contrast with the concept of another mind. If so, then the ascription of even private perceivability to bodies would involve reference to the concept of the body of another perceiver. But this would be a consequence quite compatible with our thesis. We would certainly also deny that *private* perceivability is part of the concept of body. On the other hand, such a denial is hardly incompatible with the fact that perceivability as such is part of the concept of body. There would be such incompatibility only if the natural, everyday concept of perceivability presupposed the sophisticated philosophical distinction between private and public perceivability. It seems to me obvious that it does not, just as the concept of color does not presuppose the distinction between blue and non-blue color.

Our conclusion is not, of course, that bodies are private entities, nor even that if they are publicly perceivable they would be only contingently so. We have no reason for denying that a body can be perceived by more than one person. And it is possible that one can *derive* from the content of the concept of body, together with certain assumptions, the proposition that all bodies are perceivable, somewhat as one can derive from the content of the concept of triangle, together with certain postulates, the theorem that a triangle has angles equal to two right angles. Our conclusion is merely that the concept of body does not, and must not be supposed to, include the characteristic of being publicly perceivable and, more generally, that the account of the concept of body has logical priority over that of the concept of public perceivability and over the general distinction between private and public entities.

There is a second, though closely related, reason in support of this conclusion. We are concerned with the concept of body because we are concerned with the question of the possibility and nature of our knowledge of the existence and characteristics of bodies. If publicity were part of the concept of body, then to prove that there are bodies would be to prove that certain entities (presumably the entities we perceive) are publicly perceivable. But how would one do this? Perhaps it is a matter of logical necessity that a pain can be felt by only one person. But what kind of logical necessity would guarantee to us that what we think we perceive is also perceivable by another? The fact is that, with the possible exception of certain internal feelings, we can determine whether something is or is not publicly perceivable only by determining whether *in fact* it is perceived by other persons or, more likely, whether it is of the sort of things that actually are perceived by other persons. We have no notion of a *property* of public perceivability that is not purely dispositional (that is, the presence of which in an entity can be determined in any way other than the actual occurrence of a perception of that entity, or of another entity of the same general sort, by another person). But now the only evidence we can have that an entity is actually perceived by another person is the bodily state and actions of that person, and thus the only way we have of knowing that an entity has the dispositional property of being publicly perceivable and thus can be a body is by knowing something about another body, namely, the other percipient's body. I cannot know that Smith sees the black cat on the road unless I know, directly or inferentially, certain facts about Smith's body. Consequently, if perceivability by another person is an essential characteristic of a body, then we can never know that there are bodies.

The existence of other minds and our possession of knowledge of what they perceive, think, and feel may be beyond doubt. But then even more certain would be the existence of bodies and our possession of knowledge of them. We must know that there are bodies in order to know that there are other minds. The problem of perception is logically prior to the problem of other minds. Any solution of the latter presupposes a solution of the former, even if each solution were to consist simply in saying "Of course we know that there are bodies (or other minds) as well as what (more or less) they are." If we have no knowledge of the existence of bodies, then we would have no knowledge of the existence of other persons. Consequently, no conclusions regarding the problem of other minds should be introduced as premises in a discussion of the problem of perception.

It may be said that our arguments are inconclusive. They may show that publicity is not a part of the concept of body. But they do not show that one could have the concept of body at all if bodies were not publicly observable; they do not show that public perceivability is not a *transcendentally necessary* characteristic of bodies. It may be argued that if bodies were not publicly observable then a public language would be impossible, and that if a public language is impossible then a genuine language would be impossible, including a language in which one would talk of bodies and express the concept of body. But such transcendental considerations, even if legitimate, are irrevelant to our denial that publicity is part of the concept of body. They are arguments for the proposition that bodies are public (or that at least some bodies are public and perhaps even, weakly, that some entities are public). Even if sound, they do not demonstrate that publicity is part of the concept of body, but merely that, mainly because of very general considerations about the nature of language, bodies are publicly observable, or at least that there are some publicly observable bodies. In effect, such arguments are designed to show that we do have a certain derivative knowledge that the skeptic has denied. But we are not concerned here with the truth or falsehood of skepticism. For by denying that publicity is part of the concept of body we are not committing ourselves to the unsoundness of any *argument,* transcendental or not, for the existence of public bodies. For example, we would not be doing so even if the above transcendental argument were a standard deductive argument. The fact that a triangle's having angles equal to two right angles follows deductively, in part, from the concept of triangle does not mean that the possession of angles equal to two right angles is part of the concept of triangle. In any case, a transcendental argument, as its very name suggests, is not a standard deductive argument.

It has also been assumed by theorists of perception that bodies are mind-independent entities: that it is part of the concept of body that the existence and characteristics of a body are independent of our perception of the body and that a body can continue to exist and preserve its properties even upon the cessation of our perception of it. This, too, is an extremely plausible assumption. One reason for its plausibility is the fact that the sudden disappearance or very brief existence of an alleged object of perception is often a ground for regarding the object as illusory, presumably because usually there is no explanation of such a disappearance or of an extremely brief existence of a real body. A second reason is that, as Hume saw, what is most poignantly at stake in the problem of perception is the *continued* existence of what we perceive, its existence even when it is no longer perceived. One concerned with the possibility of our knowing that there is an external world is primarily concerned with the possibility of the existence of what one has perceived even when one (or anyone) no longer perceives it and is only secondarily concerned with the general character of what one perceives (e.g., whether it is physical or mental). And if bodies were not independent of perception, they could not have continued existence.

A complete solution to the problem of perception must answer the question of continued existence. But to suppose that for that reason we must regard independence of perception as part of the concept of body would be both wrong philosophical strategy and untrue to the content of the concept of body. If we begin by assuming that nothing can be a body unless it is capable of continued existence, then as we have seen, we would find inexplicable the fact that perception provides us with prima facie evidence for the existence of bodies. But such an assumption would also fail to correspond to our concept of body, if not by being simply wrong, then at least by excessive exaggeration of what is at most a secondary feature of that concept. It is this second point that I want to develop here.

Even if a body is necessarily independent of perception, the recognition of this fact would not be at all illuminating, let alone sufficient, for our understanding the concept of body. For *what* is that which must be able to continue to exist even when not perceived by anyone? The mere fact that it must be independent of perception, however necessary, seems to suggest nothing regarding its intrinsic features. Not only do we fail to grasp the concept of body upon being told merely that a body is necessarily independent of perception but also to be told this does not even seem to suggest what that concept may contain. Independence of perception may be a necessary feature of the concept of body, but it certainly is not constitutive of that concept. The capacity to continue to exist even if not perceived is not a characteristic of a body in the way in which, as we shall see, three-dimensionality and solidity are. In a certain sense, we know what a body is when we are told that it is a three-dimensional solid entity, but we do not know what a body is when we are told that it is an entity independent of perception. In traditional terminology, independence-of-perception would be at most a *proprium,* not an essential attribute, of a body. And it is the essential attribute or attributes of a body that must be determined first in an investigation of the concept of body. We can determine what the propria of something are only if we can determine what its essence is. Consequently, independence-of-perception must not be included in the initial account of the concept of body.[12]

One motive for regarding independence-of-perception as part of the concept of body has been the assumption that mental images, pains, thoughts, and emotions are, as a matter of conceptual fact, incapable of existence when not actually objects of awareness. And it is with mental images, pains, thoughts, and emotions that we ordinarily contrast bodies. But, I suggest, this assumption is no better off than the corresponding assumption that bodies are, as a matter of conceptual fact, capable of existence when not actually objects of awareness. Consider the claim that a man under hypnosis may not feel the pain he has, or the psychoanalyst's claim that there are thoughts and feelings of which one is not aware, or the hospital patient's claim that a certain drug makes him not feel the constant pain he is in. Quite possibly, unless drastically reinterpreted, such claims are false. But surely they have prima facie intelligibility even without reinterpretation, and that is sufficient to make us unwilling to rest great weight in our inquiry on the assumption that the entities with which we typically contrast bodies are logically incapable of existence when not actually objects of awareness.

Let us suppose that we deny this assumption, that is, that we agree that mental images, pains, thoughts, and emotions may exist even if one is not aware, not conscious, of them. Would we then be even slightly less able to distinguish between cats, flowers, and rocks, on one hand, and images and pains, on the other? Would we, on this supposition, be at all unwilling to say that the images and pains that are capable of being unconscious are still images and pains? What could they be if not mental images and pains? Would we have the slightest tendency to suppose that they are bodies? Or, let us suppose, in imitation of a poor science-fiction writer, that because of the very special psychophysical conditions on a remote planet all objects on it that are smaller than a cat literally cease to exist when no one is perceiving them. Would we then say that the coins and pencils we may transport to that planet and see and touch are not really coins and pencils, that they are not bodies at all? What would a coin or pencil that exists only while someone perceives it be if not a coin or a

---

12. Thus, I suggest, we should agree with Berkeley that in claiming that houses, rivers, mountains, trees, stones, nay, even our own bodies, are ideas, in the sense that they exist only if perceived, he was not denying that houses, rivers, mountains, trees, stones, and our own bodies exist but only that they exist unperceived.

pencil? What would a mental image or a pain that can exist when one is not aware of it be if not a mental image or a pain? Would we be tempted to say that the coin or pencil is really a mental image and that the mental image is really a body? I suggest that we would not, because the essential features of the ordinary concept of body do not include independence-of-perception, and the essential features of the concept of mental entity do not include dependence on consciousness.

4. *Three-Dimensionality* *and Solidity*

THE ESSENTIAL CHARACTERISTICS of a body are very different from publicity and mind-independence. I suggest that they are two, although the first is really a complex of several characteristics. First, a body necessarily possesses a perceivable, though perhaps never as a whole, closed (spatially complete: "with back, top and bottom as well as front . . . : something which does not exist from any special place"[13]) three-dimensional surface, containing perceivable insides. Secondly, a body has causal efficacy: the space enclosed by its surface exhibits solidity, that is, resistance to the motion of other bodies through it, and perhaps certain other kinds of causal efficacy. As we shall see, in one respect, the first characteristic is primary, though, in another respect, it is the second that is primary.

The first can be understood as a set of several distinguishable characteristics, namely, (1) perceivability, (2) closed three-dimensionality, and (3) possession of perceivable insides. But these three belong together much more intimately than, for example, do three-dimensionality and solidity, and should be regarded as constituting one complex characteristic. The notion of the insides of a body is inseparable from the notion of its outside, and the outside of a body is a complete three-dimensional surface. And the notion of such a surface is not that of the "surface" of a mere geometrical solid (the notion of the latter is itself an abstraction from that of body) but that of a surface which is, so to speak, filled with, spread over by, or suffused with perceivable qualities such as color and warmth. Let us, however, consider the components of the first characteristic one by one.

13. Price, *Perception*, p. 145.

A body must be perceivable. **The** notion of a body whose surface has no perceivable qualities is unintelligible. This is why it is through sight and touch, rather than smell or hearing, that we acquire the concept of body. For it is only visible and tactile qualities that characterize the surface of a body. Smell and hearing are species of sense-perception, but they do not have as their objects surfaces of bodies, even if they can be said to have as their objects *bodies*. Taste does have surfaces of bodies as its objects, but only insofar as it coincides with touch. There is nothing unintelligible about the notion of a region in space in which peculiar phenomena (e.g., change of motion, melting, discoloration) take place; but such a region in space would not *be* a body, even if we deny that it is empty. The shape of such a region would be a geometrical, but not a perceivable, characteristic, and the region would remain merely a peculiar region of space.

Even if the existence of a certain body can be known independently of perception (e.g., by divine revelation), what would be so-known to exist would have to be capable of being perceived. If imagination is an essential feature of any kind of thinking, surely it is an essential feature of our thinking of bodies. And, as Berkeley seemed to argue, for one to imagine a body is necessarily for one to imagine also that one perceives it. Perhaps this does not prove, as Berkeley thought, that it is inconceivable, and thus impossible, for a body not to be perceived. It is a strong reason, however, for thinking that it is impossible for a body not to be perceivable. This is not to say that the so-called theoretical entities of physics cannot exist. It is merely to say that, insofar as they are logically incapable of being perceived, they are fundamentally, though of course not completely, unlike cats, flowers, and rocks, that is, that there is not sufficient similarity between them and the paradigms of the concept of body to make illuminating the application of that concept to theoretical entities, although, probably, there is sufficient similarity for the applicability to both of a concept such as that of a physical reality.

A body must have a closed three-dimensional surface. It may not be possible to observe this surface as a whole, but it must be possible to observe its parts in succession so that they could be regarded as constituting a closed three-dimensional surface. It must be noted that (bodies of) gases and (bodies of) liquids do have closed three-dimensional surfaces. That of a (body of) liquid is determined by its container. That of a (body of) gas, if the gas is at all visible, is usually not sharply delineated. But the fact that gases and liquids (as bodies, not as stuffs) do not have stable, characteristic, or even clearly defined surfaces must not be taken to imply that they do not have complete three-dimensional surfaces.

A body must have perceivable insides. An indication, though not a definition, of what this means is that any attempt to *break* the surface of the body would be unsuccessful, that any such attempt would at most result in a change in the surface of the body, and that any section of the body discloses a continuation of the "outside" surface. A body may be hollow in the ordinary sense of this word, and thus in a corresponding, though loose, sense it would not have insides. But, strictly speaking, a hollow body, in addition to the region it occupies, encloses another region without occupying it, and the latter region *is inside* the body but is not, nor does it contain, the *insides* of the body.

The second major characteristic of a body is its causal efficacy. A body must change the motion of any other body upon contact, whether its direction or velocity or both. A body must offer resistance to the motion of any other body with which it comes in contact. Without doubt, it is precisely because of this characteristic that it is popularly believed that one can prove the reality of what one perceives by touching it or pushing it or kicking it, and not because of any intrinsic superiority of the sense of touch. But while the kinematic manifestations of solidity are the most obvious, a body may also have other kinds of causal efficacy (such as the emission of heat and magnetic attraction).

Often, philosophers who have discussed the causal efficacy of a body have also attempted to *explain* it, usually by postulating the existence of a certain special entity which, rather than the body as a whole, is the real subject of the causal properties. Whether such explanations are legitimate, and how they should be understood, are difficult questions and seem to me to belong more properly in the philosophy of science. In any case, no such explanation need, or should, be included in the account of the very concept of body. What must be included in such an account is simply that certain characteristic, primarily kinematic, sorts of phenomena tend to occur in the region occupied by a body. It would be harmless to say that the cause of such phenomena is the body itself. But any specific explanation would no longer be conceptual in character, however true it may be.

Should we say that a body is an entity that (1) has a perceivable closed three-dimensional surface with insides and (2) is causally efficacious? It is important to note that these two characteristics of a body are not logically connected. For example, it is not unintelligible to suppose that another planet is populated with entities possessing perceivable complete three-dimensional surfaces and containing insides but occupying regions in which no causal efficacy is exhibited. Let us call them *apparitions*. A ghost, I suppose, would be an example of such an entity. Apparitions might even be publicly perceivable and mind-independent. We could have a geography of them. They might move, and we could study their traffic. There may be scientific reasons why there could not be such entities, but there are no conceptual reasons. Now, clearly, apparitions would not be real bodies, any more than a ghost would be a real man. Moreover, I suggest, neither would they be regarded as *real* entities of any sort.

Consider, on the other hand, another hypothetical situation: a planet on which there are no (indigenous) perceivable entities (other than the planet itself and the nonindigenous explorers), but numerous regions close to its surface offer, in varying degrees, resistance to motion. Indeed, the existence of such regions could be determined only by observation. But such observation would have as its objects bodies (nonindigenous occupants of the planet such as the explorers' bodies and their instruments) that meet with resistance in the regions but are not themselves occupants of the regions, and thus we could not say that we would observe the "solid regions" in the manner in which we observe bodies. Let us say that such regions are occupied by *unobservable solids*. We should not speak of the regions themselves as being solid, for the causal phenomena may occur in spatiotemporal series that we would describe as the motion of that which is responsible for them, whereas regions of space cannot move.

Would we regard unobservable solids as bodies? Clearly, we would not. We would not apply to such entities the concept of body, just as we do not apply it to a magnetic field or to the heat emitted by a body. Nevertheless, we would continue to believe that there are *real*, though mysterious, entities in the regions. In this respect there would be an important difference between an apparition and an unobservable solid. And this difference is merely a consequence of the fundamental difference between the two essential characteristics of a body. Both the possession of a perceivable complete three-dimensional surface containing insides and causal efficacy are constitutive of the concept of body but in very different ways. Only the latter characteristic is constitutive of our concept of the *reality* of a body, in the sense that its presence by itself guarantees the reality of something, though not necessarily of a body; the presence of the first characteristic is necessary for that something's being a *body*, but its presence by itself does not guarantee the reality of anything.

Why is it that unobservable solids would be regarded as real entities, while even public and mind-independent apparitions would not? The reason must lie, of course, in our concept of reality, which we have touched upon in section 7 of Part Two. Apparitions may appeal to our aesthetic sense. But, *ex hypothesi,* they would not *do* anything, they would not change the world around us. It is a logical fact that what is real must be at least potentially important, that is, significant to us, capable of making a difference to us and of affecting our lives. And it is a noteworthy fact about human nature that what seems important to men is largely what is capable of producing changes in their bodies or of restricting their motions. Our concern with the integrity, health, freedom, and existence of our bodies is absolutely fundamental. It is the unique importance of the human body that seems to explain the central place of solidity, and of causal efficacy in general, in our conception of a body.

Thus, in a curious yet not unclear sense, the essence of the *reality* of a body is, as Locke almost saw, its solidity or, more generally, its causal efficacy. And, in a correspondingly curious yet clear sense, the essence of a *body,* as distinct from the essence of its reality, is not its causal efficacy, but, as Descartes saw, its extension, or, more properly, its possession of an observable closed three-dimensional surface with observable insides. For it is this latter characteristic that constitutes the core of our conception of a body. We are inclined to say that an apparition is simply a body that does not offer resistance to motion and has no other causal properties. We are inclined to say that a penetrable cat is still a cat. What else can it be? An unobservable solid, on the other hand, is not an unobservable body. It is not a body at all, though it is of course something real. An apparition is something unreal, yet it can only be described as an unreal *body* (e.g., as an unreal cat or an unreal dagger). That this is so is perhaps a result of the fact that the possession of a three-dimensional closed surface containing insides is the epistemologically prior characteristic. We could not know that there are solid, causally efficacious entities, whether observable or not, unless we knew that there are observable three-dimensional entities, but we could know the latter without knowing the former. It is only through changes in observable extended entities that we learn of the presence of a solid, whether the latter be coincident with an observable three-dimensional entity or not.

Nevertheless, it is obvious that we could not say that the essential feature of the concept of body is the possession of a perceivable closed three-dimensional surface containing insides. For if we say this then we must say that mere apparitions clearly and unequivocally satisfy the concept of body, while of course they do not. On the other hand, to regard causal efficacy as equally essential would require us to say that apparitions clearly and unequivocally *fail* to satisfy the concept of body, and this again they do not. What then should our conclusion be? It should be that the ordinary concept of body has taken us as far as it could. It is too indeterminate to take us farther. At the same time, we should, for the sake of terminological convenience in this inquiry, render it determinate. We shall do so in the most natural way, namely, by defining a body as an entity that possesses a perceivable closed three-dimensional surface with perceivable insides and exhibits causal efficacy.

This definition offers no intrinsically important philosophical insight. The concept it determines is merely the logical product of the concepts of observable three-dimensional entity and causally efficacious entity. Such a concept is neither indispensable nor illuminating. A philosopher requires it only because a similar concept pervades the very foundations of ordinary thought and discourse. On the other hand, our definition of body allows for a clearer and more orderly conception of the problems of perception. It follows from it that our knowledge of bodies would be, essentially, knowledge of entities that, first, have observable closed three-dimensional surfaces containing insides and, second, are causally efficacious. Since the possession of an observable closed three-dimensional surface containing insides is the *epistemologically* primary characteristic of a body, our *knowledge* of bodies is primarily knowledge of observable three-dimensional entities and only secondarily knowledge of causally efficacious entities. For we can know the existence of the former without knowing the existence of the latter, but not conversely. The fact is that while nothing would be a body unless it is causally efficacious, we can know that a certain entity is causally efficacious, and thus that it may be a body, only by inference from certain observed motions and changes in observed three-dimensional entities. Our knowledge of the publicity and mind-independence of such entities would be further knowledge of certain facts about bodies but not knowledge of their being bodies. Thus whatever difficulties there may be regarding the possibility and nature of such further knowledge, they cannot affect the question of the possibility of our knowledge of bodies or lead us to deny that we perceive bodies.

Thus we may conclude that, contrary to the usual philosophical assumption, our knowledge of bodies is quite complex. It has as its objects a number of very different characteristics of bodies, each knowable in a very different way. The logically primary part of such knowledge is our knowledge of the existence and qualities of observable three-dimensional entities. Only if we have the latter may we also acquire knowledge of the causal efficacy, mind-independence, and public perceivability of such entities. But it is important also to note the very great differences between the ways in which we may know that what we perceive is causally efficacious and the ways in which we may know that it is public and mind-independent. While in both cases we must first know that there is an observable extended entity, our knowledge of the causal efficacy of such an entity can be the result of direct inference from perceived changes in the motions and qualities of other such entities in its vicinity. Our knowledge of the entity's mind-independence and publicity, however, cannot possibly be a direct inference from anything that we perceive about the entity or about its neighbors. There is *some* intelligibility to the claim that we perceive the causal efficacy of a body, for example, its deflecting the motion of another body. There is none to the claim that we perceive the mind-independence and publicity of a body.

It may seem that what has emerged as the first, and most important, question, regarding our knowledge of bodies, namely, whether and how one knows that there is before one an entity possessing a complete three-dimensional surface and containing insides, is a woefully emasculated and philosophically unimportant part of the problem of our knowledge of bodies. But this would be a mistake. The chief philosophical worry regarding our knowledge of bodies is whether through perception we may know something that we do not perceive. And this question is answered affirmatively if we conclude that we can know entities possessing three-dimensional surfaces and insides. For we would then know that there are parts of their surfaces and of their insides that we do not perceive. Indeed, we would not know that the body itself may exist unperceived, but at least we would have divided the question of knowledge through perception of the unperceived into two parts, one of which is logically prior to, and I believe more easily answered, than the other.

Our task, however, is not the solution of the problem of perception but the determination of the nature of primary perceptual knowledge. We have now specified what sort of knowledge we would expect to be *directly* derivable from primary perceptual knowledge, namely, knowledge of the existence of perceived entities possessing complete three-dimensional surfaces and containing insides. We have acknowledged that it is a conceptual fact about a perceiving that it constitutes prima facie evidence for the existence of such an entity, though we have not made, nor will we make, a judgment whether it constitutes genuine, real evidence. And we may assume that if any perceptual knowledge is primary, it is either knowledge of our perceivings or a part of such knowledge. Our task is to determine, What do we know when we know that a certain perceiving has taken place? It is really the question, What is perception?

5. *The Nature of Perception*

THE QUESTION, What is perception? is quite unlike the question, What is a body? As we have seen, a number of characteristics can be found in bodies. Some are clearly more fundamental than others. There are logical relations among them. Several distinguishable accounts of the concept of body can be offered, and one can be reasonably suggested as definitory of that concept. This is not the case with perception, however, the reason perhaps being that perception is not an entity at all.

At this moment the reader sees the page on which these words occur. Let him contemplate the fact he would describe by saying "I see the page on which these words occur." There is much that can be said about the page. One can describe its color, its shape, and the various marks on it. There is much that can be said also about the person who sees the page. One can describe his bodily position, his character, capacities, competencies, and the particular state of his sense organs. But none of these descriptions of what is seen or of the person who sees it would be even remotely illuminating regarding the nature of his seeing it.

We might have a complete account of the physical processes that the physiologist would call seeing. But such an account would not be even relevant to the account of the *concept* of seeing, for those physical processes are describable as the processes of seeing only by *correlation* with seeing itself and thus cannot be identified with seeing. A similar comment can be made regarding the view that seeing is a kind of behavior. Perhaps there is no mere *correlation* between such behavior and seeing; perhaps the relation is a logical one, in the sense that the behavior is a criterion (in some one of the Wittgensteinean senses of this word) of seeing. Even so, to *identify* seeing with any kind of behavior would be incompatible with the concept of seeing. In saying "He sees this page" I am not describing the position of his body and the movements of his eyes, even though the latter are my reason for saying that he sees the page. Nor am I describing any dispositions of his to behave or talk in certain ways, though I may infer such dispositions from his seeing the page; in fact, I am likely to be quite unclear about precisely what these dispositions are but very clear about what it is for him to see the page. And in saying that *I* see the page, I am not using my behavior, whether actual or dispositional, even as a reason for saying that I see the page, let alone as the subject matter of saying this.

It has also been said that perception is neither a state nor a relation nor a process, whether physiological or behavioral or mental, but rather a certain kind of achievement.[14] But even if this is true, we still must answer the question, What *kind* of achievement is perception? How is it to be described? There is a sense in which we can offer a complete description of the achievement of scoring a goal. But what do we say in offering a similarly complete and adequate description of my "achievement" of seeing this page? Do we say that I am now able to tell you what is on it? While this may be relevant, it is hardly sufficient as a description of the distinctive nature of seeing; and children, deaf-mutes, and animals may see without possessing such an ability. Do we say that I am now able to act in conformity with various truths about the page? Here we must recall what was said above about the identification of seeing with behavior. Do we say that I opened my eyes and directed them toward the page? This could be true of a blind man. Shall we add that my visual mechanisms must be normal and functioning? Ultimately we determine that one's eyes, optic nerves, and visual areas in the brain are normal and functioning by appealing, directly or indirectly, to the fact that one sees. But, in fact, it is not true that seeing is an achievement, like scoring a goal in soccer. What makes the belief that it is plausible is that the *establishment* of the seeing-situation, that is, one's *coming* to see, is an achieve-

14. See Gilbert Ryle, *The Concept of Mind* (London: Hutchinson's University Library, 1949), pp. 151–52, and *Dilemmas* (Cambridge: At the University Press, 1954), chap. VII.

ment. But *what* is so-established or achieved is not itself an achievement; it is much more like a state or process or relation. In scanning the horizon for the boat, I may exclaim, "Yes, I see it, there it is!" But then I could also say, a moment later, "Yes, I still see it, I have not lost sight of it."

One might, in exasperation, urge at this point that of course perception is neither a physiological state or process nor a kind of behavior, because obviously it is something mental. But when we acquiesce to such urging, we should still understand that by so describing perception we would have only made the first of a thousand steps toward an account of the nature of perception. It may be worth taking that step, as a way of avoiding materialism and behaviorism. But it is just one step. What kind of "something mental" is perception? An action? A state? A process? A relation? And *what* sort of action, or state, or process, or relation? The tendency of philosophers to indulge at this point in a profuse yet obviously technical use of words such as *awareness, experience, mental act, apprehension,* and *sensation* has confused, not clarified, the treatment of this question. Moreover, the description of perception as mental must be taken with caution. The paradigmatic situations of saying that someone sees something are not purely mental, for they certainly include *what* is seen, and that is not anything mental. Cats, flowers, and rocks are not like mental images, thoughts, emotions, and pains.

If no description of what is seen or of the person who sees it, whether of his body or his behavior or his "achievements," would illuminate the nature of his seeing it, may we not simply offer a description of the *seeing* itself, perhaps after we somewhat pedantically classify it, in general, as mental? We may not, simply because there is nothing that we can say about seeing as such. (The use of adverbs such as *clearly* and *distinctly* to modify the verb *see* may describe certain "accidental" characteristics of seeing, but they do not tell us at all *what* seeing is, they do not, that is, describe the essential characteristics of seeing. In fact, they probably do not describe seeing at all but rather the appearance of what is seen.) There is nothing surprising about this. There are many other things whose essence cannot be described in itself: pain, the color red, figure, individuality (i.e., the characteristic of being an individual thing). Such things are indefinable. But the reason for this is not, as commonly supposed, that they are simple, that they contain no constitutents or parts. Pink is a standard example of something simple, according to philosophers who distinguish between simples and complexes, but it can be defined quite adequately as a light red; its redness and the lightness of its redness are not constituents or parts of the quality but rather the quality's genus and specific difference. Perhaps those things are indefinable which are either summa genera or which do fall under a genus but have no specific difference that is distinguishable from themselves. An example of the latter sort is the color red: it does have a genus, namely, color, but does not seem to possess a difference distinguishable from itself. (What kind of color is the color red? Red.) Individuality, on the other hand, seems to belong to the former sort: it does not seem to have a genus (though we can verbally make one up, e.g., entity). But whatever the correct explanation of essential indescribability (indefinability) may be, the fact that some things are essentially indescribable must be recognized.

On the other hand, our inability to describe the essence of certain things must not be regarded as equivalent to ignorance or, what would be worse, to our possession of some ineffable special way of knowing them. We are not at all ignorant of the nature of the color red, or of pain, or of individuality, or of figure. And our knowledge of them is not the mere fact of our occasional awareness of them ("knowledge by acquaintance"), or of our capacity to recognize them, or of some special cognitive intuition unlike any of these. In fact, it consists in our (easily describable) knowledge of their similarities to and differences from other things— of their position, so to speak, on the conceptual map—and the proper account of their nature consists in the acceptance or rejection of, emphasis or deemphasis on, various analogies between them and such other things. Examples of such knowledge would be our knowledge that the color red is more like orange than it is like blue, that it is more like the color blue than it is like a figure, that it is more like a figure than it is like pain, that it is more like pain than it is like a field of force. To have such items of knowledge is to know something about the *nature* of the color red and not merely about certain accidents of it (e.g., that it is Mary's favorite color).

I suggest that perception is also essentially indescribable, in the above sense. It is in proposed or taken-for-granted analogies between perception and other things and in the search for such analogies, hitherto unnoticed, that we can hope for clearer, better understanding of the nature of perception. The useful theories of perception are nothing but considered and defended detailed emphases on such analogies.

There are, I suggest, at least four analogies that seem to throw light on the nature of perception. The first is the analogy with physical contact, for example, with a situation such as a book's being on a chair or someone's kicking a stone. It is the ground of Naïve Realism. The second is the analogy with subjective experience, for example, with a situation such as someone's feeling pain. It is the ground of Berkeleyan Idealism. The third is the analogy with imagination, for example, with a situation such as someone's imagining a castle on the Rhine. It is the ground of the Sense-Datum Theory. The fourth is the analogy with ordinary relative properties, for example, with a situation such as someone's being tall. It is the ground of the Theory of Appearing.

To offer an account of the concept of perception is to appraise these analogies or propose another one. By what criteria should such an appraisal be made? In respect to what, in the context of our inquiry, should the appropriateness of each analogy be determined? Clearly, in respect to the degree of illumination they throw on the possibility and nature of our knowledge of bodies. It is the derivative nature of our knowledge of bodies that occasions the philosophical problem of perception and the need for a philosophical account of the concept of perception. There must be a primary knowledge on the basis of which we may know bodies, if knowledge of bodies is to be possible at all. It is quite insufficient, though true, to say that this primary knowledge is knowledge of our perceivings, that is, knowledge expressible in perceptual statements. For saying this throws no light on the question, *How and why can our perceivings be intelligibly, even if falsely, regarded as the basis of our knowledge of bodies?* It is the appropriateness of the answers they suggest to this question that is the main criterion for the appraisal of the above four, and any other, analogies. This is why, as we shall see, the purpose of the analogies is not so much to provide us with understanding of what perception is in itself, in abstraction from its objects, but of what else is involved in the perceptual situation, of how perceiving relates to objects. For, in itself, perceiving is not philosophically puzzling. We cannot offer a useful description of it, but we know perfectly well what it is. How it fits in the perceptual situation is what puzzles us and requires philosophical illumination. At the same time, there are other, though not unrelated, criteria. The answer that an analogy suggests to the above question must also do justice to the intimate relation between bodies and perception. Specifically, it must do justice to the fact that *it is bodies that we perceive,* and to the fact that *bodies are by their very nature objects of perception.*

An acceptable account of perception must be as faithful as possible to the ordinary concept of perception, even if it must to some degree re-form the latter.

Let us begin with the first analogy, that with physical contact. If a book is on a chair, then there must be a certain chair (as well as a book). And, thus, if one knows that a book is on a chair, one has sufficient grounds for claiming to know that there is a certain chair. At the same time, if there is a certain chair, it does not follow at all that a book is on it; thus if one knows that there is a certain chair, one has no grounds for claiming to know that a book is on it. The reason it may be thought that perception is analogous to a situation such as that of a book's being on a chair is clear. Our perception of a body is generally taken to entail the existence of that body, and for this reason our knowledge that the former has taken place is regarded as sufficient grounds for our claiming to know that the latter exists. On the other hand, it is generally thought that while it is essential to a body that it be perceivable, it is not essential that it in fact be perceived.

The analogy has deep roots. It derives much of its force from the fact that in the case of tactile perception it appears to be far more than a mere analogy. And, as we have seen, tactile perception has a certain primacy regarding our knowledge of the causal properties of bodies, of the *reality* of bodies. The natural conception of ourselves and of the world around us requires that perception be regarded as a relation between an animal, not a disembodied mind, and an entity in its physical environment, and as an intimate relation, one of contact, not like that of being to the left of something or of being taller than someone. The natural conception of perception is the naturalistic one. A major trend in the history of the philosophy of perception, from Plato's account of the fusion of effluences from external things with the eye to the contemporary physiological account, is an eloquent testimony to the power of this conception. Yet, despite the eloquence of the testimony, the strength of the analogy on which it is based is not at all as great as it appears to be.

It may seem that the analogy is obviously inappropriate because it is one with a relation between bodies, while perception must be more than that if it is to serve as grounds for our knowledge of bodies. But while this observation is true, it does not by itself affect the value of the analogy. For, after all, it is an analogy; its basis is a certain kind of similarity, not identity. The crucial fact about perception which we attempt to understand by the use of an analogy is its relationship to bodies. And this relationship could be analogous to that between a book's being on a chair and the chair itself, even if a book's being on a chair is quite different in all other respects from perception.

But there is another, much more important reason for regarding the analogy as defective. The crucial logical features of the situation of a book's being on a chair are (1) that the statement "*x* is on that chair" entails the statement "That chair exists" and (2) that the statement "That chair exists" does not entail the statement "*x* is on that chair." In virtue of the second feature, the analogy provides for a crucial fact about perception, namely, that according to general assumption, though not conceptual necessity, a body may exist even if not perceived. At the same time, in virtue of its first feature, the analogy also provides for the fact that perception is regarded as the ground of our knowledge of bodies. In reality, however, the major defect of the analogy consists precisely in this first feature. For it makes it appear that the perceptual ground of our knowledge of bodies is logically sufficient, that is, that the statements describing such grounds *entail* the corresponding body-statements. But to suppose this is to suppose that our knowledge of bodies is really deductive, that our justification of body-statements is quasi-mathematical. Not only does this seem obviously false, it also renders the justification of body-statements unintelligible.

Entailment is an intelligible, indeed excellent, ground of justification whenever it is intelligible to suppose that one may know the truth of the entailing statement even if one does not know the truth of the statement entailed. For example, I can know the truth of the statement "John is taller than Peter and Peter is taller than William" even if I do not know the truth of the statement "John is taller than William." And because the first statement entails the second, the truth of the first can be regarded quite intelligibly, and with unquestionable correctness, as evidence for the truth of the second. But in many cases the entailing statement and the statement entailed are such that it cannot be intelligibly supposed that one may know that the first is true even if one does not know that the second is true. And whenever this is the case, one cannot intelligibly regard one's assertion of the statement entailed as justified by one's knowledge of the truth of the entailing statement. For example, it would be absurd for one to justify the statement that John is sitting to the left of Bill by appealing to the truth of the statement that Bill is sitting to the right of John, for it is obvious that one could not know that the latter is true unless one knew that the former is true. It would ordinarily be absurd for one to justify the statement that John is blond by appealing to the statement that all five men in the room, one of whom is John, are blond, for one could not ordinarily know that the latter statement is true unless one knew that the former statement is true.

I wish to argue that if body-statements are entailed by the corresponding perceptual statements, then this would be another case of trivial and evidentially worthless entailment. The mark of a trivial entailment is that one could not know that the entailing statement is true unless one knows that the statement entailed is true; or, we may say, that the truth of the statement entailed is a criterion for the legitimate assertion of the entailing statement. And, clearly, if the statement "I see a typewriter before me" does entail the statement "There is a typewriter before me," it could do so only trivially. It is not as if we could be independently assured of the truth of the first statement and merely *discover,* by using our deductive powers, that it entails the second. The content of the statement entailed would be simply *included* in that of the entailing statement. As the first analogy suggests, it would be like "There is a chair in my office" being entailed by "My copy of Hume's *Treatise* is on a chair in my office" and not like a remote theorem in geometry being entailed by the axioms and definitions of geometry. Indeed, insofar as in ordinary usage perceptual statements are taken to entail the corresponding body-statements, they are so taken in the sense that the truth of the corresponding body-statements is a criterion of the legitimacy of the perceptual statements. If we regard the statement "I see a typewriter before me" as entailing the statement "There is a typewriter before me," we do so only in the sense that we take the former to be asserting, in part, the latter. Unlike the case from geometry, we would then find unintelligible the supposition that one may be certain that one sees a typewriter before one but uncertain that there is a typewriter before one.

But if this is so, then any theory that claims that body-statements are justified by the corresponding perceptual statements by entailment must be false. For it would fail to do justice to the one crucial fact about perception that is not subject to controversy: that perception at least seems, can intelligibly be regarded, to constitute evidence for the existence and qualities of bodies, that is, that perceptual statements constitute prima facie, even if never genuine, evidence for the corresponding body-statements. Not only then would the truth of the statement "I see a typewriter before me" not really constitute evidence for the statement "There is a typewriter before me" but it would not even appear to do so, just as the statement "Bill is sitting to the right of John" does not even appear to constitute evidence for the statement "John is sitting to the left of Bill." At most, such a theory transforms the problem of the justification of body-statements into a problem of the justification of perceptual statements, without throwing light on either. It should be noted that whether in fact perceptual verbs are used in such a way that perceptual statements entail the corresponding body-statements is beside the point. If they are, then we should revise their meaning, or introduce other suitable terms, so that the prima facie evidential character of perception can be expressed in language. What alone is to the point is that, for the reasons we have given, there must be a logical gap between the occurrence of a perceiving and the existence and qualities of the body perceived if the former is to at least seem to constitute evidence for the latter—if the justification of a body-statement by a perceptual statement is to be even intelligible, let alone possible, we must admit that it is not the sort of justification that rests on an entailment relationship. This conclusion would play in the philosophy of perception very much the sort of role that the conclusion of the Argument from Illusion has played. For it amounts to a refutation of Naïve Realism, at least insofar as the latter consists in the defense of the analogy of perception with physical contact. By trying to make the perceptual justification of our beliefs about bodies completely unquestionable, the Naïve Realist renders it unintelligible. But such justification is not unintelligible, even if it is never genuine. Therefore, the Naïve Realist is wrong. To be even intelligible, the perceptual justification of our beliefs about bodies must always be logically questionable. But we have reached this conclusion by appealing to considerations regarding the nature of justification and not to contingent empirical facts such as that people sometimes dream or that bodies sometimes appear to have colors other than those they really have. I will return to this point in section 6 of this Part.

The analogy of perception with physical contact has an additional defect, the recognition of which leads us directly to the proposal of the second analogy, that with subjective experience. The connection between bodies and perception seems far more intimate than physical contact. While probably it is logically necessary that a chair be capable of having a book on it, such a logical necessity would be quite indirect. (It may be logically necessary for a chair to have a firm surface and that something having a firm surface be able to support a book.) One's conception of a chair does not in any direct fashion include either its having a book on it or even its capacity for having a book on it. As we have seen, the relation between a body and perception is quite different. It is essential to the concept of a body that a body be perceivable. We acquire the concept of body by reference to situations of perception. We think of bodies essentially as objects of perception. The relationship of perception to its objects is more like that of the color of the chair to the chair than like that of a book's being on that chair to the chair. The first analogy entirely fails to do justice to this fact. The recognition of it consists in taking seriously the second analogy, and Berkeley's main contribution to the philosophy of perception is to have done so.

Berkeley argues that the conception of an unperceived (not just unperceivable) sensible thing is unintelligible, self-contradictory. One of his reasons is that, in the case of sensible things, *existence* means being-perceived. But he also can be taken [15] to have another, more convincing, and for our purposes far more important, reason for holding this, namely, that one cannot imagine an unperceived sensible thing, that, for example, one cannot imagine a tree in a park unless one also imagines that one perceives it. The contradiction in question, therefore, is not a mere consequence of a definition of sensible existence. It is a contradiction in the more fundamental sense of purporting to represent an unimaginable, and thus for Berkeley unthinkable, state of affairs. A brown tree that is not brown is an unimaginable tree; and this is clearly due to the contradiction involved in the description of such a tree. A sour color is also unimaginable, but not because there is any obvious contradiction in the description of a color as sour. The case of an unperceived body, according to Berkeley, is more like that of a sour color. One need not define the word *existence* in such a way that "unperceived body" would be equivalent to "nonexistent body." An unperceived body is unimaginable regardless of the definition of *existence*. Imagine the tall tree in front of the house. To imagine it, Berkeley argues, you must also imagine that you see (or touch) it. That this is so is shown by the fact that you may only

---

15. The passage (*Principles*, § 23) is too unclear to bear out conclusively any specific interpretation. The corresponding passage in *Three Dialogues Between Hylas and Philonous* is even less clear.

imagine the tree as you would see it from a certain point of view. One's very image of a tree is part of one's image of one's seeing (or touching) the tree. And whatever the relation between imagination and thought in general may be, the intimacy of the role of imagination in thought about bodies is unquestionable.

There can hardly be stronger reasons for regarding the concepts of body and perception as inseparable. But how are we to understand their inseparability? Berkeley urges us to think of our perception of bodies as being quite like our feeling of pain. One cannot feel pain unless one is in pain. To this extent the analogy with subjective experience serves the same purpose as the analogy with physical contact. But the former goes much further. It is generally taken for granted that a pain must be felt in order to exist. Not only does the statement "I feel pain" ordinarily entail the statement "I am in pain" but the latter is usually held to entail the former, which would be to say that the two are equivalent. Now it is precisely because of this feature of the feeling of pain that Berkeley considers the latter to be the analogue to the perception of bodies. The existence of pain and the feeling of pain are inseparable because they are identical. He wishes to argue that the existence of a body and the perception of that body are identical. For how else could we understand the intimate connection between the concept of body and the concept of perception?

It does not matter that one may be unwilling (as we were, above) to admit that it is part of the concept of pain that a pain must be felt. Perhaps "I am in pain" does not *entail* "I feel pain." Nevertheless, the existence of unfelt pains is largely an academic question. Our interest in the existence of pains (to be distinguished from the existence of their physiological causes) is almost exclusively an interest in the feeling of pains. That this fact requires philosophical investigation does not diminish the value of the second analogy. Berkeley might have been satisfied with the concession that the existence of unperceived bodies is possible only in the sense in which the existence of unfelt pains is possible. But this concession cannot be made, for the second analogy has important defects, illuminating though it is.

To begin with, there is a flaw in the argument that the existence of unperceived bodies is impossible, since to imagine a body one must imagine that one perceives it. Even if we grant the premise, as well as the unimaginability criterion of impossibility, as the latter is ordinarily understood, the argument requires some additional premise in order to be sound. For, one might argue that the given premise is only trivially true, since to imagine anything is precisely to imagine one's perception of it. One might argue that this is what is *meant* by *imagining,* when we use the latter term in the narrow sense of the having of mental images and not as a vague synonym for *conceiving* or *thinking.* Imagination, in this sense, is imaginary perception. No wonder then that one cannot imagine a body without imagining that one perceives it. To conclude from this that a body cannot exist unperceived would be no sounder than concluding from the fact that one cannot be married to an unmarried woman that there cannot be unmarried women, or from the fact that one cannot *imagine,* have a mental image of, one's not imagining anything, that it is impossible for one not to be imagining anything. But while the argument is unsound as it stands, it is important. If the entertainment of mental images plays an essential role in thinking and in knowledge at all, it is in our thinking and knowledge of bodies that it plays such a role most strikingly. Berkeley's argument may not prove that unperceived bodies cannot exist, but it does draw attention to the fact that, since imagination is essentially imaginary perception and insofar as thought of bodies presupposes imagination of bodies, therefore thought of bodies is thought of bodies as perceived. This conclusion is not equivalent to the impossibility of the existence of unperceived bodies. To prove the latter we must employ an additional premise regarding the sense of *existence* when applied to bodies, a premise that can be provided only by a thorough analysis of the concept of existence. Berkeley did not provide such an analysis.

The failure of an argument in favor of an analogy is not, of course, a defect of that analogy. In this case, however, the failure of Berkeley's argument and the main defect of the analogy of perception with subjective experience are closely related. The argument fails because it does not show that the unimaginability of an unperceived body is equivalent to the impossibility of the existence of an unperceived body. The defect of the analogy is that it renders unintelligible our regarding perception as a ground of our knowledge of bodies. For perception cannot be such a ground if for a body to be is to be perceived. Let us take for granted that it is a matter of trivial logical equivalence that if one feels pain then one has pain and that if one has pain then one feels pain. (Unless we take this for granted, the analogy ceases to be distinctive.) But precisely because **we** would thus be taking for granted that the feeling of pain and the having of pain are trivially equivalent, it becomes impossible to speak of justifying one's assertion of the one by appealing to the other. It would be nonsense to attempt to justify one's assertion that one has pain by appealing to the fact that one feels pain. It would be like attempting to justify one's assertion that John is taller than Bill by appealing to the fact that Bill is shorter than John. Now, were the perception of bodies like the feeling of pain in this respect, it would be nonsense also to attempt to justify one's assertion that there is a typewriter before one by appealing to the fact that one sees a typewriter. But this is not nonsense. On the contrary, the central feature of perception is that it constitutes a prima facie ground for our knowledge of bodies, that we think we may justify body-statements by appealing to perceptual statements. For, as we have seen, our knowledge of bodies is derivative and thus stands in need of justification, and perception alone can in fact provide such justification. It may be that the justification perception provides is absolutely sufficient, yet justification it must be. Or, it may be that in fact perception provides no justification at all, that the skeptic is right; yet it must be at least intelligible to suppose that it does.

The defect of the analogy with subjective experience is thus an even severer form of the main defect of the analogy with physical contact. If perceptual statements must not be understood as entailing the corresponding body-statements, then they certainly must not be understood as logically equivalent to the corresponding body-statements. In either case violence would be done to the justificatory function of perception with regard to our knowledge of bodies. The third analogy, that with imagination, is an attempt to avoid this defect. And to be at all successful, it must offer a rather special analysis of perceptual statements. It is this analysis that is its chief merit.

A perceptual statement cannot entail the corresponding body-statement, yet it must at least seem to provide the latter with justification. Of course, as ordinarily used, perceptual statements do entail the corresponding body-statements. But, it can be argued, the reason for this is that ordinarily a perceptual statement really makes two separable assertions. One of these is the assertion of the corresponding body-statement. The other is that which the perceptual statement asserts in addition to the corresponding body-statement. That there is such a second assertion is obvious. Even if "I see a typewriter before me" entails "There is a typewriter before me," the former clearly says more than just that there is a typewriter before me. That something more is the pure perceptual residue of the content of the statement. And, since it is the only element of that content which is additional to the assertion of the corresponding body-statement, it must be the element which alone can serve as evidence for the truth of the body-statement. In addition to asserting the existence of a certain body, an ordinary perceptual statement says something else, something which alone may provide a reason for the truth of that assertion but which is neither identical with it nor entails it. Thus an ordinary perceptual statement is equivalent to, or could be analyzed as, the conjunction of a body-statement and a *pure perceptual statement.* The reason we employ ordinary perceptual statements, rather than pure perceptual statements, is likely to be the very considerable reliability of the evidence that would be provided by a pure perceptual statement; we have come to interpret what would have been pure perceptual statements as including the usual consequences of their truth, somewhat as the statement "It has been raining" is often used in such a way as to include the assertion that the ground is wet. The defender of the analogy with imagination would point out that some such analysis of ordinary perceptual statements is absolutely necessary if we are to make sense of their justificatory function and that it must be present in all plausible accounts of perception. What distinguishes such accounts is the manner in which they interpret the perceptual residue in an ordinary perceptual statement.

What then is the nature of the perceptual residue in an ordinary perceptual statement? Could it be one's inclination to believe the corresponding body-statement? But even if such an inclination is present in perception, it can hardly be that which constitutes our evidence for body-statements. For to have evidence for such statements is to have evidence for certain beliefs about bodies; and one's holding such a belief, let alone one's inclination to hold it, cannot intelligibly be regarded by itself as evidence for the truth of the belief. (One's belief that p may constitute inductive evidence for p, in the sense that one ordinarily would not believe what one is not justified in believing. But one of the premises of such inductive reasoning is that at least sometimes one has *another* kind of evidence for one's belief that p.) Could the perceptual residue be something else in the perceiver, such as his emotions, attitudes, or pains? But what would any of these have to do with the truth of one's belief about the existence of a body? The fact is that the philosophical account of the perceptual residue is really the account of the nature of perception, and thus, as we have seen, it would not consist in a discovery of some hitherto unnoticed element or in the recognition of the identity of the residue with some familiar other entity or state. Such an account may only consist in the drawing of a certain analogy. And, according to the defender of the third analogy, the proper account is provided by the analogy of perception with imagination.

One does not just imagine. One necessarily imagines *something,* usually a body. But one's imagining something is neither equivalent to, nor does it entail, the existence of what is imagined. Frequently we imagine what we *know* does not exist, yet our imagining it is in no way less genuine. Nevertheless, while what we imagine need not exist, something else must exist if imagining is to occur. That something else is the mental image, which is like, but not identical with, the object imagined. For how else would we distinguish between *imagining* something and *thinking* about it, how else would we understand the point of saying, for example, that while we may think of a thousand-sided polygon we cannot imagine one? In any case, the existence of mental images is a phenomenological fact. It should no more be questioned than should the existence of pains. To admit this is not of course to admit that it is images that we imagine rather than *what* they are images of. To imagine a certain tree I must have, I must be aware of, a mental image of that tree, but it is the tree, not the image, that I imagine.

Now what is important for the third analogy is that the existence of the image is what is essential to imagination, not the existence of the object imagined. According to it, perception of bodies is like imagination of bodies in that the existence of the body perceived is neither a necessary nor a sufficient condition of our perception of it, and what is essential for our perception of it is the awareness of another sort of entity, a sensible appearance, impression, or sense-datum, that resembles a body but is neither a part of nor identical with a body. Our awareness of such an entity does not itself present us with any problems, just as our awareness of pains and of mental images does not. With respect to such entities, one's awareness of them and their existence indeed are equivalent. Hence the former is not, nor need be, taken as evidence for the latter: to the extent to which the former is self-evident, so is, and to precisely the same degree, the latter, and conversely. Thus the third analogy has the great advantage over the first two of making quite clear the distinction between knowledge of perceivings and knowledge of bodies and of rendering quite intelligible the fact that it is of our perceivings, and not of bodies, that we have primary knowledge. According to it, our knowledge of our perceivings is like our knowledge of our pains, while our knowledge of bodies is obviously and definitely inferential.

But this advantage of the third analogy is bought at a very high price. For it completely fails to do justice to what in fact requires an account: the justificatory function of perception. However similar an image and its object may be, the existence of the former is not in any sense evidence for the existence of the latter. My having a mental image of a castle on the Rhine is in no sense intelligibly describable as evidence for the existence of such a castle. Insofar as perception is like imagination, it could not even *seem* to provide us with knowledge of bodies. Indeed, the philosophers defending this analogy sometimes do conclude, heroically, that perception is no more a ground for knowledge of its objects than is imagination, that all we really know through perception is the "images" of bodies. But even if this were true it would not be a solution of the problem. Perhaps perception does not provide us with genuine evidence for our beliefs about bodies. But, quite unlike imagination, it at least *seems* to provide us with evidence—it is at least intelligible to suppose that it does—and this fact about perception must be taken into account by any adequate theory of perception. The defect of the third analogy, and of the Sense-Datum Theory that is based on it, is not so much that it requires us to deny that perception justifies our beliefs about bodies, that it leads to skepticism, but that it requires us to deny the fact that it is intelligible to suppose that perception has this justificatory function. And this fact is the essential and philosophically most interesting characteristic of the concept of perception and cannot be subject of controversy.

Thus we seem to be left with the fourth analogy, that with the possession of relative properties, for example, a situation such as *x*'s being tall. The analogy is suggested by the existence in ordinary language of the terminology of appearing (looking, seeming). In addition to saying what the bodies we perceive *are,* we can say what they *appear* or *seem* to be, what they *look* like. In examining a hat, I can say that it is blue, but also I can say, though not equivalently, that it looks blue. There are two important facts about this terminology. First, it is plausible to suppose that my knowledge of the appearances of bodies, e.g., of the fact that the hat looks blue, is primary, while my knowledge of what bodies are, e.g., of the fact that the hat is blue, is derivative. Second, it is plausible to suppose that while what a body appears to be never entails what that body is, the former does provide us with evidence for the latter in a perfectly clear and noncontroversial way. It is not surprising, therefore, that many philosophers have described the facts of perception and of our knowledge of bodies by employing the terminology of appearing and have adopted the Theory of Appearing. But, of course, to adopt a theory of perception is not just to adopt a certain terminology. It is at least to claim that the terminology adopted allows us to understand the facts we describe with it more adequately, more clearly, more perspicuously. How could the adoption of a mere terminology do all this? Surely, only because it suggests that the subject matter to which it is applied has a certain character, a certain nature. And that suggestion is likely to amount to an implicit analogy between the subject matter in question and some other sort of situation, one with which we would not ordinarily, but in fact ought to, compare the former. Indeed, I submit, this is just what lies behind the adoption of the terminology of appearing.

Unlike the statement "This is blue," the statement "This looks blue" can be regarded as an incomplete relational statement, that is, as one that ascribes to *this* a relative property. If made logically complete, it would become a statement of the form "This looks blue to x," for example, "This looks blue to me" or "This looks blue to anyone who perceives it in the present circumstances." Thus "This looks blue" would be like the statement "John is tall." The latter is an incomplete relational statement, the complete version of which would be some statement of the form "John is taller than x," for example, "John is taller than Peter" or "John is taller than the average person." Now a statement such as "John is taller than Peter" has an intimate relationship to another sort of statement about John, for example, "John is six feet tall" or "John's height is six feet." And the point of the Theory of Appearing is that the relationship between the statements "This is blue" and "This looks blue to me" is analogous to the relationship between the statements "John is six feet tall" and "John is taller than Peter." Given that "This is blue" is a body-statement and that "This looks blue to me" is a perceptual statement and that the truth of the latter is the object of primary knowledge that serves as evidence for the truth of the former, this analogy appears to illuminate the nature of perception and to avoid the disadvantages of the other three analogies.

The statement that John is taller than Peter does not entail any statement that ascribes to John a certain definite height. Knowing the former is not the same as knowing the latter, and, often, knowing the former may mislead us into making a false judgment about the latter. Nevertheless, it certainly has an evidential relationship to such a statement. If I know the relations of John's height to the height of a sufficient and representative number of other persons, I will be able to come to know his height. And knowing one such relation is, prima facie, at least a step in achieving that knowledge. At the same time, John's actual height is independent of its relations to the heights of other persons and in fact partly determines those relations. Even if there were no other persons for him to be compared with, he would still have a certain size, and a determinate one at that. In a similar fashion, now, we may say that a body appears in a certain way to the perceiver, that the way it appears never entails what it actually is (in fact it may mislead us) yet serves as evidence for what it is, and that what a body actually is is independent of how it appears to us and in fact partly determines the latter.

But the analogy with the possession of relative properties has at least two defects. The first is that it requires us to suppose that while the occurrence of perception does not entail what characteristics the body perceived has, it does entail that there is such a body. For while x's being taller than y does not entail how tall x is, it does entail that there is something which is taller than y. Consequently, the analogy would illuminate at most how perception may provide us with knowledge of the *qualities* of bodies. It would tell us nothing about how perception may provide us with knowledge of the *existence* of bodies (unless it simply admits the entailment of the existence of bodies and thus, in this respect, collapses into the first analogy, sharing the latter's inadequacy). The Theory of Appearing has attempted to eliminate this defect by constructing such locutions as "x is appeared-to bluely" and "There appears something blue to x." But such locutions, if intelligible at all, must be understood as ascribing to x, the perceiver, a monadic property and not a relation to something else. Therefore, they are no longer the result of the analogy with the possession of relative properties. In fact, unless they are a confused version of the second analogy, that with subjective experience, they are not the result of any analogy at all, illuminating or not, but are verbal trickery.

The second defect of the analogy with relative properties is that it suggests a phenomenologically false picture of the perceptual situation. To be at all distinguishable from the analogy with physical contact, it must claim that a perceptual situation contains, in addition to the percipient, the object perceived, and the relation between the two which is called appearing, also a fourth feature or element, namely, the specific character-istic of this relation that presumably is intended by the phrase "way of appearing." [16] But what is this fourth feature? It is all very well to talk of something's appearing *blue* to me or of my being appeared-to *bluely* as long as we understand by these that I perceive or am aware of *something blue*. But it is crucial to the theory that the way x appears to y be a feature of the relation between x and y and not (or at least not in the same sense, or not necessarily) a quality of x or of any other entity. Otherwise the Theory of Appearing would collapse either into Naïve Realism or into the Sense-Datum Theory. And I think it is obvious that the perceived blue color of what I see is not a feature of my perceiving it or of the thing's *appearing* to me but of what I perceive. On this point there simply is no analogy between one's perceiving something blue and John's being taller than someone else. Being-taller-than can only be a specific feature of a relation between John and that someone else. It is not, in any sense, describable as being in John or in the other person, as their sizes are. Being blue, on the other hand, is precisely a feature of what I perceive; it is not in any intelligible sense describable as a feature of my perceiving that object or as a feature of any other relation or connection between me and the object. It is not a property of a relation.

6. *Pure Perceptual Statements*

It would be a serious mistake to suppose that the inadequacies of the above four analogies require us to simply reject them. On the contrary, it is precisely in the examination of these analogies, and in the analysis of the points at which they hold and the points at which they do not, that a genuine understanding of perception can be found. In fact, had one of the analogies been obviously adequate and the rest obviously inadequate there

---

16. The most generous interpretation of the Theory of Appearing is that appearing is merely the converse of being aware of or perceiving and thus that the perceiving itself is not a fifth element of the perceptual situation. If this is denied, then the theory is phenomeno-logically even less acceptable. There is no pair of phenomenologically given distinct relations in perception between percipient and the object perceived, one being that of perceiving and the second that of appearing.

would not have been a *problem* of perception. For example, if the analogy of perception with physical contact had been completely satisfactory, then Naïve Realism would have been obviously true, common sense would have been completely vindicated, and the justification of beliefs about bodies by means of perception would not have been of philosophical interest. If the analogy with subjective experience had been completely satisfactory, then Berkeleyan Idealism would have been self-evidently true, and we would never have sought a justification of body-statements, any more than we seek a justification of our statements that we are in pain. If the analogy with imagination had been completely satisfactory, it would have been obvious that perception does not provide us with evidence for our beliefs about bodies, and no philosopher would have been tempted to show that it does, just as no philosopher has been tempted to show that the imagining of something provides us with evidence for its existence. And, finally, if the analogy with relative properties had been completely satisfactory, then the question of our knowledge of the external world would have been dealt with in a manner similar to that of our knowledge of the exact lengths of edges, and the tendency (deplored by Hume) to believe in the double existence of the objects of perception would have been entirely absent.

Despite their inadequacies, the four analogies taken together do illuminate the nature of perception. The analogy with physical contact emphasizes the fact that perception is a *direct* ground of our knowledge of bodies, that in a certain sense in perception we are directly confronted with bodies, we are *in touch with bodies*. The analogy with subjective experience emphasizes the fact that the relation between perception and the objects of perception is an extraordinarily intimate one, that it is part of the very nature of a body that it is perceived, and that it is part of the very nature of perception that perception is of bodies. The analogy with imagination emphasizes the fact that, despite the intimacy of their relation, there is an all-important logical gap between bodies and perception, between *esse* and *percipi*. And the analogy with relative properties emphasizes that such a logical gap is not due to there being two distinct sorts of entities, namely, bodies and the actual objects of perception, as the third analogy would suggest.

But to recognize the merits of the four analogies is not all that one can do to illuminate the nature of perception. It is possible to combine them into a unified whole by offering another, fifth, analogy that possesses all of their merits and none of their defects. Unlike the other four, such a fifth analogy would not be a natural one. Were it such, it would have already been available and would have provided us with the obviously proper understanding of the nature of perception. It is an artificial analogy, in the sense that the analogue in question would not ordinarily have been considered in connection with perception. I shall attempt to provide such an analogy, but to do so I must recall the main reason that the first analogy, that with physical contact, failed.

I have argued that, contrary to what the first analogy suggests, perceptual statements cannot be taken to justify the corresponding body-statements by entailing them.[17] For such entailment could only be trivial, evidentially worthless. Let us begin by recognizing that, ordinarily, the truth of the corresponding body-statement *is* considered a necessary condition of the truth of a perceptual statement; the latter statement *is* taken to entail the former. If I assert that I see a typewriter before me and then discover that there is no typewriter before me, I would ordinarily retract my previous statement and admit that after all I did not really see a typewriter before me. But the incoherence of the claim that body-statements are *justified* by perceptual statements because the latter entail them becomes quite evident in this paradigmatic example. If the statement "I see a typewriter before me" is taken to entail the statement "There is a typewriter before me," then it would be so taken only in the sense that the truth of the latter is a *trivially* necessary condition of, a *criterion* for, the truth of the former, and, unlike the typical cases of entailment in mathematics, it is quite clear that then I could not possibly *know* that I see a typewriter before me unless I *knew* that there is a typewriter before me. I could never be entirely justified in making the perceptual statement unless I were entirely justified in making the body-statement. My grounds for believing the former could never be better than my grounds for believing the latter. In fact, they could be expected to be worse, for, since the two statements are not synonymous and the perceptual statement entails the body-statement, it might be argued that, in addition to being an assertion about bodies, the perceptual statement is also an assertion about something else and might fail to be true on account of this latter assertion. In a similar fashion, I could not genuinely justify the statement that a certain object is colored by appealing to the statement that it is red, although

17. See pp. 227–29.

being red entails being colored, for I could not *know* that the object is red unless I *knew* that it is colored, though I might know that it is colored but fail to know that it is red. Again, I could not genuinely justify the statement that Jones is in the audience by appealing to the statement that both Jones and Smith are in the audience. The latter statement entails the former, but only trivially so. I could have no grounds for believing that both Jones and Smith are in the audience that are better than my grounds for believing that Jones is in the audience, though they could be worse.

Thus, if perceptual statements really entail the corresponding body-statements, then not only would this fact not suggest a solution of the problem of the justification of body-statements by perception but indeed would render such a justification unintelligible. This seems to leave us with three alternatives: either (1) knowledge of bodies is itself an unintelligible notion, or (2) it is primary and not in need of external justification, or (3) it is justifiable by reference to something other than perception. But to accept any one of these alternatives is to accept an obvious falsehood. Yet this is just what we must do if we are to remain completely loyal to ordinary usage, in which the entailment of body-statements by perceptual statements usually does hold.

But we must not let loyalty lead us into absurdity. And ordinary usage itself encourages our breach of faith with it by containing occasional uses of perceptual statements that are not taken to entail the corresponding body-statements. In the description of dreams, hallucinations, experiences under certain psychological or physiological examinations, double vision, and the seeing of ghosts and flying saucers, it is quite natural and virtually universal to use perceptual statements even though the user not only may not believe that the corresponding body-statements are true but in fact may know them to be false. I am not appealing here to the fact that such experiences do occur, or to the existence of this feature of the ordinary use of perceptual verbs. Indeed, this feature is evident only in exceptional (though still ordinary, nontechnical, nonphilosophical) uses, but the very possibility of such exceptional uses *suggests,* though certainly does not *prove,* that an account of perceptual statements that avoids the difficulties of the account based on the analogy of perception with physical contact would have independent plausibility.

Indeed, as the analogy of perception with imagination implies, such an account can be offered. According to it, a perceptual statement ordinarily entails the corresponding body-statement not because of the intrinsic character of the perceptual content of the perceptual statement but because of a natural, though logically still accidental, *accretion* to this perceptual content of foreign matter, namely, of the content of the corresponding body-statement—an accretion made psychologically unavoidable by the contingent fact that only seldom do we discover that the body-statements we assert on the basis of perception are false and thus that we may almost always *regard* our perceptual statements as *including* the corresponding body-statements. According to this account, a perceptual statement is in effect a logical conjunction of a *pure perceptual statement* (one that does not entail the corresponding body-statement) and the corresponding body-statement itself. If this is so, then it should be possible to dissolve the conjunction and make clear the nature of that pure perceptual statement. But in doing so, we must guard against falling back into the Sense-Datum Theory, which originally suggested such an account of perceptual statements.

Either our beliefs about bodies can be justified or they cannot. If they can, then they would be justified either in themselves or by reference to some other beliefs. If they can be justified only by reference to some other beliefs, then these latter are either perceptual or they are not. If they are perceptual, then they justify the beliefs about bodies either by entailment or in some other fashion. If perceptual statements can justify their corresponding body-statements only by entailment, then no genuine, intelligible justification would be achieved at all, and the conclusion must be that there can be no knowledge about bodies. But we have another alternative: to attempt to identify an element in the perceptual statement which is logically independent of the corresponding body-statement, to try to separate it out as a distinct kind of statement, to regard this as a pure perceptual statement, and thereby to dismiss the ordinary kind of perceptual statement as a logical mixture, intellectually unwelcome though perhaps psychologically unavoidable, of a pure perceptual statement and the corresponding body-statement. Such a pure perceptual statement must have at least three characteristics: (1) it must not entail the corresponding body-statement; (2) it must nevertheless be intelligibly, even if wrongly, regarded as providing evidence for the latter; and (3) it must preserve all of the reference to perception made in the ordinary perceptual statement. It may seem that such a statement is an empty ideal and can never be actually produced. Certainly, as we have seen, this would be so if we were to identify such statements with so-called sense-datum or appear-to statements. But, in fact, there is no difficulty in providing a *nominal* definition of the sort of pure perceptual statement that we require. We can construct such a statement simply by taking an ordinary perceptual statement and conjoining with it the assertion that it is logically possible that the corresponding body-statement is false, that is, that the perceptual statement does not entail the corresponding body-statement. For instance, the following would be a pure perceptual statement: "I see a typewriter before me, but it is (logically) possible that there is no typewriter before me." Clearly, such a statement would preserve whatever pure perceptual content an ordinary perceptual statement possesses and yet explicitly exclude whatever in the content of that latter statement may entail the corresponding body-statement.

But the above definition of a pure perceptual statement is merely nominal. It does not demonstrate the possibility, the intelligibility, of what is defined. The important question before us is whether a pure perceptual statement, as so defined, is a genuine statement, whether a statement such as "I see a typewriter before me but it is (logically) possible that there is no typewriter before me" is really intelligible, whether it makes sense. That such a statement is intelligible is *suggested* by the fact that it would be quite naturally used in ophthalmological examinations and in the description of hallucinations, cases of double vision, etc. Its intelligibility when used in ordinary perceptual situations, however, can be *demonstrated* only on the basis of a conception of the nature of a perceptual situation in general that would be quite unlike the four conceptions we have already examined.

The determination of a concept of perception that can render pure perceptual statements intelligible cannot be achieved with a definition. We have argued that an account of the nature of perception may only take the form of an analogy. To make the concept of a pure perceptual statement intelligible, we require a philosophical re-formation of the ordinary concept of perception, that is, the establishment of a philosophically more useful concept of perception. Such a re-formation would consist in viewing perceptual situations as analogous to a certain other sort of situation, one to which they would not ordinarily be regarded as similar.

As we have seen, the four most familiar philosophical theories of perception rest on certain natural and immediately plausible analogies.

Their defects are due to the inadequacies of these respective analogies. Consequently, to show that pure perceptual statements are possible we must offer a philosophical account of perception by employing a more satisfactory analogy. Specifically, it must be an analogy that illuminates and does justice to at least the following four philosophically crucial features of all perceptual situations: (1) that perception necessarily has an object—that one who perceives necessarily perceives something; (2) that at least in the usual, standard cases the object of perception is a body —for example, a cat, a flower, a rock—and that ordinarily perception is perception of bodies in an immediate, direct, non-Pickwickian, obvious manner; (3) that the mere occurrence of a perceiving does not entail that there is a body which is its object nor, if there is such a body, that it has certain specific qualities; (4) that perception nevertheless can be intelligibly supposed to provide us with evidence for the existence and qualities of bodies, even if in reality it does not—that perception is a prima facie ground of our knowledge of an external world of bodies. It is not surprising that we can do justice to all four of these characteristics only by appealing to an artificial analogy. For at least two of them seem inconsistent: (3) seems to deny just what (2) seems to assert.

I shall begin by stating the sort of account of perception that would appear to do justice to all four of the above characteristics of perception. We will find that the crucial locution in that account is unintelligible if it is taken literally. Then I shall try to make it intelligible by appealing to the analogy between a perceptual situation and a certain other sort of situation.

Let us recall our discussion of the concept of body. The essence of a body is its possession of a perceivable closed three-dimensional surface containing insides; the essence of the reality of a body is its causal efficacy. But precisely this account of the nature of a body led us to admit the logical possibility that we may perceive, in addition to bodies, such entities as apparitions and that through perception we may learn of the existence of such entities as unobservable solids.[18] As long as we are concerned only with entities that it is logically possible for us to perceive, there can be no reason for refusing to acknowledge still other sorts.

Indeed, there is a fourth kind of entity that we can easily imagine ourselves knowing by perception. Although both bodies and apparitions

18. See above, p. 217.

must have a closed three-dimensional surface, it is not logically impossible for perception to have objects without such a surface. It is perfectly conceivable that there may be entities that have only an incomplete, whether plane or curved, surface. It is conceivable, for instance, that a blue rectangular entity is visible, but that if one attempts to walk around it one simply fails to see or otherwise perceive any sides or back. It is conceivable that one can touch a hard and cold entity, but that one cannot touch any sides or back. One may then, quite intelligibly even if falsely, describe such an entity as simply not having sides or a back. Whether there are entities of this sort is irrelevant to our present discussion. It is sufficient to recognize that the notion of such an entity can be explained rather easily. Clearly, such an entity would not be a body. One would be tempted to describe it as a mere surface. However, it is part of the ordinary meaning of the word *surface* that a surface must be the surface of something, while the sort of entity I am describing would really *be* a mere surface. The word *expanse* seems to convey very much the same idea, and I shall therefore refer to such entities as *perceptual expanses*. Whether perceptual expanses would exist only if perceived, whether they would be public or private, whether they would have as causes certain physiological or psychological events in the observer, are questions the replies to which are not included in the explanation of the concept of perceptual expanse. Perhaps the notion of a rainbow that might be held by one who is unaware of the physical conditions of rainbows approximates the notion of a perceptual expanse.

By perception we may know still other entities. We can imagine unobservable but solid two-dimensional entities (we may call them *impenetrable shields*); apparitions without insides (*hollow apparitions*), i.e., mere closed three-dimensional expanses; entities just like bodies but without insides (*hollow bodies*), etc. It would be pointless to describe such entities in detail or to try to provide an exhaustive list of them. What is interesting about them is not their number or their specific character, but the logical possibility of their multiplicity. For it seems plausible to assume about such logically possible objects of perception that those that would be observable form a series of increasing complexity, the members of which would not be distinguishable from one another on the basis of an individual perceiving. It seems plausible to assume that a perceiving of a perceptual expanse would not be in itself distinguishable from a perceiving of a hollow apparition, that the perceiving of a hollow apparition would not be in itself distinguishable from the perceiving of an apparition, that the perceiving of an apparition would not be in itself distinguishable from the perceiving of a body, that the perceiving of a body would not be in itself distinguishable from the perceiving of a mind-independent body, and that the perceiving of a mind-independent body would not be in itself distinguishable from the perceiving of a publicly perceivable mind-independent body.

The point of such an assumption is not that only the perceiving of a perceptual expanse would be real or direct perceiving; all of the perceivings mentioned above would be cases of perceiving in exactly the same sense, although their objects are very different. Nor is its point that the perceiving of any object other than a perceptual expanse is somehow doubtful or that the existence of any object other than a perceptual expanse is doubtful; possibly no doubt should be entertained that what we perceive are always mind-independent publicly perceivable bodies. Rather, the assumption suggests that if the problem of perception is the question, Can we know on the basis of perception that there are the mind-independent publicly perceivable bodies that we think we perceive? then the answer to that question, even if perfectly obviously affirmative, is not a simple and indivisible "Yes!" expressing some immediate simple fact but one that can be divided into several logically distinct steps each of which can be answered independently of the next, though none of which can be answered independently of the one preceding.

Let us take as an example the situation which I describe now as my seeing a cigar box before me. The first step of the problem of perception, as applied to this example, would be, Is there *at least* a rectangular blue perceptual expanse that I now see? The second step would be, Is there *at least* a hollow apparition that I now see, that is, is there at least a closed three-dimensional expanse, part of which I now see? Much, though by no means all, of what is involved in the problem whether it is bodies or sense-data that we perceive is contained in just this second question, and it is useful to be able to state it without reference to what can or cannot be doubted, or to "direct" and "indirect" perception, or to "sensing" and "perceiving." The third step of the problem of perception would be, Is there *at least* an apparition that I now see, that is, does the closed three-dimensional expanse that I now see contain insides? The fourth step would be, Is there a body that I now see, that is, is the region occupied by the three-dimensional expanse with insides that I now see also causally efficacious? The fifth step would be, Is there *at least* a publicly perceivable body that I now see? The sixth step would be, Is there *at least* a mind-independent publicly perceivable body that I now see? A seventh step might be, Is the mind-independent publicly perceivable body that I now see really a cigar box (rather than, say, a large pipe-tobacco box)? To lump all seven steps together and ask only, Is there a cigar-box that I now see? would be somewhat like asking, Is Jones the student who last year wrote an honors thesis and is married to a Japanese girl and spends much time in the library and came from Boston and prefers sociology to philosophy? To expect a simple affirmative or negative answer to the first question would be no more reasonable than to expect such an answer to the second question.

It may seem that what I have said in the last few paragraphs provides an answer to our question, What is primary perceptual knowledge? namely, that we have primary perceptual knowledge only of the existence and qualitative nature of *perceptual expanses*. But this suggestion can be immediately rejected, for a perceptual expanse is by definition neither a body nor a part of the surface of a body, and thus if we had primary perceptual knowledge only of perceptual expanses, such knowledge would not even appear to constitute evidence for the existence of bodies. But the above suggestion can be emended easily. It would be stated as follows: we have primary perceptual knowledge only of the existence and qualitative nature of entities that are *at least* perceptual expanses but may also be parts of the surfaces of bodies. A pure perceptual statement, that is, a statement of the form "*A* perceives an *x* but it is (logically) possible that there is not an *x*" would then be understood as equivalent to a statement of the form "*A* perceives an entity that is at least a perceptual expanse but possibly a part of the surface of an *x*," with the term "*x*" designating a body.

Such an account would be attractive. First, it is quite plausible to suggest that our perceptual knowledge of an entity that is at least a perceptual expanse but possibly a part of the surface of a body is a clear example of primary knowledge. For what sort of mistake in believing that one perceives such an entity would be thinkable? The notion of a perceptual expanse includes no mention of publicity, mind-independence, causal efficacy, or any unperceived qualities. Second, a perceptual expanse is just like a disconnected part of the surface of a body. Whenever one perceives a body, one would perceive something that is at least a perceptual expanse but possibly a part of the surface of a body. Whenever one perceives the insides of a body, through a section of that body, one would perceive something that is at least a perceptual expanse but possibly a continuation of the outside surface of the body. (If one could perceive that a body is causally efficacious, one would perceive the causal efficacy of the body by perceiving changes, whether in the motion or in the qualities, of an entity that is at least a perceptual expanse but may be a part of the surface of a body that is affected causally by the first body.) To perceive a body is to perceive a part of its surface. And to perceive a part of the surface of a body is to perceive the body itself. If the entity one perceives that is at least a perceptual expanse but may be a part of the surface of a body is indeed a part of the surface of a body, then one would perceive, directly, literally, and quite noncontroversially, the body itself. And one's perception of such an entity would be quite intelligibly, even if wrongly, regarded as evidence for the existence of a certain body, because what one perceives would be just what might be the front surface of a body. But such evidence would not *entail* that for which it is evidence, because the entity perceived might still not be a part of the surface of a body.

7. *Pure Perceptual Objects*

I SUGGEST THAT the above account of primary perceptual knowledge is essentially correct. But it is correct only because the analogy on which it rests is convincing, not because the account is literally true or even intelligible as it stands. The central notion in the account, that of an entity that is at least a perceptual expanse but possibly a part of the surface of a body, is not intelligible if we attempt to understand it literally. Yet it must be intelligible if the crucial assumption of the account is to be plausible. That, of course, is the assumption that a perceiving of a perceptual expanse is *in itself indistinguishable* from the perceiving of a part of the surface of a body. And this assumption seems not only implausible but obviously false. Are not the objects of the perceivings fundamentally different? And, if so, must not the perceivings be different in themselves? It would seem that they must. But if a sense can be given to the notion of an entity that is at least a perceptual expanse but possibly a part of the surface of a body, then it would be *at least intelligible* to suppose that the objects of the two perceivings, namely, the perceptual expanse and the part of the surface of a body, are the *same sort of entity* and not distinguishable in themselves; and thus it would also be at least intelligible to suppose that the two perceivings are not distinguishable in themselves.

The point of speaking of an entity that is at least a perceptual expanse but possibly a part of the surface of a body is that a perceptual expanse and a part of the surface of a body are not different sorts of entity, that they are the same sort of entity and are distinguishable only in that the former is, so to speak, isolated, while the latter is a part of a larger whole. The distinction between them is somewhat like that between a small town and a city suburb. Two such settlements need not be distinguishable in themselves but only in their relations to other settlements and to institutions. And the indistinguishability of a perceiving of a mere perceptual expanse and a perceiving of a part of the surface of a body would be somewhat like the indistinguishability between one's entering a small town and one's entering a city suburb. There is a clear sense in which one can say that one is entering what is at least a small town but possibly a city suburb. And the reason is that there is a clear sense in which a small town and a city suburb may be one and the same sort of entity, namely, small settlements, and the difference between them may be not intrinsic but extrinsic, one in respect to their relations to other things. But the notion of an entity that is at least a perceptual expanse but possibly a part of the surface of a body is very different from the notion of a settlement that is at least a small town but possibly a city suburb.

I introduced the notion of a perceptual expanse without engaging in detailed discussion because it is the notion of a merely logically possible sort of perceptible entity. To deny that there may be perceptible two-dimensional (spatially incomplete), even if curved, entities would be unreasonable. But that the notion of a perceptual expanse is intelligible does not at all mean that so is the notion of an entity that is at least a perceptual expanse but possibly a part of the surface of a body. In fact, if taken literally, the latter is unintelligible. The reason for this is not that the notion is self-contradictory. To say that an entity is at least a perceptual expanse but possibly a part of the surface of a body is not to say that such an entity is *both* a perceptual expanse and a part of the surface of a body (which would be self-contradictory, given our explanation of the notion of a perceptual expanse), any more than to say that one is entering what is at least a small town but possibly a city suburb is to say that one is entering a settlement that is both a small town and a city suburb. The reason for the apparent unintelligibility is that, however peculiar an entity a perceptual expanse may be, it is an *individual entity*, while the surface of a body and its parts do not seem to be entities at all. And even if we identify the surface of a body with its shape, size, color, texture, etc., it would still not be an individual entity, but at most a complex attribute or universal.[19] But, if so, then a perceptual expanse and a part of the surface of a body cannot be the same sort of entity at all. They would differ not only in species and in genus, but categorially. They would be distinguishable in themselves in the most fundamental and obvious manner. And so would be the perceiving of the one and the perceiving of the other. To speak of an entity that is at least a perceptual expanse but possibly a part of the surface of a body would be as unintelligible as to speak of an entity that is at least a dog but possibly a number.

But this conclusion is not as devastating as it appears. Nor should it surprise us. Had the notion of an entity that is at least a perceptual expanse but possibly a part of the surface of a body been intelligible prima facie, the above sort of account of the nature of primary perceptual knowledge would have been the self-evident one, and there would not have been a philosophical *problem* about perceptual knowledge. The mark of the sort of situation that generates a philosophical problem such as that of primary perceptual knowledge is that it does not fit comfortably in any one of the places in our conceptual framework in which it would be expected to fit. And the philosopher's task regarding such a situation is neither to force it into a place where it does not fit (this would lead to philosophical error) nor to give it a label and describe it as *sui generis* (this would mask what is in effect a refusal to attempt to understand as success at such an attempt), but rather to find what other sort of situation it is most like without going overboard by suggesting that it *is* that other sort of situation. Throughout our inquiry in this Part we have been reconciled to the impossibility of a useful literal description of the perceptual situation. It is not surprising, therefore, that we should find that the

---

19. "A surface must be the surface of something; and not merely that, it must be the surface of some material thing. Indeed, there is really no such entity as *a surface;* there are only solid things thus and thus *surfaced*. 'Surface,' it is true, is a substantive in grammar; but it is not the name of a particular existent, but of an attribute" (Price, *Perception*, p. 106).

main notion that seems required for a solution of the problem of primary perceptual knowledge cannot be understood literally. The question is whether it can be understood analogically. I suggest that it can.

The analogy required is a double one. It consists of two parts. According to the first, the relationship between a perceptual expanse and the surface of a certain body is analogous to the relationship between a removable part of a whole to that whole. The sort of relationship that I have in mind is the following. Consider an object that is a composite of parts, each of which is removable and capable of independent existence and yet is immediately identifiable as a part of that object. A *machine* is a standard example of such an object. Consider the automobile. Some of its parts, such as fenders and door panels, constitute its shell, others constitute its inner structure. Each is removable, and in fact the notion of an automotive part is more often applied to such parts as they are found on the shelves of stores that sell parts for automobiles than to such parts as they are found actually constituting an automobile. Now, what is crucial for the analogy is the fact that one can act in a number of ways with respect to a part of an automobile without the action being affected in any direct or necessary way by the part's being or not being actually in an automobile; certain actions, that is, with respect to isolated parts need not be distinguishable in themselves from such actions with respect to actual constituents of the automobile. For example, one can paint a fender which has been removed or which has never even been included in an automobile in exactly the same way as one would paint a fender which is an actual constituent of an automobile. To make the point of the analogy clearer, let us even imagine that unattached automotive parts are strewn throughout our environment (the country approximating an automotive junkyard). To say then that one is painting, touching up, drilling a hole in, or straightening an automotive part would entail nothing as to whether the part is an actual constituent of an automobile. At the same time, to be painting, touching up, drilling a hole in, or straightening an automobile one would necessarily be painting, touching up, drilling a hole in, or straightening a part of an automobile.

Now a perceiving (someone's seeing or touching something) would be *analogous* (we must remember that we are speaking of an analogy, not a partial identity) to an action such as painting with respect to an automotive part which may or may not be an actual constituent of an automobile. A perceptual expanse, or the front side of the surface of a body, or an observable section of the insides of a body would be analogous to the automotive part itself. The *surface* of a body (not the body itself) that is perceived would be analogous to an automobile. What I perceive is under no logical necessity to be an actual part of the surface or a section of the insides of a body; it is logically possible that it is a mere perceptual expanse. In a similar way, there is no logical necessity that the automotive fender I am painting is actually a constituent of an automobile; it might be just lying on a shelf. At the same time, what I perceive is not an object that is simply different from a body (e.g., a sensation or appearance) but precisely something the perception of which could be—yet logically does not have to be—described naturally and paradigmatically as the perception of a body, just as the painting of an automotive fender could be—but logically does not have to be—described naturally and paradigmatically as the painting of an automobile. And the fact that one perceives something can be intelligibly regarded as a reason, though not logically sufficient, for one's believing that there is a body that is perceived, just as one's painting an automotive fender can be intelligibly regarded as a reason, though not logically sufficient, for one's believing that there is an automobile that one is painting.

But this first part of the analogy is not sufficient as it stands. For, prima facie, there is so fundamental a difference between the surface of a body and a composite of removable parts such as an automobile that the analogy seems completely implausible. I have already mentioned this difference. A perceptual expanse is an individual entity while the surface of a body does not seem to be an individual entity at all. But both an automobile and an automotive part are individual entities. How then could the relationship of a perceptual expanse to the surface of a body be at all analogous to the relationship of an automotive part to an automobile? It is at this point that we must appeal to the second part of the analogy, without which the first part would remain weak and unconvincing.

The relationship between a perceptual expanse and the surface of a body would be analogous to the relationship between a removable part of a composite and the composite itself only if there is a prior, more fundamental analogy between the surface of a body and individual entities. For if there is this latter analogy, then there would be a sense in which the surface of a body and its parts are *like* individual entities. And to the extent to which the surface of a body and its parts are like individual entities, so too the relationship of a perceptual expanse to the surface of a body would be like the relationship of a removable part of a composite to the composite itself.

Indeed, there is a fundamental similarity between surfaces and individual entities. The mark of an individual entity is that it can be said to have, to instantiate, specific (or first-type) qualities, that is, qualities that are not qualities of qualities. As a matter of standard usage, a surface also is said to have or to instantiate such qualities. A surface can be said to be blue, rough, and chilly. And it is not obvious, even if ultimately true, that such predications can be reduced to predications of these qualities to the body itself. In fact, we make a fairly sharp distinction between the two sorts of predication. It is a familiar feature or ordinary thought and discourse that we distinguish the properties of a body from the properties of its surface. We have the notion of *surface* or *superficial* qualities of a body which we distinguish from the *qualities* of the body. For example, we are hesitant in calling a body such as a rock blue if only its outside surface and none of its inner sectional surfaces is blue; it is, we say, blue "on the outside."

I am not suggesting that the surface of a body is indeed an individual entity, one distinguishable from the body whose surface it is. It seems to me clear that it is not. But it seems to me equally clear that neither is it just a quality or set of qualities of the body. It is not simply the shape of the body nor is it the set of a certain shape, a certain outside color, and certain tactile qualities. For any such quality of the body can be said to be primarily, or more directly, a quality of the surface of the body, and only indirectly a quality of the body itself. The fact is that the notion of the surface of a body does not fit either into the category of individual entity or into that of quality. To be grasped, its similarities and differences to the entities in both categories must be noted. What is important for our purposes is that the surface of a body is indeed very similar to an individual entity: this substantiates directly the analogy between surfaces and individual things and, indirectly, that between the relationship of a perceptual expanse to the surface of a body and the relationship of a removable part of a composite to the composite. Had there not been the former analogy, the latter would have had no significant philosophical force. Now, I suggest, it does.

I conclude that, if understood through the above two-part analogy, the notion of an entity that is at least a perceptual expanse but possibly a part of the surface of a body is intelligible. If so, then we may say that a pure perceptual statement, that is, one that we nominally defined as a statement of the form "*A* perceives an *x* but it is (logically) possible that there is not an *x*," where the term "*x*" designates a body, means "*A* perceives an entity that is at least a perceptual expanse but may be a part of the surface of an *x*," or more briefly, "*A* perceives an entity that may but need not be part of the surface of an *x*." If we remember that a section of the insides of a body is a continuation of the outside surface of the body and that we perceive the causal effects of a body only by perceiving changes in entities that have perceivable surfaces, then we may say that the above sort of statement can express any pure perceptual knowledge that we may have.

I shall refer to an entity that is at least a perceptual expanse but possibly a part of the surface of a body as a *pure perceptual object*. The problem of the nature of primary perceptual knowledge is solved by saying that we have such knowledge only of pure perceptual objects. And the traditional problem of perception would be, Can I know, and if I can then by means of what principles, that a certain pure perceptual object that I perceive is in fact part of the surface of a body, which moreover is mind-independent and publicly perceivable? As we have seen, the problem is in fact a set of distinguishable questions and is not at all as simple as it is usually taken to be. In its *epistemologically* primary stage [20] it consists of the following series of questions. First, Is the pure perceptual object that I perceive part of the surface of an entity that is at least a hollow apparition? Second, Is it part of the surface of an entity that is at least an apparition? Third, Is it part of the surface of an entity that is at least a mind-independent apparition, that is, one capable of existence unperceived? Fourth, Is it part of the surface of an entity that is at least a mind-independent and publicly perceivable apparition? In its *ontologically* primary stage the problem of perception concerns the presence of causal efficacy in the region of the entity that is at least an apparition, that is, it concerns the existence of a real body.

If any of the questions that comprise the problem of perception can be answered, they must be answered by an appeal to the existence of certain pure perceptual objects. If I know that there is before me an entity with a closed three-dimensional surface containing insides, I know this on the basis of my knowledge that there is before me a certain pure perceptual object, something that may be a mere perceptual expanse but may also constitute a part of the surface, or a section of the insides, of such an

20. See above, pp. 219–20.

entity. If I know that this entity is also causally efficacious, that is, that it is a real body, I can know this only by perceiving pure perceptual objects that are moving or changing in certain ways. For the motions and changes that are our evidence for the presence of causal efficacy, must be, if perceived, motions and changes in entities that possess perceivable surfaces.

Our knowledge of the mind-independence and publicity of bodies would also be derivable, ultimately, from our knowledge of pure perceptual objects, but clearly in a very different way. As we have seen, a perceiving constitutes prima facie, even if never genuine, evidence for the existence of an entity that has a complete three-dimensional surface and insides. And if such an entity exists, then if one perceives in its vicinity a certain characteristically moving or changing pure perceptual object, this perceiving would constitute prima facie evidence for that entity's being causally efficacious. For such motions and changes would be just what one would expect to perceive if there is a causally efficacious entity before one. But there is nothing about what one perceives that has any prima facie connection with the mind-independence and publicity of what one perceives. There is no sense in which one can be said to perceive the mind-independence and publicity of the entity. But there is a clear sense in which one can be said to perceive its three-dimensional surface or insides, as well as, though much less clearly yet still intelligibly, its causal efficacy: the pure perceptual object one perceives can *be* a part of the surface, or a section of the insides, or (in respect to its motion or change) an effect of the causal powers of the entity.[21] It is to be expected, therefore, that the derivation of our knowledge of the existence of mind-independent and public bodies would be markedly different from that of our knowledge of the existence of mere bodies, that is, of causally efficacious three-dimensional entities with insides. The former is likely to be indirect and in need of premises quite different from any truths we may learn directly from perception. The latter is likely to be direct and free from the use of external principles. It is presumably because of this difference that, as I have argued, the concept of body does not include publicity and mind-independence. But, of course, the recognition of this difference must

21. But can one regard a body as causally efficacious if the body exists only through a single perceptual act? One can see that an arrow stops moving when it hits its target even if one does not think of either as having existed before they were seen or as continuing to exist when no longer seen.

not be confused with an estimate of the possibility or even specific character of either derivation. I have not attempted, nor shall I attempt, such an estimate in this book.

There are a number of observations to be made if the above account is not to be seriously misunderstood. To begin with, I am not saying that pure perceptual objects alone are actually or directly or really perceived and that bodies are not. My perception of a pure perceptual object and of a certain body may well be related somewhat as someone's being in Chicago is related to his being in the United States. On the other hand, it is only of the pure perceptual object, and thus at most of the front surface of a body, that I can have primary knowledge through perception. Indeed, even according to ordinary usage, while I see a tomato itself and not just its front surface, obviously I do not see the color of its back side but only the color of its front side. Hence, I cannot be said to have primary knowledge of what the color of the back side is, even though I may know with certainty what it is. Nor am I saying that one should, or even could, *doubt* that the pure perceptual object one perceives is actually a part of the surface of a body. I am merely saying that it is not logically necessary that it be such. It is not logically necessary that I have a headache now but this does not mean that I should, or even could, doubt that I do.

There is nothing in the analogical notion of a pure perceptual object that would suggest that such an object cannot be perceived both visually and tactilely. It would be simpler to suppose that it can. But it would be more plausible to suppose that it cannot. If we suppose the latter, then we should add to the account of the concept of body that a body must have *both* a visual surface and a tangible surface and that these two surfaces must coincide. The difficult and important question of the relationship between visual perception and tactile perception, however, has no special relevance to our topic.

Nor is there anything in the notion of a pure perceptual object that would suggest that such an object cannot be perceived by more than one person. Whether it can or cannot must be determined, in part, on the basis of a theory of our knowledge of other minds, which, as we have seen, would presuppose an independent solution of the problem of perception. There is also nothing in the notion of a pure perceptual object that would suggest that a pure perceptual object exists only when it is perceived, that it is mind-dependent. In fact, were this so, the consequence would be that bodies do not exist. For it is essential to something's being a body that it have a closed three-dimensional surface, and at least some sides of such a surface would be unperceived pure perceptual objects—some sides, that is, would be unperceived but perceivable entities that may but need not constitute parts of the surface of a body. Thus, if a perceiving is evidence for the existence of a body, it would also be, though indirectly, evidence for the existence of unperceived, mind-independent, pure perceptual objects, namely, the unperceived sides and inner sections of the body. But, contrary to what one might suppose, this does not entail that a perceiving would be, again indirectly, evidence for the existence of a mind-independent *body*. The fact that some parts of the surface, or inner sections, of a body may exist unperceived does not entail that the body itself may exist entirely unperceived. On the other hand, the fact that if there are perceived bodies, then there must be unperceived pure perceptual objects may explain why we believe that there are unperceived bodies. The thought of unperceived *parts* of the surface of a body leads naturally to the thought of a body whose surface consists entirely of such parts, that is, one that is not even partly perceived. Hence we come to our belief that it is not logically impossible that bodies exist unperceived. We may even say that *if* our perceivings constitute evidence for the existence of bodies, then they constitute evidence, though indirectly, for the logical possibility of the existence of unperceived bodies. But they would still not constitute, by themselves, evidence for the actual existence of unperceived bodies. (Though of course they may do so in conjunction with something else we know, presumably certain universal propositions.)

On the other hand, while our account of perception is neutral in regard to the question of the publicity and mind-independence of pure perceptual objects, just as it is neutral in regard to the question of the publicity and mind-independence of bodies, the purpose of this neutrality is to facilitate the answers to these, and other, questions that constitute the problem of perception and not to suggest that the questions are unimportant. Specifically, such an account of perception makes it possible for us to do justice both to the fact that it is bodies that we perceive and that perception provides us with prima facie evidence for the existence of bodies and to the fact that perception by itself never even pretends to inform us of the public and mind-independent, continued, existence of what we perceive. But it is the publicity and mind-independence of what we perceive, whether pure perceptual objects or bodies, that we really want to know. We cannot have primary knowledge of them, but whatever primary perceptual knowledge we do have is worth having only insofar as it might lead to derivative knowledge of them. This is especially obvious in regard to the mind-independence of bodies. The question of the existence of a certain body is simply unimportant unless it is assumed that such existence can have duration longer than that of even the longest perceptual act. It is not the *existence* of bodies so much that we want to know as their *continued* existence. We want to know whether there is an external world, and a *world* necessarily consists mostly of bodies that are not perceived.

It is part of the notion of a pure perceptual object that we can have primary knowledge of its existence and of its perceived qualities. The occurrence of a perceiving does guarantee the *existence* of a pure perceptual object. Indeed, we introduced the notion of such an object in order to provide an account of perception that satisfies four conditions of adequacy, one of which is that a perceiving is necessarily a perceiving of something, even if not of a body. To deny that there must be a pure perceptual object whenever one perceives would be both unnecessary and fatal to the solution of the problem of perception. It would be unnecessary because one cannot think of what it would be to be mistaken in believing that in a certain case of one's seeing or touching there is something seen or touched that may though need not be a part of the surface of a body. As I have observed above, to say that there is a certain pure perceptual object is to imply nothing about its existing even when not perceived or its being perceivable by other persons. The above denial would also be fatal to the solution of the problem of perception, because it is unthinkable what further reasons we could have for believing that there really is a pure perceptual object that we perceive. If the act of perceiving does not guarantee that there is such an object, then what else would even appear to offer such a guarantee?

For exactly the same reasons, we must also say that the occurrence of a perceiving guarantees that the pure perceptual object has the *qualities* it is perceived to have. (But we need not say that it cannot have qualities that it is not perceived to have. Whether we should or should not is a topic for a general theory of perception but not for an account, such as ours, of the nature of primary perceptual knowledge.) In this case, however, there is an additional reason. If a pure perceptual object need not have the qualities it is perceived to have, for example, a certain color and a certain shape, what could be meant by saying that *it* exists? What would be the criterion of the identity of a pure perceptual object if not, at least partly, its qualitative nature?

It follows that we are committed to the existence of very many entities that are neither bodies nor parts of the surfaces of bodies, namely, those pure perceptual objects perceived in the cases of illusory, nonveridical perception that are not parts of the surfaces of bodies. For, according to our account, an illusory perceiving would be the perceiving of a pure perceptual object that is *not* part of the surface of a body. But such ontological wealth is a fact, not a hypothesis. For illusory perception is a fact. A theory of perception should not be based on it[22] but it must not deny it. The only question is how to understand this fact. An alternative to our proposal would be the Theory of Appearing. It is no more economical than ours, for it claims that, instead of our multitude of pure perceptual objects, there is an equivalent multitude of relations of appearing, or at least of cases of minds being appeared-to. I have given my reasons for rejecting that claim. Any other theory must acknowledge a similar ontological multiplicity of *some things* if it is to acknowledge the facts of illusory perception.

In this respect there is a close analogy between our theory and the Sense-Datum Theory. Price's account of the relations of sense-data, and especially of those parts of a family of sense-data that are distortion-series, could easily be restated in terms of pure perceptual objects. (His standard solid would correspond to our closed three-dimensional surface of a body.[23]) But this similarity must not be misinterpreted. Unlike a sense-datum, a pure perceptual object may, quite literally, be part of the surface of a body. We have not denied that it can exist publicly and independently of perception. It is, of course, in no sense mental. And the notion of such an entity has been introduced in a fundamentally different manner. We have appealed neither to the Argument from Illusion nor to the dubitability of what we claim to know on the basis of perception. We have not indulged in a description of pure perceptual objects as what is "directly perceived" or "sensed." Nor is a pure perceptual object a phenomenon, that is, an entity defined by reference to actual or possible *experience*. Of course, it can be perceived. But it need not be perceived and is defined merely as an entity that may but need not be a part of the surface of a body. Thus our theory is in no sense phenomenalist. (Needless to say,

22. See above pp. 195–97.
23. See *Perception*, chap. VIII.

nothing in it suggests that a body-statement is translatable into a set, finite or infinite, of statements about pure perceptual objects.)

We have primary perceptual knowledge of pure perceptual objects. But we could also say that we have such knowledge of our perceivings of pure perceptual objects. It might seem that only the latter could be primary. For is it not the case that one knows that there is a certain pure perceptual object before one *on the basis of* one's perceiving it? But that one perceives a certain pure perceptual object entails that there is such an object and that it has the qualities it is perceived to have. And the entailment is, in this case, of the sort that makes knowledge of the entailing proposition impossible without knowledge of the proposition entailed. For this reason, one can know that one perceives a certain pure perceptual object only if one knows that there is such a pure perceptual object, and one can have *primary* knowledge of such a pure perceptual object only if one knows that one perceives it. (But one might have *derivative* knowledge of a pure perceptual object, e.g., of an unperceived part of the surface of a body; that would not, of course, be knowledge, whether primary or derivative, of a perceiving.) Primary knowledge of one's perceivings *is* primary knowledge of their pure perceptual objects, and primary knowledge of pure perceptual objects *is* primary knowledge of one's perceivings.

Does our account avoid the defects of the four other accounts we have considered and yet possess their merits? [24] It seems that it does. First, it does justice to the phenomenological fact that every perceiving, even if delusive, has an object. Second, it allows that this object need not, logically, be part of the surface of a body and thus that the occurrence of the perceiving does not entail the existence of a body that is perceived. Third, it allows us to say that we can ("directly") perceive bodies and thus preserves the core of the ordinary concept of perception, for the perceiving of a pure perceptual object could *be* the perceiving of the front surface of a body and thus of the body itself (just as the painting of an automobile fender could *be* the painting of a car, though the fact that a fender is painted does not entail that a car is painted because it is not logically necessary that the fender actually be on a car). Fourth, the occurrence of a perceiving can be quite intelligibly, even if always falsely, regarded as evidence for the existence of a body of a certain nature, for if

24. See above, pp. 239–45.

there were such a body then one would perceive precisely the pure perceptual object that one does perceive; we have primary knowledge through perception of something, that is, the pure perceptual object, that can *be* a part of the surface of a body. Our account makes the possibility of knowledge of bodies at least plausible. According to it, the logical gap such knowledge must bridge is not the awesome one between appearance and reality but the one between the existence of an expanse and the existence of a body part of whose surface is identical with that expanse.

8. Incorrigibility

WE IDENTIFIED the province of our primary knowledge of necessary truths by noting that such knowledge depends on perception, though in a very wide sense of this term. That we have primary knowledge of such truths as that three and two are five or that everything colored is extended has usually been taken for granted. In section 8 of Part Two my purpose was not to demonstrate that we have such knowledge but to make clearer its distinguishing feature, namely, its having objects whose relations and other characteristics, though universals, can actually be perceived in their instances. Derivative knowledge of necessary truths has as its objects relations of universals which cannot actually be perceived in their instances, though we know by inference that such relations would be instantiated if their relata are instantiated.

In this Part I have argued that if knowledge of bodies, which is derivative, is to be possible, then it must be based on the sort of primary knowledge that has as its objects the truths expressed by pure perceptual statements. A pure perceptual statement can be understood as describing one's perception of a pure perceptual object. In the case of such perception we can indeed admit that its occurrence entails the existence of its object and the possession by the object of the qualities it is perceived to have and thus that there can be no difference between primary knowledge of our perceivings and *primary* knowledge of pure perceptual objects.

We have primary knowledge of the pure perceptual object—its existence and qualitative nature are self-evident—because our perceiving it and its qualities constitute elements of the context of the belief that there is such an object which would be incompatible with the falsehood of the belief. In looking now at the keyboard of my typewriter, I find it unthinkable that I may be mistaken in believing that at least I see something grey *which may or may not* be part of the surface of a body. For the identity of this belief, what this belief is about, is in part determined by my perceiving the object. If there were not that grey something then I would not have perceived it, and if I did not perceive it, then my belief that there is that grey something would not have been a belief that there is *that* grey something.

That our knowledge of pure perceptual objects is primary would seem obvious. If this is denied, the reason may only be that the epistemic incorrigibility of a pure perceptual statement is taken to include also linguistic incorrigibility.[25] Indeed, if a statement expresses primary knowledge, it is epistemically incorrigible. Since it is not subject to justification by appealing to other statements, it is not subject to correction by appeal to other statements. But from this it does not follow that its linguistic propriety is not subject to correction. For no statement is linguistically incorrigible. The statement "I have a headache" and the statement "Jones has a headache" are equally corrigible linguistically. Both are subject to correction by an appeal to the dictionary. But it would be absurd to suggest that the two statements are equally corrigible epistemically. In fact, the first is not corrigible epistemically at all. This difference is evident in the fact that the question, "How do you know that you have a headache?" is either improper or is answerable simply by a repetition of the statement "I have a headache"; while the question, "How do you know that Jones has a headache?" is quite proper and is never answerable by repeating the statement "Jones does have a headache." But the argument that epistemic incorrigibility cannot be divorced from linguistic incorrigibility is too deep to be rejected without further explanation.

The argument has two premises: first, that to know something is to classify it correctly; second, that to classify something correctly is to apply to it the correct word. If both premises are accepted, then the conclusion, that a statement cannot be both epistemically incorrigible and linguistically corrigible, follows directly. But, surely, the second premise is false. To begin with, there is much that we know and that we regard as being of a certain kind even if we are quite unable to apply any sufficiently specific word to it. A patient may know that the sensation he is experiencing in his stomach is of the same kind as those that in the past preceded

25. See above, p. oo.

the flaring up of his ulcer, yet he may be quite unable to apply any appropriate word to this sensation, an inability deplored both by him and by his physician. A man of the world finds a certain expression on a person's face familiar and significant, and acts accordingly, though he could not even begin to describe it. One can know that the shade of color of a certain object would go well with the shade of color of another object even if one is unable to name the shades. One can know what specific shade of blue one's hat is without possessing an equally specific color-word with which to describe it.

Not only is much of our knowledge in fact not expressible in language but even the knowledge which is so expressible must be understood as containing a part that is distinct from, and logically prior to, its linguistic expression. Let us assume that to know that a certain object is square is to know that the word *square* is applicable to that object. But the latter knowledge is complex, and only one part of it is concerned with language. It is resolvable at least into (1) one's knowledge that the object has *that*, rather than another, determinate shape, and (2) one's knowledge that the word *square* is applicable to anything that has that determinate shape. Part (2) is knowledge inseparable from language; part (1) is not. Yet, obviously, (1) is the fundamental, logically prior component. To know that a certain word is applicable to a certain thing I must know that the thing has a certain determinate characteristic. But I may know that the thing has a certain determinate characteristic even if I do not know what word is applicable to it. For words are not applicable to things except insofar, and only insofar, as such things have certain determinate characteristics. And we cannot know that a word is applicable to a thing unless we know independently that the thing has a certain determinate characteristic. Ordinarily we are not making two judgments when judging that something is square—namely, that it has a certain determinate characteristic and that the word *square* is applicable to anything that has that determinate characteristic. Sometimes, however, we do, namely in the not infrequent cases when we attempt to find the right word with which to describe something, although we know, without the slightest hesitation, that the thing has a certain determinate characteristic which alone could be the ground of the applicability of the word to the thing. Such knowledge is independent of language, although it is a necessary condition for the applicability of language. Because it is independent of language, it is linguistically incorrigible. And if it is primary, not in need of inference or justification, then it is also epistemically incorrigible.

For exactly the same reasons, *epistemic incorrigibility* is distinguishable not only from *linguistic incorrigibility* but also, more importantly and more generally, from *memorial incorrigibility*. It has been argued that any judgment, whether expressed in language or not, involves classification and thus, though seldom explicitly, an appeal to memory of past entities or events; but no appeal to memory is incorrigible; therefore, no judgment is incorrigible. But if a comparison of an item with something remembered is to be made, the determinate characteristic of the item must be known first. And *this* knowledge cannot itself be memorially corrigible. For otherwise we should not know what to compare with what. The judgment (or belief, taking-for-granted) that *that* is the determinate characteristic of the item would thus be neither linguistically nor memorially corrigible, and if it is a judgment about a perceived characteristic of a pure perceptual object, it would not be even epistemically corrigible.

It may seem that such a judgment would not be genuine because it would no longer involve the application of a concept to the determinate characteristic of the object, and nothing can be a judgment that does not involve the application of a concept. A concept is essentially a way of classifying. To apply a concept to something is to view that thing as being of a certain kind, to regard it as an instance, as belonging with certain other things in the same group. But one can always misclassify something, because one can always wrongly think of the thing as belonging together with things with which in fact it does not belong. Consequently, it may be argued, a judgment which does not allow for error in classification is one that does not involve a concept and thus is not a judgment at all.

But to misclassify is not the same as to not-classify, and a judgment can involve the application of a concept yet both allow for the possibility of misclassification and still be epistemically incorrigible. It is such a judgment that would ultimately constitute that in the content of a pure perceptual statement in virtue of which the latter is epistemically incorrigible. I shall try to make this clear in the case of misclassification involving the application of a word.

One may erroneously call something blue because one erroneously thinks that the thing has a color that it does not have. This is not the case relevant to *pure* perceptual statements. The relevant case is that of one's erroneously calling something blue, not because one thinks that the thing has a color that it does not have but because one thinks that the word *blue* is the correct word for such a color although it is not. In that case one misdescribes the color of the object. But misdescribing is not the same as not-describing. An incorrect use of a word is not the same as a senseless use of the word. When one has erroneously called something blue because of ignorance of the meaning of the word *blue*, one need not have failed to attach meaning to the word *blue;* one might simply have attached a meaning that the word does not have in ordinary language or even in one's own practice in the past. (This is why a private language would not be a senseless language, even if there were no ways of checking the correctness of its uses. To misunderstand a word is not the same as to not-understand it.) If a small child uses the word *mom* in the sense of *woman,* he is using it incorrectly yet with understanding, and when he calls a childless woman a "mom" he is classifying her and applying a concept to her just as genuinely as would someone else in classifying her and applying a concept to her by calling her a woman. When I make up a word and establish a meaning for it in order to express or clarify something (e.g., to make a finer distinction), the word is immediately intelligible and applicable, even though it has never been applied before and even if it will never be applied again. The case of using a word incorrectly, even for the first time, is very much the same. When I so use it I am in effect giving it a new sense. And if it has been given a sense, then it does have sense.

What is necessary for classification, and thus for the application of a concept, is that the thing classified be thought of as being an instance of a kind. It is not necessary that one apply to it the word that others use, or that oneself in the past used, for such a kind. Nor is it necessary that one be correct in thinking that something one remembers is of the same kind. Such a classification or application of a concept is what a primary perceptual *judgment* would be. It would consist in one's seeing an expanse as an instance of whatever characteristics it has. And such a seeing-as, I suggest, is the same as thinking, as judging, that the expanse has such characteristics. It is not the possibility of a separate such judgment that matters to our inquiry but the presence of its content in the primary perceptual statement. The latter cannot be corrigible with respect to that part of its content.

PART FOUR

Derivative Knowledge

1. Knowledge and Rational Belief

MOST OF OUR KNOWLEDGE is not primary but derivative. We have primary knowledge of certain relations of universals, of the existence and characteristics of the pure perceptual objects we actually perceive, and of certain inner states or experiences such as pain and belief. The great mass of what we claim, or hope, to know can be known only by derivation from the little that we have primary knowledge of. That our knowledge of most mathematical and all scientific propositions is derivative has never been questioned. That our everyday knowledge of the bodies that surround us is also derivative has usually been admitted, and the few philosophers who have denied this probably confused the question whether we have primary knowledge of bodies with the question whether we have absolutely certain knowledge of bodies.

The issues with regard to which epistemologists disagree have not typically included the extent, possibility, and objects of primary knowledge. Even the controversies about the way of ideas and the existence of sense-data, which would seem to be an exception, arose in the context of the inquiry into the extent and possibility of derivative knowledge of bodies. They were concerned with the nature that primary perceptual knowledge must have if we are to have knowledge of bodies. But not even the Naïve Realist should claim that we have primary knowledge of the existence and characteristics of bodies, though he could claim that certain propositions about bodies are directly entailed by the propositions expressing primary perceptual knowledge.

The typical epistemological question, Do I know that *p*?, has not usually been asked in regard to what can be known without inference. The reason should be obvious. Primary knowledge, whether of necessary or contingent truths, consists in the immediate, unconditional unthinkability of mistake. To raise a serious question regarding the legitimacy of a primary epistemic judgment would be either to engage in Cartesian metaphysical doubt or to simply fail to find unthinkable what someone else finds unthinkable. The latter is not nearly as common among philosophers as philosophers like to suppose. Philosophers have not usually disagreed about our possessing primary knowledge of the simple truths of arithmetic, of our inner experiences, or of the "appearances" of bodies. And if they had, their disagreements would hardly have been resoluble. No argument could convince one who finds a certain simple state of affairs unthinkable (e.g., something's being both red and green all over) that it really is thinkable. Cartesian metaphysical doubt is equally uncommon, presumably because of its rather obvious profitlessness. No argument could prove that our powers of thought are adequate to truth; no argument could prove that the principles of valid argument are true.

It is with respect to derivative knowledge that doubt is really possible, and thus it is here that the typical epistemological problems are likely to arise. Such doubt takes two forms. It may be directed at the correctness of the derivation. Or it may be directed at the legitimacy of the method of derivation itself. And the fact of greatest significance to epistemology is that ordinarily neither sort of doubt arises with respect to demonstrative derivations. As a method of derivation, demonstration has unquestionable legitimacy. And while the correctness of an extensive process of demonstration may be doubted, because of its dependence on the veridicality of memory, at least the separate steps of that process can have unquestionable correctness. The reason for this is obvious. Such steps can themselves constitute instances of absolute necessity, they can themselves be objects of primary knowledge, they can be such that their being mistaken would be unthinkable.

By demonstration we need not understand only formal or analytic demonstration, that is, one such that the conjunction of its premises and the denial of its conclusion would be a formal contradiction or reducible to one by substitution of synonyms. Any inference of one proposition from another such that it is absolutely impossible that the latter proposition is true while the former is false would be demonstrative inference. The proof that something is not green from the premise that it is red would be a likely example of nonformal and nonanalytic demonstrative inference. Thus, we must not confuse the question whether there are valid nondemonstrative inferences with the question whether there are valid nonformal and nonanalytic demonstrative inferences. It seems to me that the answer to the second question must be affirmative, though nothing in this book depends on this view. It is only recently that this question has been raised seriously, and, as we have seen, it has been raised mainly because of theories about the nature of necessary truth which we have already found inadequate. The first question, however, is of great importance and the answer to it is quite properly subject to controversy.

If there are only demonstrative methods of valid inference, then the general problem about derivative knowledge would be, What categories of derivative epistemic judgments can be demonstrated? It would concern only the correctness of the derivation of certain kinds of derivative knowledge, not the legitimacy of the method of derivation itself; for no one would question the legitimacy of demonstration. Indeed, this is precisely the character of the typical problems of traditional epistemology. Can we demonstrate that God exists? That the soul is immortal and the will free? That bodies exist and have the sorts of characteristics we believe they have? That the future will be like the past, and that the past really was as we remember it? Humean epistemology has seemed to have little difficulty in showing that none of these propositions can be *demonstrated* and thus in concluding that there cannot be knowledge of the sorts epistemologists have usually been interested in.

If we find it extraordinary that traditional philosophers took for granted that demonstration is the only method for the derivation of knowledge, we may recall that, at least until Hume, demonstrative knowledge of matters of fact was regarded as possible. Necessary connections, which are the ground of any demonstration, were supposed to hold not only between ideas but also between matters of fact. For causality was supposed to be a necessary connection and was supposed to be discoverable, in principle, wherever today we regard the inductive method to be applicable. I will have more to say on this topic in section *8* of this Part. Suffice it here to observe that it is Hume's convincing argument against objective necessary connections that has led philosophers to regard the province of demonstrative knowledge as extremely limited.

But even if in fact a certain derivative epistemic judgment cannot be justified by demonstration—that is, ultimately by an appeal to the unthinkability of the falsehood of what is known in conjunction with the truth of the propositions constituting the evidence—could it be that there are other kinds of derivation, by means of which the judgment may be justified? Obviously, this question is of great importance. If it can be answered affirmatively, then we would have the opportunity of silencing skepticism by, after all, succeeding in justifying the questionable sorts of derivative epistemic judgments. It would become possible to argue that Humean epistemology has seemed unanswerable only because of its far too limited conception of justification.

As I have suggested before,[1] even if most of what we regard as derivative knowledge cannot be justified, whether by familiar or by unfamiliar methods, and thus is not knowledge at all, it does not follow that skepticism is true. In addition to the skeptic who denies that we know what we think we know, there is the skeptic who denies that we have any reasons, any genuine evidence, for even believing what we ordinarily think we know. Usually, though not always, it is the latter sort of skepticism that is interesting. What is disturbing about skepticism with regard to the rise of the sun tomorrow is not so much its claim that we do not *know* that the sun will rise, that we may be mistaken in believing that it will rise, as its claim that we have no *reason* at all for believing that the sun will rise, that it is not even more probable than not that it will rise. This is not to say that skepticism regarding knowledge is unimportant, that it amounts to the insistence that instead of saying that we know something we say that we have very good evidence for believing it. Where the truths in question are of the greatest importance, as

1. See above, pp. 59–60.

philosophical truths usually are, where what is at issue is the immortality of the soul and the possibility of eternal damnation, the existence of an external world, of other persons, of God, or of a real past, mere evidence, however good, is not enough—it is knowledge, impossibility of error, that we demand. Nevertheless, the lack of even mere evidence for any of these would be shattering. And with respect to most topics, in science as well as in everyday life, we regard good evidence as sufficient and the lack of genuine knowledge both as something to be expected and as not really important. We must, therefore, consider not only the possibility and nature of derivative knowledge but also the possibility and nature of rational belief.

The distinction between knowledge and rational belief has application only to derivative, not to primary, knowledge. In other words, it is derivative, not primary, knowledge that is contrasted with rational belief. For rational belief is belief based on evidence, though not evidence sufficient for knowledge. The evidence for such a belief must be a truth other than that constituting the content of the belief, for otherwise the belief would be *self-evident*. And our account of self-evidence clearly does not allow for self-evidence that renders the belief merely rational and not knowledge, for we explained self-evidence in terms of the incompatibility between the falsehood of the belief and the context of the belief. But in fact in no account of self-evidence is it possible to distinguish between self-evidence sufficient for knowledge and self-evidence sufficient for rational belief. Any intelligible notion of evidence sufficient for rational belief is a notion of a degree of evidence which by its very nature can vary. What sense can there be in the supposition that such evidence, whose authority can vary, need not consist of truths other than the content of the belief? Such a supposition would amount to the claim that a belief can be probable in itself, in abstraction from any relations it has to other beliefs, for the notion of probable belief is merely a specification of that of rational belief.

Thus it is only with respect to derivative knowledge that the issue of the nature and possibility of rational belief arises. It may seem that for this reason our task in this Part must be twofold. We must be concerned with derivative knowledge. And we must also be concerned with rational belief. In fact, however, we shall find that the crucial conceptual issue regarding derivative knowledge and that regarding rational belief are one and the same. It is whether there are kinds of evidence other than general (whether primary or derivative) unthinkability of mistake, whether there is room in conceptual space for other species of the concept of evidence. Only if this issue is resolved affirmatively would we be able to elucidate a sense of the word *evidence* that would allow us to speak of rational belief as distinct from knowledge, as well as of nondemonstrative derivative knowledge. In recent years, largely through the influence of Wittgenstein, this issue has been stated with the use of the word *criterion*. Granted that the unthinkability of mistake is a criterion of evidence, of a basis or good reason for belief (we may call it the *demonstrative criterion*), can there be other and equally legitimate criteria of evidence? If there can, then we may find that while some are criteria, though nondemonstrative, of evidence sufficient for knowledge, others are criteria of evidence sufficient for rational belief but not for knowledge. If there cannot, then both nondemonstrative derivative knowledge and rational belief would be impossible. It is with this more fundamental general issue of additional criteria of evidence, which, unlike that of nondemonstrative knowledge, is independent of the conclusions we reached in Part One, that I shall be mainly concerned in this Part, though I shall return to the specific question of nondemonstrative knowledge in section 7. It is the chief issue regarding the concept of derivative knowledge. If nondemonstrative evidence is impossible, then the philosophical problems of derivative knowledge would call not for an inquiry, such as ours, into the concept of knowledge but for investigations into the concepts of the specific *objects* of derivative knowledge (e.g., of body and of another mind) and for ingenious demonstrations.

In all probability, the main alternative to skepticism would then be reductionism, the view that the sorts of derivative epistemic judgments that are philosophically problematic can be derived by demonstration from the appropriate evidence, because their content, contrary to what we ordinarily suppose it to be, coincides with at least a part of the content of the judgments constituting the evidence. For example, the reductionist may insist that other persons' thoughts and feelings are merely patterns of their behavior and that for that reason our knowledge of them can be justified by demonstration from our knowledge of other persons' behavior. And he would hold similar views regarding bodies, the future, the past, and any other questionable object of derivative knowledge. The implausibility of such views requires no comment. It is unclear why anyone would have thought reductionism preferable to skepticism.

There are two ways in which there could be both demonstrative and nondemonstrative criteria of evidence. First, they could all be species of the same genus. They would be specifically different from each other. But they would also have something essential in common, namely, that in virtue of which they are criteria of *evidence*. And what they have in common would in fact be the unique *general* criterion of evidence, whose relation to the demonstrative and to the nondemonstrative criteria would be like that of triangularity to equilateral, isosceles, and scalene triangularity. Then the legitimacy of the nondemonstrative criteria of evidence would be as secure and unquestionable as that of the demonstrative criterion. But I am unaware of a serious attempt to show *what* the multiple criteria of evidence have in common. It should go without saying that to show this, one must do something more than simply apply the word *evidence*—or a synonym of it such as *reason for belief, justification, ground, support*—to all of them. One must identify, with some precision, that feature which, for example, deductive and inductive inferences have in common and which renders the premises of both evidence for their respective conclusions.

The second way in which there could be both demonstrative and nondemonstrative criteria of evidence appears far more hopeful. According to it, the multiple criteria of evidence are not species of the same genus, do not have something in common, and are, in fact, logically quite distinct. Nevertheless, they are equally legitimate, equally genuine. And their multiplicity is such that it does not render the word *evidence* equivocal, and thus remains epistemologically relevant. It is this second possibility that has attracted the attention of contemporary philosophers. I will consider it, and its ramifications, in detail, although in section 9 of this Part I will have more to say about the first possibility. The main issue in our investigation will be the intelligibility of the general concept of criterion that such a view presupposes. It is the concept of what has been called a *nondefining criterion* for the applicability of a word, and it constitutes a major departure from the sort of concept of criterion for the applicability of a word that one would ordinarily have adopted, namely, the concept of what has been called a *defining criterion*. I shall begin by delineating the way in which the latter would be introduced.

2. *The Concept of Defining Criterion*

RECENT PHILOSOPHY owes the popularity of the term *criterion* to Wittgenstein.[2] He used it, generally, as a technical philosophical term for a logical, conceptual, linguistic, conventional ground for the applicability of a word to a certain object (or for its employability, correct use, in a certain situation) and contrasted a criterion with empirical grounds, contingent evidence, for the applicability of the word to something. That there are criteria, in this very general sense, is obvious. A word has a meaning and is applicable to an object solely in virtue of ultimately arbitrary conventions that associate it with that object. That fact about the object in virtue of which it is so associated with the word is the criterion for the applicability of the word to the object. At the same time, a criterion for the applicability of a word to a certain object is also a criterion, in the ordinary, nonphilosophical sense, for the object's being of a certain kind, namely, of the kind with which the word is conventionally associated; it is not at all something of purely linguistic interest. For, that a word is applicable to an object determines *what* the object is.[3] (Although to say this, is not to say that *all* that the object is, or can be known to be, consists in the applicability of that word to it.) If this is not immediately obvious, the reason may only be the confusion of the applicability of the word to something with its actual application to that something. The latter need have nothing to do with what the object is. The former does. An object can be blue without anyone saying that it is, and one can say that a certain object is blue even if it is not.

2. The classical introduction of his notion of criterion occurs in Wittgenstein's *Blue Book:* ". . . to explain my criterion for another person's having a toothache is to give a grammatical explanation about the word 'toothache' and, in this sense, an explanation concerning the meaning of the word 'toothache.' When we learnt the use of the phrase 'so-and-so has a toothache' we were pointed out certain kinds of behaviour of those who were said to have a toothache. As an instance of these kinds of behaviour let us take holding your cheek . . . . Now one may go on and ask: 'How do you know that he has got toothache when he holds his cheek?' The answer to this might be, 'I say, *he* has toothache when he holds his cheek because I hold my cheek when I have a toothache.' But what if we went on asking: 'And why do you suppose that toothache corresponds to his holding his cheek just because your toothache corresponds to your holding your cheek?' You will be at a loss to answer this question, and find that here we strike rock bottom, that is we have come down to conventions" (*The Blue and Brown Books* [Oxford: Basil Blackwell, 1960], p. 24).

3. Cf. Wittgenstein, *Philosophical Investigations,* tr. G. E. M. Anscombe (Oxford: Basil Blackwell, 1953), §§ 370–73.

Under the influence of the ordinary, nonphilosophical usage of the word *criterion,* philosophers have often diverged significantly from the above sense. In ordinary usage, a criterion is a characteristic mark of something, a standard for judging whether something falls in a certain class, a norm by which we determine the degree to which something is a proper specimen of its kind. The word may be correctly applied to an essential attribute, a logically sufficient but not necessary condition, a necessary but not logically sufficient condition, conclusive empirical evidence, good empirical evidence, and even any merely familiar characteristic of something. And we find that in philosophical discussions the concept of a criterion for the applicability of a word is sometimes used as little more than a synonym for "reason for applying a word." But there are several and very different sorts of reasons for applying a word, and we would gain nothing by calling, indiscriminately, all of them *criteria.* Let us distinguish, very briefly, these sorts of reasons.

There would seem to be four most general considerations regarding the application of a word to a certain object.[4] (1) The characteristic of the object in virtue of which the latter is a member of the class of objects to each of which the word is applicable as a matter of linguistic convention. We may call it the *criterial characteristic.* The *fact* that the object has such a characteristic (not the characteristic itself) may be called the *criterion,* the conceptual ground, for the applicability of the word to it. The criterion must be distinguished from what may be called the speaker's *conceptual reason* for applying the word to the object, namely, his *belief* that the object has that characteristic. One may apply a word to the wrong object but for the right conceptual reason, or to the right object but for the wrong conceptual reason. (2) The feature of the total situation of the use of the word, the presence of which serves the speaker as grounds (whether inductive or deductive) for believing that the object has the criterial characteristic, that to which one would actually appeal in justifying one's application of the word. Such a feature may be called the *circumstance* of the application of the word (the word *evidence* being too general, since the criterion also can be called evidence, and Wittgenstein's own term *symptom* being too specific); the speaker's belief that such a feature is present may be called his *circumstantial reason* for applying the

---

4. For the sake of simplicity and brevity, I shall make these distinctions with respect to words that are applied to objects. Many words, of course, are not *applicable to* objects but *employable in* situations. The distinctions regarding the latter would be parallel.

word. A word may be applicable to an object though there is no way of discovering that it is; or there may be a way of discovering that it is, but one may fail to use that way. (3) The *effect* of the actual application of the word, the difference the utterance of the word makes to the situation in which it occurs, for example, the passing of information, the encouragement of a certain attitude, the hearer's being insulted, and so forth. The effect should be distinguished from (4) the *purpose* for which the speaker utters the word. The former is what the utterance in fact does. The latter is what it is intended to do. One does not apply a word to an object merely because doing so would be correct, but for a specific purpose. And sometimes the use of the wrong word has the desired effect, though at other times the use of the right word fails to have the desired effect.

The criterion for the applicability of a word, one's conceptual reason for applying it, the circumstance for its application, one's circumstantial reason for applying it, the effect of its application, and the purpose of its application are, of course, intimately related, and thus the loose labeling of all of them as "criteria for the use of the word" is not surprising. Often our description of the act one performs in uttering a word is determined by one or several of these features of the utterance. Nevertheless, they are quite distinct (though in some cases—e.g., the application of *headache* to one's own state—one and the same feature of the situation may serve both as criterion and as circumstance). In particular, it is important to recognize that only the criterion is determinative of the concept that corresponds to the word. It is natural for blue objects to look blue. But a man may call a blue object red because it looks red to him and still have perfect knowledge of the meaning of the word *blue,* perfect grasp of the concept of blue color. It is natural that a person who is called unintelligent should feel insulted. But the members of some religious sect might instead be flattered; and the word *unintelligent* is insulting *because* it means what it does—it is not *part* of its meaning to be insulting. Indeed, there are words the purposes of whose use seem determined by linguistic convention, e.g., *stupid*. But even such conventionally determined purposes are not constitutive of the concepts corresponding to the words. A stupid man is simply an unintelligent man, not a certain kind of unintelligent man, for example, one who is insulted, or is to be insulted, or deserves to be insulted.

If the concept of criterion is introduced in the above manner, then it would be obvious that a word, e.g., *evidence,* can have many and logically distinct criteria, and a speaker can have many and logically distinct conceptual reasons for its use, only insofar as it is equivocal; that the criterion for the correct use of a word is precisely that which one must describe or point out when one explains the meaning of the word; and that the criterion for something's being such and such is identical with that something's being such and such. But there may be many and logically distinct kinds of circumstances, and thus circumstantial reasons, for the use of a word; the use of a word may have many and logically distinct effects; and a speaker may have many and logically distinct purposes for his use of a word.

Thus, a criterion for the applicability of a word to a certain object would be a logically sufficient condition for the applicability of the word to that object, for the object's being such and such. The fact that y is x is a criterion for y's being m because of the rule or convention (explicit or not) that the word "m" is applicable to anything that is x. It is because the word "m" is applicable to anything that is x by virtue of a rule or convention that the fact that y is x is a logically sufficient condition of the applicability of the word "m" to y. It would be unintelligible to suppose that there is a convention for the applicability of a word and that the convention is satisfied in a certain particular case and yet that the word is not applicable in that case. But, also, either a word is equivocal, in a perfectly ordinary, straightforward sense—and then none of its criteria is a logically necessary condition for its applicability, though the disjunction of its criteria would be; or it has only one criterion—and then that criterion is not only a sufficient but also a logically necessary condition for its applicability. For, in view of the purely conventional nature of the meaning of a word, it would be unintelligible to suppose that a word is *applicable* to an object even if the object does not have the characteristic in virtue of which alone is the word applicable to anything.

The criterion for the applicability of the word "m" to something and that something's being m would be identical. To state the criterion for the applicability of the word "m" to something would be to state what it is to be m. A criterion and that for which it is a criterion would be one and the same. Suppose that y's being x is the criterion for the applicability of the word "m" to y and yet that y's being x and y's being m are not identical. Then it must be, at least logically, possible to identify y's being m without referring to y's being x; otherwise there would be no sense to saying that they are not identical. But to identify y's being m is simply to determine that y is m; to determine that y is m is to determine that the word "m" is applicable to y; and to determine that the word "m" is applicable to y is to determine that y satisfies the criterion for the applicability of "m." Therefore, either y's being x is not the criterion for the applicability of the word "m" to y or y's being x is identical with y's being m. Therefore, the criterion for the applicability of the word "m" to y and y's being m are identical. For example, if one's holding one's cheek is the criterion for the applicability to one of the phrase "having a toothache," then to have a toothache is the same as to hold one's cheek. Otherwise it should be possible to identify one's having a toothache without referring to one's holding one's cheek. But to identify one's having a toothache is to determine that one has a toothache; to determine that one has a toothache is to determine that the phrase "having a toothache" is applicable to one, and to determine that the phrase "having a toothache" is applicable to one is to determine that one satisfies the criterion for the applicability of that phrase. Therefore, either one's holding one's cheek is not the criterion for the applicability of the phrase "having a toothache" to one, or one's holding one's cheek is the same as one's having a toothache. We must reach such a conclusion, however complicated we make the alleged behavioral criteria of someone's having a toothache.

Thus, it would seem, the term *criterion* has a function similar to that of the term *definition*. If a criterion is both a logically necessary and logically sufficient condition for the applicability of a word, one could say that to *state the criterion* for the applicability of a word is to *define* the word, that to know the criterion for the applicability of a word is to know what the word means, that a criterion and that for which it is a criterion are identical. If we were to prefer the concept of criterion to that of definition, the main reason would be that a definition, being a *verbal* expression of a conventional rule of meaning, is, especially in the case of philosophically interesting terms, seldom easy to produce and sometimes actually impossible. The concept of criterion, as so explained, is that of what has been called a defining criterion.

3. The Concept of
Nondefining Criterion

THE ABOVE ACCOUNT of the concept of criterion (in the technical sense of a conceptual ground for the applicability of a word) would ordinarily have been unchallengeable. That the conceptual ground for the applicability of a word may only be a *defining* criterion would have seemed a conclusion so obviously true as to be trivial. It has been challenged, however, and especially in regard to the epistemological topics that constitute the general problem of derivative knowledge.[5] The challenge consists, briefly, in the claim that a criterion for the applicability of a word need not be a defining criterion in order to be a conceptual ground for the applicability of the word; that there can be multiple and logically distinct criteria for the applicability of a word even if the latter is not equivocal; that a criterion and that for which it is the criterion are not identical; that the criterion for the applicability of a word need be neither a logically sufficient nor a logically necessary condition for the applicability of the word.

Wittgenstein says, "To the question 'How do you know that so-and-so is the case?' we sometimes answer by giving '*criteria*' and sometimes by

---

5. A. J. Ayer writes: ". . . the necessary and sufficient conditions for knowing that something is the case are first that what one is said to know be true, secondly that one be sure of it, and thirdly that one should have the right to be sure. This right may be earned in various ways; but even if one could give a complete description of them it would be a mistake to try to build it into a definition of knowledge, just as it would be a mistake to try to incorporate our actual standards of goodness into a definition of good" (*The Problem of Knowledge* [London: Macmillan & Co., 1958], p. 34). S. E. Toulmin distinguishes between the "force" of a modal term such as "cannot," i.e., its practical implications, and the criteria, standards, grounds, or reasons by reference to which we decide in any particular context that the use of the term is appropriate; and he warns that "it will be wrong to say, merely on account of [the variation in criteria for the use of the term 'cannot'] that the word 'cannot' means quite different things when it figures in different sorts of conclusions" (*The Uses of Argument* [Cambridge: At the University Press, 1958], p. 34). R. M. Hare argues that "Since . . . it is possible to use the word 'good' for a new class of objects without further instruction, learning the use of the word for one class of objects cannot be a different lesson from learning it for another class of objects—though learning the criteria of goodness in a new class of objects may be a new lesson each time" (*The Language of Morals* [Oxford: Clarendon Press, 1952], p. 97). R. M. Chisholm officially announces that there is a "problem of the criterion" and argues that "we must not suppose that a description of [the criteria for applying 'adequate evidence'] would constitute a *definition* of 'evidence'" (*Perceiving: A Philosophical Study* [Ithaca N.Y.: Cornell University Press, 1957], p. 32). He asks a number of "difficult questions" concerning "the relation of *evidence* to . . . 'the marks of evidence'" (p. 97). Is the relation analytic, or synthetic *a priori*, or synthetic *a posteriori*, or is it merely "emotive"? Chisholm remains unhappy with all of these alternatives. Norman Malcolm denies that "when one states the criterion for something one says what that something *is*—one *defines* it." (*Dreaming* [London: Routledge & Kegan Paul, 1959], p. 60). "The criterion of someone's having a sore foot is what he does and says in certain circumstances; and *that* is not a sore foot" (*ibid*). Nevertheless, at least with respect to the criteria of dreaming, he insists that the criterion and that for which it is the criterion are not logically independent. Clearly, Malcolm's position raises the same difficult questions that Chisholm's does.

279

giving *'symptoms.'* "[6] If we use the word *evidence* in its standard and quite unobjectionable sense of a reason or ground for belief, then the Wittgensteinean concept of criterion amounts to that of a certain *kind* of evidence, namely, one that is linguistic, conventional, conceptual in nature. Such evidence bears an appealing resemblance to demonstrative evidence. Indeed, were a criterion defining, its evidential role would be demonstrative, though triflingly so. For example, if being an unmarried man is the defining criterion of being a bachelor, then we could utilize someone's being an unmarried man as demonstrative evidence that he is a bachelor. But if a criterion could be nondefini then the sort of evidence it would constitute might be of great importance. It would still be a conceptual ground for the applicability of a word, and thus would preserve its appealing resemblance to demonstrative evidence. But it would not be trifling at all. For, not being defining, a criterion would now be an entity, fact, state, or property distinct from that for which it is a criterion. For example, it may become possible to claim that someone's holding his cheek is a conceptual, and thus presumably unquestionably legitimate, ground for believing or knowing that the phrase "having a toothache" is applicable to him, that is, that he does have a toothache, even though his holding his cheek and his having a toothache are not at all one and the same. It may become possible to justify our derivative epistemic judgments about other minds, bodies, the future, the past, and thus to solve the chief epistemological problems in a novel and far more promising manner. We would be able to refute the skeptic, for he is not likely to question the legitimacy of conceptual sorts of evidence.

A discussion of the claim that there are nondefining criteria must begin with an important distinction, one which is required by the fact that the word *criterion* is itself an epistemic word referring to a certain kind of evidence. The distinction I have in mind is that between what I shall label first-order and second-order criteria. A second-order criterion is a criterion for the applicability of the word *evidence* or its synonyms; it is a criterion *of evidence,* a criterion for something's *being evidence* for something else. A first-order criterion, on the other hand, is a criterion for the applicability of a word or phrase other than *evidence* or the latter's synonyms; it is a criterion for something's being the case that is not a criterion for something's being evidence for something else. For example, someone's holding his cheek would be a *first-order criterion* for his having a toothache, as

6. *The Blue and Brown Books,* pp. 24–25.

his having a toothache is not a case of something's being evidence for something else. On the other hand, the fact that a certain proposition entails another would be a *second-order criterion* for the former's being evidence for the latter. If someone's holding one's cheek is evidence for his having a toothache, then the criterion for its being such evidence would be a second-order criterion.

The distinction is important for two reasons. The first is that the existence and even possibility of certain first-order nondefining criteria can be determined only by appealing to second-order criteria. For a first-order criterion is simply a certain entity, state, or fact that constitutes a conceptual evidence for something's being the case. And it constitutes such evidence only because it satisfies a certain general criterion of evidence, a second-order criterion. Consequently, the most important question regarding criteria, namely, whether there can be nondefining criteria, can be answered only by appealing to general criteria of evidence, by determining whether something that is not a logically sufficient or necessary condition but is a conceptual ground for the applicability of a word can satisfy any general criterion of evidence.

The question regarding the possibility of nondemonstrative derivative knowledge, for example, of bodies or of other minds, concerns primarily the criteria of evidence itself and only secondarily the separate and particular criteria for the existence and nature of bodies or of other minds. Whether there are such latter criteria and what they are may be determined only by a prior investigation of the general criteria of evidence, of that in virtue of conformity to which something would count as conceptual evidence for statements about bodies or other minds. What is at issue regarding the appeal to criteria in justifying derivative knowledge is not so much the truth of the general claim, for example, that a certain behavior is evidence that someone is in pain or that certain perceivings are evidence that it is raining, but the question *what* kind of evidence such behavior or such perceivings would be and, more specifically, in what sense, if any, can they be said to be *conceptual* evidence. To say that, for example, someone's holding his cheek is a criterion for his having a toothache is, primarily, to offer a theory, namely, a theory about a certain kind of evidence, and only secondarily to draw attention to the fact that someone's holding one's cheek is indeed evidence for his having a toothache. The theory is, as it should be, far more general than the facts it attempts to explain. It proposes that something can be conceptual evidence for something else without being a logically necessary or sufficient condition for it. The first test the theory must meet is the question whether what it proposes is even intelligible. But to question the intelligibility or truth of the theory is not to deny the facts it is designed to explain or elucidate; it is not to deny (though neither is it to affirm) that, for example, one's holding one's cheek is evidence that one has a toothache.

As long as we fail to distinguish between first- and second-order criteria and concentrate our discussion on the former, we are not under the control of fundamental notions or in a position to even begin to grasp the concepts involved in derivative knowledge. We merely take for granted that we do have such knowledge; we recognize, for example, that we can know other minds only through behavior and bodies only through perception, we admit that such knowledge can neither be deductive nor inductive, and we then conclude simply that there must be some other kind of evidence, namely, one that is both nondeductive and noninductive. The attachment of the term *criterion* to such evidence does not render this bare and, as Kant would have said, infinite judgment conceptually illuminating. To achieve understanding of these matters we must begin by asking what it is for something to be both nondeductive and noninductive evidence, what would be the content of any such criterion of evidence. And when we so begin, we are no longer free to appeal quickly to the facts of what we say or believe. For it is the proper *interpretation* and correct *appraisal* of what we say and believe that is at issue now.

We shall begin with the issue of the criteria of evidence, of second-order criteria. Our treatment of this issue will determine the view we shall adopt regarding the possibility of first-order nondefining criteria. But in section 5 of this Part we will consider this possibility independently of general considerations regarding the criteria of evidence. For it is too important a matter to be denied a full discussion.

But there is a second and more specific reason for making the distinction between first-order and second-order criteria. It allows us to separate the question whether there are nondefining criteria for such states as someone's having a toothache and the question whether there are nondefining criteria for the applicability of the word *evidence* itself, for example, for regarding a certain behavior as conceptual yet nondeductive evidence that someone has a toothache. It may be that the first question can be answered affirmatively only if the second question is answered affirmatively. Nevertheless, there is a crucial difference between the two.

Part of what is meant by a nondefining criterion, though only a part, is that it is not a logically sufficient condition of that for which it is a criterion. But while there are reasons for supposing that a first-order criterion need not be a logically sufficient condition, there are no reasons at all for supposing that a second-order criterion, a criterion of evidence, need not be a logically sufficient condition. Even if we allow that some-one's holding his cheek is conceptual evidence for his having a toothache, we must, if we are to avoid absurdity, qualify this by saying that neverthe-less a person can hold his cheek and still not have a toothache. However complex we may make the person's behavior, we must still allow that its occurrence does not logically entail that the person has a toothache. This is in part why we require the notion of nondefining criterion: to be able to say that something can be a conceptual yet nondeductive ground for something else. But it would be simply nonsense to say, and to my knowledge it has never been said, that a criterion of evidence need not be a logically sufficient condition for something's being evidence, that when a criterion of evidence is present, evidence need not be present, or need be present only "for the most part." We may allow that someone's holding his cheek can be evidence for his having a toothache even if he might not have a toothache. But we can hardly allow that whatever our criterion for one's-holding-one's-cheek-being-evidence-for-one's-having-a-toothache may be, it can be present even if one's holding one's cheek might not be the sort of thing that is evidence for one's having a toothache. To deny that a criterion for something's being evidence is a logically sufficient condition for that something's being evidence could only render us completely rudderless in the foggy waters of the logic of criteria.

But that a criterion of evidence, a second-order criterion, must be a logically sufficient condition does not entail that it must be a defining criterion, that it must also be a logically necessary condition. The tradi-tional general criterion of evidence has been the demonstrative criterion. According to it, x is evidence for y if it is absolutely impossible that while x is present (or is the case) y is not present (or is not the case). That the demonstrative criterion is a logically sufficient condition for something's being evidence—that is, that if it is absolutely impossible that x is present and y is not, then logically necessarily the presence of x is evidence for the presence of y—has never been denied. But is it also a logically necessary condition of evidence? This is the major issue in this Part of our inquiry. If it is, then the demonstrative criterion is a defining criterion. Nothing then can be evidence if it is not demonstrative. And since both derivative knowledge and rational belief must be based on evidence, nothing can be derivative knowledge or rational belief that is not demonstrable. The skeptical consequences of this view are well known, though, as I have observed above, the view is not as narrow as nowadays we suppose.

It is significant that in fact no *general* criteria of nondemonstrative evidence have been proposed. The criteria that have been proposed are explicitly limited to specific subject matters, namely, those with regard to which derivative knowledge has seemed philosophically problematic. None of the proposed criteria has been suggested by, let alone deduced from, general considerations about the nature of evidence. We have merely been told such things as that other persons' behavior is what is called evidence for other persons' thoughts and feelings or that certain kinds of observed past conjunctions of two kinds of events are what is called evidence for their conjunction in the future. What is noteworthy about such claims is not so much that they are left undefended but that they are inextricably and explicitly tied to specific subject matters, whether other minds or empirical generalizations. The demonstrative criterion is totally different in this respect. It can be stated and defended (e.g., as we did in Part One) *in general,* in abstraction from any specific subject matter. To say that x is evidence for y if it is absolutely impossible for y not to be the case if x is the case, is to make a statement that is applicable to any subject matter and thus independent of the facts about any subject matter. According to one and the same criterion, something's being an odd number is evidence that it is not divisible by two, something's being green is evidence that it is not red, something's being square is evidence that it is not round, something's being visible is evidence that it is extended. Possibly, to each of these a more specific demonstrative criterion is applicable. But any such specific demonstrative criterion would still be a species of the same genus. I do not wish to urge that the unique generality of the demonstrative criterion is a sufficient reason for denying the legitimacy of any other proposed criteria of evidence. It is, however, some reason for suspicion regarding the latter.

It may seem that the defense of the existence of nondemonstrative criteria of evidence, and thus of the view that the criteria of evidence are nondefining, is easy, obvious, and unobjectionable. We in fact use the word *evidence* (or, more likely, words such as *knowledge* or a phrase such as *reason for believing*) according to different criteria in regard to different subject matters. Such usage is standard and quite common. To deny the existence or legitimacy of such criteria is either obviously false or a case of the influence of a mystical belief that the real meaning of a word is determined by reference to something other than its standard use. Consider the following derivative epistemic judgments, all of which would be, in an appropriate context, regarded as based on evidence. (1) I know that it is raining outside. (2) I know that 16 times 11 is 176. (3) I know that she loves him. (4) I know that I was in Washington in the summer of 1955. (5) I know that one ought to pay one's debts. What criterion would we employ in determining that what we regard as the evidence supporting such judgments is really evidence? It seems that there is no *one* criterion that we could so employ regarding all five cases, that in fact five fundamentally different, logically entirely distinct criteria of evidence would have to be employed. The evidence supporting (1) is, let us suppose, one's observation of the rain; in the case of (2), the self-contradiction of the denial of the arithmetical statement; in the case of (3), the observation of what she says and does (not the observation of her love for him); in the case of (4), one's memory of the past event; in the case of (5), perhaps the social consequences of one's not paying one's debts. All five are quite different, it is difficult to find any similarities among them. They are completely and unquestionably logically distinct and in no sense species of one and the same genus. The criteria in accordance with which they are correctly called evidence are, therefore, themselves completely and unquestionably logically distinct and in no sense species of the same genus. Each is applicable only to its appropriate specific subject matter, with regard to which its legitimacy is unchallengeable. The criterion of evidence with respect to bodies is observation; with respect to mathematical truths, self-contradiction of denial; with respect to other persons' thoughts and feelings, observation of their bodies; with respect to past events, memory; and with respect to morality, the social consequences of action. Nevertheless, only one is a species of the demonstrative criterion, namely, the self-contradiction of denial.

But such a defense of nondemonstrative criteria of evidence is quite insufficient. Even if the use of *evidence* in nondemonstrative contexts is a matter of standard practice, and thus in a sense there are nondemonstrative criteria of evidence, skepticism may still be true. For there may be such a multiplicity of criteria of evidence simply because *the word "evidence" is equivocal*. And if it is, then the multiplicity of the criteria of evidence need be of no greater epistemological significance than the multiplicity of the senses of *know* which we examined in Part One, section 2, most of which we found to be epistemologically irrelevant. The mere existence of a sense of *evidence* in which it would be correct to say that *x* is evidence for *y* need have no bearing on the problems of derivative knowledge. Suppose that through some sort of philological accident the word *evidence* came to have, in addition to its present senses, one in which it would be synonymous with *belief*. Then it would be perfectly correct for someone to say that he has evidence that God exists if he believes that God exists. But such a philological accident would constitute no theological advance.[7]

In fact, the defenders of the multiplicity of the criteria of evidence have been careful to avoid leaving the impression that what they are defending is that the word *evidence* is equivocal. And the reason for this has been not so much their awareness of the inability of equivocation to support epistemological theses, but the obvious fact that the word *evidence* is not equivocal. In the above five statements, whether I am appealing to deduction, or observation of bodies, or memory as my evidence for asserting something, I am using the word *evidence* in the same general sense. The claim that there are nondemonstrative criteria of evidence must, therefore, be understood as denying that the multiplicity of criteria of evidence is the result of equivocation with the word *evidence,* and thus as asserting that they are nondefining. When so understood, it becomes a philosophical thesis of considerable importance. I shall call it the *thesis of nonequivocating multiple criteria of evidence.*

If true, the thesis would serve as the basis of a solution to the traditional epistemological problems and consequently of a refutation of skepticism. For by insisting that the criteria of evidence are "field-dependent," that they are to be discovered in the very modes of reasoning we actually employ and not through some independent insight into the nature of evidence, the thesis legitimizes the usual methods of justifying the most general kinds of claims to knowledge or to rational belief. And it also makes the philosophical inquiry into the nature of evidence seem virtually identical with an inquiry into the actual uses of the word *evidence.* For

---

7. Indeed, in sacred theology the word *evidence* does seem to be governed by a distinct criterion, namely, occurrence in Scripture. An atheist would not change his views upon learning of the existence of such a criterion.

the multiplicity and diversity of the criteria of evidence, according to the thesis, are such that their discovery may only be achieved by a description of how the word *evidence* (or a synonymous expression) actually functions in discourse.

It may be worth recalling that the really serious kind of skepticism consists in the denial that anything can be sufficiently like the absolute impossibility, the unthinkability, of mistake to be nonequivocally called evidence.[8] Using the concept of criterion, we may now say that the skeptic denies that there can be criteria of evidence sufficiently like the demonstrative criterion to be still counted as criteria for the application of the same concept; he denies that the word *evidence* can be applied nonequivocally to both demonstrative and (any sort of) nondemonstrative evidence. But the legitimacy of the demonstrative criterion is unquestionable. Its relevance to the appraisal of belief and the choice of action, which are the typical context of the employment of the concept of evidence, is undeniable. Consequently, the skeptic concludes, nothing that is unlike the demonstrative criterion can be a criterion for the applicability of the concept of evidence. It is difficult to deny the skeptic's premise that any nondemonstrative criteria of evidence (e.g., past conjunctions in the case of inductive inference) are quite unlike the demonstrative criterion (i.e., the unthinkability of mistake, whether in premises or in inference). Therefore, it has seemed that if the skeptic is to be answered, this must be done by denying his other premise, namely, that if certain criteria for the applicability of a concept are quite unlike, then they cannot be criteria for the applicability of the same concept. The thesis of nonequivocating multiple criteria is intended to deny just that premise. It claims that there are multiple and logically distinct criteria for the applicability of the word *evidence* even though the word remains unequivocal, that the criteria of evidence, the second-order criteria, are nondefining.

4. Nonequivocating Multiple Criteria of Evidence

THE THESIS OF nonequivocating multiple criteria of evidence rests obviously on an important assumption: that there can be a relation such as it

8. See above, pp. 59–60.

claims there is between the criteria of evidence and evidence itself. What it tells us about this relation is (1) that a criterion of evidence is a conceptual, conventional ground for the applicability of the word *evidence* to something; (2) that a criterion of evidence is a logically sufficient condition of something's being evidence (even if such a something is not itself a logically sufficient condition of that for which it is evidence); and (3) that there can be (indeed, that there are) many and logically distinct criteria for the application of the word *evidence* even though this word is not equivocal, that is, that a criterion of evidence is not a logically necessary condition of something's being evidence.

The first feature of the relation is required if the thesis is to be *relevant* to the philosophical issue for which it is proposed, namely, the account, elucidation, and justification of the application in certain subject matters of the concept of evidence. The second feature is required if the thesis is to provide a definite *solution* of that philosophical issue; for example, even if the occurrence of a certain behavior need not entail that someone is in pain, surely, whatever our reason for regarding such behavior as evidence that someone is in pain, it must entail that, *settle* the question whether, the behavior is such evidence. The third feature is required if the thesis is to be saying something *distinctive and novel*. For, of course, no one would have denied that there must be conceptual, conventional grounds for the application of the word *evidence* to something and that the presence of these grounds is logically sufficient for the applicability of the word to that something. To be saying something new, the thesis must claim that there is more than one kind of such conceptual grounds. The demonstrative criterion unquestionably provides such a ground, and if there can be only one criterion of evidence, then nothing can be nondemonstrative evidence. And the thesis must also hold that this multiplicity of criteria of evidence is not due to equivocation of the word *evidence*. For not only is it false that that word is equivocal but such equivocation could render the correctness of our calling something evidence irrelevant to the epistemological question whether it is evidence, whether its role in the appraisal of belief and the choice of actions is at all like that of demonstration. (In a similar fashion, the correctness of calling an automobile accident the "end" of a certain journey is irrelevant to the question what the goal of that journey was.)

To make the third property of the relation clearer, we should specify that if the criteria of evidence are logically distinct, then, *at least*, (1) the satisfaction of one of them in any particular case does not entail the satisfaction of any of the others, and (2) they are not species of the same genus. The reason for (1) is obvious. Condition (2) is necessary because if the criteria for the applicability of a word are species of the same genus, then clearly the latter is the essential something that all the criteria have in common and thus is the real and *only* criterion for the applicability of that word. We should also say that, in the context of the thesis, if a word is equivocal then, *at least,* it has two or more senses such that (1) its use in one of them does not entail that it is also used, in the same particular situation, in any of the others, and (2) they are not species of the same genus. These conditions of equivocation are necessary because we wish to avoid saying, for example, that the word *triangle* is equivocal because it means both a closed plane three-sided figure and a closed plane figure possessing three angles, or because it refers with equal legitimacy to equilateral, isosceles, and scalene triangles.

Now what can a relation which has the above three properties be? Let us consider what it *cannot* be. It cannot be a relation of identity. A criterion and that for which it is a criterion cannot be identical. For then it would be impossible that there be many and logically distinct criteria for one and the same thing. Nor can it be a relation between a species and its proper genus, for example, in the sense in which something's being an equilateral triangle might be said to be a criterion for its being a triangle. The species of a genus do have something essential in common, namely, their genus, and *that* would be the real and only criterion. Nor can it be a relation between an essential property and its subject, for example, in the sense in which something's being a closed plane three-sided figure is a criterion for its being a triangle. For such an essential property is precisely what would be described in the definition of the subject, and thus if there were many and logically distinct criteria for the applicability of a word, then there would be many and logically distinct definitions, and many really different senses, of the word.

Nor can the relation between a criterion and that for which it is the criterion be that of a necessary, though not essential, property and its subject. For then either there could be only one criterion of evidence, or the word *evidence* would not be applicable unless what it was applied to satisfied *all* of the many logically distinct criteria of evidence; for example, if one mathematical proposition were to constitute evidence for another, it would have to, absurdly, both entail it and have the sort of specific relation to it that a proposition about a person's behavior may have to a proposition about that person's thoughts or feelings. Of course, the *disjunction* of all of the criteria of evidence would be a necessary condition of the applicability of the word *evidence,* but this would be the case also if the word is simply equivocal or the criteria are species of the same genus.

And now we come to the last and most important thing that a criterion, in the sense required by the thesis of nonequivocating multiple criteria of evidence, cannot be, although, as we have seen, it must be. It cannot even be a logically sufficient condition for the applicability of the word. The satisfaction of the criterion cannot *entail* that the word is applicable to the object. (E.g., the deducibility of one proposition from another cannot entail that the latter constitutes evidence for the former.) For what sort of entailments could these be? Clearly, they must be due, at least in part, to the sense, if not explicit definition, of the word *evidence.* (The unlikely suggestion that the entailment is synthetic a priori will be considered presently.) Now there could be such entailment if the proposition entailed by each of several other propositions is simply equivocal. But this case is excluded by the requirement that the word *evidence* be nonequivocal. There could be such entailment if the entailing propositions are such that they also entail each other. But then the criteria would not be logically distinct. There could be such entailment if the criteria were related to that for which they are criteria as species of one genus. But this possibility has also been excluded. Nor can the relationship be like that of p and q with respect to $p \vee q$, and of $(p \supset q) \cdot p$ and $(r \supset q) \cdot r$ with respect to q. In such cases, either the consequent is a disjunction or it contains only expressions which occur in the antecedent. The thesis can avail itself of neither option. The first would make it applicable only to disjunctive properties, the names of which would be standard examples of equivocation. And the latter would involve it in "criterial circularity," that is, the description of the criteria for something would include the description of the something for which they are criteria. I suggest that there is no sense in which a nondefining criterion of evidence can be a logically sufficient condition for the applicability of the word *evidence.* Yet, as we have seen,[9] it must be such if the thesis of nonequivocating multiple criteria of evidence is even to purport to be relevant to epistemological issues and if it is to be at all plausible.

Might not the relation between a criterion and that for which it is the

9. See above, pp. 282–83 and 288.

criterion be nonconceptual yet still noninductive? Could it, despite the original reasons for introducing the term *criterion,* be synthetic a priori? No, because then it should be possible to understand, explain, and apply the concept of evidence without appealing to the satisfaction of any criterion or even without knowing any of its criteria, just as, if the statement "The shortest distance between two points is a straight line" is synthetic a priori, it should be possible to understand and explain what a straight line is and to identify straight lines without appealing to the fact that a straight line is the shortest distance between two points (although of course it would be necessary that what one so understands or explains or identifies *be* the shortest distance between two points).

Could the relation between a criterion and that for which it is a criterion be *sui generis,* in principle unlike any other relation and thus quite unclassifiable? There certainly could be such relations, and one of them perhaps could be described as that holding between a criterion and that for which it is a criterion. But why then would any reference to such a relation between a criterion for the applicability of a word and the applicability of the word be relevant to the explanation and justification of the applicability of the word? Why would it have any conceptual significance? To be relevant to such an explanation, to have conceptual significance, the relation between a criterion and that for which it is the criterion must itself be conceptual. And we must not forget that it is for the purpose of explaining the content of the concept of evidence and the conditions that legitimize the employment of the word *evidence* that the notion of criterion of evidence was introduced in the first place.

It won't do to suggest that the relation is one of which we are directly aware and which thus requires no explanation. The evidential status of something with regard to something else is not like a color, smell, or taste. It is something that can be grasped only through judgment. Moreover, even colors, smells, and sounds can be described and classified and their similarities and differences can be explained.

I have enumerated the various possible relations that may hold between a criterion of evidence and that for which it is a criterion and have found that none can be what is required by the thesis of nonequivocating multiple criteria of evidence. This is not surprising. It is in fact not unlike the conclusion reached by the distinguished defender of that thesis, R. M. Chisholm.[10] To have reached such a conclusion is not, however, to have

10. See *Perceiving,* chaps. 3 and 7; and *Theory of Knowledge,* chap. 4.

described or elucidated the relation. It is to have demonstrated that, unless one can specify some other possibilities, the relation is a thoroughly unintelligible notion and thus that the thesis itself is absurd. It is useless to retort that we in fact *know* that behavior is evidence for other persons' thoughts and feelings, that perceivings are evidence for the existence of bodies, that self-contradiction-of-denial is evidence for the proposition denied, and that we also know that the word *evidence* is not used equivocally with respect to these and that nevertheless they are logically distinct kinds of facts, entities, or states. We cannot know what we cannot understand.

5. *Nondefining Criteria in Specific Fields*

WE HAVE CONCLUDED that the notion of a nondefining second-order criterion, that is, of a nondefining criterion for something's *being evidence for* something else, has not been made intelligible and thus must be rejected. But if the criteria of evidence must be defining and the word *evidence* unequivocal, then there can be only one criterion of evidence. If so, then, in reality, we have no choice regarding its identity. Clearly, the one and only criterion of evidence would be the demonstrative criterion or a more general criterion to which the demonstrative criterion would be related as a species to a genus,[11] for it is unquestionable that the demonstrative criterion *is* a criterion of evidence. We seem to have no notion of such a more general criterion. And insofar as we do not, we must, at least provisionally, conclude that nothing can be evidence unless it is demonstrative evidence. From this a further conclusion follows: that nothing can be the sort of evidence that a nondefining *first-order* criterion, that is, a state or entity which is conceptual evidence for another state or entity, is supposed to be, that there cannot be nondefining first-order criteria. Being *nondefining,* such a criterion neither is intended to be a formally or analytically demonstrative evidence for, that is, a logically sufficient condition of, that for which it is a criterion,[12] nor can it be such evidence or

11. We paid some attention to this possibility above (p. 273) and will return to it below (pp. 213–315).

12. See above, pp. 279 and 283.

condition, for the same reasons a nondefining second-order criterion cannot.[13] At the same time, being a *criterion* for the applicability of a word, it must be a conceptual, logical, conventional evidence for the latter and thus cannot constitute a nonformally and nonanalytically demonstrative evidence for it.

It may now be reasonably remarked that the conclusion that there cannot be nondemonstrative sorts of evidence and, specifically, that there cannot be nondefining first-order criteria is epistemologically too important and too disturbing to be allowed to rest only on the above abstract and indirect grounds. But nondefining first-order criteria can also be rejected on more immediate grounds. The fact is that our reasons for regarding the notion of nondefining *second-order* criterion as unintelligible are also reasons for regarding the notion of *any* nondefining criterion, including any specific *first-order* one, as unintelligible. Indeed, we should find the description of a nondefining first-order criterion even more puzzling than that of a nondefining second-order criterion. For in the former case, in addition to the obscurity of the general view that something can be a conceptual, noninductive, yet also nonformal and nonanalytic, ground for the applicability of a word, there is the obscurity of the likely additional view that such a ground need not even be a materially sufficient condition, that at least sometimes it is present even though the word is not applicable.

Let us once again take as an example the alleged criterial relation between a certain kind of behavior, such as one's holding one's cheek, and a certain psychological state, such as one's having a toothache. The defender of nondefining criteria assumes that the relation is not one of inductive evidence. In any case, were it one, our knowledge of other minds would be a special and particularly difficult case of inductive knowledge, and if there is a philosophical problem of evidence regarding it, it would be that regarding inductive evidence in general. Nor is there a suggestion that the relation might be synthetic a priori; it simply is not of that sort at all. So, it must be a logical or conceptual relation. But it cannot be formal or analytic, for such a relation can exist only between states the descriptions of which have the same kind of conceptual content, or are about roughly the same things. But the statements "He is holding his cheek" and "He has a toothache" are not about the same things at all; they are not even about the same categories of things. A toothache is in no

13. See above, p. 290.

sense a holding of one's cheek, a pain is in no sense a pattern of behavior. So the relation must be conceptual—one holding in virtue of linguistic conventions—yet not formal or analytic. And, finally, the relation must be such that it need not be the case that whenever the criterion is satisfied that for which it is the criterion is present, or vice versa. For, a man may hold his cheek or engage in any other kind of behavior, however complex, and still not have a toothache. And a man may have a toothache and still not hold his cheek or engage in any specific kind of behavior. So the required relation would be noninductive, conceptual, nonformal, and nonanalytic, and even weaker than material implication. I suggest that the opacity of the view that there is such a relation is unsurpassed in the history of philosophy.

The defender of such a notion of criterion may try to break through the logical fog that surrounds him by saying that the satisfaction of the criterion for the applicability of a word does not entail the applicability of the word, but *justifies,* because of the very meaning of the word, the actual application of the word, and thus that the fact that one is justified, in this sense, in applying the word is not the same as the fact, if it is a fact, that the word is applicable. On the other hand, the fact that one is justified in applying the word and the fact, if it is one, that the word is applicable obviously cannot be unrelated. Hence the further and really unavoidable claim is made that while it is not a necessary truth that all statements made in accordance with the criterion are true, it is a necessary truth that they are generally true, or that any one such statement is almost certainly true.[14]

---

14. Rogers Albritton suggests that, according to Wittgenstein, "That a man behaves in a certain manner, under certain circumstances, cannot entail that he has a toothache. But it can entail something else, which there is no short way of stating exactly, so far as I can find. *Roughly,* then: it can entail that anyone who is aware that the man is behaving in this manner, under these circumstances, is *justified in saying* that the man has a toothache, in the absence of any special reason to say something more guarded. . . . Even more roughly: That a man behaves in a certain manner, under certain circumstances, can entail that he *almost certainly* has a toothache" ("On Wittgenstein's Use of the Term 'Criterion,'" *Journal of Philosophy,* LVI [1959], 856; but see also the postscript to this article in the reprint of it in *Wittgenstein,* ed. George Pitcher [Garden City, N. Y.: Doubleday, 1966], pp. 247–50). Albritton expresses doubt that there are criteria in this sense, that there are the necessary propositions that there would have to be if there were such criteria. A similar conception of criterion is utilized by Sydney Shoemaker in *Self-Knowledge and Self-Identity* (Ithaca, N. Y.: Cornell University Press, 1963). He claims, for example, that ". . . it is a necessary (logical, or conceptual) truth, not a contingent one, that when perceptual and memory statements are sincerely and confidently asserted, i.e., express confident beliefs, they are generally true" (p. 229).

But this defense of nondefining criteria rests on a sleight-of-hand. It makes us believe that it is telling us one thing, which is rather exciting, while in fact what it tells us is something quite different. Having failed to make intelligible how something can be the sort of conceptual evidence for something else that a nondefining criterion is supposed to be, the defender of nondefining criteria has now told us, in effect, that something can be such conceptual evidence in the sense that it is conceptual evidence for *justifiably asserting* that something else. For we are told that while one's holding one's cheek does not entail that one has a toothache, it does entail that it can be justifiably said of one that one has a toothache. Thus, in effect, what was supposed to be a *nondefining* criterion for someone's having a toothache is now offered as a *defining* criterion for the justified assertion that he has a toothache. But, *ex nihilo nihil fit*. To be at all relevant to our understanding of what a nondefining criterion may be, this proposal must be supplemented with the claim that there is also a relation, presumably noninductive and conceptual, between one's justifiably asserting that someone has a toothache and someone's actually having a toothache. And this relation would probably turn out to have very much the same characteristics as the original criterial relation was supposed to have: for example, it cannot be one of entailment, for then, by hypothetical syllogism, one's holding one's cheek would entail one's having a toothache.

In fact, it is even worse than that. When we are told that someone's holding his cheek is a criterion, that is, a conceptual evidence, for his having a toothache in the sense that it "justifies" the assertion that he has a toothache, what could the word *justifies* possibly mean? Surely, it means the same as "constitutes evidence for." And what must this latter phrase be taken to mean, if it is to be at all suited for a defense of the possibility of nondefining criteria? Surely, it must be taken to mean "constitutes conceptual evidence—*of the sort a nondefining criterion is supposed to be* —for." Indeed, the phrase "justifiably asserting that *p*" may mean many and very different things: being morally justified in asserting that *p*; being for certain practical purposes justified in asserting that *p*; its being false or at least unlikely that one may deny that *p* without exhibiting ignorance of the meaning of the sentence "*p*"; or asserting that *p* with a certain degree of evidence. It could not be that the defender of the view uses the phrase in either of the first two senses. What is at issue is neither the morality of lying nor the practicality of optimism. Nor could the third sense be the relevant one. It is just false that, for example, any kind of behavior by a person *entails* that someone else who denies that the person is in pain is ignorant of the meaning of the word *pain;* and far too many kinds of behavior make this merely *likely*—kinds that no one would think conceptually related to the person's being in pain—namely, many kinds of behavior that Wittgenstein would have called symptoms of his being in pain.

It is the fourth, epistemic sense of the phrase "justifiably asserting that *p,*" namely, that of asserting *p* with a certain degree of evidence, that alone could be relevant. But it is just in this sense that the use of the phrase in explaining the criterial relation can throw no light. To say that one's holding one's cheek entails that someone else can assert with evidence that one has a toothache is merely to repeat the original view: that one's holding one's cheek is, in virtue of a criterion for the use of the word *evidence,* what is meant by evidence that one has a toothache, and, once again, that since clearly it cannot be inductive or formal or analytic evidence, nor even something which is always accompanied by what it is evidence for, it must be a conceptual but not analytic evidence and even not a materially sufficient condition.

As long as we fail to recognize the ambiguity of the word *justification* and the fact that it is only in its epistemic sense that it is relevant to the topic of criteria, we are tempted to "think of concepts as being determined by their justification-conditions (rather than their truth-conditions)" [15] and to suppose that we have discovered a noncontingent yet nondeductive relation between the criterion for applying the concept to something and the applicability of the concept to that something. But, in the epistemic sense of *justification,* the justification-conditions of a concept are simply those that constitute evidence for the satisfaction of the truth-conditions of the concept; they can neither be understood independently of the truth-conditions nor can they by themselves illuminate the sort of relation they have to the truth-conditions.

We should note that what is at issue in the present discussion is not whether, for example, a certain kind of behavior is evidence that someone is in pain. Unless one embraces complete skepticism regarding other minds, one would certainly agree that it is. What is at issue is a certain philosophical claim about the *sort* of evidence behavior can be for some-

15. See John L. Pollock, "Criteria and Our Knowledge of the Material World," *Philosophical Review,* LXXVI (1967), 28–60.

one's being in pain, namely, that it is conceptual and noninductive, yet nonanalytic and even materially nonsufficient, evidence. This philosophical claim can be rejected, on the grounds that it is unintelligible, without for a moment questioning that a certain behavior does constitute evidence for someone's being in pain.

Could it be that the existence of nondefining criteria should be regarded as a hypothesis required for the explanation of how the learning of a public language is possible? But, there are many other hypotheses that can serve such an explanatory function, if it is *hypotheses* that we want. Let us take the case of psychological words. Perhaps we make inductive inferences to other persons' inner experiences from the connection between our own behavior and inner experiences. Perhaps the very young child (who is really the interesting case, for it is mainly in early childhood that we acquire the ostensive basis of language) is capable of telepathic experiences of his mother's, or someone else's, inner experiences. Perhaps the connection is made as a result of lucky guesses which are immediately reinforced, the probability of the occurrence of such guesses and their reinforcement being great considering the length of time and multitude of situations involved. Even if such hypotheses are unlikely, they are better than unintelligible ones.

The notion of nondefining criterion may also be defended by means of the quasi-Kantian transcendental arguments that are sometimes used to refute skepticism.[16] The general form of such an argument can be stated as follows. Let "p" be the proposition which the skeptic rejects (whether it be that something is the case or that we know that it is the case). If "p" is false, i.e., if the skeptic is right, then p is meaningless. So either what the skeptic asserts is false or his assertion is meaningless (if p is meaningless, then so is not-p). For example, if the proposition "Other persons can have pain" is false, then it is meaningless. For its being true is a necessary condition of there being a concept of pain. Therefore, the skeptic's denial of it is either itself false or, since it employs the word *pain*, it is meaningless.

Now such an argument may suggest the possibility of introducing the notion of (nondefining) criterion as follows. "That p is a criterion for the fact that q" means: if it is false that if p then (at least usually) q, then q is

---

16. Perhaps the best-known such arguments are employed by P. F. Strawson in *Individuals: An Essay in Descriptive Metaphysics* (London: Methuen, 1959). See pp. 34–35 and pp. 105–6.

meaningless. For example, to say that someone's holding one's cheek is a criterion for his having a toothache would be to say that if it is false that if someone is holding his cheek then (at least usually) he has a toothache, then it is meaningless to say of someone that he has a toothache. Such a notion of criterion would serve the purpose for which the notion of nondefining criterion was introduced. For, taking for granted that *q* is not meaningless, we should be able to consider *p* as evidence for *q* in the very clear sense that if *p* is true then (at least usually) *q* would be true. The notion of such a relationship between two propositions has considerable plausibility when applied to specific situations. For example, we may be told that if it were false that if someone exhibits a certain behavior then, ordinarily, he is in pain, then there could not be an established meaning of the word *pain,* and thus the statement "He is in pain" would be meaningless. And this may be taken to constitute a refutation of the skeptic, although in fact, if at all true, it would show only that we would not have an established, public concept of pain if we could not know that other people are in pain on the basis of their behavior, a fact which seems to me to have been denied by no one.[17] In any case, this fact (if it is one) throws no light whatever on *how* we may know that other people are in pain on the basis of their behavior, or on the *sort* of relationship that holds between a person's behavior and his being in pain; specifically, it does not even suggest that the relationship in question is a noncontingent, conceptual relationship. This becomes quite clear when we consider the above general definition of a nondefining criterion. Perhaps the larger

---

17. The familiar sort of transcendental argument does not prove that skepticism is *false,* even if we assume that if skepticism is true then there cannot be meaningful discourse about the objects of skepticism. Take as an example of such an argument A. C. Danto's: ". . . if it is impossible to have knowledge—as it would be on the skeptic's theory . . . then it is impossible to have understanding. But it cannot be to the skeptic's interest to deny that we have understanding . . . , since he could not then state his position" (*Analytic Philosophy of Knowledge* [Cambridge: At the University Press, 1968], p. 187). Let us grant the premises of the argument. Nevertheless, from the fact that skepticism cannot be both true and stateable it does not follow that skepticism is false. And, surely, the goal of an argument against skepticism is to show that skepticism is false, not that it is unstateable. We may win a rhetorical victory over the skeptic if we convince him that if he is right then what he says is nonsense. But it would not be a philosophical victory, for of course he would immediately point out that our denial that he is right is also nonsense. Skepticism cannot be refuted with debater's ploys. At most, the transcendental arguments have shown us that traditional skepticism leads to skepticism regarding the meaningfulness of all discourse. They have not shown that the latter is wrong, and thus have not shown that the former is wrong. In fact, they have not even won a psychological victory. One who doubts the existence of a material world, including that of his own body and of other persons, is not likely to demur at doubt about the meaningfulness of one's discourse.

conditional *If it is false that (if p then usually q) then q is meaningless* itself is conceptually true; for our concept of meaning may be such that, for certain values of "*p*" and "*q*," it renders this conditional analytic. But from the conceptual character of the truth of this conditional nothing follows regarding the character of the truth of the smaller conditional that occurs in its antecedent, namely, that if *p* then usually *q*. That conditional may be conceptually true but it may also be contingently true; the truth of the larger conditional would suggest nothing about that. And, certainly, we have no reason for supposing that it is noncontingently and conceptually, yet nonanalytically, true, nor do we as a result of our assent to the larger conditional have any clearer conception of how there might be a noncontingently and conceptually, yet nonanalytically, true conditional.

I doubt that the defenders of nondefining criteria would claim to have made the notion of such a criterion intelligible. Rather, they seem to regard the existence of nondefining criteria as a hypothesis that must be accepted if we are to avoid certain philosophical consequences. What are these consequences? First, that certain standard kinds of knowledge, such as that another person is in pain, are impossible. Second, that certain standard segments of language, such as third-person psychological statements, are meaningless. But the problems of epistemology, for example, that concerning our knowledge of other minds, demand theoretical understanding and conceptual illumination. Where practical concerns, even if only the desire for predictive success, are relevant, there may be reason for the adoption of an *ad hoc* hypothesis whose intelligibility is questionable. Where understanding and clarity are alone relevant, as surely is the case in epistemology, the adoption of such a hypothesis achieves nothing but further confusion. It also tends to mask the alternative solutions and to discourage further exploration of them.

6. *Are Epistemic Terms Evaluative?*

ONE REASON for the initial plausibility of the thesis of nonequivocating multiple criteria of evidence is the plausibility of the similar thesis regarding evaluative terms (due largely to the distinction between evaluative and descriptive meaning) together with the relatively novel suggestion that epistemic terms such as *evidence* and *knowledge* are themselves evaluative, normative. I shall not discuss here the question of the criteria of evaluative terms, or the distinction between the descriptive and evaluative meaning of such a term,[18] but I will argue that the classification of epistemic terms as evaluative is mistaken and thus that the thesis of nonequivocating multiple criteria of evidence can gain nothing from any plausibility of the similar thesis regarding evaluative terms. At the same time, it may be well also to remember that the latter is motivated, and defended, by reference not to fundamental considerations about the nature of meaning and of language as such but to special problems regarding the subject matter of ethics.

It is curious that epistemology should seek illumination from ethics. The reverse has usually been the case. And the chances of epistemology for success seem gloomy if it must depend on aid from ethics. Gloomy or not, however, such a prospect must be investigated.

It is natural, perhaps inevitable, to think that one ought to (or at least has the right to) believe what one has evidence sufficient for knowing or what one at least has good evidence for, that better supported beliefs are worthier, that the truth no less than the good should guide our actions. We have appealed to this connection between epistemic and evaluative concepts ourselves.[19] But to recognize all this is not at all to recognize that epistemic terms are evaluative. There are obvious ways of preserving epistemology from the pitfalls of an "ethics of belief" and still accounting for the obligations and rights that knowledge and evidence seem to place on belief and action. Indeed, it can be admitted, one ought to believe what one at least has good evidence for. But it is not self-contradictory to deny this. In many contexts, for example that of religion, such a denial would not be even surprising.[20] An immediate consequence of this is that there is not an analytic relationship between the concepts of what is worthy of belief or what ought to be believed, on the one hand, and the concepts of evidence and knowledge, on the other.

The traditional task of epistemology is to account for the nature,

18. It may be worth noting that any distinction between different meanings or different aspects of one meaning, however legitimate it may be, is inherently unable to offer support to the view that a term may be employed in accordance with a number of logically distinct criteria without a corresponding equivocation with the term. If we say that what remains invariant through the uses of a term (e.g., *good* or *evident*) is only its evaluative meaning or its "force" while its descriptive meaning varies, then we are no longer faithful to that view.

19. See above, pp. 43–44.

20. See Roderick Firth, "Chisholm and the Ethics of Belief," *Philosophical Review*, LXVIII (1959), 493–506.

degrees, and kinds of evidence and knowledge. This can be done, certainly no less well than can the account of any other fundamental philosophical topics, without the use of evaluative terms; although, given the *moral* assumption, to be justified by the moral philosopher and not by the epistemologist, that one ought to believe, and perhaps act in accordance with, what one at least has good evidence for, the epistemologist's conclusions would also be grounds for determining what one ought to believe and how one ought to act. In a somewhat similar fashion, we may investigate the nature, kinds, and degrees of happiness, and especially the means for the achievement of happiness, without making reference to how one ought to live; although, given the moral assumption that one ought to promote happiness, the results of our investigation would also be grounds for deciding how one ought to live. But the investigator of happiness (who hopefully would be a psychologist, not a philosopher) need not be concerned with the difficulties of proving or even explaining the proposition that one ought to promote happiness.

This may become clearer if we distinguish between categorical and hypothetical evaluative statements. Even if epistemic statements were evaluative, they would be hypothetical evaluative statements and thus their content would be essentially nonevaluative, non-normative. Let us grant that the following are typical epistemic statements: "One ought to believe what one sees." "One ought to believe what the Bible says." "One ought to believe that a man is in pain if he is writhing on the floor and screaming." "One ought to believe that a proposition is true if its denial is self-contradictory." I suggest that such statements are analogous to statements such as "One ought to take a daily walk" or "One ought to study foreign languages" rather than to statements such as "One ought to love one's fellow man" or "One ought to promote happiness." Whatever the proper analysis and justification of the latter two statements may be, the former two are analyzed and justified in perfectly ordinary, non-normative ways. "One ought to take a daily walk" probably means "If one is to be healthy one should take a daily walk," and its justification would make reference to medical facts, not to any principles about how one ought to live. In a similar fashion, a statement such as "One ought to believe what one sees" should be understood, if it is an epistemic statement at all, to mean "If one is to believe what is true then one should believe what one sees." And the justification of such a hypothetical statement would consist in showing that what one sees is, or is likely to be, true, and would be quite independent of the question whether one ought to believe what is true.

The task of the epistemologist is to determine whether the alleged ways of finding truth are legitimate and reliable—whether, to what extent, and why what one sees, or what one finds in the Bible, or a proposition with self-contradictory denial, is true. Determining this is not the same as determining that one ought to believe what has been shown to be true; although, together with the principle—to be explained and justified by the moral philosopher and presumably in very different ways—that one ought to believe what is true, this too would be determined. If there are essentially evaluative, normative epistemic statements at all, there is only one: "One ought to believe what is true or at least likely to be true." And that statement, I suggest, does not belong in epistemology.

7. *Nondemonstrative Criteria of Knowledge*

WE HAVE BEEN concerned with the view that there are criteria of evidence other than the demonstrative criterion, that is, other than the impossibility of mistake—the view that something can be evidence for something else without entailing it, whether formally or nonformally, analytically or synthetically a priori. As we have seen, this is a view regarding both derivative knowledge and rational belief. We have concluded that it has not been made intelligible. But may it not be the case that there are multiple criteria for the impossibility of mistake itself? Such criteria would be criteria of knowledge, and not of rational belief, for knowledge consists in the impossibility of mistake. So, curiously, perhaps skepticism regarding rational belief cannot be refuted, but skepticism regarding knowledge can. It may be that in fact we know, in the strict sense of the word, far more than we suppose, for much more might count as impossibility of mistake than we usually suppose; but that far fewer of our beliefs are rational, based on genuine evidence, than we would expect. Such additional criteria of knowledge would not be alternatives to the *unthinkability* of mistake. Were they that, they would be dismissed, in virtue of our arguments in Part One. They would be also additional criteria of the unthinkability of mistake. For a liberalization of the criteria of the impossibility of mistake could be understood as being also a liberalization of the criteria of the unthinkability of mistake.

Such a view would, in effect, apply the philosophical reasoning that lay behind the thesis of nonequivocating multiple criteria of *evidence* to the more specific topic of the criteria of *knowledge*. We have argued that, whatever the case with evidence insufficient for knowledge may be, evidence sufficient for knowledge must be evidence that guarantees the truth of what is asserted as known, that knowledge consists in the absolute impossibility of mistake (or, ultimately, in the unthinkability of mistake). But, it may be said, there are different kinds of absolute impossibility (or of unthinkability) and thus different kinds of knowledge. One supposes otherwise only because of one's mistaken belief that only logical impossibility is real, absolute impossibility. Perhaps the word *impossibility* applies to the other kinds of impossibility in different senses. But this does not entail that such nonlogical kinds of impossibility are less strong, that inferences based on them are less legitimate. For example, the kind of impossibility involved in the bombing of New York City by the air force of North Vietnam is fundamentally different from the kind of impossibility involved in finding a rational square root of 2. Yet they are equally strong, equally genuine; the first kind of impossibility is not less real or less genuine than the second kind. Both cases would be equally impossible and equally unthinkable. Appeals to both would be equally persuasive.[21] But this argument is quite unsatisfactory.

The argument is based on the supposition that the criteria for the use of *impossible* (or of *unthinkable*), and thus for the use of the phrase *impossibility of mistake,* are themselves multiple, even if the criteria of evidence are not. Now, as we have seen in section 4 of this Part, the view that a term can have multiple criteria without ordinary equivocation is indefensible. Consequently, if the above supposition were true, then the

21. This sort of argument can be found in Toulmin, *The Uses of Argument,* p. 36. Toulmin, however, presents it in the context of his distinction between the criteria and force of a term. The criteria of the term *impossible* would be field-dependent, though its force would be field-invariant. In the above two examples the criteria are different, but the force of the use of the term *impossible* is the same. According to Toulmin, the force of a modal term is "the practical implications of its use" (p. 30). It seems to me to be what I have called above (pp. 276–77) the effect and the purpose of the use of a word, and to be neither part of the conventional meaning of the word nor constitutive, even in part, of the corresponding concept.

term *impossibility* (or *unthinkability*) would be equivocal, and the multiplicity of its criteria probably epistemologically irrelevant. But, in any case, the supposition in question is not true.

Impossibilities in different fields can be compared, not only in accordance with their relative degrees in the respective fields (e.g., a Chinese air attack on New York City is not as impossible as a North Vietnamese air attack, while a rational square root of 2 is as impossible as any mathematical impossibility; hence a rational square root of 2 is, relative to its field, more impossible than is a Chinese air attack on New York City, relative to its field), but also in accordance with a common, absolute standard. An attack on New York City by the air force of North Vietnam may be the strongest impossibility in that "field." Even so, it is not nearly as strong an impossibility as a rational square root of 2. There is an obvious test of this.[22] A knowledgeable man would surely prefer to bet that there cannot be a rational square root of 2 than that New York City cannot be bombed by North Vietnam. Why? Because he would know that the former is "more impossible" than the latter. And the criterion he would use for making such a choice is the real, field-invariant, common and absolute criterion of impossibility.

A man may assert in a particular context with equal energy and forcefulness that there is no possibility of his being mistaken (1) that if John is taller than Bill and Bill is taller than Peter, then John is taller than Peter; (2) that he has a headache; (3) that 15 times 17 is 255; (4) that he saw his wife entering a house of prostitution; (5) that he turned off the oven before leaving for Florida; (6) that he can lift a certain large table off the floor if he tries; (7) that Johnson is happily married; (8) that environmentally produced changes are not inherited. Now, I am not concerned with the question whether, in the sorts of situation in which all of these assertions may be made by the same person, they would be justified. I am concerned with the question whether, *in such situations,* a man who would make them, with the usual sort of justification available for each of them, would regard what he means when he

---

22. "The usual touchstone, whether that which someone asserts is merely his persuasion—or at least his subjective conviction, that is, his firm belief—is *betting.* It often happens that someone propounds his views with such positive and uncompromising assurance that he seems to have entirely set aside all thought of possible error. A bet disconcerts him . . . . If in a given case, we represent ourselves as staking the happiness of our whole life, the triumphant tone of our judgment is greatly abated" (Kant, *Critique of Pure Reason,* B852–53, tr. Norman Kemp Smith). See also Harry Frankfurt, "Philosophical Certainty," *Philosophical Review,* LXXI (1962), 303–27.

uses the phrase "impossibility of being mistaken" in making each such assertion as different in kind, and not in degree, whether the impossibilities in question are analogous, for example, to different kinds of furniture rather than to different approximations to white or to circularity. And it seems obvious that, in the usual sort of contexts in which he might make all of them, he would find it perfectly natural to make an arrangement of such assertions in accordance with the *degree* of the impossibility of their being mistaken. In fact, it is likely that the arrangement he would choose is the one given above, though this is not essential to my thesis. Let us imagine that he is asked to bet his life against ten dollars that each of the above eight assertions is true. Only a fool would accept such a bet with respect to assertions (8) and (7). Only a reckless gambler would accept it with respect to (6) and (5). A mature, rational man may accept the bet with respect to (4) and (3), though I think he probably would not. And one might support oneself for life by making such bets with respect to (2) and (1), if one could find takers. But if this is so, then surely the notion of impossibility of mistake is applicable paradigmatically only to the highest degree of such impossibility. For impossibility is a matter of degree in the way in which circularity and whiteness are,[23] and not in the way in which temperature and power are a matter of degree. The notion of something's being less impossible or less circular or less white than something else is only a misleading version of the notion of something's being less *like* an impossibility or a circle or a white thing than something else is. It is not a notion of a *kind* of impossibility or circularity or whiteness. To admit that the alleged logically distinct criteria of impossibility of mistake can differ in degree is to admit that only one, namely, that of the highest degree, is the genuine criterion of impossibility of mistake, the rest being only "criteria" of *approximations* to impossibility of mistake.

One reason the view that the notion of impossibility is governed by multiple criteria has appeared plausible is that a similar view has had wide currency for a very long time. I have in mind the view that there are two kinds of impossibility, logical and empirical. The former, it is said, consists in incompatibility with the laws of logic, the latter in incompatibility with the laws of nature. The distinction between the two has often rested on the confusion, to which I have drawn attention before, of the

---

23. See above, pp. 55–56.

impossibility of the falsehood of a proposition with the impossibility of our being mistaken about it. A proposition is logically impossible, it is said, if it is self-contradictory; but there is nothing self-contradictory about a proposition such as "There is not a table before me now" or "I do not have a headache," and yet it is surely just as impossible that I am mistaken in believing that there is a table before me or that I have a headache as it is that I am mistaken about the truth of some logically true propositions. But to say that a logically true proposition is necessarily true, that it is impossible for it to be false, is not to say merely that I cannot be mistaken about its being true—it is, primarily, to say that the proposition cannot be false, that regardless of circumstances and events it may only be true. Obviously, this is the content of the notion of logical impossibility. And if a notion of empirical impossibility is to be given content which would make it a companion concept to that of logical impossibility, then this content must have to do with the nature of the truth of the proposition itself, not with the question whether one can be mistaken in believing that the proposition is true. In fact, in terms of the usual account of empirical possibility, not only is it logically possible that there is no table before me or that I do not have a headache, but it is also empirically possible. For empirical possibility is defined in terms of conformity to laws of nature. And the laws of nature allow for the possibility of the nonexistence of a table before me and of my not having a headache now.

But if we define the empirically impossible as that which is incompatible with the laws of nature, then empirical impossibility and logical impossibility would not at all be two separate and equal kinds of impossibility. The reason is that the so-defined concept of empirical impossibility is really a derivative concept of logical impossibility. To say that it is empirically impossible that p would be to say, at least, that it is logically impossible that both the laws of nature are such and such and p is false. And this means that the impossibility of p is not a *kind* of impossibility, distinct from but on the same conceptual level as logical impossibility, but what would be far more properly described as conditional or indirect *logical* impossibility. The only possible way to show that there is a distinctive and underivative concept of empirical impossibility would be to consider the laws of nature themselves and to discover that there is a sense in which it is impossible for them to be false, though not logically impossible. Such a task would seem to be hopeless. If by *laws of nature* we mean the fundamental propositions actually accepted by contemporary scientists, then to say that it is impossible for such propositions to be false is either to make nonsense of the experimental character of science or to indulge in an irrelevant prognostication about its total future development. If by *laws of nature* we mean certain necessary fundamental truths about the world, whether or not they are known to us, then we allow for the possibility that we could never be sure in applying the concept of empirical impossibility to any proposition, for while we know which are the fundamental principles that scientists now accept, we do not know which are the laws of nature that cannot be false. And, in any case, we would have no idea what sort of nonlogical necessity such laws could have, for the only conception of such a law that we possess is that of a possible principle of empirical science. And we have no idea of a relevant sense in which a principle of empirical science can be necessary.

8. *Induction*

I HAVE CONCLUDED that there cannot be nonequivocating multiple criteria of evidence. As we have seen, this amounts to the startling conclusion that the demonstrative criterion is the only clear, intellectually visible criterion of evidence that we have, and thus that, as far as we can understand these matters with the conceptual materials at our disposal, the criteria of evidence in general and the criteria of derivative knowledge are the same —that we can have evidence only for what we can know, and that all (derivative) knowledge is demonstrative knowledge. In the face of such conclusions, it may be well to ignore our general arguments and consider in its own right the familiar specific claim that induction constitutes a second and equally clear and equally legitimate criterion of evidence— that inductive inference is an equally legitimate mode of derivation of knowledge or at least of rational belief, even though it is not equally strong (it does not render mistake absolutely impossible) and even though the sense in which it is legitimate may be different from the sense in which demonstrative derivations can be said to be legitimate. What is especially impressive about induction as a criterion of evidence is its wide applicability. For example, we ordinarily attempt, and should be happy to succeed, to solve the problems regarding our knowledge of bodies and other minds by showing such knowledge to be inductively justified.

The recent arguments in favor of induction usually take the form of the rhetorical, perhaps even *ad hominem,* claim that the insistence on a single criterion of knowledge and the identification of it with the absolute impossibility of mistake is merely the result of an obsession with the sort of knowledge one can achieve in logic and mathematics and of the attempt to apply the criteria suited for it to other, quite different sorts of knowledge. The *general* traditional problem of epistemology has been, What is the justification of inferences that are not formally valid? But in fact there is no such general problem, we would be told; there are only problems concerning the justification of inferences indigenous to the various fields or bodies of knowledge, and these problems are soluble by reference to the relevant standards of valid derivation, of valid argument, in such fields. And the basis of the argument would be the proposition that formally valid inferences are not the only paradigm of valid inference, that they have been thought to be such only because of the influence of the mathematical sciences in which they are the appropriate kind of inference, and that it is simply a mistake to require of all other inferences that they be like formal inferences. Inductive reasoning, we would be told, has its own standards of validity.

But formally valid inferences have been regarded as unquestionably valid because of a reason, not because of some vague influence of the mathematical sciences; and this reason has been the fact that their denial has been thought unintelligible, unthinkable, inconceivable. The skeptic does not simple-mindedly assume that if an inference is not formally valid then it is invalid; he does not merely assume that whatever is logically possible *is* really possible. He requires a *reason* for supposing that nondemonstrative inferences are valid, that their conclusions should be believed, that acting in accordance with them would be rational; he asks for a reason for supposing that what is merely logically possible need not be really possible. For the validity of demonstrative inferences there is a clear reason of unquestionable authority: the unthinkability of the premises' being true and the conclusion false. The skeptic is the first one to recognize that this, by definition, cannot be a reason for the validity of nondemonstrative inferences. But his recognition of this fact is not his ground for denying the validity of such inferences. His ground is his inability to find *any other* reason for asserting that such inferences are valid, his inability to understand any other way in which an inference can be valid. In this he may be mistaken. Perhaps there are such reasons. But his mistake is not that of carelessly modeling validity in general after the validity of formal inferences.

It is reported, with approval,[24] that Wittgenstein likened the philosophical demand for a justification of induction to the ancient demand for something on which the earth may stand. And, indeed, there is a parallel. But it has not the slightest tendency to show the senselessness or even hopelessness of the former demand, for there is nothing senseless or hopeless about the latter. Of course, if the latter is interpreted as a demand for a *thing* on which the earth rests, then it might be hopeless since it might be involved in an infinite regress. But then what is analogous to it would be the interpretation of the former demand as one calling for an *inductive* justification of induction, the hopelessness of which was immediately recognized by the very philosopher who first brought to our attention the problem of induction. But, of course, the proper interpretation of the problem of induction is that it demands an explanation of the acceptability, the intellectual groundedness, of induction as such. And what corresponds to this is the perfectly proper demand for an explanation of why the earth keeps its place, a demand which was satisfied by showing not that the earth rests on another thing but that its position is preserved by certain forces. What was never an intelligible alternative would have been the frivolous claim that in talking about what the earth may stand on we are simply misusing the ordinary notion of *standing on*. In the same manner, while it may be senseless to attempt to justify the principle of induction inductively, it is not at all senseless to argue that grounds must be given for supposing that it is true. To argue thus is not to allow for the possibility that within the mode of inductive reasoning all arguments may be invalid. It is to allow for the possibility that inductive reasoning as such may be invalid, that is, cognitively worthless.[25]

24. S. E. Toulmin, *An Examination of the Place of Reason in Ethics* (Cambridge: At the Universtiy Press, 1964), p. 206.

25. Toulmin himself admits that this may be the case with at least one "mode of reasoning," namely, religion, that one may allow for the distinction between proper and improper arguments in religion and still deny that religion has cognitive worth. "The propriety of particular arguments within a mode of reasoning is one thing: the value of the mode of reasoning as a whole is another" (*Place of Reason in Ethics*, p. 221). Skepticism regarding induction is skepticism regarding the value of the inductive mode of reasoning as a whole. This is why we must resist the powerful rhetoric of § 481 in Wittgenstein's *Philosophical Investigations*: "If anyone said that information about the past could not convince him that something would happen in the future, I should not understand him. One might ask him: What do you expect to be told, then? What sort of information do you call a ground for such a belief?"

The fact is that induction is not even regarded by common sense as a self-sufficient and intrinsically legitimate mode of inference. The problem of induction was born in the eighteenth century through the reflections of David Hume. It is still discussed in the framework of Hume's argument. But an essential feature of that framework is left out of most modern discussions, the result being either a skepticism less interesting than Hume's or a hasty, nervous reassurance that really there is no problem of induction at all. Contemporary Humean skepticism is less interesting than Hume's, for the former fails to recognize, as Hume's did not, the importance of the notion of necessary connection. And the usual proffered solutions of the problem are quite unconvincing because, again, they fail to provide for what Hume himself regarded as indispensable, namely, necessary connection.

Hume wished to discover the nature of what he thought was the only inference that could lead us to (derivative) knowledge of matters of fact, namely, causal inference. The crucial demand in the pursuit of such knowledge is that we be able to infer the existence and nature of entities and events that we do not observe, either because they are still in the future, or because they are in the past, or because though present they are in fact not being observed. He believed that such an inference may only be causal in nature, that the entity or event so inferred must be either the cause or the effect (proximate or remote) of an entity or event that is in fact observed. But what is the nature of the relation between cause and effect in virtue of which such inference is possible? It is not the spatiotemporal contiguity of the cause and the effect, nor the fact that the cause must precede the effect. Nor could it be the mere constant conjunction of the two kinds of entity or event. There is something more than these that we require of a causal relation, and that additional element is indeed the essential one: the *necessary* connection between the cause and the effect.

It is not merely that, as Hume admitted, the notion of necessary connection is part of the notion of causality. What is even more important is that, as Hume himself saw, causality can perform its function as the foundation of factual inference only insofar as it is a kind of necessary connection. Indeed, once this is recognized, it becomes evident that the other characteristics of causality are necessary only because they are *consequences* of the presence of necessary connection. Spatiotemporal contiguity seems essential only if we think that spatiotemporally distant events or entities cannot be necessarily, *really* connected. The precedence of the cause seems needed for distinguishing this kind of necessary connection from other sorts of necessary connections, including those in logic and mathematics; the connection is one that takes place in time and holds between nonsimultaneous entities. The constant conjunction is entailed by the presence of necessary connection and thus may serve as a *sign* of the existence of such a connection. Thus, a causal inference would be a demonstrative inference; because of the necessary connection between cause and effect, if the cause is present, it would be absolutely impossible that the effect may not occur.

Hume failed to discover such a necessary connection between the objects or events that we call cause and effect, though of course he found the other characteristics of the causal relation. For this reason he thought that there can be no justification of factual inference. But he also thought it necessary to inquire why we think that such inference is justified. For, he argued that mere constant conjunction neither justifies inference nor in fact is taken by anyone to do so. Only necessary connection can be appealed to in such a justification. We think that causal inferences are justified, Hume argued, because we think that necessary connections are objectively present, and we think the latter by confusing a subjective feeling of necessary connection with an objective necessary connection.

Philosophers since Hume, with the notable exception of Kant, have thought that the problem of induction is that of justifying factual inference by appeal to constant conjunction. They have ignored Hume's own (and Kant's) conviction that only a causal, necessary connection can in fact provide such a justification. They have, surprisingly, also failed to see that in fact even in ordinary thought and discourse observed constant conjunction is regarded only as *indirect* evidence for factual inference— that only when we think we can first infer from the observed constant conjunction the presence of a causal or necessary connection do we think we can infer the factual conclusion of the original inference. Some contemporary philosophers have argued that it is part of the very notion of rationality or of evidence that the fact that A and B have been constantly conjoined in the past makes rational, or constitutes evidence for, the conclusion that they will be so conjoined in the future.[26] They

26. See P. F. Strawson, *Introduction to Logical Theory* (London: Methuen, 1952), pp. 248–63.

have neglected the power and fundamentality in ordinary thought and discourse of the all-important notion of *accidental constant conjunction.*[27] And so they have ignored the fact that we regard constant conjunction in the past as evidence supporting factual inference only if we regard the conjunction as *non-accidental*. And to regard a constant conjunction as non-accidental is precisely to regard it as a consequence of a necessary connection which itself is what actually renders the factual inference justified.[28]

It is not surprising, then, that the so-called problem of induction has seemed insoluble. Contemporary philosophers have taken for granted that a solution would consist in showing that constant conjunction by itself can serve as a ground for inference, but not only can constant conjunction by itself not be such a ground, it is in fact not regarded as such a ground by anyone, even in his nonphilosophical moments. If inductive inference can be justified, it can be justified only by appealing to necessary connections, by appealing to the applicability of the demonstrative criterion of evidence. It is not part of our task to inquire whether this can be done. Suffice it to say that it can only if Hume's argument against the very idea of an objective necessary connection can be refuted.

9. *Skepticism*

I HAVE NOW completed my argument that the chief issue regarding derivative knowledge, namely, the possibility of nondemonstrative criteria of evidence, cannot be solved by appealing to the existence of logically

27. I am not referring here to the continuing attempts in the philosophy of science to provide an "explication" of the distinction between accidental and nomic universal statements. (A familiar and representative example of such an attempt can be found in Ernest Nagel, *The Structure of Science* [New York and Burlingame: Harcourt, Brace & World, 1961], chap. 4). As the term *explication* suggests, these attempts aim at discovering the actual criteria scientists use in distinguishing between these two kinds of statement (e.g., that the statement occupy a place in a scientific system), not at an elucidation of the natural concept of lawful connection in terms of which we evaluate the adequacy of such proposed criteria. (The logical connections of a universal statement with other confirmed universal statements should be regarded as *evidence* that the statement does not merely happen to be true, not as what is *meant* by saying that it does not merely happen to be true.)

28. That induction, insofar as it is a rational procedure, presupposes necessary connections in nature, is an important thesis in W. Kneale's *Probability and Induction* (Oxford: Clarendon Press, 1949). But he does not seem to appreciate sufficiently Hume's argument, not to the effect that there are no necessary connections in nature but that we have no *idea* of such a connection, that there is in conceptual space no room for such an idea.

distinct multiple criteria of evidence. The specific nondemonstrative criteria that have been proposed, chiefly the inductive criterion but also the behavioral criterion for other persons' thoughts and feelings, either presuppose the demonstrative criterion or lack any intellectually visible content. And the general thesis that there can be logically distinct multiple criteria of evidence seems acceptable only if we are willing to regard the word *evidence* as equivocal. But if we do, then the existence of nondemonstrative criteria would be epistemologically irrelevant. For it is not the applicability of the word *evidence* as such that matters but its applicability in a sense that is relevant to the appraisal of the truth of beliefs and of the rationality of actions. It is beyond question that the sense in which the absolute impossibility of mistake is called evidence is relevant in this way. It is completely clear why we should accept and act in accordance with what it is unthinkable that we should be mistaken about. If anything else is to be relevantly called evidence, it must be so called in more or less the same general sense, in conformity to what would be, at least roughly, the same general concept of evidence. This is why the thesis of nonequivocating multiple criteria of evidence insisted on the possibility that the use of the word *evidence* may be governed by multiple and logically distinct criteria without being equivocal. This is why the thesis has very considerable philosophical importance. But we have seen that such a possibility has not been made intelligible.

I have already mentioned that the existence of nondemonstrative criteria of evidence may be defended in another way.[29] We may accept the multiplicity of the criteria of evidence but argue that they are not logically distinct and do not render the word *evidence* equivocal by claiming that they are species of one and same genus, the latter being the one and only *general* criterion of evidence. This would seem to be the traditional view, although, to my knowledge, it has only been assumed and never explained or argued. It is not a plausible view. For it does not consist merely in the claim that the word *evidence* is correctly applied in both demonstrative and nondemonstrative contexts without equivocation. This claim may be false, but certainly it is not implausible. It consists in the claim that the demonstrative and the nondemonstrative criteria of evidence have something in common, that demonstrative and nondemonstrative inferences have an identifiable common feature. For example, such a common

29. See above, p. 273.

feature must be found in the relationship of the premises of a formally valid argument to its conclusion; in the relationship of the proposition that the sun has always risen in the past to the proposition that it will rise tomorrow; in the relationship of the proposition that someone is writhing and screaming on the floor to the proposition that he is in pain; in the relationship of the proposition that I seem to remember that I was in Washington in July of 1955 to the proposition that I was in Washington in July of 1955; in the relationship of the proposition that I see a blue pure perceptual object to the proposition that there is before me a body whose front side is blue; perhaps even in the relationship of the proposition that paying one's taxes promotes the happiness of the greatest number to the proposition that one ought to pay one's taxes. It seems incredible that all of these relationships, or even some of them, have any common feature that could constitute their being evidential, and it is chiefly this fact that has prompted so many contemporary philosophers to seek refuge from skepticism in the thesis of nonequivocating multiple criteria of evidence. For, of course, one does not show that there is such a common feature simply by saying that all of the above are *evidential* relationships, or by using some synonym of *evidence* such as *ground* or *justification*. Nor is there any plausibility to the possible claim that the common feature is a certain simple and indefinable property, that the relationship of the general criterion of evidence to its species is like that of color to red, yellow, and blue and not like that of triangularity to equilateral, isosceles, and scalene triangularity. There simply does not seem to be such a property. Had there been one, we would hardly have had the interminable epistemological controversies about the genuineness of certain alleged kinds of evidence. We do not find ourselves tempted to insist, for example, that only blue is a color or to question the propriety of calling both red and yellow colors.

To demonstrate that there is a unique general criterion of evidence, one of whose species is the demonstrative criterion and the others various nondemonstrative criteria, one must provide the notion of such a general criterion with a clear, intellectually visible content. If one cannot do this by offering a useful definition, at least one should be able to provide enlightening analogies. To my knowledge, this has not been done; nor can I think of a way of doing it. It is a crucial fact, to which I have repeatedly drawn attention, that the one unquestionable criterion of evidence is that for evidence sufficient for knowledge, namely, the absolute impossibility, the unthinkability, of mistake. Thus for anything else to be a criterion of evidence that belongs to the same genus, it must be *like* a case of absolute impossibility of mistake without *being* one. Only if the nondemonstrative criteria of evidence are similar to the demonstrative criterion can they all be legitimate and epistemologically relevant. Only then can there be *rational* belief, a belief that falls short of being knowledge yet resembles knowledge and thus can be a substitute for the latter wherever it is unattainable. Only then would the really serious sort of skepticism be false. But how could there be such similarity?

In Part One I argued that the concept of knowledge belongs to both of two important classes of concepts: those that are typically employed for the purpose of influencing actions and attitudes and those that constitute standards or ideals. It thus resembles both the concepts of love and good and the concepts of white and circle. This double resemblance is, of course, not accidental. Impossibility of mistake is the intellectual ideal. It is also the ground par excellence of rational action. For, as we have argued, the most important context in which we employ the concept of knowledge is that of one's appraisal of one's beliefs and one's choice of actions. The typical looseness of the everyday employment of the concept of knowledge is the result both of the convenience of regarding a standard as satisfied where the divergence from it seems insignificant and of the practical necessity of encouraging (one's own or someone else's) action even where its basis in truth is uncertain.

But this is an explanation of the looseness of the use of the concept of knowledge, not a justification of that looseness. A justification would consist in the demonstration that the cases of such loose usage are indeed approximations to the standard case of absolute impossibility of mistake. That we believe that there are such approximations and that they are common is beyond question. In this fact lies the explanation of why we are generally honest in our loose use of the concept of knowledge and thus the explanation of the commonness of such use. Were our belief in the existence of such approximations obviously true, then the concept of knowledge would have indeed been very much like the concept of circularity. That certain figures are more like circles than are certain other figures is obviously true, and the looseness of the everyday use of the concept of circularity is not only easily explainable but clearly justified. But there is nothing obviously true about our belief that certain cases are more like cases of absolute impossibility of mistake than are other cases.

On the contrary, it seems unintelligible to speak at all of something's being *like* the absolute impossibility of mistake but not *being* such impossibility. It is in this fact, I suggest, that the deeper root of philosophical skepticism is to be found. It is because of it that there are difficult and perhaps insoluble problems regarding rational belief. As I have pointed out above, the cause of epistemological concern is not so much the fact that we know so very little, but the possibility that we may not have any reason at all for believing anything that we do not know. It is rational belief, not knowledge, that we may lack.

That this is so has been obscured, first, by our tendency to confuse the epistemic notion of probability, which is nothing but the notion of rational belief, with the mathematical notion of probability as relative frequency or proportion of alternatives, and, second, by the fact that belief, which is the genus of knowledge, is very clearly and quite unquestionably a matter of degree. Probability as relative frequency or as proportion of alternatives is a sufficiently clear notion, and it is in a very obvious fashion a matter of degree, a degree subject to precise calculation. But that degree of probability, in this sense, is also a degree of *evidence* can be assumed only on the basis of a solution of the problem of induction. If it is unclear why the fact that the sun has always risen in the past should constitute evidence that it will rise tomorrow, then it is even less clear why the fact that someone smokes cigarettes should make it more likely, "closer to knowledge," that he will die of lung cancer than had he not smoked cigarettes.

The second cause of the plausibility of the view that there are approximations to knowledge is the connection between the notion of impossibility of mistake and the notion of confidence or belief. If I have what I recognize as perfect knowledge that *p*, then ordinarily I am completely confident that *p*. But if I have only what is sometimes called "probable knowledge" that *p*, then I might be considerably less confident. For confidence, belief, is a matter of degree. And since knowledge is a certain kind of belief, it too *appears* to be, qua knowledge, a matter of degree, very much in the way in which whiteness is. But this is only an appearance. Impossibility of mistake is one thing, confidence is another.[30] And while it is clear what would be a mere approximation to perfect confidence, it is

30. This is why it is useful, though wrong, to insist that knowledge is not a species of belief, that it is not a belief that has reached a certain degree, that has become perfect.

not at all clear what would be a mere approximation to perfect, absolute impossibility of mistake, perfect knowledge.

This is why the common trend in contemporary (though not in traditional) epistemology to define the concept of knowledge in terms of the notion of evidence is a peculiar, though deep-seated, conceptual perversion. While in our preliminary reasoning in Part One we employed the notion of evidence in reaching an account of the concept of knowledge, the result of that reasoning made no use of that notion. We neither appealed, nor should we have, to the notion of evidence (or support, or justification, or basis, or ground) in our final account of the nature of the impossibility of mistake. There is, of course, room in our account for a notion of evidence, namely, as a brief description of the knowledge to which we appeal in *demonstrating* claims to derivative knowledge. For it is mainly with respect to derivative knowledge that the notion of evidence is useful, and in our account it is no more problematic than is the legitimacy of demonstrative inference. But as long as we have no clear notion of evidence other than that which renders mistake absolutely impossible, a definition of knowledge in terms of evidence would be either obscurantist or ultimately redundant.

The belief that a useful conception of evidence, in terms of which both knowledge and rational belief are to be understood, can be established has seemed to philosophers unquestionable because of their awareness of the fact that we do employ the word *evidence,* seemingly unequivocally and quite correctly, in a number of very different sorts of situations, only one of which is that of demonstration. We may be tempted to say that it is just a brute fact that the word *evidence* is applicable, equally legitimately and without equivocation, in both demonstrative and nondemonstrative contexts. But, as I argued at the beginning of this book and as we found in our discussion of the usage of *know,* that a word has certain uses does not in itself constitute a conceptual fact, whether brute or civilized. It does so only when clear and distinct criteria for such uses can be identified, only when a corresponding concept becomes intellectually visible, only when a certain room in conceptual space is found for it.

It may seem that our account, especially our claim that the absolute impossibility of mistake is the only clear, intelligible criterion of both evidence and knowledge, leaves us no hope of escape from the clutches of extreme skepticism. But it is unnecessarily dramatic and peculiarly shortsighted to think of the business of epistemology as devoted exclusively to refuting the skeptic. We should be willing to accept the truth about any subject matter, even if in the case of epistemology the truth is on the side of skepticism; the task of epistemology is not the refutation of skepticism but the discovery of the truth about the nature and extent of knowledge. And the problems of epistemology are sufficiently difficult to require for their solution long and arduous preparatory work rather than impatient manifestoes. It seems incredible that we could solve them, almost instantly, by providing convenient definitions of epistemic terms and equally convenient criteria for their application, or by hasty abstract arguments from the nature of language or the dictates of common sense to the effect that of course everything is all right. The Moorean argument that our certainty regarding the propositions the skeptic doubts is always greater than our certainty regarding the skeptic's premises is either irrelevant or a *petitio principii*. It is irrelevant if by "certainty" is meant confidence; the skeptic does not question the degree of our confidence in the propositions he doubts but the rationality of that confidence. And the argument would be a *petitio* if by "certainty" is meant knowledge, that is, if the argument is that we have better, more solid knowledge of what the skeptic questions than we have of his premises.

From a purely theoretical discipline such as epistemology, one free from the practical demands for courage, risk-taking, occasional reliance on hunches, and the healthy conservatism of respecting common opinion more than ingenious argument, we expect *solutions,* not bare though comforting proclamations. To assert that *of course* we know far more than the results of our inquiry would suggest is merely to cut a pose, not to offer a philosophical judgment. For a judgment is philosophical only insofar as it is a consequence of careful analysis and criticism. The philosophical question is not what do we believe but what can we explain. Philosophical convictions are numerous, be they true or false. Adequate philosophical explanations are less common.

My purpose in this Part has been neither to attempt specific solutions of the familiar epistemological problems regarding derivative knowledge and rational belief nor to reject the possibility of such solutions. It has only been to consider these problems insofar as their solutions may depend directly on the account of the very concepts of knowledge and evidence; it is this account that has been the task of this book. More specifically, I have been concerned with the possibility that there are nondemonstrative criteria of knowledge, and of evidence in general, that would legitimize those derivative epistemic judgments and rational beliefs that seem incapable of demonstration. And I have argued against the tendency to short-circuit inquiry into the particular epistemological problems by conceptual fiat. But I have not argued that solutions of at least some of these problems may not, after all, be found by employing the demonstrative criterion; it is not so obvious to me, for example, that our knowledge of other minds is not inductive and that the principle of induction cannot itself be demonstrated by appeal to causal, necessary connections. Nor have I argued that an intelligible concept of nondemonstrative evidence cannot be offered; it is not obvious to me, for example, that demonstrative and inductive evidence are not species of the same genus and thus that both are not genuinely and unequivocally evidence, although it is obvious to me that to show that this is so one must make the concept of such a genus intellectually visible and not merely appeal to the fact that both sorts of evidence are called evidence.

This is why the outcome of our investigation is not skepticism. We are not denying that we know or at least have evidence for much more than we can conceptually ground, though neither are we affirming this. Such denials and affirmations are not our business. We have merely concluded that so far there is no adequate philosophical criticism of the concepts of knowledge and evidence that renders the claim to such wider knowledge intelligible, and that the only clear notions of knowledge and evidence that we have allow knowledge and rational belief much less scope than it is usually supposed. This is the only sort of conclusion that it is our business to reach.

The central task of philosophy is somewhat like the putting together of a jigsaw puzzle, the pieces being the most general and fundamental concepts with which we understand ourselves and the world. Sometimes the problem is to fit a piece that we have. At other times, the problem is to find a piece that we need for completing the picture. The concept of a nondemonstrative criterion of evidence is of the latter sort. Philosophers have not yet made intelligible such a concept. But from this we should hardly conclude that there is not such a concept, or, even worse, that there is not room for one. Despite our subjective estimate of the length of the history of philosophy, philosophy may still be in its infancy. And an infant must be allowed to grow naturally, not by envelopment in the pretensions and illusions of an artificial adulthood.

Index

Acceptance, 30–31. *See also* Belief

Acquaintance, 21, 23, 66; knowledge by, 21, 224. *See also* Awareness; Consciousness

Albritton, Rogers, 294

Analogy, method of, 13, 129, 142, 175, 192, 224–25

Analysis, conceptual, 6–7, 11

Analyticity Theory, 107–11, 125, 129, 136–42

A posteriori: knowledge, 4, 75, 93–97, 178, 183, 185–86; nonempirical propositions, 104; propositions, 102–5, 165–66

Apparitions, 217, 219, 245, 247; hollow, 246

Appearance, 195, 198–99, 202, 235, 253, 262

Appearing, Theory of, 204, 225, 236–39, 260

A priori: empirical propositions, 104; knowledge, 4, 64, 75, 93–97, 178, 183, 185–86; propositions, 102–5, 165–66; Theory of the, 105

Argument: epistemically serious, 35, 62–63, 89–90; from Illusion, 185–97, 229, 260; philosophical, 190–92; transcendental, 211, 297–99

Aristotle, 170, 180

Assent, 30–31. *See also* Belief

Austin, J. L., 14, 41, 54, 190, 201

Awareness, 21, 178, 182–83, 223–24; direct, 65; sensory, 189–90. *See also* Acquaintance; Consciousness; Ego; Self

Ayer, A. J., 85, 194, 196, 279

Behavioral account of knowledge, 19–21

Belief, 30–32, 43, 51, 59, 67–69, 85; acts of, 19; context of, 68–77, 86, 93, 183, 185, 262–63; dispositional, 19; ethics of, 300; justified true, 46; objective reality of, 69, 74, 86; occurrent, 19–20; probable, 43, 271; rational, 43–45, 50, 53, 59, 271, 284, 302, 316; states of, 20; true, 25, 33–34, 44, 50; true rational, 26, 44–45, 47, 52–53, 58. *See also* Acceptance; Assent; Conviction, feeling of; Opinion

Index

Believe, episodic uses of, 20
Bergmann, Gustav, 156
Berkeley, George, 180, 200, 206, 213, 215, 230, 231, 240
Berkeleyan Idealism, 240
Black, Max, 94, 119
Bodies, 186, 197–221; continued existence of, 211–12, 259; hollow, 246
Body-statements, 203, 261

Carnap, Rudolf, 11
Cartesian circle, 93
Causal Theory of Perception, 204
Causality, 145–46, 270; principle of, 82
Chisholm, R. M., 64, 155, 279, 291
Classification, 6, 8–10, 263–66
Coherence Theory of Truth, 35
Colors, incompatibility of, 155
Common sense, 5, 204, 207, 310
Conceivability Theory of Necessary Truth, 123–24, 131, 164
Concepts, 5–6, 14, 99, 265–66, 276; clarity of, 13; distinctness of, 13; justification-conditions of, 296; philosophical, 12, 191; truth-conditions of, 296
Consciousness, 21, 23–24, 178, 182. *See also* Acquaintance; Awareness; Ego; Self
Constant conjunction, 311–12
Constructional philosophies, 11. *See also* Carnap, Rudolf; Goodman, Nelson
Conventions of language, 80, 123–40 *passim*
Conviction, feeling of, 30
Correspondence Theory of Truth, 95, 165
Counterevidence, 68
Criteria, 272, 274–78; defining, 273, 274–78, 279, 295; first-order, 280–83, 292–93; nondefining, 273, 278–87, 293, 295, 297–99; second-order, 280–83, 292–93
Criteria of evidence, 272–73, 280–83, 292–93; demonstrative, 272–73, 282–83, 287, 292, 302, 307, 312; general and specific, 273, 313–16; nondemonstrative, 273, 285–87, 312–13, 319; nonequivocating multiple, 60, 285–92, 312–14; thesis of, 60, 299, 314
Criticism, conceptual, 6–8, 10–11

Danto, A. C., 63, 64, 298
Deductive mode of reasoning, 53–54
Deductive proof, 53–54
Definition, 278; implicit, 109–11, 125
Demonstration, 269. *See also* Criteria of evidence, demonstrative

Denial, Theory of, 111–13
Descartes, René, 67, 68, 71, 84, 88, 93, 181, 187, 200, 218, 268. *See also* Cartesian circle; Doubt, metaphysical
Dispositions: behavioral, 19–20; doxastic, 19; epistemic, 19
Doubt, 46, 67–68, 268; grounds for, 68; impossibility of, 46, 67, 71, 74; metaphysical, 84, 93, 268; unreasonable, 46. *See also* Descartes, René; Cartesian circle
Dreaming, 195

Efficacy, causal, 214, 216–21
Ego, 8, 84–85, 178. *See also* Acquaintance; Awareness; Consciousness; Self
Egocentric predicament, 34
Empiricism, 119, 180
Entities: abstract, 169–70; mental, 24, 214; non-spatiotemporal, 169; nontemporal, 149–66, 171–72; recurrent, 155
Episodic uses: of *believe,* 20; of *know,* 20
Epistemic judgments, 4, 35–36; derivative, 4, 34–35, 95; first-order, 89–90; first-person, 21, 33, 36, 41–42; past-tense, 48; present-tense, 48; primary, 4, 34–36, 61–96; third-person, 21, 33, 36, 41–42
Epistemology, 3–5, 268–69, 299–302, 318
Essences, 7, 123–24
Essentialist Theory of Necessary Truth, 123
Ethics, 300
Evaluative statements, 301
Evaluative terms, 299–302
Evidence, 25–26, 28–29, 32–34, 60, 79, 200, 272, 317; demonstrative, 280, 292–93; empirical, 94; knowledge without, 29, 34; nondemonstrative, 287–88, 292–93; nonempirical, 94; sufficient, 25–26, 45–46, 51, 54, 89. *See also* Criteria of evidence; Self-evidence
Excluded middle, principle of the, 109
Existence, 172–77, 230–32; conditional, 177; fictional, 177
Expanses, 246; perceptual, 246–55
Experience, 23, 63, 223; immediate, 63, 72–73, 75; inner, 267, 268, 297
Explication fallacy, 11
External world, 186–87, 212, 259

Facts, 64, 117–21
Fichte, Johann, 8
Firth, Roderick, 300
Formal Truth, Theory of, 112–19, 125, 130
Forms, Platonic, 21, 170
Frankfurt, Harry, 304

Index

Game Theory of Necessary Truth, 108, 111, 124–40, 142–43, 168
Gettier, E., 58
Goodman, Nelson, 11

Hallucination, 193
Hare, R. M., 279
Hartland-Swann, J., 19
Heidelberger, H., 58
Hintikka, J., 15
Hume, David, 8, 24, 50, 104, 119, 199, 206, 211, 240, 269, 270, 310, 311, 312

Idealism, 198, 206–8; absolute, 84; Berkeleyan, 240; transcendental, 9
Identity Theory of Universals, 171
Illusion: argument from, 185–97, 229, 260; perceptual, 188–89, 192–93, 260
Images. See Mental images
Imagination, 82–83, 215, 230–32. See also Mental images; Unimaginability
Immutability, 148–49, 172
Impenetrable shields, 246
Impossibility: absolute, 50–51; conditional, 306; empirical, 305–7; kinds of, 50, 302–7; logical, 77, 303, 305–6. See also Mistake, absolute impossibility of
Inconceivability. See Conceivability Theory of Necessary Truth; Unthinkability of mistake
Incorrigibility, 35, 262–67; epistemic, 262–65; linguistic, 35–36, 262–65; memorial, 265
Indistinguishability, intrinsic, 190, 194
Individuality, 155
Indubitability, 46, 67, 71, 74
Induction, 307, 309; principle of, 309; problem of, 310–12, 316
Inductivism, 204
Inductivist Theory of Necessary Truth, 168
Inference, 35; causal, 310–11; demonstrative, 311; formal, 308–9; inductive, 307–12; nondemonstrative, 5, 308

Joseph, H. W. B., 153, 159
Judgments: collective, 153; enumerative, 153, 159. See also Epistemic judgments
Justification-conditions of concepts, 296

Kant, Immanuel, 141–42, 187, 282, 304, 311
Kneale, W., 312
Know: episodic uses of, 20; exaggerated uses of, 54; strong sense of, 68; weak sense of, 46, 57–58

Knower, 22, 24. See also Ego; Self
Knowing, acts of, 19
Knowing-how, 17–19
Knowing-that, 17, 19
Knowing that one knows, 27–28, 54, 88–93
Knowledge: by acquaintance, 21, 224; a posteriori, 4, 75, 93–97, 178, 183, 185–86; a priori, 4, 64, 75; 93–97, 178, 183, 185–86; behavioral account of, 19, 21; claims to, 42–43; of contingent propositions, 72; demonstrative, 72; derivative, 4, 34–35, 61, 202, 267–74; without evidence, 29–34; false, 25, 29; intuitive, 74, 178–83; of matters of fact, 269–70, 310; of necessary truth, 66, 72, 75, 96–97, 99, 178–83, 185–86, 262; nondemonstrative, 272, 281; of perceivings, 186, 202–3; perceptual, 4, 96; primary, 4, 34–35, 72, 78, 94, 180, 182–83, 201–2, 261, 267; propositional, 15, 25; of pure perceptual objects, 261–63; retrospective appraisals of, 47

Language: conventions and rules of, 80, 124–40 passim; private, 266
Lehrer, Keith, 30, 58
Lewis, C. I., 73, 106
Linguistic propriety, 35–36
Locke, John, 85, 108, 180, 183, 187, 218
Logic, principles of, 106, 109, 115
Logical form, 112–19
Logical impossibility, 77, 303, 305–6; conditional, 306

Malcolm, Norman, 46, 68, 279
Material things, 186, 197. See also Bodies
Matters of fact, knowledge of, 269–70, 310
Meaning, descriptive, 299–300; evaluative, 299–300
Mental acts, 223
Mental entities, 24, 214. See also Belief, acts of; Knowing, acts of; Mental acts; Mental events
Mental events, 19. See also Belief, acts of; Knowing, acts of; Mental acts; Mental entities
Mental images, 181, 207, 213–14, 232, 235–36. See also Imagination; Unimaginability
Metaphysics, 7
Mind, 85, 88, 208
Mistake, absolute impossibility of, 51–53, 56–61, 66, 71, 76, 78–79, 87, 287, 302–

5, 315–17. *See also* Unthinkability of mistake
Moore, G. E., 318

Nagel, Ernest, 312
Nature, Laws of, 306–7
Necessary connection, 270, 310–12
Necessary Truth, 64, 66, 72, 75, 76–88, 93–97, 99–183 *passim;* Analyticity Theory of, 107–11, 125, 129, 138; Conceivability Theory of, 123–24, 131, 164; Contradiction-of-Denial Theory of, 111–13; Essentialist Theory of, 123; Formal Truth Theory of, 112–19, 125, 130; Game Theory of, 108, 111, 124–40, 142–43, 168; Inductivist Theory of, 168; knowledge of, 66, 72, 75, 96–97, 99, 178–83, 185–86, 262; logico-linguistic theories of, 105–24, 139, 164–65; Nonpropositional Theory of, 119–23, 125, 129; Rules Theory of, 168; Transcendental Theory of, 123
Necessity: causal, 145–49; eternal, 148
Nominalist Theory of Universals, 171
Noncontradiction, principle of, 80, 109, 111–13, 125–26
Nonpropositional Theory of Necessary Truth, 119–23, 125, 129

Objects. *See* Physical objects; Perceptual objects
Observation, 47–48
Opinion, 30. *See also* Belief
Other minds, 208

Pain, 37–39, 207, 213, 231, 297–98; knowledge of, 37–39; unfelt, 231
Pap, Arthur, 108, 161
Parallel postulate, 82
Perceivings, 186–88, 197, 202–3, 225, 252; primary knowledge of, 261–62
Perception, 21–23, 63, 179, 182–83, 185–265 *passim;* auditory, 189; Causal Theory of, 204; direct, 198, 205, 247, 260; gustatory, 189; illusory, 188–89, 192–93, 260; indirect, 205, 247; nonveridical, 260; olfactory, 189; problem of, 187, 198, 203–7, 221, 240, 247–48, 255; realist theories of, 200, 206–7; tactile, 226; veridical, 188–89
Perceptual objects, pure, 255–62, 267; primary knowledge of, 261–63
Perceptual residue, pure, 234

Perceptual statements, 203; ordinary, 234, 243; pure, 234–38, 239–49, 254–66
Phenomenalism, 204–60
Phillips-Griffiths, A., 20
Physical objects, 186, 197. *See also* Bodies
Pitcher, George, 294
Plato, 21, 34, 61, 66, 68, 71, 161, 170, 176, 179, 180
Pollock, John L., 296
Price, H. H., 63, 199, 214, 260
Prichard, H. A., 54
Probability, 79, 316
Property-universals, 155–56
Propositions: analytic, 106–11, 140; a posteriori, 102–5, 165–66; a priori, 102–5, 165–66; contingent, 72; empirical, 104; enumerative, 159; essential elements of, 114, 159; factual, 114–15; inessential elements of, 159; logical, 106–8, 119–23; nontemporal, 149–66; self-contradictory, 80, 111–12; synthetic, 106; synthetic a priori, 140–42, 204, 291; universal, 153–54, 159; vacuously true, 114–15

Qualities, tactile and visual, 198
Quinton, Anthony, 109, 112

Rationality, 79, 311
Realism, Naïve, 204, 225, 229, 239, 268
Reality, 14, 195, 218, 226. *See also* Existence
Reasoning, modes of, 309; deductive, 53–54; inductive, 304; religious, 309
Reductionism, 272–73
Resemblance, 9
Resemblance Theory of Universals, 171
Right to be sure, 29
Rules Theory of Necessary Truth, 168
Russell, Bertrand, 21, 160, 161
Ryle, Gilbert, 19, 222

Schopenhauer, Arthur, 187
Self, 8, 24. *See also* Ego; Knower
Self-evidence, 40, 62, 61–76, 271
Sense-data, 190, 192, 198–99, 202, 205, 235, 260, 267–68; families of, 260
Sense-Datum Theory, 190, 192, 194, 204, 236, 239, 243, 260
Sensibilia, Theory of, 204
Sensing, 205, 223, 247, 260
Shoemaker, Sydney, 294
Similarity, 9
Simples, 223–24

Index

Skepticism, 5, 45, 59–60, 84, 204, 207, 211, 233, 236, 270–73, 285–87, 297–99, 302, 308–10, 312–19

Solidity, 212, 262–67

Solids, unobservable, 217, 245

Solipsism, 208

Spinoza, Benedict de, 191, 192

Statements. *See* Body-statements; Evaluative statements; Perceptual statements

Strawson, P. F., 112, 297, 311

Surfaces, 214–21, 246, 251–56; tangible, 257; visual, 257

Symptoms, 275, 280, 296

Syntactical structure, 114, 125

Synthesis, conceptual, 6, 11

Tactile qualities, 198

Telepathy, 208, 297

Toulmin, S. E., 279, 303, 309

Transcendental idealism, 9; linguistic, 9; psychological, 9

Transcendental Theory of Necessary Truth, 123

Truth, 29–30, 51, 95, 144, 165; a priori, 64; Coherence Theory of, 35; conceptual, 99; Correspondence Theory of, 95, 165; discovery of, 53; Formal, Theory of, 112–19, 125, 130; having, 48–49, 54, 84, 87; search for, 53. *See also* Necessary Truth

Truth-conditions of concepts, 296

Truth-sufficient reference, 157–66

Truth-tables, 108–9

Unimaginability, 82–83, 230–32. *See also* Imagination; Mental images

Universals, 102, 155–56, 161–62, 166, 167–78, 179, 262, 267; formal, 155–56; Identity Theory of, 171; Nominalist Theory of, 171; property-, 155–56; Resemblance Theory of, 171; uninstantiated, 162, 170–73

Unthinkability: of mistake, 75–88, 87, 93, 183, 268, 272, 287, 302–4, 315; principle of, 76–88, 92, 100, 164. *See also* Conceivability Theory of Necessary Truth

Visual qualities, 198

Wittgenstein, Ludwig, 11, 37, 126, 222, 272, 274, 275, 279, 294, 296, 309

Word, applicability and application of a, 275; criterion for, 275–78; purpose of, 276

Words: descriptive, 6, 8, 114, 125; logical, 114–15, 125; nondescriptive, 114